JA92

Operation Just Cause

Operation Just Cause

The Storming of Panama

by

Thomas Donnelly
Margaret Roth
Caleb Baker

LEXINGTON BOOKS
An Imprint of Macmillan, Inc.
NEW YORK

Maxwell Macmillan Canada
TORONTO

Maxwell Macmillan International
NEW YORK   OXFORD   SINGAPORE   SYDNEY

Front jacket photo: Rangers of C Company, 3d Battalion, 75th Ranger Regiment, prepare to assault La Comandancia from porch of gymnasium across the street, 3:45 P.M., 20 December. Photo courtesy 75th Ranger Regiment.

Library of Congress Cataloging-in-Publication Data

Donnelly, Thomas (Thomas M.)
Operation just cause : the storming of Panama / by Thomas
Donnelly, Margaret Roth, Caleb Baker.
p.   cm.—(Issues in low-intensity conflict series)

Includes bibliographical references and index.
ISBN 0-669-24975-0 (alk. paper)
1. United States—Foreign relations—Panama.   2. Panama—Foreign
relations—United States.   3. Panama—History—American invasion,
1989.   I. Roth, Margaret (Margaret C.)   II. Baker, Caleb.
III. Title.   IV. Series.
E183.8.P2D66   1991
327.7307287—dc20   91-2732
                                                           CIP

Lexington Books
An Imprint of Macmillan, Inc.
866 Third Avenue, New York, N. Y. 10022

Maxwell Macmillan Canada, Inc.
1200 Eglinton Avenue East
Suite 200
Don Mills, Ontario M3C 3Nl

Macmillan, Inc. is part of the Maxwell Communication
Group of Companies.

Printed in the United States of America

printing number
1 2 3 4 5 6 7 8 9 10

For William F. Donnelly,
Margaret Gibson Roth, and
Linda Marie Harrington

Contents

List of Figures

Photographs

Photo section follows page 220.

Foreword

On the evening of 16 December 1989, one day after the National Assembly of "Corregimiento" representatives declared Panama in a state of war, Marine First Lieutenant Robert Paz was shot and killed by members of the Panama Defense Forces. Manuel Antonio Noriega, the self-proclaimed "maximum leader" of Panama, had established the climate in which this reprehensible act took place. Noriega's disregard for the democratic process, his disdain for the good offices of the Organization of American States and his contempt for the United States emboldened his subordinates to precipitous and lethal action against American citizens. Lt. Paz's murder culminated a pattern of harassment of U.S. citizens by the Panama Defense Forces and was the trigger event for Operation Just Cause, the overthrow of the Noriega dictatorship of Panama.

As a result of these actions, the president of the United States ordered the armed forces into Panama to create an environment safe for Americans there, ensure the integrity of the Panama Canal, provide a stable environment for the freely elected Endara government, and bring Noriega to justice.

At 12:45 A.M. on 20 December, U.S. forces began the assault on Noriega's forces. The operation was characterized by the introduction of overwhelming combat power on a host of targets simultaneously during the hours of darkness. The goal was to minimize casualties on both sides and to incapacitate the Panama Defense Forces and its leadership as quickly as possible. Noriega surrendered himself to U.S. forces at 8:50 p.m. on 3 January 1990. Operation Just Cause was essentially over.

The Republic of Panama was reborn as a democratic nation after twenty-one years of military dictatorship. Twenty-three U.S. servicemen gave their lives so that the Panamanian government could begin the task of rebuilding democratic institutions and economic opportunities for all of the Panamanian people.

The authors have captured the events leading to Operation Just Cause and the heroic actions of the troops during the operation. Americans fought and died so that all the people of Panama could prosper democratically. It was an unusual opportunity for America and for Panama. It was noble work performed magnificently by outstanding American soldiers, sailors, airmen and Marines.

This is their story.

Maxwell R. Thurman
General, U.S. Army (Retired)
Washington, D.C.

Preface

This is a story about the United States military, particularly its Army, one of the least understood institutions in modern-day America.

Although set primarily in Panama, this is not about the sufferings of that tortured country. Nor is this a story about Manuel Antonio Noriega, although he is the main villain of the piece. The tale of Panama's descent at the hands of the dictator, his connections to the drug trade, his problematic relations with various agencies of the U.S. government, and the way Noriega bedeviled the Reagan and Bush administrations has been admirably chronicled in two recent books, *Divorcing the Dictator* by Frederick Kempe and *Our Man in Panama* by John Dinges. Readers searching for one soldier's view of *Operation Just Cause* should seek out 1st Lt. Clarence Briggs's *Operation Just Cause, Panama December 1989: A Soldier's Eyewitness Account.*

This is a story about how military men and women successfully planned and executed a complex operation in pursuit of ambitious goals, against a tumultuous political backdrop with changing directives. These service members should be considered both as individuals and as the products of their training and professional experiences in the all-volunteer force.

The success of Operation Just Cause has its deepest roots in the failures of Vietnam. The principal architects of the campaign were senior generals like Maxwell Thurman, Carl Stiner, and Colin Powell, who learned the frustrations of defeat as young commanders in the jungles of Southeast Asia.

The men and women of the armed forces—again, particularly the Army—also are products of the Vietnam schoolhouse. Ronald Reagan gave his Pentagon more than $1 trillion to rebuild America's military forces from the post-Vietnam slough; the soldiers, sailors, airmen, and Marines who fought in Just Cause are the fruits of that investment, as are their equipment and training.

Just Cause represents not only a culmination of years of effort and expense, but points the way for an American military so victorious in the cold war that tens of thousands of service members are about to be removed from overseas bases. Just Cause is nothing less than a radical change of mission for a Defense Department prepared to fight long-studied battles in the Fulda Gap and accustomed to the nightmarish mathematics of nuclear exchange. The U.S. military's experience since Just Cause reinforces this dramatic change in mission.

Although this book was written before Operation Desert Shield and the subsequent victory in Operation Desert Storm, it is clear that U.S. military forces in the future must be able to react quickly to global conflicts. Indeed, the Persian Gulf war showed that there is much work yet to be done if the Department of Defense is to shift its attention from the plains of central Europe to regional hot spots.

Had Iraq decided in August to drive into Saudi Arabia, the United States would have been hard-pressed to thwart the attack. Desert Storm reinforced at least one significant lesson from Just Cause: In a world where superpower tensions no longer apply, contingency operations like the wars in Panama and the Middle East may well become the Pentagon's central focus.

This book is the product of hundreds of interviews with the participants in Just Cause. From first-term soldiers to four-star generals to the families who supported them, those who planned, fought, and endured the battle for Panama have a part in this book.

We must also acknowledge those who helped us in the research for and writing of this book. First and foremost comes the staff of *Army Times,* particularly Marla Ollieu, Murphy Coome, Liz Rathbun, and Katherine McIntire; Bonnie Benwick of *The Washington Post* also helped edit the manuscript. And thanks are also due Joanne Osteendorf and Cristina Rivero for their maps and graphics and Doug Pensinger for his photographs.

The U.S. military was extraordinarily helpful in providing access to its troops at all levels. Army Chief of Staff Gen. Carl Vuono and Gen. Gordon Sullivan, now Army vice chief of staff, deserve special thanks in that regard. Thanks also to Lt. Col. Jim Fetig and Col.

Raoul Alcala of General Vuono's staff and to Col. Bob Killebrew for their insightful assistance.

Finally, we must express our appreciation to the men and women of Just Cause for answering our questions with patience and candor. As reporters who focus daily on soldiers and the business of fighting, we find ourselves occasionally treating war as a more rational undertaking than it truly is. In the days after 20 December 1989, to scramble down the burned-out streets of downtown Panama City, to see parachutes caught in the trees at Rio Hato airfield or to scale the same hills that paratroopers did under heavy fire was to feel a chill. This book tells how our men and women made themselves masters of those killing grounds.

Prologue: The Only Warfighting CinC

General Maxwell Thurman arrived at his brother Roy's house in the Washington, D.C., suburb of Alexandria early in the evening. He had just completed yet another in a wearisome series of flights from Howard Air Force Base in Panama City, where he was commander in chief of U.S. Southern Command (SOUTHCOM).

Though he flew in four-star style on a C-20, the military designation for a Gulfstream executive jet, the last months of 1989 had taken a toll on the wiry general.

But this trip, on 16 December, was going to be a mixture of business and holiday pleasures, insofar as the hard-driving Thurman allowed himself to step entirely off duty. He was looking forward to five days of relative relaxation, with only a few Pentagon meetings to discuss how to translate George Bush's anti-drug policy into a plan for controlling the South American drug trade.

Talk of Andean drug strategy would be leavened by a chance to enjoy his two beloved Shetland sheepdogs, Rax and Dundee, and conversation with Roy and family friends. Then Roy would accompany the general back to Panama for Christmas.

Around nine-thirty, the telephone rang, and Thurman said he had to go to the Pentagon for a while. Roy Thurman, himself a retired lieutenant general, knew well the ceaseless demands of command. He didn't think twice about the call until Max returned home two hours later.

His holiday mood had evaporated. Clearly his mind was set on some distant problem. "I have to go back to Panama," a subdued Max Thurman told his brother.

Though the two bachelor brothers share an affection that can at times be joyful, Thurman does not waste words.

The severe life of a four-star general only heightened the monkish devotion that is central to Max Thurman's personality. It is a cliché among those who have known and worked for Thurman that he is married to the Army. If he had not joined the service, the joke goes, he would have joined the priesthood.

The brothers often travel together, accompanying each other on the long car trips that are commonplace for officers transferred every two years. Max could drive for hours without a single word. But the silence that night, as they drove to Andrews Air Force Base in Maryland, was excruciating.

"Anyone else awake?" asked Roy, referring to the late-night session at the Pentagon.

"Colin's there," replied Max, speaking of Gen. Colin Powell, chairman of the Joint Chiefs of Staff.

The miles swept by over the familiar route to Andrews Air Force Base: past the Pentagon, across the Potomac River, through one of the poorest sections of Washington and into Maryland. At last, Max spoke.

"Do you realize that I'm the only warfighting CinC"—after almost a decade at the highest levels of the Army, this commander in chief's speech was laced with acronyms—"in the American forces?"

Roy Thurman assumed his brother was talking about the drug war. Whatever had happened at the Pentagon that night was related to the battle to stop cocaine trafficking, Roy thought.

Max Thurman kept his real purpose a secret, even from his brother. Upon returning to Panama, he would assume command of the largest military action by U.S. forces since Vietnam, and lead his men into a new kind of war far removed from the ideological struggles of the cold war. The following afternoon, President Bush ordered more than 26,000 men and women to attack Panama to eliminate the brutal Panama Defense Forces and topple their notorious leader, Manuel Antonio Noriega.

Operation Just Cause

1

The Man on Horseback

The president's decision to send troops to Panama was merely the latest in a long series of U.S. and European interventions in the area. Indeed, but for the United States, there may never have been a republic called Panama.

The area was discovered by the Spanish in 1501 on an expedition led by Rodrigo de Bastidas. When the first Spaniards arrived, there were perhaps 750,000 inhabitants of various tribes in the region; the native word *panama* is thought to mean "abundance of fish." The first Spanish attempt at settlement, begun a year later by Christopher Columbus near the present-day province of Darien, fell prey to disease and greed.

But by 1510, Vasco Núñez de Balboa had established a successful colony. Nine years later, Panama Viejo, the predecessor of Panama City, was founded on the Pacific Ocean, and the Spanish administration moved to the present-day area of Panama City. The new settlement quickly became a trading center, and its booming business in South American gold and silver attracted pirates.

British raiding parties preyed upon the Panamanian coastline until the late seventeenth century. Sir Francis Drake, himself, was buried at sea off Portobelo, on the Caribbean coast.

Over the next century, the Spanish commercial and colonial empire withered. In 1821, led by Simón Bolívar, Panama declared its independence from Spain. Though the new country quickly merged with Colombia, the yearning for independence soon returned. During the 1830s, Panama attempted three times to secede from Colombia.

U.S. interest in Panama surged with the California gold rush of 1849. The prospectors who traveled to California via the southern route through Panama brought an economic boom to the isthmus. The United States built a railroad across Panama in 1855, a project that gave rise to the Atlantic port city of Colon.

Soon the idea of a canal linking the Atlantic and Pacific oceans took hold. In 1879 a French diplomat, Ferdinand de Lesseps, received a commission to begin a canal like the Suez, which he had completed in Egypt ten years earlier.

A second such triumph was not within de Lesseps's reach. The canal project was called off in 1889 in the face of insurmountable financial, engineering, and health problems. The task of cutting through densely wooded mountains infested with disease-carrying mosquitoes had claimed the lives of thousands of laborers, and skilled labor was in short supply.

Beyond the formidable tasks inherent to the project, instability in Panama proved another obstacle to progress. Between 1850 and 1900, Panama struggled through forty political administrations, fifty riots, five more attempts at secession from Colombia, and thirteen U.S. interventions. All the while, U.S. interest in a canal was building, although several attempts to negotiate a deal with the Colombians fell through.

In 1903, when the Colombian senate delayed ratifying a treaty, the United States lent its support to the Panamanian secessionist party, extending it formal recognition as the legitimate government of Panama on 6 November. A canal treaty was concluded less than two weeks later, a treaty that allowed the United States to build a canal and gave it perpetual control over the zone surrounding it.

Again, the Panamanians immediately regretted the deal and sought to renegotiate the treaty almost from the start. Work on the canal took another decade, and the waterway was opened on the fifteenth of August 1914 under U.S. control.

A turbulent but democratic and constitutional series of governments ruled in Panama from independence in 1903 until 1968. On the eleventh of October of that year, Arnulfo Arias, who had been elected twice before only to be ousted by the Panamanian military, was thrown out of office yet again after just eleven days in power. The military junta was led by Col. Omar Torrijos.

The military, starting with the Guardia Nacional, would dominate the Panamanian political system until the United States drove Noriega from power with Operation Just Cause.

U.S. military involvement in Panama began in 1903, when Marines were sent to protect the railroad crossing the isthmus. The Marines remained to provide security for the canal construction, and were augmented in 1911 by the Army's 10th Infantry Regiment. These forces established Camp Otis on the Pacific side of the isthmus. The Marine battalion left in 1914 to join an expedition against Pancho Villa.

Artillery units took their place. As the canal was completed, fortified coastal gun emplacements were established at both the Atlantic and Pacific ends of the canal.

A year later, the Army established a formal headquarters, the Panama Canal Department, based on Ancon Hill in Panama City, and in 1916 the command moved to Quarry Heights on Ancon Hill. The facility is now home to United States Southern Command, known as SOUTHCOM, the U.S. military's headquarters in Latin America.

The Panama Canal Department became a regional command of the Army the following year. It remained the senior Army command when a superior command, Caribbean Defense Command, was created in 1941 to assume operational control for air, land, and sea forces in the area. The Panama Canal played an essential strategic role during World War II, and by 1943, 68,000 personnel were assigned to defend the canal from more than one hundred bases in Panama.

After the war, the United States was reluctant to give up many of these installations, despite pressure from the Panamanians. Caribbean Command was retained under the newly organized and created Department of Defense, but troop strength in Panama shrank steadily, reaching a low of 6,600 in 1959.

In 1963, rising tensions in Central America and increasing interest in the military theater of Latin America led to the creation of SOUTHCOM, a fully integrated command including Army, Navy, Air Force, and special operations units, of which the Army component, now called U.S. Army South (USARSO), was the largest. Since 1975, SOUTHCOM has encompassed an average of ten thousand personnel. Traditionally the SOUTHCOM commander has been an Army general.

The chief mission of SOUTHCOM has always been the defense of the Panama Canal. Over time, however, a significant mission developed to help install pro-U.S. leaders in Latin American militaries through training and weapons sales.

The command now runs sixteen security assistance organizations throughout the region, whose primary functions are to maintain ties with local militaries and with the U.S. diplomatic hierarchy in those countries. Each team of military advisers reports to the U.S. ambassador in that country and to the director of the Defense Security Assistance Agency.

This change naturally affected the kind of military leaders assigned to SOUTHCOM. Despite the potential threat from Cuba and later from Nicaragua, U.S. strategy in the theater has been to encourage local solutions to local conflicts. Particularly since the Vietnam War, with its taint of foreign intervention, SOUTHCOM commanders have seen themselves as diplomats as much as warriors.

Yet despite Panama's close ties to its northern neighbor, the United States had a poor relationship with the Guardia Nacional. As Panamanian nationalism began to reassert itself after World War II, tension between the two militaries grew. The hostility reached new heights when, in 1964, U.S. troops fired on Panamanian protesters, killing twenty-eight and wounding more than three hundred. U.S. officers felt that the Panamanian troops had allowed the protesters to riot, perhaps even encouraged them.

The Guardia Nacional was developing an identity of its own, independent of Panama's ruling elite, which had dominated both its officer corps and the missions of the force. Yet even as the Guardia's hostility toward the U.S. military increased, it often served U.S. interests. Foremost among these was the ousting of Arnulfo Arias from the presidency of Panama. First elected president in 1940, Arias was a fascist and populist, an open admirer of Hitler and Mussolini. A coffee farmer from the western province of Chiriqui, he was openly hostile to the U.S. presence in Panama. He was expelled from office in 1941, but in 1949 was again elected president. Ousted in 1951, Arias won a third chance at the presidency in 1968.

For the oligarchy and military, his time was up. The leader of the Guardia, Gen. Bolívar Vallarino, the last Panamanian leader to come from the upper classes, was determined to see Arias deposed once and for all.[1] An attempt to rig the 1968 election failed, however, and Arias won 60 percent of the vote. When Arias made it clear he would purge the Guardia, senior military leaders resolved to stage a coup to be led by Maj. Boris Martínez.

Martínez acted in concert with Torrijos, a romantic, vaguely socialistic officer with great dreams for his country and the Guardia. For all his eccentricities, Torrijos understood power and wore it well. After the successful coup, Torrijos took command of the junta ruling the country and in short order ousted Martínez also.

Helping Torrijos to depose Martínez was Capt. Manuel Antonio Noriega, like Martínez an intelligence officer. The young Noriega had worked for Martínez, running intelligence operations in Chiriqui province.[2] Noriega had a long association with the U.S. Army. He began working with members of the 407th Military Intelligence Brigade in the mid-1960s, taking courses from U.S. officers in Panama and at Fort Bragg, North Carolina, in 1967.[3] Later, he worked for the Central Intelligence Agency, providing airfields and money to support CIA director William Casey's campaign to arm the Nicaraguan contras. From the early years of his military career, Noriega was often in trouble for his drinking and sexual adventures, which had come to the attention of the U.S. military community.

Among U.S. officers in Panama, Noriega came to be viewed as a most unattractive ally. According to officers with extensive experience in Panama, such as Gen. Frederick Woerner, who served a number of tours in the region and was SOUTHCOM commander from 1987 to 1989, a favorite cocktail party pastime during the 1960s was to speculate on the power struggles within the Panamanian military. "The worst scenario was that Noriega would come to the number one position," says Woerner. "But general wisdom was that he would not, that he had the power to, but he would always keep a front man as a lightning rod."

To the Americans, Noriega seemed comfortable as a subordinate to Torrijos, who did much to check Noriega's crude and brutal behavior. Yet as Torrijos consolidated his power through the 1970s, boosting his popularity to new heights with the negotiation of the

1977 treaties promising control of the canal to Panama, Noriega expanded his own base, rising to lieutenant colonel and chief of intelligence on the general staff.

When Torrijos died in a plane crash in August 1981, the checks on Noriega disintegrated. The Guardia collapsed in a power struggle. Torrijos's plan to introduce a form of democracy, based largely on his own impressive popularity, died with him. He had intended to hold elections in May 1984. Although they were to be free elections, Torrijos and his associates in the Guardia established their own political party to ensure continued military power.

Inheriting Torrijos's post as commander of the Guardia Nacional was Col. Florencio Flores, who was barely able to control the ambitions of Noriega, chief of staff Lt. Col. Rubén Darío Paredes, and Lt. Col. Roberto Díaz Herrera, Noriega's cousin and executive secretary of the general staff. Not only did these officers have their eyes on leadership of the Guardia, they worried that Flores would permit the military to become subordinate to the civilian government. In league with the Guardia's chief of operations, Lt. Col. Armando Contreras, the three decided Flores had to go. In March 1982, they "retired" Flores and several officers loyal to him in a bloodless coup.

No longer would the military be able to exercise power by force of personality alone, as Torrijos had.

To ensure continued military rule while technically upholding the commitment to civilian government, the three ringleaders worked out a deal whereby Paredes, who had succeeded Flores, would resign from the Guardia and run for president in the 1984 elections. The Guardia leadership would pledge itself to support the Paredes ticket. Noriega, Paredes, and Herrera signed a pact to this effect, drafted by Noriega and called Plan Torrijos.

"It is agreed that today's comandante and tomorrow's president Paredes will remain committed, in close and determinant connection with the successive comandantes, to preserve the rights, aspirations, feasible advantages, and ethical and reasonable privileges of the general staff members who leave active service," the agreement read.[4] In other words, to share the wealth. When Paredes's presidential term expired in 1989, Noriega and Diaz Herrera would be in a position to succeed him.

The Guardia change of command took place in grand, if not pompous, style on 12 August 1983, with Noriega replacing Paredes.

Noriega quickly moved to tighten his grip on the force and reassert its position in Panamanian society, which had slipped since Torrijos's death. In a speech at the elaborate ceremony, Noriega hinted at the need for the Guardia amid the turmoil caused by the guerrilla wars in El Salvador and Nicaragua. "We, the national defense forces, cannot be indifferent . . . to the Central American tragedy," Noriega said.[5] "We cannot be mere spectators in this drama. We will be in our barracks, as groups opposed to the regime demand with their outcries. However, it would be unacceptable, hypocritical pretension to say that, having played an important role in our national life, this force would remain idle in the task of achieving reconciliation among Panamanians."

Paredes formally announced his candidacy a week later. His campaign, such as it was, quickly fizzled. He had virtually no political base other than the Guardia. His pledged ally Noriega disappeared and Díaz Herrera went so far as to meet with opposition parties to signal the Guardia would take no active role in the elections. Paredes's candidacy evaporated without a trace.

Noriega now stood alone at the head of the Guardia. Upon taking power, he moved quickly to mold the institution to his liking, promoting himself to the rank of brigadier general while advancing Díaz Herrera to full colonel. Noriega also renamed the Guardia the Panama Defense Forces, or PDF. He had come to dislike the term Guardia Nacional, which in Latin America rarely meant a military force. To him, it sounded amateurish. At the same time, he wanted to maintain the image of the force as purely defensive. Perhaps above all, Noriega was thinking of the Israeli Defense Force, which he greatly admired.

Within six months of assuming command, Noriega maneuvered to secure political as well as military power, though he was careful to hold forth a civilian front man in the person of presidential candidate Nicolás Ardito Barletta. Noriega assigned Díaz Herrera the job of seeing that Barletta defeated the opposition candidate, Arnulfo Arias.

As the 6 May election neared, the race appeared to be close, with Barletta's slick campaign and professional political organization—bolstered by American image makers—seeming to balance Arias's genuine popularity and haphazard campaigning style. However, as election results trickled in, Díaz Herrera realized Barletta was headed for resounding defeat. Fortunately, the PDF controlled the voting apparatus. He suspended the vote count and set about to rig the results. In the official tally, Barletta won by fewer than 2,000 votes out of 600,000 counted.

Such transparent fraud drove Panamanians into the streets, but their demonstrations did not last. Having tightened his grip on Panama, Noriega was constrained by few rivals, either military or civilian. Nor did the United States present a serious threat to his machinations. For the Reagan administration, trying to stamp out communism in Central America, the problem of Noriega's corruption was less important than his aid in supporting the Nicaraguan contras against the Sandinista government and in backing the Salvadoran army.

Noriega was a known commodity who had assisted U.S. intelligence and military operations throughout his career. CIA director William Casey and National Security Council aide Lt. Col. Oliver North found Noriega invaluable. Barletta was no stranger, either, having studied at the University of Chicago school of economics under none other than George Shultz, Reagan's secretary of state. The United States was willing to accept the theft of the election—not to mention Noriega's increasing role in the drug trade—and recognize Barletta as the president of Panama.

Shultz flew to Panama in October 1984 for the inauguration of his former student, with the aim of securing Panama's aid in isolating the Sandinistas and supplying the contras. With Reagan on the verge of an overwhelming reelection victory, the administration looked to Panama as the strategic linchpin of its unflagging anticommunism in Central America.

The evolution of Panama into a strategic focal point was having a profound effect on SOUTHCOM as well. The command found itself no longer a sleepy backwater, responsible primarily for defending the Panama Canal and keeping track of intrigues within the Panamanian military, but a frontline participant in Reagan's battle against communism. The command became a significant base for special operations forces and military assistance specialists.

But Noriega's methods became more than the United States could ignore. Barletta was not as pliable as Noriega had reckoned, and by mid-1985 the two were often at odds.

Far more difficult was the September 1985 murder of Dr. Hugo Spadafora, a romantic revolutionary companion of Torrijos and a hero to many Panamanians—but a long-time enemy of Noriega. Spadafora had openly attacked the general for trafficking in cocaine. On 14 September, the doctor's headless, battered body was discovered in Costa Rica just a few yards from the Panamanian border.

News of the brutal slaying galvanized Panama. Spadafora's father, Carmelo, charged that Col. Julio Ow Young, Noriega's successor as intelligence chief, had executed his son on Noriega's order. While Noriega was out of the country at the time of the murder, the charge was widely accepted as true. Huge crowds mourned Spadafora; thousands greeted the return of his body to Panama City. Still more watched his funeral on national television. Díaz Herrera was furious, convinced Noriega had left the country so that he could pin the blame for the murder on him.

Envious of Noriega's power, Díaz Herrera decided this was the time to move against the PDF *comandante*. He ordered the elite Battalion 2000 to move from Fort Cimarron, just east of the capital, into the city. If the coup failed, Díaz Herrera could claim he had moved in troops to quell the demonstrations. The troop movement prompted a hurried phone call from Gen. John Galvin, SOUTHCOM commander in chief, to Díaz Herrera. Galvin wanted to know if Noriega was being ousted. Díaz Herrera backed down for lack of support among senior PDF officers. Noriega returned to Panama.

To cover his tracks, Díaz Herrera tried to focus Noriega's attention on his problems with Barletta, who was caught between popular clamor to investigate the Spadafora killing and the need to appease Noriega and the PDF. Added to this conflict was the need to salvage Panama's rocky economy. While Díaz Herrera was moving on Panama City, Barletta was in Washington, meeting with Shultz, assistant secretary of state Elliott Abrams, and other officials. They warned him that Díaz Herrera was trying to make him a scapegoat amid the outcry over Spadafora's death. When Barletta returned to Panama, Noriega and Díaz Herrera forced him to resign.

Their new choice for president was Eric Arturo Delvalle, a sugar magnate and one of Panama's wealthiest businessmen. For the time being, Noriega would find him compliant enough.

The Barletta firing was a turning point for Abrams, a committed neoconservative convinced of the need for a forceful U.S. presence in Central America. He had urged Barletta to hold on, hoping he could face down Noriega. When Barletta fled the country, he left Abrams to handle Noriega for the Reagan administration.

On 12 December 1985 Abrams and National Security Adviser Adm. John Poindexter flew to Panama to warn Noriega of U.S. concerns about his overarching power, his growing army, and his continuing involvement with drugs. The three men met at Howard Air Force Base, the main U.S. airstrip in Panama. Poindexter was new to his job, having just replaced Robert McFarlane as national security adviser.

Abrams says the main purpose of the trip was to tell Noriega that the United States would not tolerate increasing corruption within the PDF. "That was the first serious message to Noriega," he later told a House committee disturbed by the general's reputed involvement with drugs.[6]

Abrams had an uphill battle, for Noriega retained powerful allies within the CIA and Defense Department by virtue of his role in the contra operation. With Congress shifting on its commitment to aid the Nicaraguan rebels, the Reagan administration was reluctant to press Noriega too hard. Not until the Iran-contra scandal broke and the contra operation broke down did Noriega's abuses begin to outweigh his usefulness.

Supporting Noriega became increasingly difficult in early 1986 as Congress, particularly Senator Jesse Helms, began to investigate reports of corruption, brutality, and drug trafficking by Noriega and the PDF. Helms, a staunch opponent of the canal treaties, in March began a series of hearings intended to dramatize Noriega's excesses. In the face of mounting congressional criticism of Noriega, Abrams tried to minimize the damage. But with the widely reported hearings, Helms proved to have fired the first shot in what was to become open season on Noriega.

More serious blows followed in quick succession. In the 12 June edition of *The New York Times*, Pulitzer Prize-winning reporter Seymour Hersh detailed Noriega's role in the killing of Spadafora, the cocaine trade, and arms sales to Colombia guerrillas.[7] Other national newspapers followed suit, expanding on Noriega's simultaneous ties to the CIA and Cuba.[8]

The Reagan administration tried to rally support for Noriega, who hired a public relations firm to help with the damage control, but Helms succeeded in getting passed legislation requiring the CIA to report on the charges, including the PDF's role in the death of Spadafora. A remarkable coalition of the Senate's most liberal and conservative members voted for the bill.

Over the next year, the strain eased slightly in large part because of the Panamanian participation in various drug arrests. Noriega met regularly with the U.S. ambassador to Panama, Arthur Davis, and with General Galvin at the Quarry Heights headquarters of SOUTHCOM. Then, early in 1987, Noriega began to move against Díaz Herrera, his chief of staff and principal rival for supremacy in the PDF.

Díaz Herrera had kept a low profile since his aborted coup attempt.[9] He had been stripped of most of his power within the PDF. Adrift, the colonel sought refuge in the teachings of an Indian guru, Satya Sai Baba, inviting one of the guru's disciples to Panama. Díaz Herrera became a vegetarian and a devoted family man. He lost weight. Simultaneously, whatever trust Noriega still had in Díaz Herrera slipped away. It was time for another "retirement."

On 25 May Noriega summoned Díaz Herrera to negotiate the details of his departure with the PDF staff, although there was little room for debate. The assembled staff said Noriega had approved a deal that would provide well for Díaz Herrera by making him ambassador to Japan. On 1 June the announcement was made. But on 5 June, a friend called Díaz Herrera to warn him Noriega would renege on the deal. His disgrace would be complete.

The next day, SOUTHCOM changed hands. The new commander in chief, Gen. Frederick F. Woerner, Jr., continued the tradition of soldier-diplomats in the post. A West Point graduate and infantry battalion commander in Vietnam, he is fluent in Spanish. He holds a masters degree in history and a degree from the Uruguayan General Staff College, and has had a number of assignments focusing on Latin America. Woerner looked forward to the SOUTHCOM assignment as the capstone on his military career.

He intended to do what he could to help reform the PDF, and would begin the effort with his change-of-command speech, to be delivered in both English and Spanish. The speech would outline the U.S. view of the military's proper role as subordinate to civilian authority.

Woerner was not new to Panama, nor to Noriega and his career. He gave a copy of the speech to his brand-new aide, whom he had just met, and told him to put the text on the podium. As Woerner rose to speak, he realized the speech was not there. Having prepared it himself, he was unfazed. He had no trouble remembering what he intended to say on a topic he cared about so deeply. Woerner was determined to make a point to Noriega.

Woerner's message was none too subtle. He cited the U.S. armed forces as a noble example of a professional military. "Never, in our history," he said, "have we had a man on horseback, but have always been subordinate to civilian authority as elected by the populace. This ingredient of legitimacy is a fundamental underpinning of a professional military."

Because of its particular relevance to Noriega and the PDF, many in the audience interpreted the speech as a message from Washington directly to Noriega. Though Woerner says the ideas were his alone, the Panamanian dignitaries assembled at Howard Air Force Base heard Woerner's message as a *yanqui* rebuke. Noriega stomped off without paying his respects at the reception that followed.

While General Woerner was giving Noriega a taste of strong medicine, Díaz Herrera was preparing a near-lethal dosage for him of some strong medicine of his own.[10] Angered by Noriega's treatment of him and perhaps shamed by his own past excesses, Díaz Herrera struck back at Noriega through the press. He invited several Panamanian journalists to his house and began to lay out the myriad corruptions of Noriega's rise to power and the intrigues of the PDF. Díaz Herrera spoke of his own role in the stolen elections of 1984 and Noriega's part in the killing of Spadafora, and even charged Noriega with assassinating Torrijos.

These revelations had a cataclysmic effect on the Panamanian people. Although Díaz Herrera himself was no darling of opposition politicians, his charges gave voice to the broad but cowed majority of Panamanians who hated Noriega and the brutalities of the PDF. Whatever the truth of this barrage of charges, the effect was to rally diverse opposition groups to demonstrate in unison. A group of protesters assembled outside Díaz Herrera's house. Although they were relatively few in number, Noriega moved like lightning to suppress them. He sent his fiercest riot squads, "the Dobermans," to disperse the crowd with rubber hoses, tear gas, and finally bird shot. The demonstrators would scatter, only to reassemble. The gathering, and Noriega's reaction to it, unified the opposition as no previous event had.

Noriega ordered Delvalle to declare a state of emergency and to suspend nine articles of the Panamanian constitution guaranteeing civil liberties. The PDF now could make arrests without warrants and detain people without charges. Freedom of movement, assembly, and expression, all tenets of the constitution, were canceled. Alarmed by this escalation of political warfare, the U.S. Senate that June passed a resolution urging the restoration of constitutional rights.

Noriega's reaction was more of the same. In a move that may well have forced U.S. leaders to abandon him forever, he engineered an attack on the U.S. embassy in Panama City. Shortly before noon, in a carefully staged scene reminiscent of the 1964 riots, demonstrators began to hurl rocks at the embassy compound and to wreck cars while PDF policemen stood aside and watched. Following the incident, the Reagan administration directed the CIA to sever its ties with Noriega. From now on, he was to be a "target" rather than an "asset."

But Noriega still had ample domestic power. In the summer of 1987, he enjoyed almost total authority in Panama, with little to restrain him from using it. On 10 July, a day that Panamanians came to call "Black Friday," Noriega showed the extent to which he would oppress his country. The Civic Crusade, a coalition of Anti-Noriega groups, had called its boldest demonstration yet for that day, on the eve of Noriega's daughter's marriage. In response, the PDF took to the streets, shooting and arresting thousands of protesters in another flogging of civil liberties.

Noriega also stepped up the harassment of U.S. servicemen and women. In early October, the PDF arrested six airmen and three sailors, taking them to the PDF general headquarters, known as *La Comandancia,* in downtown Panama City. After holding them for three hours, the PDF transferred the nine men to a police station in Balboa, below SOUTHCOM headquarters. From Balboa they were moved again to nearby Fort Amador at 4:00 A.M., where PDF troops questioned and photographed them. All nine were released later that morning. Throughout their detention, the PDF denied the servicemen's requests to make telephone calls or talk to an English-speaking PDF member. Thus began a pattern that would continue until the United States forcibly removed Noriega from power.

In Washington, Elliott Abrams set about to convince the Reagan administration that Noriega would have to go. Top State Department officials talked of his removal as fundamental to any solution of Panama's festering economic problems.

Though some agreed in principle, there was little agreement on the means of removing the dictator. Abrams and others at the State Department were coming to the conclusion that the only way would be a surgical military strike by special operations teams. Officers in SOUTHCOM were adamantly opposed, and ridiculed Abrams's attempts to devise tactics for such an operation. The SOUTHCOM staff called it a "Rambo operation." Only on the eve of the invasion would this argument be resolved.

2

"You Know, Woerner, You Better Be Prepared."

Despite Woerner's warning shots and the demonstrations aroused by Díaz Herrera's revelations, few officials in Washington were in a hurry to discipline Noriega. Lt. Gen. Colin Powell, who had replaced Admiral Poindexter as national security adviser—the choice of another military officer had been a controversial one because of Poindexter's role in the Iran-contra scandal—was not sure there were clear alternatives to Noriega. He felt the United States could not improve the situation until the elections scheduled for May of 1989, and the best plan would be to focus efforts toward the election.

To Woerner, this policy of procrastinating until the election meant there was no comprehensive and cohesive political-military strategy for Panama. The one firm policy was, by decision of President Reagan, a prohibition on the use of military force. Nonetheless, Woerner could see that Noriega's PDF could very well become the enemy. As SOUTHCOM commander in chief, he felt he should prepare against that contingency.

This turned the SOUTHCOM world on its head, for a large part of its mission had been encouraging ties with the Panamanian military. Woerner was trying to build cooperation between the two forces, and many Panamanian officers had been to U.S. Army schools. The command now had to consider the possibility of fighting the forces it was trying to educate and train.

As SOUTHCOM commander, Woerner had assumed leadership of one of the more peculiar American military institutions. Its primary fighting forces were under its Army component, known as

U.S. Army South, or USARSO. Its principal military task had been, since 1914, defense of the Panama Canal, a mission that had not been a dominating American concern since World War II, despite continuing crises within Central America. During the Reagan years its profile had been raised by the crises within the region, but its largest combat unit remained a single brigade of just two battalions, the 193d Infantry Brigade. Air Force participation in SOUTHCOM was minor, although the Navy had a substantial fueling facility in Panama. As the Army and other services bought new weaponry during the Reagan buildup, SOUTHCOM was low on the list of needs in comparison with the confrontation with the Soviet Union in Central Europe. Many in the Pentagon regarded Panama as a halfway house for soldiers whose careers were going nowhere and who were due to retire. Faced with a growing crisis on its hands, SOUTHCOM had two strikes against it: its own bureaucratic structure and a lack of confidence back in Washington.

Woerner himself was not well known in high circles in Washington, though after serving in Colombia, Guatemala, and Uruguay as well as Panama he was an expert on Latin America. He also held an advanced degree in Latin American studies and had been the director of Latin American studies at the U.S. Army War College. Compared to his immediate predecessor, General Galvin, who had gone on to lead U.S. and NATO troops in Europe, Woerner was less influential. Also, Adm. William Crowe, the chairman of the Joint Chiefs of Staff, had very definite ideas about Panama. Crowe did not see American strategic interests as being engaged by the situation there, and was opposed to confrontation. He was against the use of U.S. bases to aid the Panamanian opposition. To observers such as Elliott Abrams, Crowe shared Woerner's desire to find a Panamanian solution to a Panamanian problem.

Woerner's director of operations and plans at SOUTHCOM was Brig. Gen. Marc Cisneros, another Spanish-speaking officer, being of Mexican descent from southern Texas. As his relations with the United States deteriorated, Noriega targeted Cisneros in his psychological operations against Americans, constantly featuring him in articles in the government's newspapers as a Latin traitor, a genocidal general.

As the crisis developed, Cisneros was given the task of revising SOUTHCOM's contingency plans, which, oriented on defense of the Panama Canal, did not include a scenario where the PDF was the enemy. This was a sea change in the institutional thinking of SOUTHCOM, and it did not go smoothly. The worst contingency thought about the PDF previously was how to control anti-American popular demonstrations if the PDF were to just stand aside.

Even as he began to plan against them, Cisneros did not think the Panamanians would fight to the death for Noriega. As he watched Panamanian television, observed the growing popular support of the anti-Noriega forces, and talked to some of their officers, Cisneros became convinced that Noriega did not have much of a constituency among his own forces.

Led by Brigadier General Cisneros and Maj. Gen. Bernard Loeffke, the USARSO commander, discussions got under way in November 1987. Loeffke, too, is a soldier-diplomat, but with a paratrooper's spirit and confidence. He speaks five languages, including Russian and Chinese, and has trained with Chinese paratroopers. Also a veteran of several Panama tours, he had a keen understanding of Latin American politics and culture, and subsequently went on to head the Inter-American Defense Board.

Woerner gave overall direction to the planners. He felt he was a man out on a limb—the Reagan administration, in the person of Admiral Crowe, had clearly stated it did not intend to use force in Panama. Still, Woerner felt the need to plan for contingencies. "Every bone in my body said, 'You know, Woerner, you'd better be prepared. As a military commander, you'll look kind of silly if you get an order to do something and you don't have any plans,'" he recalls.

One of the first decisions I faced was between the strike, [a] commando-type operation, or an intervention of force. And I weighed this very, very carefully. Because of the greater control over violence, over collateral damage, I would have preferred the strike operation. But the one thing that I did not want, a dominant factor that led me away from that was—even if I succeeded, much less if I failed to get Noriega—I had a population of 50,000 Americans scattered throughout the country and I could not guarantee their protection against a PDF that might be a little upset with us, seeing that we would have just kidnapped their commanding officer. I could not resolve the problem of security with a strike-type operation, successful or not.

Crowe also told Woerner he would not approve "a surprise attack." Crowe wanted any operations to be the result of a deliberate buildup. "If we were to make the decision to intervene militarily, we build up the force," Woerner recalls.

> We make no secret of it. We start flowing it in. That would give us one final chance at having Panama solve the problem themselves. In other words the PDF says, "Hey wait a minute. We're not going to die for this guy." And I would have let it be known to the PDF, to the rank and file, that you have one way to stop this invasion: take Noriega out. So I felt that the initiation of the force, prior to the stage of intervening, could have forced the Panama Defense Forces to act. And then, you know, we never would have had to say publicly whether we had intended to invade or not. Plausible denial: "It's another training exercise."

The SOUTHCOM plans themselves, first code-named *Elaborate Maze,* then changed to *Prayer Book,* covered a wide range of combat and post-combat operations. The combat portions of the plan, called *Blue Spoon,* came to include varying options and troop lists, ranging from forces already stationed within Panama to very large forces coming in to augment them. Elaborate plans were made to cover a range of contingencies from conducting a surgical operation oriented on Noriega all the way to full-scale combat operations. Other concerns were having to establish a military government or reconstituting a civilian government in a situation where all services had broken down.

These options included some very large forces indeed. Cisneros was concerned that such operations could quickly grow beyond the ability of SOUTHCOM to manage them, threatening unity of command. To carry out the options that called for troops outside of Panama, SOUTHCOM would have to pry troops from other commands and commanders naturally reluctant to let them go. In the course of reviewing the war plans, Cisneros reminded Woerner that "here in SOUTHCOM we're sort of the poor cousins. . . . Most of our forces are augmentations. They come from different commands. All the commands have their peculiarities. All of them want to get involved in how they're going to run your troops."

Though there was general agreement in Panama as to what kind of military operation Blue Spoon should be, the issue of who or what organization should be in command was still at issue. Loeffke was most concerned about the operations in Panama City and believed that USARSO should therefore be in charge of what he called Joint Task Force–Panama. Cisneros retained his reservations about the command structure.

By the end of 1987, the Panama planners were ready to flesh out their plans by discussing them with the various Army organizations that would serve as augmentations to the force in Panama. Key among these was the Army's primary force for contingency operations, XVIII Airborne Corps, headquartered at Fort Bragg. In January 1988, representatives of the corps planning staff traveled to Panama to discuss Prayer Book/Blue Spoon, as did members of the staffs of Forces Command, from Fort McPherson, Georgia, and Training and Doctrine Command from Fort Monroe, Virginia. Few of these staff officers had a good idea of what Blue Spoon was, but were anxious to learn what planning needed to be done in the event of an operation or deployment to Panama and what role each command was to play.

The planning staff from XVIII Airborne Corps, including the corps commander, Lt. Gen. John Foss, and his operations officer, Col. Tom Needham, were sure they would become an operational headquarters if there were to be fighting in Panama. But as their representative, Lt. Col. Tim McMahon, chatted with the Forces Command staff on the plane to Panama, he was surprised to learn that Loeffke had other ideas. Loeffke wanted USARSO to be the warfighting headquarters, subordinate to SOUTHCOM, and had gone so far as to prepare an operations order of his own in support of the SOUTHCOM plan. Loeffke called his organization Joint Task Force–Panama.

This revelation inspired a range of questions in the minds of McMahon and others from the corps. They saw USARSO as rife with the same organizational problems Cisneros saw in SOUTH-COM—while USARSO was a legitimate, decent, viable theater Army headquarters, it just was not structured for running an operation the size of a full-scale Blue Spoon, they thought. Loeffke, too, understood the shortcomings of USARSO—he had served as chief of staff of XVIII Airborne Corps—but thought they could be remedied by augmenting the USARSO staff by attaching forces from other Army units in the United States.

XVIII Airborne Corps found itself very reluctant to give up much, as it had to focus on contingencies all over the world. "We couldn't give away the corps's capability to do that," says McMahon. "But we still felt that there was a requirement, it was also good for us, to rotate some folks in various positions, not only within the USARSO staff but within some of their operations as well, their signal organization, their military intelligence organization, and so forth."

Loeffke wanted more, especially intelligence officers. Because of the familiarity between Panama and the United States, the growing ties with the PDF, and the American predilection to overlook the abuses of its constant ally within an unstable region, the Panamanian military had not been considered a worthwhile intelligence target. What CIA activity there was in Panama was aimed at higher-level targets. The PDF "order of battle," such as it was, had been a lower priority. The corps was reluctant to give up these units, arguing that it would inhibit their ability to deploy rapidly.

Loeffke also wanted relief from longstanding exercise commitments. As the Army component of SOUTHCOM, USARSO was obligated to run a number of command post exercises within the theater, with various Central and South American countries. The USARSO staff would be tasked to send a group of officers and work the command post exercises with the staff college in Chile or Venezuela or another country. The burden often fell on the 193d Infantry Brigade, which now was becoming more concerned with operations in Panama. Yet the brigade's focus remained on local security concerns rather than on designing a broader campaign.

While the XVIII Airborne Corps was reluctant to provide much relief for USARSO, the command had other options for calling on stateside units for help. In addition to being the Army component of a unified command in SOUTHCOM, USARSO was a major organization under the Department of the Army. As such, they could appeal to the department for troop levies from other Army commands, and in this case the department told Forces Command to supply USARSO's needs. The result was that staff officers from units such as the 10th Mountain Division, stationed at Fort Drum in upstate New York, were finding themselves taking long weekends in Central and South America for the command post exercises. These staff augmentees, called "filler angels" for their role in filling out USARSO's needs, included active and reserve officers and came from other Army commands as well. A captain from the Army's armor school at Fort Knox, Kentucky, might find himself with a brief summer vacation in the dead of winter, shifting his focus from stopping the Russian hordes in the Fulda Gap to the problems of fighting in the streets of Panama City as an augmentee to the Joint Task Force–Panama staff.

In these initial meetings, the Army planners felt there was little urgent need to resolve the many issues raised by the possibility of an operation in Panama. They were soon caught out when, on 4 February 1988, two Florida grand juries—one in Miami, one in Tampa—indicted Noriega on separate charges rising out of his connection with the drug cartels. Each set of charges was the fruit of investigations by ambitious U.S. attorneys who appeared to care little about the foreign policy implications of their cases.

The first fallout from the indictments was to further heighten the spiraling rivalries within the Reagan administration. Though all agencies were aware of the pending charges, the policymakers had little advance warning. Abrams and Woerner learned the charges would be brought in one of their routine meetings just twenty-four hours before the indictments were to be released. Many officials were to criticize the charges after they were brought, but no serious opposition was voiced in a meeting with U.S. attorney Leon Kellner. President Reagan was briefed only after the fact—by then-Lt. Gen. Colin Powell.

The foreign policy effects of the two drug indictments were swift in coming. On 25 February, after goading from Elliott Abrams and William Walker, Panamanian president Eric Arturo Delvalle, a man who had given his blessing to Noriega's "Black Friday" of the previous summer, fired Noriega, saying he had placed himself "above the nation," and installed the PDF chief of staff, Col. Marco Justine. As hated as Noriega was, Delvalle was seen as a corrupt member of Panama's elite, tarred by association with Noriega, and despised by the upper-class members of the Civic Crusade, who sought the ouster of Noriega. Delvalle had no credibility with the Panamanian people, and certainly few took to the streets after his firing of Noriega. Finally, Delvalle himself was a weak-willed man, incapable of a direct confrontation with Noriega.

Though the United States had coaxed Delvalle into his timid attempt to get rid of Noriega, the American government again found itself paralyzed and unable to capitalize on even this slight opportunity of its own making. Though President Reagan swiftly expressed his support for Delvalle and condemned Noreiga's "efforts to perpetuate military rule," he would not buttress his words with any action. The Defense Department thought backing Delvalle was a bad idea. For six weeks, the United States dithered over economic sanctions.

Noriega felt no such paralysis. The day Delvalle "fired" him, he stepped up the pace of harassment of U.S. servicemen in Panama. During that week, thirty-three service members were detained by the PDF while on the way to work, ostensibly for wearing their uniforms while traveling in public. Under a provision of the Panama Canal treaties of 1977, wearing uniforms while traveling to military facilities was permitted, and the roundup took SOUTHCOM by surprise. In response, Woerner restricted the movements of his soldiers.

The Delvalle affair also gave the State Department the pretext for securing one of its long-held goals: severing the ties between SOUTHCOM and Noriega. Woerner and the Defense Department had wanted to maintain communications, even though they had eroded to a minimal level. Moreover, formal notification to the Panamanian government of upcoming exercises was required under the Panama Canal treaties.

Typically, Woerner would meet with Noriega in Noriega's office at Fort Amador, a base shared by both the U.S. Army and the PDF. But they would also meet at military functions in the region. According to Woerner, Noriega

> always abided by the rules. Well, he also knew that if he didn't, he might get that one shot at me but there wouldn't be any more. And he was interested in maintaining it.
>
> He was using me as a vehicle of reminding the U.S. government of what a loyal ally he had been over the years, and how he had helped us on a series of sticky problems: the shah of Iran, the intelligence-gathering activities, the counterdrug [operations], etc. And he would reassure me—I'd get the same speech about the [Torrijos] revolution that began in 1968 and would be completed with the elections in 1989, full restoration of democracy. I got the same lecture each time. Half the talk would be straightforward. He can be disarmingly honest at times. And any day-to-day issues that we had were handled straightforwardly.

But when we got into the philosophy of the role of the military and all, then it was pure smoke. The one exception I remember well on the philosophic smoke was when he told me about the military returning to the barracks in 1989. He said, "Remember. This is not the United States. This is Panama. The democracy will not be the democracy of the United States. It will be the democracy of Panama." And he said the military, for the next year or so, will have an important political role. And he paused for a second, and he said, "No. For the next decade." And he paused another second or two, and he looked at me and he said, "No. Forever." It was the one moment of reality in my periodic philosophic sessions with him.

Woerner felt he could not impress Noriega with how he was jeopardizing his position with the United States. "I sensed that he thought it was just something that he could wait out. . . . The way those meetings would usually go, Noriega would call or he'd frequently send a message through a mutual friend or acquaintance. And it would be kind of low key: 'There are difficulties emerging. And it's important that we maintain communications. We've always been friends. We have to talk.' It would be these kinds of things."

The Noriega-Delvalle standoff prodded the Army and SOUTH-COM to step up planning, especially of the special operations projected. Army special operations forces were conducting a series of exercises at Hurlburt Field, Florida, called *Casino Gambit,* when the Delvalle firing occurred, and commanders quickly added long hours of planning in the nights to their days in the field. Working for weeks on end, the special operators quickly cobbled together what would become known as the Joint Special Operations Task Force, or JSOTF. The senior leaders, including Gen. James Lindsay, then commander of U.S. Special Operations Command, decided that the current SOUTHCOM special operations forces organization was too small to handle an operation of the size they were planning, and those in Panama agreed. The planning continued for several weeks after the Casino Gambit exercises were over and most of the troops had returned to Fort Bragg.

The worsening situation also pushed other plans along. The Prayer Book plan was being completed, and it had evolved into a complex series of operations. The actual fighting portion of the plan was code-named *Blue Spoon,* but its scenario depended upon another part of the plan called *Elder Statesman* and later changed to

Post Time. This was a plan for the buildup of forces, on a piecemeal basis, over a week. It actually would have taken twelve to nineteen days to execute in full and from a standing start, because it would take that long to mobilize the backup forces required from the Air Force. Also, the buildup would be strung out by the deployment of Marine amphibious forces from the west coast of the United States.

The core of the force that would supplement the Army's 193d Infantry Brigade permanently stationed in Panama would be units from the 7th Infantry Division (Light), stationed at Fort Ord, California. Woerner, Cisneros, and Loeffke felt comfortable with these "light fighters," who had been on several deployments to Central America. However, they would require a secure airfield and a longer warning time to deploy to Panama than would the 82d Airborne Division, the heart of XVIII Airborne Corps's quick reaction capability. But SOUTHCOM and USARSO preferred to lead their troop roster with the 7th Division rather than the paratroopers. Following on the heels of the 7th Division would be a Marine expeditionary force and carrier air power.

The second element in Prayer Book was known as *Klondike Key.* This portion of the plan called for what is known as a "noncombatant evacuation operation," or NEO. As SOUTHCOM envisioned it, not only did the families of American soldiers have to be secured and evacuated, but also the tens of thousands of U.S. citizens throughout Panama City. To the soldiers stationed in Panama, who would be living, as it were, in the war zone, this was an important ingredient of the plan. They had to be sure their families and loved ones were safe, and were concerned with the likelihood that a strike on the PDF or Noriega would mean that hostages would be seized in retaliation.

Other commands questioned the idea, or at least how it was to work. Planners at the XVIII Airborne Corps believed the slow troop buildup would alert the PDF to any operation and that that would be the trigger for hostage taking. The SOUTHCOM planners had not made it clear whether the evacuation operation would be run simultaneously with combat operations, diffusing the main effort, or before, or even after. Any of the options would require huge numbers of troops, they argued. They thought the NEO plans were nebulous, at best.

"There's also the question of whether you're going to have a hostile or a non-hostile NEO," recalls one corps planner. "Are you going to have to fight to get thousands of U.S. citizens, and protect them at the same time, out of Panama? If so you've got to secure them as well or else you'll be fighting your way through to a departure area. I don't recall that we've done anything like that on a large scale."

Another controversial plan in the Prayer Book series was called *Krystal Ball,* and later *Blind Logic.* This was the plan for stability and civil affairs operations to be conducted after the fighting was over. The Krystal Ball plans were also believed to be nebulous. They called for a combat force, a tactical unit to clear an area of the city, after which the civil affairs people would move in. The civil affairs specialists would assume operational control of the military force as they did civil affairs tasks. Of all the elements of SOUTHCOM's Prayer Book series, this plan was least liked by the XVIII Airborne Corps, and perhaps the least specific. "I don't know if they were going to build strategic hamlets in the neighborhoods but there just wasn't the follow-through in thinking in the whole plan," says the war planner. The corps regarded stability force operations as an integral part of any campaign, not separate operations in themselves. Their objectives should be in support of specific operational goals, such as reestablishing governmental infrastructures such as the police force or other agencies, or allowing private businesses to begin functioning after hostilities were ended.

Woerner admits this phase of the plan was weak.

> We worked at it, but we worked to the limits of our own ability, and it was one of the most important phases. And the reason we could not develop that past a certain level was because I was not permitted to enter into plans with the Department of State, for security reasons. Remember, we're now planning an invasion of a friendly nation with whom we have diplomatic relations from bases internal to that country. Pretty sensitive issue, especially when you've got base negotiations going on in the Philippines.

Beyond the issues of unity of command, the Joint Chiefs of Staff (JCS) operations staff was uneasy with the Prayer Book series. They regarded it as too complex, some even finding it incomprehensible. In its first version, the plan was not approved by the joint chiefs. Cisneros would make four trips to the Pentagon to brief the JCS on Prayer Book/Blue Spoon.

Lt. Gen. Thomas Kelly, then director of operations for the JCS, and his staff were unhappy with the slow pace of Post Time, the deployment phase of Prayer Book. "The key part of this was that we were going to go down there with 22,000 troops roughly; it would take up to twenty-two days to introduce them into theater," says Kelly. "[Woerner] insisted on using the 7th Infantry Division, which was sort of major in Panama, all of which we disagreed with. The thing we disagreed with the most was that he was going to use JTF-Panama with USARSO as the [headquarters] that would manage this force."

The JCS operations staff considered Prayer Book to be an extremely complicated plan. This reinforced the feeling that USARSO could not manage the operation. Says Kelly: "[The] USARSO [headquarters is] four hundred guys, but what have they been doing all their lives? They've been administering security assistance in Latin America. So I made that clearly known in very, very strong terms with Cisneros that I thought they needed to reconsider command and control."

Cisneros agreed with Kelly, but was unable to convince Woerner of the need to bring in outside help in the form of the XVIII Airborne Corps, a difference of opinion that in time widened into a major dispute. And Woerner's refusal to change the command structure, along with the complexity of the command structure for Prayer Book/Blue Spoon, began to erode his credibility in Washington. The difference in outlook between the kind of officers of the JCS operations staff and those in Panama was dramatic. The operations staff considered the military component the centerpiece of any operation. Proper planning should center around the need to fight successfully if need be. Woerner and Loeffke, mindful of the exposed American community in Panama, looked for other routes to resolve the conflict, considering combat only a last resort.

Cisneros found himself caught in an uncomfortable middle ground. He wanted to confront Noriega more directly than Woerner would let him, and wanted to have the option of overwhelming force if needed. And the personal attacks upon him in the Panamanian press rankled Cisneros. Yet, like Woerner, he felt there was a possibility for a local solution, and that a "Panamanian answer" would survive longer than one imposed by Americans.

Cisneros also felt that SOUTHCOM should press ahead with a plan despite the direction from Crowe and the Reagan administration that military force was not an option. "I think that sometimes your higher headquarters will never lay out things for you very clearly and tell you exactly A, B, C, and D and do that. My view is that you take your mission, and you take risk and you do it," says Cisneros.

Yet the Prayer Book/Blue Spoon plan raised more questions than it answered for many in the Pentagon. To Kelly, it represented

an exaggerated sense of what they could do. You talk about bringing in air sorties off a carrier, you introduce Marines into the theater, bringing in the 7th Division, trying to do all those things. . . . We kept trying to talk [Woerner] into using the XVIII Airborne Corps head-quarters, and actually, Gen. John Foss, the corps commander, was also trying to put together a joint task force that could respond to Panama's requirements, but we never could get that done.

As the plan evolved, a kind of compromise emerged, but it was one that satisfied no one. Says Kelly: "We got it to the point where [SOUTHCOM] agreed that at a certain point they would introduce that corps headquarters, but it would not be until they thought [the operation] exceeded their capability. Changing command during an operation is pretty tough."

In the event Prayer Book/Blue Spoon was approved, it would first only be approved for execution planning. This meant that JCS has approved the concept for more detailed work, and that Cisneros was free to call on outside forces to prepare supporting plans, in-cluding those of other services.

Almost immediately, Cisneros ran into resistance. The Prayer Book/Blue Spoon plans called for a Navy aircraft carrier to stand off Panama to provide close air support in the event Howard Air Force Base, the prime Air Force field in Panama, came under artil-lery or mortar fire. But getting the Navy to agree to a unified com-mand structure would be a difficult task, and it fell to Cisneros.

"I put in the concept that it would be under our operational con-trol, and this upset the Navy to no end," he says.

There was a series of very nasty messages between the Navy and my-self as [the SOUTHCOM operations director] that went back and forth on it. General Woerner was not involved. He just gave me the mission to go on it, and then I was fighting that battle, but I learned later that the Navy's responses to me were being cleared at the highest levels. They thought General Woerner was personally involved in it. I said, "General Woerner gave me the mission and I went to it: get control of the Navy. Whatever Navy assets, I want them under my control."

But the Navy was not about to let an Army general control the operations of one of its capital ships and made that clear when the Prayer Book series first was briefed to the Defense Department. The arguments became heated within the JCS meeting room, known as "the tank." Says Cisneros:

> If the Navy force comes in here, they will be under our operational control. The Navy fought that because it said first of all, "We own the waters. Therefore the [ships are] in our waters, so they're under our operational control. You just give us a mission and we'll do it." My argument was that you, the Navy, are oriented where the ships are. Where the ships are is not important. The mission that the aircraft are doing, and the mission of where they're going to be regarding force presence, is the important thing. The mission that you're here for is to support us here in Panama. Therefore, you should be under our operational control.
>
> They fought that very hard, because I think they honestly felt we were going to give them rudder orders and since we're primarily an Army command, they were very reluctant. And our argument was, "Well, you have a commander. You have a Navy commander of that force. We'll give him the orders and he'll comply with them. We're not going to individually give you rudder orders for each ship." That got into a big donneybrook, and finally Admiral Crowe voted in our favor, and the plan was approved where the Navy carrier, if it came in here, would be under our operational control. I personally had to go up there and argue this in the tank, and the Navy was really shooting arrows at me from all directions. [Then] I got a call from JCS. It said the chairman has approved the concept, they will be under [the operational control] of [SOUTHCOM].

So for a rare moment in the history of the U.S. military, a Navy carrier would come under the operational control of an Army commander in chief. Nevertheless, the Navy kept fighting the idea, in official and other channels, and the issue would not be resolved for more than a year.

The plan was not very satisfactory to the XVIII Airborne Corps, either. All of the units involved were "holding their cards rather closely," as corps planner Lt. Col. Tim McMahon puts it. During the planning and as the negotiations over troop rotations to Panama evolved, they resembled an elaborate mating dance, with the officers of the various organizations keeping a wary eye on each other.

None was more wary than the XVIII Airborne Corps, for Foss and his staff were convinced that if the situation in Panama ever required military intervention, they would be called on, and would bear the bulk of the responsibility. "From our perspective, we felt that if military operations were directed, that [the] XVIII Airborne Corps was going down there as the joint task force headquarters without regard to what anybody had written, without regard to what SOUTHCOM had written in its plans, without regard to what USARSO as a provisional joint task force had written in their plans," says McMahon. "General Foss was convinced of that and that's why our initial planning focus was different at the outset from what SOUTHCOM had been planning in Blue Spoon, and what USARSO as Joint Task Force–Panama had been planning."

The corps also had questions about tactical aspects of Prayer Book/Blue Spoon. If executed in full, the force buildup would have been massive, involving more than twenty thousand troops. At the slower pace, says one corps planner,

We would have tipped our hand much earlier. [Under] Post Time, we were bringing in forces through strategic air lift to Howard Air Force Base on a piecemeal basis over several days. We were concerned that this would have tipped our hand very clearly, that kind of airlift.

Also, we weren't certain that the forces in the Blue Spoon plan were tailored correctly for the missions. We thought they were a little heavy at first. We thought that we needed to go in according to the way the XVIII Airborne Corps operates. Our warfighting philosophy is overwhelming firepower but delivered very rapidly and decisively. We didn't feel that that plan met our own warfighting philosophy. . . .

I think there was almost a presumed benign nature of operations as a matter of fact. Howard Air Force Base was looked at as the sole arrival air field. If anything were to happen to destroy that continued air flow, to slow down or prevent the continued air flow, we'd be in trouble.

To try to give some muscle to its backing of Delvalle, the Reagan administration began to tighten the financial screws on Noriega, working to gain control of Panamanian government assets in the United States. On 3 March, nearing collapse, Panamanian banks closed. The U.S. dollar served as Panamanian currency, and what was once a strength of the country's economy became Noriega's weakness. Though he fought for his financial life, Noriega could not raise money fast enough. As a result of the sanctions, on 15 March Noriega for the first time failed to pay government employees, and a general strike was set for the next day. So was a coup, also a first for Noriega.

The coup was led by a Major Fernando Quezada, one of the shining lights of the PDF staff. Quezada recruited a number of other up-and-coming staff officers, mostly majors, and Col. Leonidas Macias, chief of the PDF police.

The smooth and sophisticated staff officers bungled their coup attempt badly. Many observers believe Noriega must have been on to the plot, for he fooled Quezada into thinking Noriega would sleep that night in La Comandancia. On the morning of the sixteenth, Macias seized control of the Comandancia's weapons storeroom, but got himself locked in by a Noriega loyalist; his co-conspirators grabbed other parts of the headquarters building and arrested the leader of the garrison troop, then-captain Moisés Giroldi, but the coup quickly fizzled. By noon all were under arrest and Noriega firmly in control of the situation.

But if the coup attempt permitted Noriega to consolidate his hold on the PDF, it also alerted SOUTHCOM to the depth of the divisions within the Panamanian force. Cisneros was the American general officer who was meeting with the Panamanian general staff. "I was getting a lot of signals, and some feelings that they just had a man that they really wanted to get rid of, but they just didn't know how to go about it in an honorable manner or in a manner that was fairly safe for them to do so," he says. The coup revealed how big the fracture was.

SOUTHCOM's attention during the coup period was divided because other elements of the Reagan strategy for Central America were unraveling. Fighting between the Nicaraguan contras and Sandinistas was peaking. The communist Sandinistas were staging a drive to root out rebel resistance in the northwest region of Nicaragua, and were extending their attacks across the border into Honduras. The day after the Panamanian coup attempt, President Reagan authorized Operation Golden Pheasant, an emergency deployment of 3,150 troops from the 82d Airborne Division and 7th Infantry Division to Palmerola air base in central Honduras.

While the primary focus of Golden Pheasant was to ensure stability in Honduras and to intimidate the Sandinistas, it also was a test of the compatibility of the units leading the troop roster for the Prayer Book plans.

Yet even as Golden Pheasant was under way, the growing concern with security in Panama led to the deployment of the 503d Military Police (MP) Battalion and 21st and 108th MP Companies—all part of the 16th MP Brigade from Fort Bragg and the XVIII Airborne Corps—on 18 March, along with various support troops. Marine and Air Force security forces were also sent. These moves boosted the local security effort, greatly increasing patrols and beefing up guard posts at the gates of U.S. installations. While the Army units stationed in Panama welcomed the help, the deployment heightened their awareness that the threat from Noriega easily could outstrip their ability to defend themselves, their families, and other Americans in Panama. To officers like Cisneros, the need for outside help—in the form of the XVIII Airborne Corps—was becoming more obvious.

Noting Noriega's strength in surviving the coup attempt, the Reagan administration moved to step up its economic warfare on Noriega, finally invoking formal sanctions on 8 April. The State Department continued to urge a surgical military strike against Noriega, and Elliott Abrams wanted to set up an anti-Noriega radio station, to be run by the Panamanian opposition, on a U.S. military base. Crowe objected to the plan on the grounds that it would endanger U.S. basing rights elsewhere at a time when there was growing opposition around the world, and especially in Europe, to the presence of American forces.

The military had begun a series of exercises in Panama, called *Total Warrior,* to assert U.S. rights under the Panama Canal treaties and to make clear that the harassment of Americans in Panama City would not be tolerated. From 12 March through 12 April, elements of the Puerto Rican and Florida Army National Guards would conduct maneuvers in Panama.

The need for security began to swallow troops as fast as the

Defense Department could send them. In the first week in April, 400 Marines from Camp Lejeune, North Carolina, were sent to further bolster SOUTHCOM's security effort, but no sooner had they arrived than armed bands of intruders infiltrated the Navy's sprawling, eight-hundred-acre Arraijan fuel tank farm near Howard Air Force Base.[1] The Marines and the intruders exchanged fire on the nights of 11 and 12 April, and one Marine, Cpl. Ricardo Villahermosa, was caught in a crossfire and killed—by a fellow Marine. The gun fights, which ranged all over the tank farm and lasted more than two hours, involved about fifty intruders and as many as one hundred Marines who returned fire with mortars as well as rifles. Other, similar incidents occurred the following week.

The incidents sounded alarm bells within SOUTHCOM, because the intruders were either Cubans or PDF led by Cubans. In the period after the coup, Noriega had begun to cement his ties with Cuba, and Cubans were aiding in the training of Noriega's Macho de Monte. During the week prior to the tank farm raids, Noriega had staged an display of Dignity Battalion devotion in the Panama City district of San Miguelito. Chanting their motto: "To die for the Fatherland is to live," several hundred local Dignity Battalion trainees went for a run through the neighborhood and were given rudimentary training in the use of automatic rifles.[2]

But the tank farm raids were another matter entirely, one that prompted a special investigation by USARSO's Joint Task Force–Panama. Several intruders were wounded by the Marines. The intruders, clad in black uniforms, also impressed the Marines as professional soldiers: "They were highly professional. They were good," recalled Marine 1st Sgt. Alexander Nevglovski.[3]

Noriega's psychological warfare was beginning to unnerve the SOUTHCOM community, particularly soldiers' wives and families. The pattern of harassment was disturbing. As commander, Woerner was drawing most of the blame, and senior officers began to refer to the command derisively as "WIMPCOM." Woerner did his best to calm the atmosphere, telling a group of families of "contingency plans for the movement of 39,000 Americans to safety by air, land, and sea [that] could be taken off the shelf if needed."[4] Yet he still believed Noriega would not push the United States to a military response, and he had standing orders from Washington that the use of force was out, despite what Elliott Abrams said.

Woerner felt like he was caught in a box and he was looking for a way out.

In response to his dilemma, Woerner tried to craft a comprehensive strategy to remove Noriega nonviolently or at least without direct American military intervention. This was Woerner's interpretation of U.S. policy or intent. While now determined to offer policies of his own making, he continued to complain about the lack of clear guidelines from the Reagan administration.

Woerner called his plans *Fissures,* and they, like Prayer Book and Blue Spoon, were to go through several stages and revisions. The overall thrust was to try to facilitate "a Panamanian solution," either by a PDF removal of Noriega or by the strengthening of the civilian opposition. Washington refused to approve the first draft of the plan, but liked bits and pieces of subsequent versions. The message to Woerner and SOUTHCOM, however, was confusing. Woerner first tried to rally support within the U.S. bureaucracy in Panama. *Fissures One* was developed with the U.S. embassy staff and coordinated with the State and Defense departments in Washington and with the CIA.

Woerner also tried to make a distinction between the two goals of removing Noriega and "restoring democracy." He thought that grossly underestimated the challenge or was deliberately dishonest. "The removal of Noriega, though it was an absolutely essential first step, unto itself merely created a promotion potential for the next thug," says Woerner. "It didn't change institutional attitudes. And secondly, 'Restore democracy,' as we mentioned, presumed the presence but temporarily displaced underpinnings of democracy. And I didn't believe that they existed."

Woerner called his strategy the "Panama Triad." The most important leg of that triad was to be the development of an internal opposition. The second leg was to be U.S. support, and the third, internationalization of the issue. He argued that a legitimate Panamanian opposition with increasing international and American support created "synergism," in that the three legs of the triad would naturally support one another. American moves would count for nothing unless in support of Panamanian "people power," and without the opposition, internationalization would be impossible. "In other words," says Woerner, "the Panamanian opposition was the figleaf that legitimized our support. And if that wasn't viable, if that had no credibility, then we were just intervening in Panama for our own national interest. Those three dimensions had to be in harmony."

Woerner's plan went nowhere fast. Says the retired commander, "What we did get was: 'Implement selective elements of the plan.' We got back tactical decisions, rather than a decision on a strategic concept."

Woerner, Loeffke, and Cisneros got so frustrated with the response that when they forwarded a *Fissures Two* plan of their own making, they wrote that the strategy should be approved in its entirety, that it should be treated as a coherent package, a whole. Woerner asked that if certain elements were found wanting that substitutes be suggested. "What you can't do is tell me to execute one, two, or three, or four, or five elements of this plan and think that you have a strategy," he told Washington. "And I got back: 'Implement paragraph 3A, 4C.' But that was exactly what I said would not work."

Neither plan was ever approved or disapproved, but drifted in a bureaucratic limbo. Without a decision, all of the interagency coordination was a waste of time and energy, for carrying out a plan would require cooperation among many government organs. Beyond their content, the plans did not satisfy Elliott Abrams's desire for a quick ouster of Noriega.

But Abrams could convince neither his boss, Secretary of State George Shultz, nor President Reagan to move against Noriega. In the late spring of 1988, their sights were focused on the upcoming summit with Soviet General Secretary Mikhail Gorbachev in Moscow. Reagan had begun to look on the summit as the crowning foreign policy achievement of his eight-year administration. Reagan had made the "Evil Empire" back down; the man who once joked on a radio broadcast that "the bombing [of the Soviets] begins in five minutes" was being hailed as a peacemaker.

During meetings with his security advisers and other leading figures in the administration on 21 and 22 May, Reagan reviewed the options in Panama.[5] The efforts at economic warfare were failing to hurt Noriega, but they were ruining the businesses and lives of Panamanian civilians. The drug indictments were going nowhere. Harassment of U.S. service members ebbed and flowed according to Noriega's whims and the State and Defense departments were at loggerheads. But Reagan was determined to break the impasse.

After he outlined the policy options, Reagan made clear his decision: the United States would drop the drug indictments if Noriega would agree to step down in Panama.

While Reagan's decisiveness impressed those at the meeting, the decision itself angered many, particularly Vice President George Bush, whose campaign to succeed Reagan as president already was being hampered by the indictments. For Bush, the prospect of letting a drug-dealing dictator out of the indictments looked like political suicide. He was being tarred with the Noriega brush because during his tenure as CIA director he had met briefly with Noriega.

Nor was the Congress happy when news of the possible deal was leaked. Senator Robert Dole, challenging Bush for the Republican presidential nomination, was leading a charge in Congress against any such deal.

Reagan stood fast. Deputy Assistant Secretary of State Michael Kozak would be sent back to Panama to renew negotiations with Noriega. Noriega had been telling Kozak that he would step down if the drug indictments were dropped. Kozak felt this promise was genuine,[6] but others in Washington and in Panama had their doubts. In sum, the deal proposed that when the United States announced the end of the economic sanctions, Noriega would agree to resign by August. Civil liberties would be restored, and Noriega would leave Panama before the elections scheduled for 7 May 1989.

As Kozak began his final negotiations with Noriega, the Panamanian leader began to stall on some of the details. As the days dragged on, and the summit approached, Reagan and Shultz grew warier of Noriega's gamesmanship. When details of the deal were leaked to the press, criticism in Washington quickly mounted. Noriega's final offer was to announce his "retirement" when Reagan returned from Moscow. But the president had already left for the summit. Shultz turned the offer down.

This was to be Noriega's last chance to work a deal with the Reagan administration, for when the summit was over, the administration began to turn to the task of getting Bush elected. For his part, Bush had chosen the Noriega deal as the ground on which he would make his break from Reagan. With his campaign at a low ebb, Bush needed to establish himself as a politician in his own right. There would be no deal that would allow Noriega to step down peacefully.

3

"We've Got to Start Paying Attention to Panama."

The Reagan administration's preoccupation with the presidential campaign meant that Noriega and Panama were relegated to the back burner. Woerner was told in no uncertain terms that his job was to keep the situation as quiet as possible. This didn't prevent Noriega from keeping up his harassment of American soldiers, including illegal detentions and occasional beatings. But at "WIMP-COM," the message was one of appeasement, directed from Washington.

In the Pentagon, too, doubts rose over SOUTHCOM's Prayer Book series of plans, especially over USARSO's ability to act as a joint task force headquarters. Though the JCS had given its approval for detailed planning, in June of 1988 Cisneros convinced Woerner that the XVIII Airborne Corps would run the operation from start to finish.

The corps's director of operations, Col. Tom Needham, and Lt. Col. McMahon were asked in June to visit Cisneros's planners under the impression they were to describe the corps's capabilities. Their briefing was not necessarily to be focused on Panama, but on capabilities throughout the theater. Shortly after the meetings had begun, Cisneros "laid it on the table that they were looking at us for a more specific agenda than we supposed," says McMahon. "That specific agenda was for us to be the base for joint task force headquarters not only for operations in Panama but throughout the theater. We said we could do that."

Needham, McMahon, and corps commander Foss had expected to get the call in time, and were relieved that they would have the opportunity to design an operation to their own standards. The corps planners had done some preliminary thinking about how they would conduct such an operation if left to their own devices. But now, with the green light from JCS, they began to plan in earnest.

McMahon was given the central responsibility for a Panama contingency, and he was joined by Maj. David Huntoon, a brand new addition to the corps planning staff. Their missions remained essentially the same—the protection of the Panama Canal and American lives—and they set about drafting a set of objectives to accomplish those missions.

"Even at that time we had the sense at least that we didn't have to kill every darn member of the PDF," says McMahon.

> We thought as a matter of fact even at that time that there would be less actual shooting, hooking, and jabbing than there was. Many would just roll over if we took out not only Noriega—and by "take out" I mean remove him from power—but his coterie, this clique of bad guys. I don't think we recognized at that time, perhaps we should have, but many of the members of the PDF were and probably still are tainted.

Despite the fact that the corps was rotating intelligence forces in and out of Panama, it was only beginning to draw a rudimentary picture of its opponent. Indeed, gathering practical, tactical intelligence was to remain a difficulty, even as planning advanced. As with the CIA stations in Latin America, the SOUTHCOM intelligence staff was targeted on American strategic interests within the theater, particularly in South America. Knowing the order of battle of the PDF and its Byzantine politics and jealousies was not considered a high priority. What relevant information was collected sometimes remained compartmented and therefore was kept from the planners. The most valuable information was collected by soldiers in the course of day-to-day living in Panama.

The task of designing a task force structure fell to Huntoon. The XVIII Airborne Corps has a handful of such task force models that it uses as the basic building blocks for planning purposes and which it can tailor depending upon the size and scope of operations and other factors such as the number of other services involved. It regularly exercises these model task forces under its normal training regimen.

To fit the models to the requirements of a Panama contingency, Huntoon looked at what special skills were needed. One initial modification was to add civil affairs and psychological affairs units, considered to be lacking in the Prayer Book series. Overall, though, the operation retained a defensive orientation, attempting to isolate and block PDF units, keeping them away from the canal and U.S. bases and housing areas.

"At that time we didn't feel that there was an imminent danger that we had to execute a contingency plan," says Huntoon, "but of course, we've always had a contingency plan on the books to defend the Panama Canal and protect U.S. lives and citizens." The first objective was to establish the XVIII Airborne Corps as the headquarters for the sprawling Prayer Book/Blue Spoon task force.

While SOUTHCOM and the corps were struggling to sort out their command relationship, Noriega's enemies in Washington were looking for other ways to remove their nemesis. In July, Elliott Abrams and Richard Armitage, assistant secretary of defense for inter-American affairs, led an effort to draft a presidential intelligence finding, which Reagan approved, for CIA covert action in support of a coup by senior PDF officers. Acknowledging Noriega might be killed by rebel officers, Abrams and Armitage anticipated skepticism from congressional intelligence oversight committees, which would have to be briefed on the plan. Later in the month, Armitage, Abrams, Undersecretary of State for Political Affairs Michael Armacost and CIA clandestine services chief Richard Stolz went before the Senate Select Committee on Intelligence to win support for the finding.

Minutes into the briefing, the senators' opinion was made perfectly clear. "They were snarling like mad dogs," recalls one participant. At the briefing table, Armitage turned to his companions and drolly observed, "I think they have their enthusiasm under control."

In addition to the trouble that might be caused by Noriega's death, the committee was worried that its own fingerprints would be found on an operation that might fail. It was not an unreasonable assumption; after all, the PDF officer corps was not an airtight, trustworthy organization, and Noriega was quite competent at counterintelligence. The operation required funding, and as a result, had to be approved as part of a supplemental defense spending law authorizing the reprogramming of Pentagon funds from other accounts. The Defense Department comptroller's office had already been to the House and Senate armed services committees for approval, but the intelligence panel members found themselves in an awkward position. It was an election year, and they would be on the spot if they approved the mission and it went awry in a public way. The finding died as quickly as it was conceived. There would be no covert operation to topple Noriega.

Over the course of the summer, the military continued contingency planning with a stepped-up sense of urgency driven by the troubling pattern of harassment. As the season wore on, the incidents of PDF abuse increased steadily and by late August totaled three hundred for 1988. In one celebrated incident in June, a PDF officer assaulted a U.S. soldier and his wife at gunpoint, forced the man into the trunk of his car, and then beat and raped the soldier's wife. Anger among U.S. forces stationed in SOUTHCOM was growing daily, as was their frustration at Washington's failure to halt the harassment. Woerner's standing among his soldiers was slipping, even among those who knew his predicament.

As the summer drew to a close, XVIII Airborne Corps planners began to search for a new version of Prayer Book/Blue Spoon that would allow them to assemble combat power in Panama more rapidly. The issue went beyond problems with command and control; the pace of the buildup still left planners uncomfortable.

But despite their misgivings about the Prayer Book series, the corps was not in position to change the troop roster and the issue was again buried when Maj. Gen. Carl Stiner in October was promoted to lieutenant general to replace Foss as corps commander.

Stiner, like Foss, had been commander of the 82d Airborne Division. Prayer Book had not been a major concern for Stiner as division commander because his division was merely a reinforcing element to the task force built around the 7th Light Infantry Division. Even when the corps was given responsibility for Panama planning in June, "I didn't pay much attention to that at that particular time because XVIII Airborne Corps had thirty-seven war plans already and we were the worldwide contingency force. And we had a full plate with all of our exercises that were going on and all of our [emergency deployment readiness exercises]. [But] I was advised of this and I said, 'OK, fine. We've got to start paying more attention to Panama.'"

Stiner was even less receptive to the concept of Prayer Book than Foss had been. Stiner's background included extensive tours with special operations units, including leadership of the Army's Special Operations Command. His entire orientation was toward swift, violent kinds of operations rather than the kind of drawn-out, piecemeal operation envisioned under the current version of Prayer Book/Blue Spoon.

Stiner also knew and had confidence in the capabilities of his corps. Upon assuming command, he developed what he calls "a contingency capabilities briefing," which he gave to every regional commander in chief. "I said: 'Here's how we operate. We maintain this kind of readiness all the time. We are your contingency force regardless of what the situation is, you call and we will be there. Wheels up in eighteen hours at night, forced entry, with overwhelming combat power. This is our philosophy and this is the way we train 365 days a year.'"

In the course of the Golden Pheasant exercise, the relationship between the XVIII Airborne Corps and SOUTHCOM had improved dramatically. And despite the institutional wariness in the matter of command of the Prayer Book/Blue Spoon task force, Huntoon had managed to craft a structure that SOUTHCOM approved and was willing to take before the JCS.

The joint task force structure developed by Huntoon called for the XVIII Airborne Corps to be augmented by officers of USARSO and the 12th Air Force, the small Air Force contingent located in Panama. Huntoon's first draft was completed in July, and he flew to Panama in August to discuss it with Cisneros and the planners at SOUTHCOM and USARSO. They agreed to it, and won JCS approval in November. The XVIII Airborne Corps would be the standing task force headquarters for a contingency in Panama.

To consummate the marriage of the XVIII Airborne Corps and SOUTHCOM, General Woerner wanted to exercise the new structure in a series of command post exercises to be run in Panama. The corps, too, was anxious to find out how they would handle such large forces brought in over an extended period of time, but were leery of tipping their hand to Noriega. "The way we normally play a plan is with a corps headquarters and the commanders and staffs of all the units involved," says Stiner. "We like to spread this thing out to real world distances if possible so that we exercise the communications and everything else." Moving a command structure of such size to Panama would have created a massive "signature," as Stiner puts it, especially with the involvement of the 7th Infantry Division, which would have to travel from California, and the Marines. All parties involved recognized the problem, and a month later the XVIII Airborne Corps proposed conducting the exercise at an American installation. But no agreement was ever reached and the exercise never happened. The presidential election was approaching, and although Bush had rallied from his summer doldrums, Panama was still an unwanted problem for the Republican White House and the campaign. Bush had successfully blunted Michael Dukakis's attacks on the Bush-Noriega connection and SOUTHCOM was still on the back burner.

And there it would stay for the time being, even after Bush in November 1988 was elected president in a landslide: Woerner again advanced his "Fissures" schemes, but again they fell on deaf ears. Eric Delvalle, the centerpiece of Elliott Abrams's strategy to oust Noriega, was permanently on the back burner. His calls for action against Noriega won him nothing more than a farewell session with Ronald Reagan and George Bush. The administration was looking to the May 1989 elections in Panama for their next attempt to oust Noriega.

Senior military officials in Panama doubted this strategy. "By the time President Bush became president, we were too far down the line to do anything eventually except what happened, in my view, because things had gone too far," says Cisneros. "Noriega was too entrenched then. His hoods, he had already started Dignity Battalions, and he felt very strong because he had been able to survive and he felt very confident and egotistical about it."

Or, as Delvalle told Bush in their final session: "Noriega will not have an election only to lose it."[1]

Early in 1989, Woerner continued his crusade for a comprehensive policy toward Latin America. In his testimony before the House Appropriations defense subcommittee on Bush's first defense budget in February, Woerner argued such a strategy should be anchored in an understanding of the region and its effects on American economic and political interests as well as military concerns. He told the panel that SOUTHCOM's role was to help Latin militaries not only to become more professional but to accept a role subordinate to civilian authority.

During a subsequent trip to Washington later in the month, Woerner went public with his criticisms of U.S. policy in Panama. Speaking to the American Chambers of Commerce, Woerner charged that the United States was "ill prepared" for the coming elections because "we have a vacuum in Washington."[2]

Woerner went on to say that Panama, "is so important regionally and to the United States strategically, I believe that we should be seriously debating and deciding now what our actions are to be on May 8 given a variety of scenarios. We ought to know what we plan to do in the event of a reasonably honest election, a grossly dishonest election, a postponed election, or any other possible outcome."

Woerner's speech accurately described the situation, but it provoked a firestorm when it was reported in the *New York Times*; such direct criticism of the president by a serving military officer was out of bounds. Reaction from Bush was quick and violent. Woerner had criticized the administration for its delay in filling Elliott Abrams's vacant post at the State Department, and Bush was under fire for being slow to fill many senior slots in his administration. Bush sent an angry message to Admiral Crowe—and though Crowe had made common cause with Woerner, he was no fan of the general's—and whatever credibility Woerner still retained began to slip away rapidly.

While Woerner was pushing both Congress and the administration for clear marching orders, Noriega began again to step up his campaign of harassment of American soldiers. In early February, a Navy civilian employee living in the Atlantic port city of Colon was beaten by PDF members in the Colon customs police station. Threatened with death, the Navy worker was handcuffed, beaten with a rubber hose, and kicked in the head by a PDF lieutenant, who then threatened to hang the worker up by the heels. Two weeks later, Navy Lt. Roger Muskat, on temporary assignment to SOUTHCOM, went bird watching in the marshes near the Tocumen military airfield. The lieutenant was taken into custody at the PDF 2d Infantry Company's post at the airfield headquarters. He was accused of being a spy, beaten, and strip-searched by PDF intelligence. Muskat was released after being held for nine hours.

From 19 January through the end of February, SOUTHCOM had logged about sixty incidents of harassment by the PDF, bringing to more than one thousand the number of incidents recorded since early 1988. While many were petty harassments, some were not, and the pattern of incidents was alarming to soldiers and their families. On 16 March 1988, the Panamanian wife of a Marine corporal was wounded by a PDF shotgun blast fired into her residence. On 1 August an Air Force sergeant and his father were arrested and later beaten. In early 1989 the tempo increased: on 26 January a soldier was detained at gunpoint; on 25 February another in an official vehicle was arrested and held in Panama Viejo.

The worst incident came on 3 March. Six American forces school buses, two of them loaded with school children, were detained by the PDF for alleged traffic violations. One bus driver did not have a Panamanian driver's license and was threatened by the PDF for refusing to produce one. PDF soldiers brandished automatic weapons while the children's buses were held up for several hours.

The threat from the PDF was becoming a part of daily life for the American military community in Panama. Bomb threats were so routine at Balboa High School, a Defense Department school in Panama City, that school officials asked teachers to prepare "bomb-threat lesson plans" for the school's football field.[3] The threats, running as high as fifteen per day, were so frequent that teachers and administrators stopped evacuating students unless they felt a special sense of danger. The *Tropic Times,* the SOUTHCOM newspaper, published articles directing soldiers how to behave if detained by the PDF.

Woerner did not believe the incidents would go beyond harassment; his judgment was that Noriega would not dare to risk an American response. "I did not feel that Americans were threatened life and limb," he says.

Had I felt so, I would have recommended a total evacuation of all people off post and all families on post, probably. I did not feel that. What there was, without any doubt, was an aggregation of harassments that we had to address. The problem in addressing them was, what we saw as their provocation and our reaction to [that provocation], they of course were seeing as their reaction to our provocation of, first, economic sanctions, and political isolation and military posturing.

Woerner thought he would be driven into a confrontation, but that Washington was never going to accede to the use of force.

Indeed, reaction among soldiers and their families to the PDF was mixed; some felt Americans were letting the Panamanian bullies get to them. "A lot of the harassment stories, unless they were officially documented, were rumors," says Sharon Gragg, wife of Col. Larry Gragg, who was leader of the military community in Panama. "Some were just plain stupid," she says, comparable to walking down a dark alley in a bad neighborhood.

Throughout her five years in Panama, she says, she was never harassed.

Yet there was an insidious quality to living among a police force that offered not protection, but danger.

The hatred Noriega inspired among U.S. service members in Panama paled in comparison to the hatred felt for him by Panamanians. Despite Noriega's attempts to paint himself as a nationalist, the heir of Torrijos standing tall in the face of *yanqui* imperialism, the collapse of the Panamanian economy wrought by U.S. sanctions had caused widespread misery. An anti-Noriega coalition of candidates, headed by the rotund, easy-going Guillermo Endara, and his two vice-presidential running-mates, Ricardo Arias Calderón and Guillermo "Billy" Ford, was genuinely united and remarkably popular. The coalition stood a real chance of victory in the May 7 elections.

For American policymakers, the elections were a long-hoped-for event, one which they prayed would deliver them from their Noriega problem. The U.S. government had tried to help the opposition campaign with $10 million in aid. As the election neared, a delegation of American senators and congressmen, including experts in Central American affairs like Senators Christopher Dodd and John McCain and Congressman John Murtha, flew to Panama to observe the election. They were in a hopeful mood when their plane touched down at Howard Air Force Base and General Woerner came aboard to greet the delegation as a matter of protocol.

But Woerner had a warning for a welcome. "We have information that if you observe the election, you may be arrested and thrown in jail," he told the congressmen.

"What do you recommend we do?" asked McCain and Murtha.

"I'm just passing that along to you," replied Woerner.

Woerner's response stunned the delegation. Here was the commanding American general in the country telling them he could not guarantee their safety. As McCain, a former naval officer, Naval Academy graduate, and Vietnam prisoner of war, met with SOUTHCOM officers during the visit, he was treated to the "WIMPCOM" joke, and the testimony of senior officers as to their anger and disgust at what they saw as SOUTHCOM's failure to act in the face of the harassment. The sad news deeply affected McCain. Although the congressional delegation was not threatened during their stay, McCain gained the impression that Woerner was too close to the issue and paralyzed at the thought of conducting a large-scale operation, as outlined in the war plans his command had developed.

Endara and the opposition coalition would win the election handily, according to independent observers, but the victory would not stand. Noriega, who had miscalculated the amount of fraud required to win, now had reason to tighten his grip on both the country and the PDF. Military officers tasked to ensure the election of Noriega's chosen candidate, Manuel Solis Palma, had grown tired of their leader's increasing demands. Personal loyalty among the PDF was strong, but Noriega wanted his soldiers to turn a three-to-one defeat—in the estimation of the Catholic Church—into a sweeping victory. The PDF officers had ensured Noriega that the vote count was adequately rigged in a pre-election meeting, and the loss frustrated the Panamanian leader. He was forced to take drastic measures.

PDF soldiers, many in civilian clothes, seized ballot boxes, raiding the places where the votes were being tabulated and making off with whatever they could lay hands on. The opposition party retaliated in kind. The extent of the fraud soon became clear, and was verified by former U.S. president Jimmy Carter, who also had come to Panama to observe the election.

Carter estimated Noriega

was prepared to cheat about 10 percent. And he thought that that would be more than enough to cover any sort of misjudgment on his part. . . . First, the military came [to the voting places] in uniform. Then they left and a few minutes later men came in with guns, out of uniform, and just simply took by force the actual, legitimate documents. What Noriega has done is stolen the accurate records, and substituted totally false records without any attempt at subterfuge, substituting his own will for the democratically and freely expressed will of the people.[5]

When the extent of the fraud was revealed, Endara, Ford, and other opposition leaders met with the U.S. congressional delegation to discuss the situation. "What should we do?" Endara asked.

The American lawmakers counseled him to lay low for awhile, but the blatantly rigged election results only served to step up opposition to Noriega; Endara and the two vice presidents believed they had the opportunity to force Noriega from power. Noriega was the one who chose to lay low, and the opposition party took to the streets on 10 May in a rally that took them toward the main PDF headquarters in Panama City, La Comandancia. Thousands of Panamanians cheered them on as they approached Santa Ana Square.[6]

As they were about to enter the square, the PDF "Doberman" riot police halted the caravan that carried the candidates. While Endara, Ford, and Arias Calderón negotiated with the police, scores of Noriega's Dignity Battalions, carrying sticks, hoses, and pipes, swarmed into the square. After a slight pause, they swooped down upon the opposition party, shooting and killing Billy Ford's bodyguard. The bodyguard threw up blood on Ford. The violence was captured by a photographer and later immortalized on the cover of *Newsweek* magazine.

Harassment of Americans continued in the aftermath of the elections. The most serious incident was the 8 May robbery and assault of a sailor by a band of PDF armed with Soviet-style AK-47 assault rifles. The sailor had tried to prevent the Panamanians from accosting his girl friend, whom he had just dropped off at a bus stop near the main gate of Howard Air Force Base. Three PDF soldiers forced the sailor into his car at gunpoint, drove to another location, struck him with rifle butts, and questioned him about American weapons being sent to the Panamanian opposition party.

During the election crisis, SOUTHCOM came close to executing the Prayer Book/Blue Spoon contingency plan. At the direction of Stiner, Maj. David Huntoon was sent from Fort Bragg to head a team the XVIII Airborne Corps had sent to monitor events. SOUTHCOM went through a week-long battle drill where all the senior staff reviewed the plan with General Woerner. "We reviewed Blue Spoon line by line, target by target," says Huntoon.

But if SOUTHCOM was at full alert, it did not register in Washington. Some of the congressmen who had come to Panama to observe the election reported back to Bush upon their return to Washington. In a meeting at the White House with Bush, CIA director William Webster and National Security Adviser Brent Scowcroft, McCain asked Bush to consider dropping the drug indictments against Noriega: "What is it we want to accomplish in Panama? We want Noriega out. If he would leave, . . . it might be worth it."

McCain and Murtha also were outspoken in criticizing Woerner. "Mr. President," said McCain, "I've never said this before, but you must replace the man in charge down there. That man is no damned good."

Bush would not drop the indictments, but he was near to being convinced that Noriega could not be finessed out of power. On 11 May Bush reacted. He recalled Ambassador Arthur Davis and ordered 1,881 soldiers and Marines to Panama, saying in a televised announcement: "We will not be intimidated by bullying tactics, brutal though they may be, of the dictator Noriega. I do not rule out further steps in future."

The deployment, known as Operation Nimrod Dancer, sent the headquarters of the 1st Brigade, 7th Infantry Division. The task force also included an infantry battalion and battery of towed field artillery from the 7th Infantry Division; a battalion of mechanized infantry with armored personnel carriers, tracked mortar carriers, and more than one hundred other vehicles of the 5th Infantry Division (Mechanized) from Fort Polk, Louisiana; and a Marine company of 165 infantrymen with Light Armored Vehicles (LAVs) from Camp Lejeune, North Carolina. The light infantry, Marines, and one mechanized company would be deployed by air, while the remaining mechanized forces would be shipped from Beaumont, Texas.

Bush also directed about six thousand U.S. servicemen, civilian Defense Department employees, and dependents onto U.S. bases, under an emergency sponsor program. The move helped to relieve some of the tension among the families. "A lot of people [felt] really reassured, especially teachers and Panama Canal personnel" who feared they might be targets of harassment or worse, recalls Cecilia George, a science and math teacher at Balboa High School in Panama City. Security was stepped up around the housing areas at Fort Amador and elsewhere.

Still, about four thousand Panama Canal employees and families were not covered by the order, and not everyone was reassured, even when the first of several C-141 Starlifter cargo planes touched down at Howard Air Force Base with a load of Marines and their eight-wheeled LAVs. "You can see some parallels between what's happening here and what happened in Iran," where fifty-two Americans were taken hostage in 1979, said one Army officer at the time.[7]

Despite Bush's rapid decision and deployment, some Pentagon leaders, including Crowe, were trying to downplay the confrontation. "The last thing we need to do is bomb and invade," one high-ranking officer told *Washington Post* reporter George Wilson.[8] "It would only take a skirmish to defeat Panama's army, but we'd be breaking laws and helping Noriega paint us to Latin American countries, which also want to get rid of him, as the old Yankee imperialists. He's real good at using the psychology war we taught him. And the press would end up blaming us."

Others tried to emphasize the exposure of Americans in Panama, and spoke of the slow response time planned under Prayer Book/Blue Spoon. "I don't want to get caught in the same mess we had when we tried to evacuate Americans from Vietnam," another planner told Wilson. "People got killed who didn't have to get killed. We've got to get the ships off down to Panama in case we need them. You just can't get them there overnight. We've dusted off our old [evacuation] plans."

Limiting that exposure quickly became a high priority. SOUTH-COM plans for evacuation under normal circumstances had envisioned a very slow process. Senator McCain had raised the issue with Woerner as the congressional delegation of election observers was preparing to depart the country. The meeting again took place on the delegation's plane.

But, as the Pentagon spokesman Dan Howard put it, "the deteriorating security situation" made evacuating dependents "a prudent move," and 16 May, the order was given.

Tied up with the effort to limit exposure in Panama was a Pentagon move to speed up permanent change of station transfers. These troop transfers are often done during the summer, to allow soldiers and their families to get settled in a new community during school summer holidays. In SOUTHCOM, moves planned for July and August got pushed forward to June. This was to cause manning problems during the following fall and winter months.

On 23 June Brig. Gen. Marc Cisneros replaced Loeffke as USARSO commander, and later promoted to major general. Woerner and Cisneros both gave speeches at the change-of-command ceremony blasting Noriega, Cisneros calling Noriega a "dimestore dictator" and Woerner saying "if U.S. citizens or our treaty rights in Panama are threatened, we will assert whatever force is needed to protect them."

The speeches broke a longstanding SOUTHCOM rule of psychological warfare on Noriega's grounds—in public. Woerner's Fissures plans had emphasized trying to turn the minds of PDF officers against Noriega, but Cisneros wanted to confront the Panamanian dictator in the open and at all turns. He was also concerned about the morale of the troops under his command.

The feisty Cisneros also had been chomping at the bit to go on the offensive, and Woerner had begun to let him loose. Since the deployment of additional forces in Nimrod Dancer, Cisneros had pushed a plan to conduct exercises that would enforce to the limit of the letter of the law American maneuver rights under the Panama Canal treaties. He called the exercises *Purple Storm,* and later *Sand Fleas,* sand fleas being endemic to Panama and well-known disease carriers.

"Sand Flea was to sort of be an irritant and cause them to react so we could judge their reaction plan and also to get moral ascendancy over them, showing them that we were willing to stand up," says Cisneros. "It also provided a tremendous base for us to, number one, exercise our contingency plans, but also to do joint operations with the headquarters that were here."

The exercises often turned into confrontations with the PDF, and were sometimes dangerous situations. "What scared you was we had young soldiers, locked and loaded, facing PDF, also locked and loaded, where any one person on either side could easily get scared or do something wrong, and start a fight," recalls Col. Mike Snell, commander of the 193d Infantry Brigade.

"We did a lot of those intimidation games, where we tried to intimidate them and they tried to intimidate us. They used females, foul language; we tried to counter with professionalism. We were doing this three or four times a week for six months. It was a real emotional strain. We spent a great amount of time talking to soldiers, making sure they understood what we were doing."

The Air Force sent A-37s to circle over Rio Hato, "just to watch and see what they would do," says Lt. Col. Earl E. Whitt, Jr., chief of operations and training of the 24th Composite Wing, who participated in one of the missions. The PDF ran to their antiaircraft artillery sites. The two A-37 pilots could hear PDF radio traffic warning that the aircraft were circling overhead, and read out their altitude correctly. The A-37s were flying legally, more than four thousand feet up, above restricted air space, and according to a filed flight plan. The PDF filed its usual complaint about the overflights, "but that was standard," Whitt says. The Air Force, in turn, repeated the exercise wherever there was a PDF installation—David, Coclecito, Bocas del Toro—with similar results. "Mostly the reactions were paperwork reactions," Whitt says.

"The Sand Fleas were mostly an opportunity for us to go out and practice that visual reconnaissance and use the visual reconnaissance, come back and debrief what we saw."

The Sand Fleas quickly had the desired effect. One 4 July exercise at Madden Dam, a critical structure that controls the level of the water flowing through Panama from the Atlantic and Pacific Oceans, provoked a response from the Dignity Battalions. The day following the exercise, about two hundred Dignity Battalion members blocked the entrance to Fort Clayton, the home of USARSO, and delivered a letter denouncing Cisneros.

Several days later, Cisneros gave an interview to the *Tropic Times* SOUTHCOM's command newspaper, saying "I've been thinking more and more that the United States should impose a military solution that would give [Panama] an opportunity to have a government that isn't criminal. This is my personal opinion."[9]

It was an opinion that was at last gaining currency in Washington as well. But President Bush determined that General Woerner was not the man to find such a solution. While Cisneros was taking on Noriega in the streets, he made the decision to remove Woerner as leader of SOUTHCOM.

The job of giving Woerner the news fell to Army Chief of Staff General Carl Vuono. In the middle of July, while on a trip to visit Army units in the southeast, Vuono diverted his C-20 to Howard Air Force Base. Vuono explained to Woerner that he was no longer trusted in Washington, and that his honorable option was to resign rather than be removed.

The news came as a bitter blow to Woerner. His career had been tailored to do this job. He understood the region, its culture, its politics. He had been directed by his military superiors not to pursue a military option, that the presidents he had served would not authorize force. For his pains, he became reviled as "WIMPCOM commander."

Rather than hang on, Woerner agreed to resign and "get on with the rest of my life." He saw only confrontation in store in Panama, and a good likelihood of war.

4

"Carlos, You Are My Man."

Maxwell Thurman is quite a different man from Frederick Woerner.

It was often said of bachelor Thurman that he was married to the Army. That was merely one of the clichés. He was a detail man. The essence of a "staff weenie." A man who would call a staff meeting on Christmas Eve night, expecting every officer to be prepared for whatever briefings he might require. His nickname was Mad Max. When Thurman entered the room, you knew it; any officer who worked with Maxwell Thurman, even for one briefing or meeting, knew the Thurman Effect.

In his career, Thurman tackled one thankless job after another, including the toughest assignment the service could offer in the 1980s: as the head of Army Recruiting Command, he was told to make the all-volunteer force work. The famous slogan: "Be All You Can Be" was created while Thurman headed Recruiting Command. In typical Thurman style, he took one of the Army's most dismal commands, often considered a career-ending assignment, and stood it on its head.

Thurman had risen to be Army vice chief of staff, and after that assignment, left to lead Army Training and Doctrine Command, a picturesque post on the water at Hampton Roads, Virginia, centered around Fort Monroe, a moated Revolutionary War relic, and with a giant colonial red-brick, white-columned commanding general's quarters. But in the summer of 1989, Thurman was preparing to end his thirty-six-year Army career and, indeed, had already announced his intention to retire.

During the first weeks of July, Thurman was vacationing at idyllic Holdern Beach, North Carolina, with his brother, Roy Thurman, a retired Army lieutenant general. The Thurmans were born and raised in North Carolina, and Max had attended North Carolina State before joining the Army, while Roy went to West Point. Lieutenant General Stiner, XVIII Airborne Corps commander, even had volunteered to retire Max at Fort Bragg.

The Thurmans had been vacationing in Holdern Beach for years. Max had no specific plans about what he would do after his retirement ceremony, but was inclined to live with Roy in Roy's modest home in suburban Virginia outside Washington, D.C., just a few miles from the Pentagon. The two brothers had put down some roots in the Washington area, and Max thought he'd like to be there. It was relatively near the Delaplane, Virginia, farm of retired Gen. William Depuy, one of Max's close friends.

On the first weekend of July, a call came through from General Vuono's office in the Pentagon. "Would General Thurman please hold for the chief of staff?" the aide asked. Vuono wanted to discuss the Southern Command job. Max Thurman said he would fly to Washington on Sunday to give General Vuono his answer.

Around the beach house kitchen table, the two Thurman brothers discussed the pros and cons of going to Panama.

Roy urged Max to take the job. "You're the right man, at the right time," said Roy. "You'll be Bush's choice. You'll have a clear mandate."

"I won't go as a caretaker," replied Max. "If I go, it's going to be the standard CinC tour of two years," he said.

"It won't be a problem," countered Roy. "You won't have any baggage. You're well known in Washington, on the Hill."

Recalling the conversation, Roy Thurman remembers that he thought at the time of his brother's characteristic of revealing to others only what he wants them to know. Roy was sure when he went to bed that night that Max would take the job at SOUTHCOM.

And so he would. General Thurman flew to Washington and told Vuono that he would indeed, answer the call to replace Woerner in Panama. Vuono in turn discussed the matter with Admiral Crowe, and the JCS chairman approved.

Thurman was not the most obvious choice to run SOUTHCOM,

for he had made his name not as a troop commander but, first as director of program analysis and evaluation, then at Recruiting Command, and finally as deputy chief of staff for personnel and vice chief, in a succession of staff jobs. His highest field post had been as commander of divisional artillery for the 82d Airborne Division.

What Thurman did possess, as his brother had pointed out to him, beyond his own keen intellect and devotion to work, was something Woerner had never had: the trust of senior leaders in Washington, both at the White House and in the Pentagon. As Thurman himself says, "I did know the Washington scene and the JCS from my tour as vice chief of staff of the Army; I was familiar with the JCS process. I guess they had some confidence in me. I was a guy who'd been around. It wasn't my first four-star job." On 22 July the announcement was made at the Pentagon.

Thurman's last day at Training and Doctrine Command was to be 5 August, but he would not assume command in Panama until 30 September. In the intervening months, he set about studying for his new post in typical Thurman fashion. Thurman took what he calls his "Garden Leave" between assignments—Thurman is an admitted Anglophile and had picked up the term and, in this case, the practice, from the British military—to study and understand the complexities of the job he was approaching.

His first move was to Roy Thurman's house, which became his base of operations. One of his first calls was to Admiral Crowe, who told him: "I want you to look at our defense policies in Latin America and review and assimilate what's happened recently. Come back to the [Joint Chiefs of Staff] before you go to Panama and report out what kind of things you would recommend when you become CinC." Crowe knew Thurman from their dealings when Thurman was Army vice chief of staff—the vice chief often substitutes for the service chief in JCS meetings—and said he believed "a fresh look from a guy not involved in the day-to-day business of Panama was in order."

He also made the rounds of the various agencies: JCS, the State Department, the National Security Council, and even the Drug Enforcement Agency and the CIA. For Thurman, it was a time of learning. "I'd only been to Latin America a half dozen times or so, and those were the kinds of trips I took as [vice chief of staff]," he says. He obtained a translation of Noriega's book on psychological warfare, and took intensive Spanish instruction from the Defense Language Institute.

Thurman also took a look at the organization he would command. He concluded that SOUTHCOM, with a total staff of 380, did not have the manpower to do detailed warplanning.

Another stop for Thurman during his garden leave was Fort Bragg. Stiner had wanted Thurman to discuss contingency operations for Panama. Stiner was increasingly uncomfortable with Prayer Book/Blue Spoon and wanted to discuss a different concept. Stiner was away when Thurman arrived, but Lt. Col. Tim Mc-Mahon, and Maj. Gen. Will Roosma, Stiner's deputy commander at the XVIII Airborne Corps, handled the briefing. Thurman agreed with the corps concept of replacing the slow Blue Spoon operations with one featuring the rapid application of overwhelming combat power. As he heard the comparison of the two plans, Thurman was reminded of the piecemeal operations he had observed as a young officer in Vietnam. As Thurman learned about the problems of Panama and Noriega, he began to feel Stiner could solve them. Encouraged by Thurman's favorable initial review of their plan, the corps feverishly set about detailed planning.

About a week later, Thurman was replaced at Training and Doctrine Command by Gen. John Foss, Stiner's predecessor at the XVIII Airborne Corps. Stiner flew up to Fort Monroe for the change of command ceremony.

Even as he was saying goodbye to Fort Monroe, Thurman's mind was on the business of Panama. As the ceremony ended, Thurman strode off the reviewing stand and made a beeline for Carl Stiner. Thrusting a finger in Stiner's chest, Thurman said,

> Carlos, I've talked to the chief and I've talked to the chairman, and you are my man for everything that has to be done there. I'm putting you in charge of all forces and you've got it: planning, execution, the whole business. I have looked at my staff and I have told the chairman and I have told the chief that it cannot run a contingency operation. He said you can have it and I'm holding you responsible.

Thurman's direct charge to Stiner stunned the corps commander. Though he had known Thurman for many years, counted him a friend, and knew well the Thurman Effect, Stiner was taken aback by the sureness of Thurman's decision. Maybe the months, the years of wrangling over the details of Prayer Book/Blue Spoon had left Stiner too focused on minutiae. Panama planning had been a long-running headache for the XVIII Airborne Corps, going back to General Foss's tenure as corps commander. The job was now his: "Carlos . . . you are my man for everything."

Stiner and his planners now could do what they had wanted all along. It had been their war to run and now they were going to be able to develop their own plan, according to their own philosophy, not be called in to run someone else's plan.

For Stiner, there was much to dislike about Prayer Book/Blue Spoon. Stiner, with his steely, slit-eyed gaze and Tennessee twang, is a backwoods warrior straight out of central casting. His background was in special operations, going back to Vietnam, and like Thurman, he loathed the idea of a gradual, piecemeal military operation. The SOUTHCOM plan went against his every instinct, all of his training.

Stiner had deep confidence in his philosophy of fighting. Strike the enemy before he strikes you. Make him fight your kind of battle, not his. Attack at night. Force your way into his backyard. Maintain surprise but hit him with overwhelming combat power at precise points of decision. Paralyze his ability to react. Get it over with quickly. Speed would win you the support of the American people, save your soldiers' lives, and end hostilities on favorable terms without undue enemy casualties.

To Stiner, this philosophy was a tailor-made solution to American problems on Panama. "Here was a situation where we were maybe going to have to fight our friends," he says. "There's nothing wrong with the Panamanian people, but they had just been misled. And that's a heck of a difference than fighting someone who is your arch rival, your adversary."

Of all the elements of Prayer Book/Blue Spoon, the least attractive was the pace of the operation and the compromise of security that would inevitably accompany it. The naval forces, especially, took too long to build up, thought Stiner. The shipping was to come out of Hawaii, and go to Camp Pendleton, just above San Diego, California, to pick up the Marine amphibious brigade. That would take weeks. At the same time, a Marine air alert battalion would be airlifted from Camp Lejeune into Panama. "At the tune of five hundred sorties of C-141's and C-5's [cargo aircraft], there's a heck of a signature associated with that," says Stiner. "Then you have aircraft carriers, one sitting in the Pacific and one on the Atlantic to provide air support. I didn't feel we needed air support if we went at night and we maintained the element of surprise as much as possible."

To do the detailed planning for the operation, Stiner turned to McMahon and Huntoon, the two officers who had monitored Prayer Book/Blue Spoon for the XVIII Airborne Corps. These two planners, like others at the corps and an increasing number of division-level operations officers within the Army, were graduates of the service's School of Advanced Military Studies program at Fort Leavenworth, Kansas. This program selects the best and brightest students at the Army's Command and General Staff College and extends their studies for a second year. The second-year course, a recent addition to the Army's officer professional development program, is a controversial one, its critics claiming it smacks of elitism, along the lines of the Prussian general-staff concept. Successful completion of the course also guarantees these officers important troop assignments such as battalion commands, positions that traditionally have meant sure promotion and rapid career progress. McMahon and Huntoon would test whether the advanced program would truly produce the kind of incisive operational planning that it had been designed to.

The core of the second-year course is to create officers who are capable of designing military campaigns. This goes beyond the successful conduct of the military operation to include the political, economic, cultural, and social ramifications that can either undermine or support the combat itself. The heart of the course is an intensive study of military history, a search for linkage between successful tactics and successful strategy and a study of the operational level of warfare.

McMahon and Huntoon started their planning from scratch, roughing out ideas on blackboards and legal pads. In the stifling heat of a Fort Bragg August, the two planners were closeted with their team in the small classroom-style cells at the corps's red-brick headquarters. "We were very concerned about the political [aspects], and the business of keeping the commander focused on victory," says Huntoon. "So we looked at it as a campaign with a series of objectives, and not as one set-piece battle. So we looked beyond the first D-day strikes and thought about all the things we would have to accomplish in the next several days. It was clearly something that was going to be happening on several levels, not just a military level."

The first thing the two tried to determine was what the end of the war should look like. From there they worked backwards, identifying large objectives such as the security of Americans, protection of the Panama Canal, and so forth.

While setting McMahon and Huntoon to work, Stiner wanted to get a feel for the situation in Panama and the SOUTHCOM forces. Stiner may have wanted to change SOUTHCOM's war plans, but he knew that the forces stationed in Panama would form the backbone for any contingency force, no matter how large and how rapidly it was deployed. He wanted to play to SOUTHCOM's strengths and complement its weaknesses.

This would be a delicate business. "I didn't want to take the whole corps headquarters there for signature reasons," he says. "I wanted to draw on their expertise and make them feel a part of a team effort. We didn't want to create an adversary relationship or the atmosphere of a bunch of know-it-alls coming in trying to take over. I didn't want that at all."

That trip began an exhausting, once-every-two-week cycle of flights from Fort Bragg to Howard Air Force Base. "I would take one or two C-20 loads," says Stiner.

> You can put about twelve people on a C-20. We'd fly out of Fort Bragg right after dark, or fly out in time to land in Panama after dark at Howard. Then we'd take Black Hawk helicopters to Fort Clayton, go inside where those folks who were there who were in the know would be assembled along with the commanders on the ground. We would plan all night long. We would coordinate the next day and continue to plan and then leave there the next night and come back into Fort Bragg.

From SOUTHCOM, Stiner and his planners got essential information on targeting. These operation needed to be precise; three of the U.S. installations in Panama were shared with the PDF. "We knew we had to secure the locks along the canal," recalls Stiner.

"We could not afford to let the canal get blocked. We had to secure the seat of government, our own embassy."

These were similar goals to the Prayer Book/Blue Spoon plan, but Stiner wanted to accomplish them quite differently. He and his planners wanted to minimize the required defensive maneuvers by complementing them with offensive action to eliminate the threat from the PDF and Noriega. With fifteen thousand Americans—all potential hostages—in the Panama City area alone, the defensive mission would be a nightmare, all but impossible. Better to neutralize the Panamanians to prevent them from striking. Stiner's instinct told him that the PDF could not react to such a challenge.

To accomplish this goal, says Stiner,

> there were certain key things that we had to do. We knew we had to knock out the [PDF central headquarters in Panama City, La] Comandancia, to neutralize the command and control. We knew we had to take down the police and most of the institutions of government because they, too, were run by the PDF. We knew that we had to take on those PDF units that could influence this action. If we did that— and we did it all simultaneously to completely paralyze them and neutralize them—anything left would be sitting out there with no guidance, no connectivity, no instruction. We could then go after them separately.

During Thurman's August visit to Fort Bragg, he had suggested that another element of Prayer Book/Blue Spoon needed to be changed: unity of command between special operations and conventional forces. Under Prayer Book/Blue Spoon, the two kinds of forces were separate but equal partners reporting to the regional commander in chief, not the commander of the joint task force. While the unity of command is a time-honored military principle and a specific tenet of American doctrine, combining the efforts of separate services and conventional with unconventional forces has proved to be a difficult chore. For a range of reasons, from the petty-bureaucratic to valid concerns of institutional integrity, the integration of special operations with conventional forces has been especially hard—there is an endemic lack of trust between the two communities. Despite the difficulties, Stiner and Thurman were convinced—with the encouragement of General Vuono, Army chief of staff—that this was a profound drawback to the Prayer Book/ Blue Spoon plans and, with thorough planning and coordination, Stiner could control both kinds of forces.

Stiner's extensive special operations background ideally suited him for the job, and indeed, his conception of the operation was as a special operation writ large. He was well respected by the special operators and by the airborne and light infantry community he led as corps commander; no one in the entire Army would have been better trusted. Stiner could convince the unconventional force leaders they would be employed properly and the conventional force commanders that they wouldn't have special operators running around uncontrolled.

By the beginning of September, Stiner and his planners had made the rounds and were prepared to draft a plan, designated Operation Plan, or OPLAN, 90-1. One of the conditions that the planners established for a unilateral U.S. action in Panama was that it would not be in support of a coup. The most likely trigger was to be, as Huntoon puts it, "Noriega really running out of control or losing control and making a direct threat to U.S. lives. That was what we could anticipate as giving us the direction to execute this particular plan."

For contingency operations, and especially a plan meant to react to such a threat, the driving factor is time: how much force can you bring to bear, and how quickly? The XVIII Airborne Corps had developed models that allowed for a range of options and phases meant to allow for immediate response to quick and massive application of military power, giving national leaders a range of options.

The time line the planners modeled had three phases: pre-crisis action, crisis action, and deployment. Pre-crisis actions might include additional forces moved to Panama as a hedge against possible future needs. Crisis actions would be broken down further, but would largely be based on in-country forces. Additional deployments following after a crisis, or in response to a crisis, would mean forces flown in from the United States. As they assembled the plan, it was when the situation permitted additional rapid deployments that Huntoon and McMahon began to feel they were coming up with "war winners."

The planners also broke their task into phases. The first would be assault force operations that would include forces stationed in

Panama, reinforced by Army Rangers and other special operations forces and the 82d Airborne. Huntoon allowed for three days of assaults. Following that would be airlanded forces with the mission of restoring stability to Panama. This might include additional combat, but would include more police-like operations, too, technically called stability operations. These might last up to thirty days.

Stiner and the corps planners were not perfectly sure what would qualify as a trigger mechanism for the assault. "We knew that in order to implement the full plan that it would take some kind of a trigger that would be acceptable as morally justifiable—like protecting lives—in the minds of the American people and the world," Stiner recalls. "We knew that kind of thing would have to happen. Now we didn't know what it would be, but we felt that sooner or later there would be some Americans killed or there would be some taken hostage. That was just our feeling."

Stiner realized if the action had to be taken on short notice it would have to be much more defensive in nature. As a result, he strongly preferred, as did Huntoon and McMahon, the deployment option. "We couldn't take down the Comandancia, we couldn't do a rescue, hit Modelo prison, or anything like that," says Stiner.

The second stage would allow fourteen to sixteen hours of notice. That would allow time to add many of the special operations forces, Delta Force units, a Navy Sea-Air-Land, or SEAL, team from Norfolk, Virginia, and the permanent special operations aviation Task Force 160 from Fort Campbell, Kentucky. "We couldn't take on the whole PDF," asserts Stiner.

> We could have knocked out the Comandancia but not searched it. But when it came to securing Americans who were not inside of a compound but out in the city, or maintaining law and order in the city, or taking on other PDF units or blocking them, we couldn't do that. We'd just have to do those things in the city and hang on till we could get more there.

The third stage called for forty-eight hours warning. "The third option was the full blown. Give us forty-eight hours so we can get all of our airplanes assembled and we'll go do it right," says Stiner.

By the end of the month, Huntoon, who had primary responsibility for creating the plan, had produced a draft that had been reviewed by McMahon and Stiner. Huntoon's design used a more conservative command structure—what contingency planners call a "pure joint task force"—than the one hinted at by Thurman. Stiner would still be task force commander, but, because the overwhelming portion of the forces would be Army forces, there would be a separate Army force commander under him. The task force was to be based around the 82d Airborne Division, with follow-on air-landed forces of the 7th Infantry Division. The special operations forces would remain separate but equal.

Even as McMahon and Col. Tom Needham, the chief of operations for the XVIII Airborne Corps, began to review Huntoon's structure, they began to lay the ground work for the integration of the joint special operations task force, called JSOTF, with the overall task force structure. Word of Thurman's intent had spread, and the planners wanted to be ready if he made the instruction clear.

So the corps planners and their counterparts in the Joint Special Operations Command (JSOC), also at Fort Bragg, began to take some cautious steps toward one another. McMahon instructed Huntoon to write in the JSOTF organization, but to do it delicately, setting broad goals and designating targets. "We don't want to change their operational method. We don't want to change their concept," said McMahon. "So we're going to work with them until we figure out what we have to tell them to do so they will do what they are going to do anyway."

As it happened, several of the special operations planners were, like Huntoon and McMahon, graduates of the second-year course at Fort Leavenworth. It gave the officers a common frame of reference to help break down the normal institutional barriers. Maj. Jim Delany, himself a second-year graduate, was designated as the liaison officer from the corps to the special operations task force.

Max Thurman was not the only Army four-star general preparing himself for a new command. In August, Colin Powell had been chosen to replace Admiral Crowe as chairman of the Joint Chiefs of Staff. Powell, possessed of a keen intelligence and an unerring sense of how to operate with the highest levels of the government, had served a short stint as commander of U.S. Forces Command since leaving the National Security Adviser's job in the Reagan White House. Politically savvy and armed with the new clout given the JCS chairman by the 1986 Defense Reorganization Act, General

Powell was readying himself for a position of extraordinary power.

Reflecting on that new job, Powell discovered he had a nagging problem that had been bugging him for a year and a half: Noriega. Through the course of the summer, the Panamanian strongman had often skirted the line of provocation, keeping up his war of nerves with the U.S. military. On 8 August American forces in Panama arrested twenty-nine Panamanians who were interfering with one of the "Sand Flea" military exercises. PDF vehicles shadowed a Marine convoy heading for Empire Range, an Army installation. The U.S. convoy was doing reconnaissance to "check condition of roads and confirm it could move along certain routes," according to the official SOUTHCOM explanation, but it was also testing PDF response to American movements with an eye toward the Prayer Book/Blue Spoon plan. After the convoy was well within the range complex, the PDF members halted the lead vehicle. The Panamanians, nine of whom were in uniform and twenty in civilian clothing and thought to be members of the Dignity Battalions, were carrying automatic rifles, grenades, pistols, and other weapons. The confrontation broke into chaos as dozens of Marines took firing positions in an attempt to ward off the PDF. The PDF, in typical reaction to Sand Flea exercises, screamed at the U.S. soldiers, but then retreated under the guns of U.S. firepower. The Marine convoy reported no shots fired, and took a number of PDF hostages. Among those detained as Maj. Manuel Sieiro, a brother-in-law of Noriega.

Two days later, the PDF retaliated by arresting two American Military Police (MP) officers at Fort Amador, an installation jointly operated by the Army and the PDF. Under direction from Cisneros, the Army answered by arresting two Panamanian MPs on duty at Amador's front gate. While these incidents and arrests ended quickly and all those detained by both sides were released relatively rapidly, tensions were mounting once again. With 1 September— the date when the government chosen in the May elections was to take office—fast approaching, Noriega was once again trying to stoke anti-American sentiments to divert Panamanian public attention from his theft of the election and continuing corrupt rule.

Noriega's psychological warfare was having more success with opinion outside Panama than among his own countrymen. On 23 August delegates of an Organization of American States (OAS) negotiating team created after the May elections to try to resolve the political standoff in Panama announced they were giving up their efforts. Foreign Minister Diego Cordovez of Ecuador, leader of the delegation, claimed military maneuvers by the United States were partly responsible for their failed efforts to coax Noriega from power. In its report explaining its inability to remove Noriega, the team claimed the series of Sand Flea exercises conducted by U.S. troops in Panama had a "negative effect" on negotiations for a transfer of power. Without questioning the legality of the exercises under the Panama Canal treaties, the OAS delegation called them "inopportune."

"It is essential to avoid the possibility of an incident that, in the present circumstances in Panama, might thwart all efforts to achieve a peaceful solution," the report stated. "The mission is of the opinion that at this time it is essential to avoid actions that could exacerbate the situation."

Foreign ministers from throughout the hemisphere met in Washington to consider the situation in Panama. The Bush administration had never believed that the OAS mission could oust Noriega, and concluded that multilateral diplomatic efforts were a failure.

Four months after Noriega's annulment of the presidential election, Francisco Rodríguez assumed office as the civilian president of a provisional Panamanian government. Rodríguez had risen to become the comptroller of the Panamanian treasury department after holding a number of bureaucratic jobs in the successive Noriega-backed governments. Rodríguez, fifty-one, had attended school with Noriega. He became the seventh president of Panama in seven years.

The day after, President Bush announced the United States would not recognize the government installed by Noriega. "Panama is, as of this date, without any legitimate government," said Bush. "The United States will not recognize any government installed by General Noriega. Our ambassador will not return and we will not have any diplomatic contact with the Noriega regime."

The mood in the White House was gloomy. To the president's two top military advisers, Admiral Crowe and National Security Adviser Brent Scowcroft, there seemed to be no way to maneuver Noriega out of power short of a military confrontation. After a mid-September meeting of the National Security Council, Crowe re-

turned to the Pentagon with a warning for his top operations officers, Army Lt. Gen. Tom Kelly and Rear Adm. Ted Schaefer, then
director of intelligence in the JCS.

"I am absolutely 100 percent convinced that the only way the
situation is going to get resolved in Panama is with military force.
You guys better be ready," Crowe said. "I can't tell you when it is
going to happen and I can't tell you what the trigger is going to be,
but I'm convinced that's the only way it's going to be resolved."

General Powell was coming to a similar conclusion. He had wres-
tled with the Noriega problem for years, first in his White House
years with the National Security Council, then at U.S. Forces Command. In those posts his role had been first as an adviser to the
president and then as a general whose job it was to make sure that
the commanders who might be charged to fight in Panama had adequate troops and training for the mission. But as chairman of the
JCS, Powell would be forced to advocate a policy. He would be the
president's top military man; he could not shrink from the spotlight.

Powell had never cared for the Prayer Book/Blue Spoon scheme.
He thought the planners were being too clever, and too dependent
upon the scenario unfolding as they anticipated. "Frankly, I always
thought that one day something would happen and we got to be
prepared to go right out, like in an hour," says Powell. "And you
had better have a one-hour plan, whereas a lot of the plans being
talked about would take three months to do. I didn't want to be left
with the option of saying to the president, if ever asked, 'Yeah, we
can do something in about three months.'"

On Thursday, 28 September, just days before they were to assume
their new commands, Powell and Thurman met with Stiner to discuss Panama plans. Powell made it clear to his two generals that he
was prepared to look at the entire range of contingency plans. Powell had somewhat contradictory expectations. The notion of a surgical strike to remove Noriega had been the preferred option with
Elliott Abrams and others in the Reagan administration, and those
under Bush who were pushing to get rid of the Panamanian leader
had picked up the cry. Powell admits that his thinking was colored
by White House thinking: "I was thinking more in terms of a more
elaborate plan perhaps, a more surgical kind of plan."

But at the same time he did not see any attractive alternatives to
Noriega within the PDF. This reasoning was driving him away from

the surgical strike option, and he wanted new choices from Thurman and Stiner. Powell was a Vietnam-generation officer just as the other two were. He instinctively loathed the notion of a piecemeal operation if another way could be found, and he doubted that removing Noriega would by itself do the trick, ease his Panama headache. "I thought that what we would have to do eventually was take it all down," he says. "We would really have to take the PDF down or else you couldn't solve the problem. And I came into office with that mind-set. That there were lots of budding Noriegas throughout the PDF and to take out Tony just wouldn't do it." Still, as Powell readied himself to become the nation's highest-ranking officer, he was not possessed by a sense of impending crisis in Panama. There might be trouble coming for which he did not feel adequately prepared, but trouble had not arrived yet.

Thurman had spent the last week in September immersed in SOUTHCOM policies not only for Panama but for the entire SOUTHCOM region. Beyond troubles with Noriega, there were the Sandinistas still to worry about, and the president's Andean drug initiative to disrupt the cocaine trade in Colombia, Peru, and Bolivia. On Friday, 29 September, he gave a half-hour briefing to the JCS in their meeting room, "the tank."

Thurman tackled the task with an analyst's precision. The southern theater was "a mosaic of extremes," he said, mixing rural and urban societies that ranged from near stone age to fully modern. It suffered from some of the densest population centers on the planet and some of its most sparsely populated wilderness. Theirs was a wide divergence of wealth and poverty.

Almost every nation in SOUTHCOM suffered from constant turbulence, Thurman continued. Active and insidious insurgencies thrived in countries whose fragile economies were riddled with pervasive debt. Democratization was the hope of the region, but developing the institutions of the region would be a mighty struggle. Drugs, especially the cocaine trade, were debilitating to these efforts. The drug cartels were shadow governments in partnerships with the insurgents. They were also a serious threat to the United States, the cost measured in lost and wasted lives and hundreds of billions of dollars each year.

Next came Panama. It was another strategic key, said Thurman. The Carter-Torrijos treaties called for the Panama Canal to revert to the Panamanians in ten years. The canal remained an important route for world trade, and was therefore key to the strategic security of the United States.

Thurman had discussed his plans for Panama with Admiral Crowe. Crowe, echoing his warning to the JCS operations staff, had told Thurman that he should expect to be called on to take military action. It was just a matter of when. Thurman now said he intended to clear the decks by reducing military dependents. He would shape up SOUTHCOM. He would be back in thirty days with specific recommendations.

That evening, General Thurman flew to Howard Air Force Base in Panama. At eleven o'clock Saturday morning, 30 September, he assumed command of SOUTHCOM. He hit the ground running. Almost the moment of the change of command ceremony was over, Thurman switched from his Class B uniform—the military equivalent of a businessman's coat-and-tie—to combat fatigues, and ordered that everyone do likewise. As his first act of command, he had called in all the military groups and officers from the embassies around Latin America, the regional foreign area officers, "for a dump Saturday and Sunday. I will work nights and weekends," said Thurman. He intended to shake up his staff.

After two days of meetings and a healthy dose of The Thurman Effect, the new commander in chief dismissed his staff.

At 10:00 P.M. that Sunday night, Brig Gen. William Hartzog, the SOUTHCOM director of operations, alerted Thurman that there would be a coup against Noriega the next day, led by Maj. Moisés Giroldi, PDF chief of security. Giroldi had played a central role in foiling the 1988 coup attempt, and in meetings with CIA agents in Panama, procrastinated about going through with the attempt on Noriega. Thurman spoke to these agents for several hours that night and with the CIA near Washington. He was trying to get a sense of the situation before calling the Pentagon for instructions, and he also had his doubts about Giroldi's plans and his intentions.

Thurman spoke to Powell at 2:00 A.M. Monday morning, and Powell subsequently spoke to Defense Secretary Richard Cheney and National Security Adviser Brent Scowcroft.

Giroldi told the CIA agents that he wanted limited U.S. help, and that Panama should seek its own solution. But he did want to have the roads blocked, because he feared that PDF units at and near

Fort Amador, and the PDF 7th Infantry Company at the western base of Rio Hato, would try to rescue Noriega. He also wanted a bloodless coup, to convince Noriega to retire as Noriega had his predecessors. Giroldi had no intention of turning Noriega over to the Americans.

Thurman concluded that the coup was ill-motivated, ill-conceived, ill-led, and fatally flawed. His reading of Noriega's book on psychological warfare had given him a healthy respect for Noriega's talents in that realm. He could not believe Giroldi wanted to talk him into retirement to some ranch in the country. Thurman also found Giroldi's motivation for the coup to be suspect. Giroldi said he wanted to retire Noriega for violating the twenty-five-year limit in Panamanian law on serving in the armed forces. "There was no talk of democracy or anything like that. It was not for the people but for the PDF," says Thurman.

Thurman also quickly realized that he could only support the surprise coup with a piecemeal response, the one thing he wanted most to avoid. Cisneros, on the other hand, argued that the coup attempt would give them an opportunity that might not come again. He called La Comandancia, asking to speak to several PDF officer he knew, including Colonel Guillermo Wong, chief of intelligence for the PDF, Noriega's old post. Cisneros had worked with Wong on exercises when Cisneros held the SOUTHCOM operations post, and wanted to pump Wong for information. Wong was not in his office, and Cisneros began to have doubts about the coup plotters as well.

In Washington, Colin Powell was equally unimpressed by the coup plot. Despite the opportunity to achieve a "Panamanian solution" to his Noriega problem, he remained convinced that Giroldi or any other senior PDF leader would be as bad as Noriega, if perhaps not as clever. The idea that "we would allow Tony Noriega to go off into a hacienda somewhere while his buddy"—Giroldi had quashed the 1988 coup attempt on Noriega—"takes over the government" left Powell with no doubts at all. He would do nothing to intervene that was not consistent with the protection of Americans. He told President Bush that the United States should take no active role in the coup.

Says Powell: "A great power doesn't throw the weight of its prestige and authority behind some guy who walks in, doesn't ask for your help, and says, 'I'm gonna do this whether you like it or not. And if I ask you would you block a couple of roads?' When the time comes and there is believed to be a requirement to do this, we do it on our agenda for our purposes. Not for somebody else's purposes."

When he was briefed on the situation Monday morning, George Bush's instincts were in tune with Powell's recommendation. Thurman would be allowed to make blocking movements consistent with the protection of American lives and installations, but no more.

When Giroldi decided to postpone the coup, the Americans backed further away from what they were now convinced was a half-baked plan. In any event, there was little opportunity to help Giroldi, for the coup collapsed quickly. On Tuesday morning, Noriega surprised Giroldi by appearing at La Comandancia, while Giroldi's men—the 4th Infantry Company and the "Doberman" riot police—secured the building. At about 11:00 A.M., Giroldi broadcast news of the coup on Panamanian radio.

But Giroldi had made a number of errors that were to prove fatal to the coup and to him. Before he could be arrested, Noriega made phone calls to allies ordering reinforcements to retake the PDF headquarters. Further, Giroldi couldn't bring himself to assassinate Noriega. Even as Giroldi proclaimed the coup on the radio, Noriega loyalists were flying to his rescue. By mid-afternoon, the coup was over, and shortly thereafter, Giroldi was dead.

5

A Lot of Moving Parts

General Thurman flew to Washington on the day after the coup was over to confer with Powell and the JCS. Panama could no longer be relegated to the back burner. It was Thurman's job to protect American lives and interests while the country was disintegrating around him.

It was time to get Stiner and his planners in high gear. Before he left for the Pentagon, Thurman instructed Hartzog, his director of operations, to prepare overall guidance to set Stiner formally to work. Thurman would return to Panama the next day, 5 October, for a conference with Stiner and the XVIII Airborne Corps operations staff. Also attending were Maj. Gen. Gary Luck, the head of the Joint Special Operations Command, and his planners.

Thurman's charge to Hartzog was to stick to the big picture; this was Thurman's conception of a theater commander's job. Hartzog's job was to express what Panama should look like when the war was over, and he responded with a short operations order, twenty-five pages of general guidance that shaped the nature of the operation but did not describe how the operation should be conducted. "Stuff like—minimize collateral damage. That was a change from the earlier notion that SOUTHCOM would do detailed war planning," says Thurman.

The planning session started late at night. The Fort Bragg contingent arrived before Thurman, just after 10:00 P.M., and went directly to the SOUTHCOM command post at Quarry Heights. Called "The Tunnel," the command facility was dug hundreds of yards into the rock of Ancon Hill, a huge formation that rises from the heart of Panama City. The corps and JSOC staffs were still creating slides for their overhead projectors when Thurman returned.

Thurman had two points to make. He announced that Stiner would be overall commander, in charge of both conventional and special operations. "Carl Stiner is my warfighting friend. Everybody got that?" And he wanted to "decapitate" the PDF by eliminating its leadership and severing its command structure with an airborne strike. "I spent eleven years in airborne operations, six right in the heart of [the division], as a company-grade officer, and two years as a colonel. We think we understand the PDF and I think we can finish the operation in short order," he said.

Stiner and Luck then began the briefing, with their staffs switching and projecting slides as fast as they could make them on instructions from Hartzog. Stiner acted as master of ceremonies, padding his narrative as necessary to keep the flow of the discussion going.

"Meanwhile we're running off slides and saying here's the next slide and we're putting it up there," recalls McMahon. "The idea there, and again we're getting into Thurman's logical focus, was to take a look at these various triggers for an operation." Despite his disdain for reacting to the unpredictable behavior of the PDF hierarchy, and his confirmed view that the Giroldi coup was a mess, Thurman had come back from Washington with the understanding that he might be told to grab such an opportunity the next time. Says McMahon: "The triggers we were looking at ran the gamut from a serendipity coup—'Hey, here's a good thing that's happening. Let's jump on it and how soon can we respond there'—to a coordinated coup, to a U.S. unilateral action that is not linked to a coup."

In the course of the sessions, the planners identified four different levels of force they could bring to bear, depending upon the scenario. It also was abundantly clear that, in attempting to integrate special operations forces with conventional forces, American unilateral action was vastly to be preferred, and most likely—given the nature of politics and coups in Panama. The consensus was that an overwhelming, knockout punch could be delivered within forty-eight hours, and that if a reasonable level of operational security could be preserved, the PDF could indeed, be "decapitated."

After many hours' work, the session broke up; Thurman needed to fly to Washington again to alert the joint staff concerning the direction he was heading in his contingency planning. And with the entire operation squarely in their laps, McMahon and Huntoon needed to get to work fleshing out a task force structure and an operational plan and send it to the units who would be carrying it out for review.

Before wrapping things up, Thurman again made several major points about what he called "non-war-winners." If a U.S. soldier's wife or child were to be killed on a U.S. military installation, or part of the Panama Canal system destroyed or disabled, that would off-set any other victories and the operation would be judged a failure.

By the time they returned to Fort Bragg, McMahon and Huntoon had just a few days to rework their previous operations plan, 90-1, to accommodate changes that resulted from the performance of the PDF in the Giroldi coup. Seeing the coup unfold had given Thur-man, Stiner, and the planners invaluable insights into how the PDF command structure would react in a crisis and which units were most loyal to Noriega.

In facing down Giroldi and the men of the PDF 4th Infantry Company, Noriega had summoned the "Macho de Monte"—loosely translated as "The Mountain Men"—of the 7th Infantry Company from their base at Rio Hato, about one hundred miles from Panama City on the Pacific Coast, and where Noriega had a beach house. Also moving to rescue him was Battalion 2000 from Fort Cimarron, east of the city. He had also moved his UESAT coun-terterrorist troops from Flamenco Island near Fort Amador to Pan-ama Viejo, the oldest part of Panama City. The plan needed to be rewritten to accommodate the change. The ability of Noriega and these loyal troops to respond to a crisis so rapidly and so decisively impressed the American planners, and would significantly compli-cate their task.

Perhaps preventing the movement of the Macho de Monte from Rio Hato was the toughest challenge. It was a long way from the central PDF headquarters, La Comandancia, in downtown Panama City, but they could not be allowed to influence that fight, which would be the central objective of any attempt to dismember the PDF command structure. Under 90-1, Rio Hato had been a secondary target for the Marines of Task Force Semper Fi, whose main charge was to seize Noriega's Farallon beach house nearby. And there were additional troops at Rio Hato: the 6th Infantry Company, an NCO academy, and a training facility for PDF recruits. The original plan called for a blocking position west of Panama City, based on the assumption that any reinforcements from Rio Hato would have to move by road, most likely the Pan American Highway.

During the coup, Thurman had established a blocking position at the Bridge of the Americas, where the highway crossed the canal at the southern end of Panama City. But the ability of the Macho de Monte to deploy by air—they had flown to the Torrijos/Tocumen airport complex east of Panama City, then moved by ground routes—meant that greater effort had to be expended against the Rio Hato facility. They could not merely be blocked; they had to be attacked in place if they were to be prevented from reinforcing Panama City.

The bearded "Mountain Men", uniformed in black shirts, were among the toughest soldiers Noriega could call on, and they were stationed at the Rio Hato facility removed from the intrigues of the PDF staff in Panama City to ensure that they would remain loyal to the Panamanian general. Members of the two companies often served as guards when Noriega visited his beach house. The Macho de Monte had been given extensive training in commando tactics and had a gruesome initiation ceremony in which they poured buckets of blood over the heads of new recruits. They were commanded by Capt. Cholo Gonzalez.

Their mobility and unswerving loyalty had convinced Maj. Federico Olechea of Battalion 2000—the unit was so named for the date when the PDF would take charge of the defense of the Panama Canal—that he should stand by Noriega during the Giroldi coup; Giroldi had counted on a pledge of neutrality from Olechea. Battalion 2000 had marched right behind the Macho de Monte to La Comandancia to rescue Noriega, and while they were of more questionable loyalty, or at least less likely to initiate action in the shadow of American forces, they loomed as the larger threat. Huntoon and McMahon decided they needed not only to be blocked at the Pacora River Bridge—yet another important site on the Pan American Highway east of Panama City and Torrijos International Airport—they needed to be assaulted in their base at Fort Cimarron. Fort Cimarron was just northeast of the Pacora River Bridge.

Finally, Noriega had strengthened the PDF garrison at Panama

Viejo, the site of the first European settlement in the country and the home of the PDF 1st Cavalry Squadron, equipped with V-150 and V-300 armored cars, four- and six-wheeled vehicles made by Cadillac Gage, an American arms company. This made the unit one of the most mobile and best-equipped in the entire PDF. After the coup Noriega had moved his UESAT commandos from Flamenco Island near Fort Amador and a company of Battalion 2000 to the Panama Viejo base. He wanted units he could trust in that important location.

Of these three major moves, the toughest to tackle would be the Rio Hato base. It would require a major diversion of force and another parachute drop site. To seize Rio Hato rapidly would require a major effort, and Stiner, despite his desire to strike as many targets as possible with as much force as he could muster, did not have infinite resources. Stiner decided the Rio Hato target would go to the 75th Ranger Regiment, the Army's finest light infantry. Under the original plan, the Rangers had been given a number of targets, including the clearing of La Comandancia. Now they would have to concentrate a good portion of their troops in the assault on Rio Hato.

The need to strike Fort Cimarron and Panama Viejo quickly made the use of the 82d Airborne Division almost mandatory. Airborne troops can be deployed and assembled much more rapidly that airlanded troops such as those of the 7th Infantry Division (Light). After parachuting into Torrijos/Tocumen airfields, the 82d would be loaded onto helicopters for air assaults against Fort Cimarron and Panama Viejo. This would, according to the plan, take place under the cover of darkness the same night as the initial assault onto the airstrip.

Another target that grew in importance was the sprawling facility at Tinajitas, also east of Panama City in an area intensely loyal to Noriega. The home of the PDF 1st Infantry Company, Tinajitas was also thought to be the place where Noriega had imprisoned and possibly tortured some of the soldiers and officers whom he suspected of complicity in the coup.

The coup did resolve the question of how to target the 4th Infantry Company, the unit normally stationed in La Comandancia. It had backed Giroldi in the coup and, in the aftermath, Noriega purged it from the PDF. The headquarters complex was still manned by a substantial force of PDF troops, but the 4th Company was no longer a target.

As Huntoon and McMahon sat down to rework their operations plan, they faced PDF that were primarily ground forces and were organized into thirteen military zones totaling two battalions, ten other independent infantry companies, the cavalry squadron, the Doberman riot control company, and a special forces command consisting of the UESAT forces and other assorted commandos. In addition, there were the paramilitary Dignity Battalions, whose strength was not precisely known. Noriega's navy consisted of twelve vessels, including fast patrol boats, and a company of naval infantry marines. The PDF air force boasted thirty-eight fixed-wing aircraft of various types, seventeen helicopters, and an assortment of air defense guns, the most threatening of which was the Soviet-designed ZPU-4, a four-barreled gun something like an old American "Quad-fifty" machine gun.

On the U.S. side, the XVIII Airborne Corps, to be designated as Joint Task Force–South, or JTF-South, could call on an impressive array of forces. Forces already in Panama numbered about thirteen thousand, and were mostly assigned to USARSO, but these included the infantry of the 7th Infantry Division (Light) and 5th Infantry Division (Mechanized) that had been deployed under Operation Nimrod Dancer. These forces had been sustained and rotated through the summer, as had the MPs, special operations forces, and intelligence units that had slowly augmented USARSO. An additional battalion's worth of forces could come from the U.S. Jungle Operations Training Center, headquartered at Fort Sherman at the Atlantic end of the Panama Canal.

The planners wanted to deliver a large number of additional forces as fast as they could. If they could arrange the forty-eight hours of preparation time they had determined was necessary, they could bolster the attack with the entire 75th Ranger Regiment and the divisional ready brigade of the 82d Airborne, for a total of approximately five thousand additional soldiers. That could be supplemented on D-day by an airlanded brigade of the 7th Infantry Division—yet another five thousand or so soldiers—and would call for the final brigade of the 7th Division as a reserve. Within forty-eight hours of the initial assault, JTF-South could field a force of more than 26,000.

One major problem would be mobility within Panama, for most of these units were infantry with very few vehicles, save for the mechanized 4th Battalion, 6th Infantry Regiment, of the 5th Division from Fort Polk. After the initial assaults, movement would be best by helicopter, but the Army's helicopter fleet in Panama was by no means equal to such a task. USARSO had but a single battalion of transport helicopters, and those were Vietnam-era CH-47 Chinooks and UH-1 Hueys. Additional UH-60 Black Hawks, the service's most advanced troop transport used for air assaults, had been deployed as part of the Nimrod Dancer force, but this amounted to slightly more than a battalion's worth of lift. In any operation, these aircraft would be taxed heavily.

The nature of the operation would also require extensive use of special operations forces. The increase in special operations activities in SOUTHCOM to support the anti-drug effort and the training and assistance missions to other Central American armies had brought a significant buildup of special operations forces, primarily Army Special Forces, to Panama in the middle and late 1980s. An independent command, Special Operations Command–South, was permanently based in Panama, as was a forward-based battalion of the 7th Special Forces Group from Fort Bragg. The special operations component of JTF-South would be given a wide range of targets.

One of those targets would be Noriega himself, "decapitate the snake," in the words of Col. "Jake" Jacobelly, the commander of special operations forces stationed in Panama. If the full Panama contingency force were deployed, snatching Noriega would be of lesser priority, for he would have few soldiers left to command. Trained as an intelligence officer, Noriega was always tough to track, rarely sleeping in the same location two nights in a row. In the wake of the coup, he had become even more watchful. With so many other targets to worry about, the JSOTF planners directed that the effort to get Noriega be "apropos" and in balance with the size of the rest of the operation.

By the second week of October, Huntoon and McMahon had their plan, designated Operations Plan 90-2. They had a task force structure. They had Stiner's approval. And they had quite a laundry list of targets.

Joint Task Force–South would have four major components: Army, Navy, Air Force, and Joint Special Operations, all reporting directly to Stiner. If the plan were executed in full, the conventional ground component would consist of four major task forces: Task Force Atlantic, Task Force Pacific, Task Force Bayonet, and Task Force Semper Fi. They would be supported by the helicopters of Task Force Aviation.

Task Force Atlantic would include the elements of the 7th Infantry Division deployed to Panama in Nimrod Dancer, the battalion training at Fort Sherman, and MPs. They would strike targets in the central and northern regions of the Panama Canal.

The ready brigade of the 82d Airborne would lead Task Force Pacific into Torrijos and Tocumen airfields after these had been secured by elements of the 75th Ranger Regiment. They would then be airlifted to strike Panama Viejo, Fort Cimarron, and Tinajitas.

Army troops stationed in Panama would form the bulk of Task Force Bayonet, augmented by the mechanized infantry from Fort Polk, and they would attack targets in Panama City, including La Comandancia. They would also secure the U.S. side of Fort Amador while attacking the PDF side.

The Marines in Task Force Semper Fi would have a variety of blocking missions, including the Bridge of the Americas and areas around Howard Air Force Base. The aviation units would support all the ground forces as needed, including flying air assaults into Fort Amador, Panama Viejo, Fort Cimarron, and Tinajitas.

The special operations component was made up of four major task forces: Task Forces Red, White, Black, Blue and Green. Task Force Red designated the Rangers, broken into Task Force Red-R striking Rio Hato and Task Force Red-T hitting Torrijos/Tocumen. Task Force White would be the Navy Sea-Air-Land, or SEAL, units of SEAL Team 6 and SEAL Group 2, from Dam Neck, Virginia. Task Force Black would be the 3d Battalion, 7th Special Forces Group; Task Force Green would be the ultra-secret Delta Force.

While Huntoon and McMahon were sweating long days and nights at Fort Bragg, another kind of temperature was rising in Washington, and George Bush was on the hot seat. The administration's handling of the coup was sharply criticized by many in Congress, who thought it a bungled opportunity. Conservative Senator Jesse

Helms, the ranking Republican on the Senate Foreign Relations Committee, claimed the rebels asked for U.S. assistance and to remove Noriega from La Comandancia.

Congressional critics also had harsh words for Thurman, claiming SOUTHCOM should have anticipated the route the troops loyal to Noriega would take in riding to the rescue of their commander. To these observers, the United States had taken entirely too passive a stance in support of Giroldi.

Some lawmakers even questioned whether the administration would reveal the true story.[1] Senator David Boren, chairman of the Senate Intelligence Committee, told Molly Moore and Joe Pichirallo of the *Washington Post*: "I am convinced the full facts have not been laid out for us or the American people." Boren charged that Giroldi and the rebels waited for American assistance during the short hours they held Noriega. When the help was not forthcoming, "Five hundred members of a motley crew came in and took control," ending the rebellion. Boren angrily said that would never have happened if SOUTHCOM had acted.

Thurman spent a lot of time in Washington trying to explain his actions to the House and Senate armed services committees and to the JCS. And he wanted Stiner to give him a workable plan he could take to the JCS as soon as possible.

In the second week of October, Stiner, Thurman, and the XVIII Airborne Corps planners reviewed their ideas with senior Army leaders, including General Vuono, the chief of staff, and others on the Army staff. When Thurman was satisfied, he scheduled a meeting with General Powell. It was fixed for Sunday, 15 October.

All the principals scrambled to be in Washington. Stiner was attending his daughter's wedding in Tennessee on Saturday when he was called out of the reception and told to be at the Pentagon the next day. Needham, McMahon, and Huntoon flew in from Fort Bragg. As they drove to the Pentagon on Sunday morning, they were halted by D.C. policemen who told them to take another route; the Army was running its annual ten-mile race, an event that attracts thousands of runners, and they would have to find another way round. With hours still before the meeting, there was plenty of time to find a detour.

The meeting would be held in the National Military Command Center, the nerve center of the joint chiefs. The center, where the

U.S. military monitors the world and runs operations, more resembles a modern office than a Strangelovian command post. Officers work in small cubicles decorated in subdued tones, at personal computers linked together, and under dimmed lights.

Thurman and Stiner led the briefing, Powell, who had brought along Lt. Gen. Tom Kelly, the JCS operations director, quickly grasped the concept of the plan, said he thought it was complicated, that it "had a lot of moving parts."

Stiner was sure of the plan and his men. "We can do it," he said. "I know these forces and I know what they can do. I feel confident with this plan, provided we've got the airlift and can do it all at once." Stiner stressed that if at all possible, he would prefer to go with the full-scale plan if required to execute. "I will not be party to a piecemeal operation," he told Powell, adding that the smallest forces he was prepared to move with would be battalion-sized task forces. Stiner asked Powell to make sure Military Airlift Command came through with the aircraft needed within thirty-six hours—he knew the plan called for forty-eight hours, but wanted to be sure that would be met.

"That was a big issue," recalls Stiner. "In developing the lift, the load data for the forces, we paired our forces down to the minimum that we felt that was absolutely necessary to do this job, in order to keep the demand for airlift to a minimum for a couple reasons. One, this airlift is out all over the world all the time doing things, and two is the signature associated with it when you start trying to assemble all of it."

At any given moment, about 80 percent of the Military Airlift Command fleet is performing some mission, and Stiner was asking for a lot of airlift. Kelly, however, was sure of their ability to react, and sure that they could be made to meet Stiner's need. Knowing Stiner and Thurman, he had been suspecting they would present this kind of a plan. "We can make that happen," said the blunt operations director. "I'll just tell the Air Force," he joked.

And the word did go forth. The following week, Stiner briefed Air Force General Hansford Johnson, chief of U.S. Transportation Command, on his planned operation in Panama. Johnson agreed that he could provide the lift and tasked the Air Force to sort out the requirements.

Two days later, on 17 October, the XVIII Airborne Corps published a draft version of Operations Plan 90-2. It was circulated to the component commanders, and the planning conference was scheduled for 20 October in the Tunnel (see figure 5–1).

The draft gave the component commanders what are known as "mission-type orders." A key concept in the U.S. Army's notion of how to command in wartime, such orders tell soldiers what their commander wants them to do, not how to do it. How to accomplish the mission is left to the subordinate, as are the tactics he thinks appropriate. This preserves the lower commander's freedom to react to changing situations, essential in contingency operations.

Mission-type orders are meant to communicate the superior commander's intent. For example, Operations Plan 90-2 told commanders to neutralize their assigned targets. In different situations, "neutralize" could mean quite different things. As McMahon puts it: "Specifically we said, 'isolate, neutralize and/or destroy.' Isolate means, 'Hey, you guys here are sitting this one out? Good.' We may leave two soldiers there just for the radio. Over here, these guys aren't sitting this one out. We'll take care of them. 'Neutralize' can run from surrender, or you capture some of them and the rest of them surrender, to destroy, if the boys really want to duke it out."

At the planning conference, the component commanders for both the conventional forces and the special operations forces, the division and brigade commanders, gave back-briefs on how they planned to handle their assigned targets.

Task Force Bayonet would be commanded by Col. Mike Snell of the 193d Infantry Brigade, the main fighting force of USARSO. Snell was an old Panama hand, formerly a commander in the 3/7 Special Forces. His main targets would be the Comandancia, the PDF barracks at Fort Amador, and various smaller PDF stations within Panama City.

Snell broke his force down into subordinate task forces. Task Force Gator, consisting of the mechanized battalion from Fort Polk plus C Company, 1st Battalion, 508th Regiment (Airborne), of the 193d Infantry Brigade, would isolate, then seize and secure the La Comandancia complex. The tracked M113 armored personnel carriers of the 4th Battalion, 6th Infantry Regiment, would provide some protection for the U.S. soldiers as they moved through the streets of Panama City toward the PDF compound.

U.S. SOUTHERN COMMAND

JOINT TASK FORCE SOUTH
(HQ XVIII Airborne Corps)

NAVAL FORCES, PANAMA	AIR FORCES, PANAMA
MARINE FORCES, PANAMA	ARMY FORCES, PANAMA

TASK FORCE SEMPER FI
(MARINE FORCES, PANAMA)
6th Marine Expeditionary Bn .... Camp Lejeune, N.C.
   Company K, 3/6 Marines
   Company I, 3/6 Marines
   Company D, 2d Light Armored Inf Bn (-)
   Dets. G and H, Bde Service Support Group 6
1st Pln, First Fleet Anti-Terrorist
   Security Team .... Norfolk, Va.
Marine Corps Security Force Company .... Panama
534th Military Police Company (Army) .... Panama
536th Engineer Bn (Army) .... Panama
Battery D, 320th Field Artillery (Army) .... Panama
2/27 Inf (-) (Army) .... Fort Ord, Calif.

TASK FORCE BAYONET
HQ/HQ Company, 193d Inf Brigade .... Panama
5/87 Inf .... Panama
1/508 Inf (Abn) .... Panama
4/6 Inf (M), 5th Inf Division (M) .... Fort Polk, La.
59th Engineer Company .... Panama
519th MP Bn .... Fort Meade, Md.
   HQ/HQ Det., 519th MP Bn .... Fort Meade, Md.
   209th MP Company .... Fort Meade, Md.
   555th MP Company .... Fort Lee, Va.
   988th MP Company .... Fort Benning, Ga.

TASK FORCE ATLANTIC
HQ/HQ Company, 3d Bde, 7th Inf Division .... Fort Ord, Calif.
4/17 Inf .... Fort Ord, Calif.
3/504 Inf (Abn) .... Fort Bragg, N.C.
Battery B, 7/15 Field Artillery .... Fort Ord, Calif.
Battery B, 2/62 Air Defense Artillery .... Fort Ord, Calif.
Company C, 13th Engineer Bn .... Fort Ord, Calif.
Company C, 7th Medical Bn .... Fort Ord, Calif.
Company C, 707th Maintenance Bn .... Fort Ord, Calif.
Company C, 7th Supply & Trans. Bn .... Fort Ord, Calif

TASK FORCE AVIATION (HQ Avn Bde, 7th Inf Division)
1/228 Avn .... Panama
Task Force Hawk (HQ 3/123 Avn, 7th Inf Division)
   3/123 Avn (-) .... Fort Ord, Calif.
   Company E, 123 Avn (-) .... Fort Ord, Calif.
Task Force Wolf (HQ 1/82 Avn, 82d Abn Division)
   1/82 Avn (-) .... Fort Bragg, N.C.
   Troop D, 1st Squadron, 17th Cavalry .... Fort Bragg, N.C.
   1/123 Aviation (-) .... Fort Ord, Calif.

JOINT SPECIAL OPERATIONS TASK FORCE

Task Force Red (HQ 75th Ranger Regt)
HQ/HQ Company, 75th Rgr .... Fort Benning, Ga.
1/75 Rgr .... Hunter Army Afld, Ga.
2/75 Rgr .... Fort Lewis, Wash.
3/75 Rgr .... Fort Benning, Ga.

Continued on next page

FIGURE 5–1

Joint Task Force–South: Table of Organization

JOINT SPECIAL OPERATIONS TASK FORCE (cont.)

Task Force Black (HQ 3/7 Special Forces Grp)
- 3/7 SF Grp   Panama
- Company A, 1/7 SF Grp   Fort Bragg, N.C.

Task Force White (HQ Nav. Spec. Warfare Grp 2)
- Teams 2, 4, Nav. Spec. War. Grp 2   Little Creek, Va.
- Naval Special Warfare Unit 8   Panama
- Special Boat Unit 26   Panama

Task Force Green (Army Delta Force)

Task Force Blue (Navy Special Mission Unit)

7th SF Grp (-) (Arrived D+10)   **Fort Bragg, N.C.**
- HQ/HQ Company, 7th SF Grp
- 1/7 SF Grp (-)
- 2/7 SF Grp
- Support Company, 7th SF Grp
- 112th Signal Bn (-)   Fort Bragg, N.C.
- 528th Support Bn   Fort Bragg, N.C.
- 160th Aviation Grp (-)   Fort Campbell, Ky.
- 617th Aviation Detachment   Panama

ELEMENTS UNDER DIRECT CONTROL OF JTF-SOUTH
- 1st Battlefield Control Detachment (-)   Fort Bragg, N.C.
- HQ/HQ Company, U.S. Army South   Panama
- 16th MP Bde   Fort Bragg, N.C.
  - 503d MP Bn   Fort Bragg, N.C.
    - HQ/HQ Detachment, 503d MP Bn
    - 21st MP Company
    - 65th MP Company
    - 108th MP Company
  - 92d MP Bn   Panama
    - HQ/HQ Detachment, 92d MP Bn
    - 549th MP Company
- 470th MI Bde   Panama
  - 29th MI Bn
  - 746th MI Bn
  - 747th MI Bn
- 525th MI Bde (-)   Fort Bragg, N.C.
  - Company A, 319th MI Bn
  - 519th MI Bn (-)
- 35th Signal Bde (-)   Fort Bragg, N.C.
- 1st Corps Support Command (-)   Fort Bragg, N.C.
  - 44th Medical Bde   Fort Bragg, N.C.
    - 5th Mobile Army Surgical Hospital   Fort Bragg, N.C.
    - 32d Med. Supply & Optical Maint. Unit   Fort Bragg, N.C.
    - 36th Medical Company (-)   Panama
    - 142d Medical Bn (-)   Panama
  - 41st Support Group
    - 193d Support Bn
      - 1097th Transportation Company
  - 46th Support Group (-)   Fort Bragg, N.C.
    - 2d Support Center   Fort Bragg, N.C.
      - 330th Transportation Center
    - 7th Transportation Bn   Fort Bragg, N.C.
- 4th Psychological Operations Group (-)   Fort Bragg, N.C.
  - 1st Psyop Bn
  - 90th Psyop Company
  - 94th Psyop Company
- 96th Civil Affairs Bn   Fort Bragg, N.C.
- 1109th Signal Bde   Panama
  - 154th Signal Bn
  - 1190th Signal Bn

FIGURE 5–1 (continued).

AIR FORCES, PANAMA
830th Air Division	Panama
1st Special Operations Wing (AC-130)	Hurlburt Field, Fla.
24th Composite Wing	Panama
CORONET COVE (A-7D Air Nat'l Gd rotation)	
Det., 114th Tac. Fighter Grp	S.D. ANG
24th Tac. Air Support Squadron (OA-37)	Panama
61st Military Airlift Group	Panama
VOLANT OAK (C-130 rotation)	Various
310th Military Airlift Squadron	Panama
Det. 1, 480th Recon Tech. Group	
(FURTIVE BEAR)	Panama

NAVAL FORCES, PANAMA
Naval Security Group (Galeta Island)	Panama
Mine Division 127	Panama

ARMY FORCES, PANAMA (HQ XVIII Airborne Corps)

82D AIRBORNE DIVISION (-) — Fort Bragg, N.C.
HQ/HQ Company, 82d Abn Division (-) — Fort Bragg, N.C.
1st Bde, 82d Abn Division (+) — Fort Bragg, N.C.
1/504 Inf (Abn)
2/504 Inf (Abn)
4/325 Inf (Abn) (-) (+)
Company A, 3/505 Inf
Battery A, 3/319 Field Artillery (-)
Battery A, 3/4 Air Defense Artillery (-)
Company C, 3/73 Armor
Company A, 307th Engineer Bn
Company A, 782d Maintenance Bn
Company B, 307th Medical Bn
Company A, 407th Supply & Service Bn
Company A, 313th MI Bn
Company B, 82d Signal Bn (-) — Fort Bragg, N.C.
82d MP Company (-) — Fort Bragg, N.C.
401st MP Company — Fort Hood, Texas
511th MP Company — Fort Drum, N.Y.
1st Bde, 7th Inf Division (Manchus) — Fort Ord, Calif.
HQ/HQ Company, 1st Bde
1/9 Inf
2/9 Inf
3/9 Inf
Company A, 13th Engineer Bn
Company A, 707th Maintenance Bn
Company A, 7th Medical Bn
Company A, 7th Supply & Trans. Bn

7th INFANTRY DIVISION (LIGHT) (-) — Fort Ord, Calif.
HQ/HQ Company, 7th Inf Division
7th MP Company (-)
2d Squadron, 9th Cavalry (-)
2d Bde, 7th Inf Division (-)
HQ/HQ Company, 2d Bde
5/21 Inf
3/27 Inf
6/8 Field Artillery
Battery A, 2/62 Air Defense Artillery
Company B, 13th Engineer Bn
Company B, 7th Medical Bn
Company B, 707th Maintenance Bn
Company B, 7th Supply & Trans. Bn
127th Signal Bn (-)
13th Engineer Bn (-)
107th MI Bn (-)

Joanne Ostendorf and Cristina Rivero

FIGURE 5–1 (continued).

Task Force Red Devil, A and B Companies, 1/508 Infantry (Airborne), would move against Fort Amador. Two platoons would move by truck to secure the main gate while the remainder of the force would air assault onto the fort's golf course; the Panamanian and American facilities at Fort Amador were separated by the width of a fairway.

Task Force Wildcat was the final force under Snell's command. The three companies of the 5th Battalion, 87th Regiment, 193d Infantry Brigade, plus A Company, 4/6 Infantry, would neutralize PDF customs police headquarters at Ancon Hill and Balboa and the Ancon Hill traffic police station.

Task Force Pacific would be commanded by Maj. Gen. James Johnson, also commander of the 82d Airborne Division. His paratroopers would drop into Torrijos International Airport and Tocumen Military Airfield about forty-five minutes after it had been secured by elements of the 75th Ranger Regiment. The three battalions of the division's ready brigade would then use the airfield to conduct air assaults, one battalion each to Tinajitas, Panama Viejo, and Fort Cimarron. The Rangers who had secured the airfields would come under Johnson's control for follow-on missions.

Task Force Atlantic would be led by Col. Keith Kellogg, then commander of the 3d Brigade, 7th Infantry Division. His task force had a slew of smaller targets scattered throughout the northern and central sections of the Panama Canal Zone. Many of them were in the vicinity of the port city of Colon, a free-trade zone with an abundance of rough neighborhoods.

Coco Solo was the home of the PDF marines. They would be assaulted by C Company, 4th Battalion, 17th Infantry Regiment, 7th Division, along with an additional platoon drawn from whatever unit was rotating through the jungle training center. They would be augmented with MPs and two Vulcan air-defense squads. The Vulcans, which feature 20mm Gatling guns, were designed for air cover, but their rapid rate of fire makes them an excellent ground support system as well.

A second target was Fort Espinar, another PDF installation at the north end of the Panama Canal. It was the home of the PDF 8th Infantry Company. A Company, of the 4th Battalion, 17th Infantry, would make the assault. The task force had other important blocking missions. One was the Boyd-Roosevelt Highway, the main north-south artery between Colon and Panama City. It would be secured by Headquarters Company of the 4th Battalion, 17th Infantry, along with mortar and engineer support. B Company would secure "The Bottleneck," a narrow isthmus at the entrance to Colon, with MPs of the 549th MP Company and a platoon of engineers. The antitank and scout platoons of the 4th Battalion, 17th Infantry would seize France Field, the main Colon airstrip. Other targets included securing Madden Dam, the Cerro Tigre logistics center, the town of Gamboa and Renacer Prison. Other elements of the 549th MPs would secure the Gatun, Miraflores, and Pedro Miguel Locks in the central canal region.

The Marines of Task Force Semper Fi would be augmented by Army MPs, engineers, and artillerymen for their blocking missions at the Bridge of the Americas. They would move to their designated positions quickly in their Light Armored Vehicles. A second Marine rifle company would patrol the hills in the rear of Howard Air Force Base, an important security mission, as Stiner was very concerned about mortar attacks on the base that would serve as the hub of huge helicopter and fixed-wing air operations. The Marines, who had learned much about PDF tactics and the close terrain in their defense of Arraijan tank farm, would be ideal for this difficult hide-and-seek mission.

The Joint Special Operations Task Force would be commanded by Maj. Gen. Luck, or Maj. Gen. Wayne Downing, who was due to relieve him in December. The largest of the special operations forces would be Col. William "Buck" Kernan's 75th Ranger Regiment, Task Force Red. Kernan assigned his 1st Battalion and C Company, 3d Battalion, to the assault on Torrijos/Tocumen as Task Force Red-Tango, while the 2d Battalion and A and B Companies, 3d Battalion, 75th Ranger Regiment would form Task Force Red-Romeo against Rio Hato. In the west they were to be relieved within hours by a second brigade of the 7th Infantry Division, under division commander Maj. Gen. Carmen Cavezza, who would begin to move farther west into Panama while the Rangers were held for subsequent missions.

The Navy SEALs of Task Forces White and Blue would get several important missions. The largest would be an assault by sea on Paitilla Airport, a small strip in Panama City where Noriega kept his own private jet. SEALs also would disable the fast patrol boats at Coco Solo and Noriega's private yachts in Balboa harbor, snatch Noriega if he happened to be at Farallon beach house at Rio Hato, and protect the Bridge of the Americas from below.

Delta Force formed Task Force Green. Its targets would be Carcel Modelo prison, where American Kurt Muse was held. Muse had led a radio propaganda effort against Noriega that helped rally support for the Panamanian opposition. Task Force Green was also the central reserve in the effort to snatch Noriega. If reconnaissance teams located Noriega at any of his known hideouts, Delta Force teams on alert in helicopters would swoop in to get him.

Green Berets of the 3/7 Special Forces formed Task Force Black. In addition to many reconnaissance missions, they would seize the main Panamanian television tower at Cerro Azul to prevent Noriega from rallying his forces by television broadcast. They also would block the Pacora River Bridge on the ground to prevent Battalion 2000 from moving from Fort Cimarron into Panama City.

The plan did indeed have "many moving parts," as General Powell had said, and the commanders expressed a number of concerns at that first planning conference. The largest concern was airlift, both to Panama and for the forces already there. With nearly 250 special operations helicopter and AC-130 gunships, conventional and unconventional troop transport helicopters, C-130 and C-141 cargo planes to drop paratroopers and supplies, and Air Force attack aircraft in support, the skies over Panama City were going to be packed. Sorting out that traffic was going to be a nightmare and threatened to be a disaster if not done properly.

Supporting such a potentially large force was also a challenge. Stiner was adamant about maintaining tactical surprise, and any logistics buildup would surely tip off the PDF. The same was true if extra helicopter support for air assaults was moved in. Yet there was just not enough fire support, especially for the attack on La Comandancia. Despite the risk, Stiner agreed that four Sheridan tanks and six AH-64 Apache attack helicopters could be smuggled into Howard Air Force Base.

One final problem had to be addressed: communications. With so many units performing dozens of missions at night, and with the freedom to shape tasks according to necessity, every unit had to know how to raise other units. Such communications had been a severe problem during the 1983 U.S. assault on the island of Grenada. Yet in the intervening years little work had been done to develop the models for such a large communications scheme. These plans, called Joint Communications and Electronics Operating Instructions, are the key to preventing two units from trying to use the same frequency, and getting varying units from different services to use similar communications security. The Army's 35th Signal Brigade, the signal unit of the XVIII Airborne Corps, was given the task of developing the communications plan. Without it, agreed the commanders, such a complex operation could easily find itself in trouble.

The planning conference adjourned with many issues unresolved. Yet Stiner and his planners felt they had accomplished a huge task in a short period of time. The hard work had been done. The plan needed fine-tuning. It was complex, so it needed detailed rehearsals. And it needed to be blessed in Washington. Stiner and Thurman owed General Powell an update.

6

"Let's Do It."

A week after the first planning conference in Panama, Stiner was back in Washington to review his plan with Powell. In the wake of the Giroldi coup, rumors of other attempts kept the JCS staff on alert. After the blasting the Bush administration and the Pentagon had taken throughout the month of October, there were plenty of hopes that some PDF officer would let the Americans off the hook. Yet Powell, confident in his own analysis, was uninterested in aiding another half-baked coup. "Great powers should not be at the mercy of a gang that couldn't shoot straight," he said.

Powell was impressed with Stiner's plan. Yet he remained concerned about the ability to respond to a rapidly breaking situation; the chairman did not want to be at the mercy of events he could do little to control.

What if there is a terrorist attack against American citizens or a U.S. installation and I don't have time to assemble the airlift you need? Powell asked. Must you do it all at once?

Stiner replied that he did not want a piecemeal operation; it would cause more casualties and take longer to accomplish the mission.

The two generals debated the issue back and forth, Powell pushing Stiner to consider every possible scenario, Stiner sticking to his guns. He did not want to deploy anything less than a complete task force. Powell agreed.

Four days later, on 31 October, Stiner convened a second planning session at Fort Clayton, to refine the operation and work out details. The commanders continued to discuss the air assault operations and talk about other follow-on targets. A draft of the communications plan was published for review and specifics of the fire support plan hammered out. Shortly before the meeting ended, Stiner warned, "It won't go exactly as planned."

Still, a detailed plan was emerging. The following day, Stiner briefed the full operation to Lieutenant General Kelly and the JCS operations staff, in preparation for a presentation to the complete Joint Chiefs of Staff on 3 November.

By now, the script was well rehearsed. "I am not a war fighter," Thurman had told Kelly. "I need a war fighter. Carl Stiner is my war fighter and everybody in Panama carrying a gun works for Carl Stiner." Substituting the 82d Airborne for the 7th Infantry Division had raised some eyebrows. "A lot of people went around saying, 'Well, you know Max is an old airborne guy and Carl Stiner can't spell anything but airborne,'" recalls Kelly. Some in the Marine Corps questioned the elimination of the Marine expeditionary force from Panama contingency planning, and various Marine generals had called Stiner offering additional forces. "The fact is, we could get an airborne division on the ground in ten minutes or we could get an airlanded brigade in a day and a half. If you're going to do that you have to work fast. We realized that we had to take down the PDF; that became the catch phrase," says Kelly. He, too, was happy with the plan.

The final hurdle was the meeting in the JCS "Tank" in the bowels of the Pentagon. Stiner conducted the briefing, but the outcome was a foregone conclusion. With Powell's strong presence and the increased power given to the JCS chairman by defense reform laws, his blessing ensured the plan's acceptance by the full panel of service leaders. "That was really a pro forma meeting where they all saluted because General Powell clearly liked the plan," said one participant. Operations Plan 90-2 was published that same day.

Thurman had directed Stiner to create a war plan that could last for ten years, or until the United States ceded sovereignty of the Panama Canal to Panama. He was sure Stiner's plan would fit the bill.

Additional planning conferences were scheduled in Panama for 18 November and 18 December. The first would work out final bugs, including the communications plan, and set the stage for rehearsals. Each component unit was directed to incorporate the new plan in its normal training schemes. By mid-December, rehearsals and their after-action reviews would be complete, allowing commanders to discover any glitches in the plan and discuss needed changes.

Of continuing concern was the shortage of highly qualified helicopter pilots and gunners within USARSO units. Stiner's plan relied heavily upon pilots' ability to fly extended and repeated missions using night vision goggles, keeping tight formations in air assaults with helicopter running lights completely blacked out. Because of the Pentagon's stated rotation policies, and the traditionally low priority of SOUTHCOM, there was a severe need for experienced pilots to fly these demanding missions. Pilots and crewmen were gradually being sent to Panama on temporary duty, but the moves were taxing the Army's small pool of senior flight warrant officers.

The sheer number of aircraft required in the plan stunned Air Force airspace managers. "It was kind of unreal," says Lt. Col. Earl Whitt, Jr., airspace manager for Howard, who was introduced to the battle plan in late November. "I started reading it and my eyeballs fell out. There was an unbelievable amount of traffic that was coming through here."

Radar would be shut down to prevent damage from jamming. Pilots would be flying blacked-out. "Nobody was going to see anybody unless they had goggles on, and even then they were only going to see straight ahead," Whitt says.

At Tocumen Airfield alone, on hostile territory, the plan required fifty C-141s for airdrops or landings, plus C-5s, several AC-130s, and helicopters. "And we had to make sure nobody was going to go bump in the night," Whitt says.

Not only was the airflow almost overwhelming, but the advanced state of planning took airspace planners by surprise, he says. "Up until that point, there had been little or no coordination with the Air Force from the XVIII Airborne Corps, from USARSO, SOUTHCOM, anybody."

An airspace control plan was developed that would regulate everything in the air—fixed-wing aircraft, helicopters, artillery and other projectiles—by altitude, timing, and routes. Army pilots would fly along air highways, consisting of parallel one-way routes with exit points for their targets. The airspace managers for each task force component assembled at Bergstrom Air Force Base near Austin, Texas, around a large wall chart to identify and adjust colliding routes and "sanitize" target areas to keep aircraft away from friendly fire.

One result of the discussion was the decision that any use of air space not already written into the plan before the operation would require permission from the air operations center at Howard.

The day following the November conference in Panama, Thurman issued an order aimed at getting the number of American military dependents in Panama below five hundred. On the afternoon of the Giroldi coup, the SOUTHCOM commander had had his hands full trying to protect 4,500 school children scattered around the canal zone, and he wanted to clear the decks as best he could before a full-scale combat operation. Because of the turmoil at the Comandancia, children had stayed at school until seven-thirty on the evening of the coup attempt, underscoring to Thurman the vulnerability of dependents in Panama.

On the same day as the order to reduce dependents, the secret deployment of Sheridan tanks, Apache attack helicopters, and three OH-58 scout helicopters was completed. On the nights of 15 and 16 November, giant C-5 cargo planes brought in the tanks and helicopters. The Apaches were kept in hangars at Howard, while the tanks were moved to their marshalling area and parked in tents.

No sooner had Stiner returned to Fort Bragg from the planning conference than he was summoned again to Panama. On 15 November, he got a call from Brig. Gen. Bill Hartzog saying General Thurman, who was in Washington, wanted Stiner to come down immediately.

"How come? I'm coming down in three or four days," asked Stiner.

"We've got some intelligence that you should be aware of."

Hartzog and Stiner met at Fort Clayton just before midnight. Hartzog said a Colombian informant with ties to the drug trade had come in to claim there were ten car bomb attacks planned against Americans in Panama, and that the cars were planted in warehouses. SOUTHCOM was skeptical of the charges, but the informant had passed a polygraph examination. The Colombian also claimed there was a woman agent working on U.S. military installations with access to U.S. military blank identification cards. Someone was going to infiltrate an installation and detonate one of these car bombs.

When Thurman returned the next day, he activated JTF-South. Stiner was in business. "I'm going to stand you up and I'm going to hold you responsible for all defensive measures," Thurman told him. Stiner sent for his command team, moved into the command center, and put SOUTHCOM on the highest state of alert. They decided to set the rehearsal cycle in fast motion, especially the special operations forces, who were housed in a hangar at Howard Air Force Base. They went to a high state of readiness, flying and exercising repeatedly at night.

Every element of the task force prepared major exercises. Stiner flew back to Fort Bragg during the final days of November to watch the 82d Airborne stage a brigade-sized airdrop and follow-on air assaults into mock-ups of the targets at Tinajitas, Fort Cimarron, and Panama Viejo.

Task Force Atlantic had been conducting its rehearsals since early November and continued them into December. The securing of Madden Dam was practiced 6 and 23 November, then again on 11 December. Three Cerro Tigre rehearsals were conducted as well. On 14 December, paratroopers conducted a mock assault on Renacer Prison, along with a SEAL reconnaissance and surveillance team. The entire task force ran through its plan 6 December, under operation "Get Some."

The 75th Ranger Regiment conducted a rare regimental-sized exercise to rehearse a large airfield take-down at Hurlburt Field in the Florida panhandle, where the Air Force stations its special operations aircraft. The "Sand Flea" exercises were given new life and new routes of reconnaissance.

Most elaborate were the aviation rehearsals. Night after night the helicopters flew. They did not go toward their actual objectives, but flew representative distances and representative legs, allowing the planners to confirm where they should establish forward area refueling points, essential for the 82d Airborne's air assaults. Because of the small helicopter fleet in Panama and Stiner's refusal to tip his hand by bringing in more choppers, the refueling operation had to be able to fill up twenty Black Hawk helicopters in less than twenty-five minutes. By 1 December, Stiner felt the aviation plan was in good shape.

The possibility of mortar fire by the PDF continued to plague Stiner. PDF mortars in Tinajitas could range the Torrijos/Tocumen airstrips; other known positions could bring Howard Air Force Base under fire. During the first weeks of December, Stiner tried to assemble the fire-finding radars that would pick out mortar locations and practice the countermortar techniques that could silence the PDF mortars quickly.

For many families in Panama, the bomb scare marked the pinnacle of misery and frustration. Getting on and off military posts was a nightmare because of the additional security measures now in force. At Fort Clayton, for example, all traffic was routed in one gate and out another, creating lines down Gaillard Highway. Guards checked cars coming on posts with mirrors. Dozens of dogs were shipped into Panama to sniff for bombs. The parking lots at the Corozal post exchange and commissary were blocked off to keep potential car bombs away from shoppers, so shoppers had to carry groceries several blocks to their cars.

People were tired. They were stressed. Many had been separated suddenly from their friends by Blade Jewel, the rapid, forced move of 6,300 service members and their families to the States in May, June, and July. Now, with this new disruption in day-to-day life, "It was a very pessimistic feeling here," says Lettie Raab, wife of Col. Larry Raab, commander of MPs in Panama. That period, she says, "was probably harder to live with than a lot of the things that went on during Just Cause."

The Thanksgiving car bomb scare subsided, but the level of tension in Panama remained high. Noriega was attempting his tried-and-true tactic of shifting the blame for his country's problems to the yanquis. Stiner recommended to Thurman that the Sand Flea exercises be scaled back. The forces were well rehearsed, and Noriega was using them as an opportunity to trot out his Dignity Battalions and confront U.S. troops. At last, SOUTHCOM was developing something of an intelligence capability against the PDF, and what officials were discovering was a force deep in turmoil. Noriega was losing his grip while resorting to ever harsher methods; talk of a coup was everywhere.

American pressures were mounting on the Panamanian dictator. On 15 December, Noriega deposed Francisco Rodríguez and installed himself as head of government, declaring before a Panamanian legislature packed with his cronies that Panama was in "a state of war" with the United States.

While his statement was worded as a clever provocation to infuriate the Americans, the subtleties were lost on the rank and file of the PDF. The Panamanian military was in disarray; now it would spin irrevocably out of control.

The night after Noriega's declaration, Marine Lt. Robert Paz, a Colombian by birth, and three companions were driving along Avenue A in downtown Panama City. The streets were packed, and the crowds agitated. Just after 9:00 P.M., they were stopped at a PDF roadblock. Seeing the Michigan license plates on the faded and rusted Chevrolet, about forty Panamanians surged toward the car. The PDF guards at the roadblock waved the few cars ahead of the Americans through the checkpoint, but demanded that the Americans halt. The PDF began waving their AK-47 assault rifles at the Marines and tried to pull them from the car. The driver panicked and slammed on the accelerator pedal. The PDF guards fired at the car as it sped away.

One of the rifle bullets pierced the car's trunk lid, just above the license plate. It tore through the thin sheet metal and into the passenger compartment. Paz, sitting in the left rear seat, was struck in the spine. Another round grazed a Marine officer's ankle. The driver raced to the Gorgas Army Community Hospital emergency room, but Paz was mortally wounded. Although doctors worked on him for about fifteen minutes, Paz was pronounced dead.

About half an hour before the shooting, a Navy lieutenant and his wife had gotten lost returning to Rodman Naval Station after dining out. When the couple stopped at the same roadblock, the PDF demanded to see their identification cards and pulled them to the side of the street while their identification was verified.

The lieutenant and his wife witnessed the Paz shooting, and the PDF knew it. After the shooting, a Panamanian officer returned to the couple and took them to a nearby PDF office. Blindfolding them with masking tape, they whisked the Americans into the back of a pickup truck and took them to another location, which the lieutenant thought to be La Comandancia. The PDF began an interrogation that was to last four hours. During the session, the lieutenant was repeatedly beaten and kicked in the groin and head. He was told he would be killed if he did not provide details about his assignments and his unit.

The PDF interrogators turned to the officer's wife. They slammed her against a wall, opening a cut on her head. Forced to stand against the wall with her arms over her head, she collapsed to the floor, exhausted. The PDF stood over her, grabbing their crotches and taunting her. At about one o'clock in the morning, the Panamanians gave up and released the couple on Fourth of July Avenue, three blocks from La Comandancia.

Southern Command reacted first to news of the Paz slaying. Thurman was again in Washington, briefing Defense Secretary Richard Cheney on his plans for the drug war and making Christmas plans with his brother, Roy. Brig. Gen. Bill Hartzog was standing in for Thurman. When he heard of the incident, Hartzog telephoned the National Military Command Center in the Pentagon.

The USARSO leadership in Panama was enjoying a cherished evening of relaxation when Cisneros learned Paz was shot.

The traditional Christmas ball at Fort Amador had almost been canceled, but the leadership felt that families in Panama had had enough disruptions in their lives. The community was ready to get on with Christmas, to try to have a good time. The guests were even permitted to flout the curfew. The Raabs, master and mistress of ceremonies, planned to announce that a commemorative wine glass with the U.S. Army South galleon painted on it would be a pass back on base after the 11:00 P.M. curfew. Amid the festivities in the ballroom of the Fort Amador Officers' Club, Noriega was all but forgotten as the guests finished their dinner and looked forward to hearing an American children's choir sing Christmas carols.

About one-third of the way through the program, the children were singing "Feliz Navidad" when a soldier came in and whispered something to Cisneros. Barbara Pote, sitting with a clear view of the head table, saw Raab mouth the words, "Oh, my God" and her face blanch. After a couple of minutes, Cisneros walked up to the choir director and asked him to conclude the program.

When the music stopped, Cisneros announced calmly and apologetically that a serviceman had been shot. While saying nothing about Paz's death, he asked the soldiers to return to duty immediately and advised their wives to go home and stay inside. Some people sitting in the back of the room, unable to see the head table, at first didn't believe the news. But the wave of dress-blue uniforms heading for the door made it clear this was no joke.

"You never saw a place empty out so damn fast," Pote says. Soldiers hurried to the next room to confer while their wives gathered their coats and arranged rides home. The soldiers disappeared to work, not to return home in many cases until several days later, and then only momentarily until the end of December. "For the people that were in Panama, that was the beginning," says Lettie Raab, whose husband dashed off to Gorgas Army Community Hospital to interview Paz's companions. "From the sixteenth on, you saw your husband occasionally."

Just before 10:00 P.M., Cisneros put SOUTHCOM on the highest state of alert, and moved the forces in Panama to their ready positions under Operations Plan 90-2. Soldiers manned defensive positions at Fort Clayton and Fort Amador. Hartzog also called Stiner at Fort Bragg.

Cars sped into the military posts as MPs stood in the road, waving them in. When she walked into her home on Fort Clayton, Pote tried to be nonchalant about the fact that her husband, Maj. Rob Pote, executive officer of the 1st Battalion, 508th Infantry Regiment (Airborne), was going to work on a Saturday night. She was concerned that Rob's parents, visiting from Pontiac, Michigan, would be unnecessarily alarmed. She told her mother-in-law, Glenden Pote, only that "something happened."

Thurman, Powell, and Kelly assembled at the Pentagon command center, where they reviewed the situation and the range of options in the plan. The three generals discussed the situation until midnight, when Thurman called for a plane to take him back to Panama. Thurman left saying he would communicate "in a couple of hours, after I get back on the ground and see what else goes on tonight." Powell and Kelly began preparations for the meeting they knew would come the next day.

At the White House, National Security Adviser Brent Scowcroft woke President Bush to tell him of the Paz killing. Bush was visibly upset. Later in the night, word came in about the harassment of the Navy lieutenant and his wife.

In his eighty days as JCS chairman, Powell had changed, and the world had changed. The Soviet bloc was crumbling and America's strategic focus was shifting. When he was National Security Adviser, he had agreed with his predecessor at JCS, Admiral Crowe, that Panama was of secondary importance. But now, he felt that America should hang out a shingle saying "Superpower lives here."

In thinking and talking through their options that night, Powell and his military advisers began to feel strongly that a move against Noriega was called for. The next day, they would go to the president and recommend implementation of the full plan.

Kelly called Stiner, to review the concept and details of the operations plan. "They are going to brief the president," said Kelly, adding that they were going to recommend implementation of the plan. "Will you let Wayne Downing know?" he asked.

Sure, replied Stiner, who had a request of his own. "Will you please pass one thing to the chairman, a request from me? He's smart enough to know this, but tell him there is nothing we can do to bring Lt. Paz back. The damage has already been done. The best thing that we can do is to do this thing right and give me forty-eight hours. That's my request, so we can get our planes together and get our forces there, and I'll do it right." Kelly agreed.

Powell and his lieutenants reconvened in the command center early the next morning to hear Thurman's update. He had gotten back to Panama at 5:00 A.M., and had yet another beating to report, of a soldier who was shuttling a mail truck to the Panama City airports. SOUTHCOM also had sent Powell a transcript of the Navy lieutenant's debriefing, adding an edge to the cold reasoning demanded by the policy questions before the chairman.

The first meeting would be with Cheney and his policy deputies, Undersecretary of Defense Paul Wolfowitz and Carl Ford, principal deputy assistant secretary for international security affairs. The State Department and National Security Council also sent representatives.

Powell laid out the plan, and his recommendations to strike with the full package of forces. Cheney initially was undecided, while the others were generally against action, though not vehemently. What about a smaller operation? Powell worked through the arguments, as had Major Huntoon, Lt. Col. McMahon, Lt. Gen. Stiner, and General Thurman: the PDF was the problem, even more than Noriega; a larger force reduced the probability of high casualties; the situation in Panama had deteriorated beyond Noriega's control; and the threat to Americans was serious.

Cheney's advisers suggested that the Paz killing and the beating of the Navy couple were not sufficient grounds to act: Was the lieutenant where he shouldn't have been? Did the Marines have guns?

What was really going on? In the end, Powell prevailed. Cheney was convinced of the need to act, and act forcefully.

The day's second meeting would be at Powell's stately residence at Fort Myer in Virginia. Powell and his wife, Alma, were having a Christmas party that day. Attending were the four service chiefs: Army general Carl Vuono, Marine general Al Gray, Air Force general Larry Welch, and Admiral Carlisle Trost. Also attending was Air Force general Robert Herres, the vice chairman of the JCS. These senior four-stars picked over the plan, commenting on various details. Marine commandant Gray summed up the meeting when he urged them not to tinker. "Leave it alone," he said.

The decisive meeting would be with the president at two o'clock at the White House. The meeting was pure Bush: an intimate gathering of trusted officials, a thorough briefing, complete with huge maps of Panama and the targets to be attacked. It was designed to let the president sort through his options methodically. Dressed in a blue blazer and gray trousers, Bush had just come from a brunch with family, friends, and Vice President Dan Quayle. He had told Quayle of his intention to move against Noriega. Attending the meeting were Quayle, Secretary of State James Baker; John Sununu, White House chief of staff; National Security Adviser Scowcroft; Robert Gates, Scowcroft's deputy who was also acting as the representative of the intelligence community; Powell; Kelly; and White House Press Secretary Marlin Fitzwater.

Conspicuously absent was CIA director William Webster. Bush was not happy that a plan for a covert operation against Noriega, called Panama 5, formulated and approved by Bush in the aftermath of the Giroldi coup, had been leaked to the press.

The meeting was also in keeping with Bush's modus operandi: exhaust every policy option almost to the point of humiliation, then strike decisively when he felt his back against the wall. Bush sat in his office, under "The Peacemakers," a favorite painting depicting Abraham Lincoln and his generals near the end of the Civil War. He wanted Noriega, his longtime nemesis. He also wanted the Panamanian government of Guillermo Endara to be a credible democracy. "How can I do that?" he asked.

The first issue was whether to respond at all. Secretary of State James Baker laid out what he thought the response would be around the region, in Europe, the Soviet Union, and elsewhere in the world. There was a strong feeling that some response was necessary. But what response?

Powell laid out the plan (see figure 6–1). He urged the use of hammerhead military force, saying it was most likely to guarantee a rapid success. A surgical strike aimed solely at Noriega would not suffice, he contended. Noriega was both leader of the PDF and a product of its corruption; eliminating Noriega alone would merely open an opportunity for another strongman.

And Noriega was an elusive target, with an intelligence officer's skill and natural talent at deception. It might take a while to catch him, said Powell.

Scowcroft, a former Air Force lieutenant general, instinctively grasped the complexity of the plan, and became something of a devil's advocate. Bush was concerned about the number of casualties, both among American soldiers and Panamanian civilians, from fighting on the cramped streets of Panama City. Powell and Kelly said there might be as many as seventy soldiers killed.

But Powell persisted that the overall operation was a job that his troops knew how to do. "We trained for it, we practiced," he said, outlining the thorough rehearsals that had just been completed.

Scowcroft agreed a surgical strike could work, but at much higher risk. "We haven't trained for it. We can never be that certain where Noriega is at any particular time," he pointed out.

Bush was convinced that the situation in Panama was degenerating. All intelligence reports were now painting Noriega as increasingly desperate and paranoid. To the president, Noriega's claim to the title of "Maximum Leader" and declaration that Panama was in a state of war with the United States apparently had given his followers the green light to resume harassment of Americans. It did not seem that Noriega was in control.

Ultimately, Powell convinced Bush, Baker, and the others at the meeting. Ever since the coup, Bush had thought it would come down to this. "This guy is not going to lay off," said the president. "It will only get worse."

"Let's do it," Bush said quietly.

The meeting broke up at around 4:00 P.M., with Powell and Kelly returning to the Pentagon. Powell called Thurman, who was in the

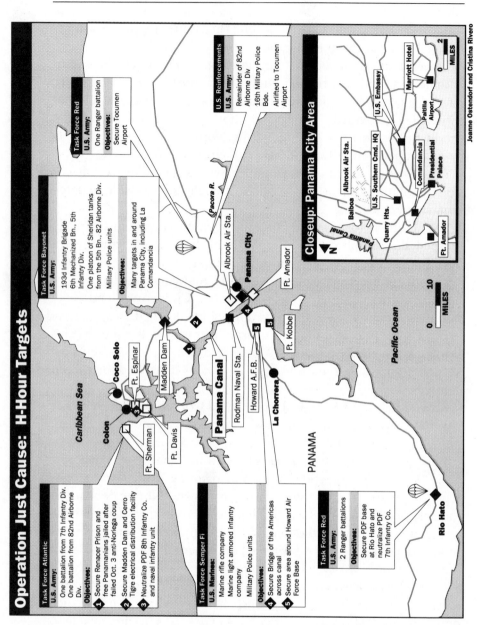

Operation Just Cause: H-Hour Targets

Task Force Atlantic

U.S. Army:
One battalion from 7th Infantry Div.
One battalion from 82nd Airborne Div.

Objectives:
1. Secure Renacer Prison and free Panamanians jailed after failed Oct. 3 anti-Noriega coup
2. Secure Madden Dam and Cerro Tigre electrical distribution facility
3. Neutralize PDF 8th Infantry Co. and naval infantry unit

Task Force Bayonet

U.S. Army:
193d Infantry Brigade
6th Mechanized Bn., 5th Infantry Div.
One platoon of Sheridan tanks from the 5th Bn., 82 Airborne Div.
Military Police units

Objectives:
Many targets in and around Panama City, including La Comandancia

Task Force Red

U.S. Army:
One Ranger battalion

Objectives:
Secure Tocumen Airport

U.S. Reinforcements

U.S. Army:
Remainder of 82nd Airborne Div
16th Military Police Bde.
Airlifted to Tocumen Airport

Task Force Semper Fi

U.S. Marines:
Marine rifle company
Marine light armored infantry company
Military Police units

Objectives:
4. Secure Bridge of the Americas across canal
5. Secure area around Howard Air Force Base

Task Force Red

U.S. Army:
2 Ranger battalions

Objectives:
Secure PDF base at Rio Hato and neutralize PDF 7th Infantry Co.

Caribbean Sea

Coco Solo
Colon
Ft. Espinar
Ft. Sherman
Ft. Davis
Madden Dam
Pecora R.

Albrook Air Sta.
Panama City
Ft. Amador
Ft. Kobbe

Panama Canal
Rodman Naval Sta.
Howard A.F.B.
La Chorrera

PANAMA

Pacific Ocean

Rio Hato

0   10
MILES

Closeup: Panama City Area

Balboa
Quarry Hts.
U.S. Southern Cmd. HQ
Albrook Air Sta.
U.S. Embassy
Marriott Hotel
Paitilla Airport
Comandancia
Presidential Palace
Ft. Amador

0   2
MILES

N

Panama Canal

Joanne Ostendorf and Cristina Rivero

FIGURE 6–1

Operation Just Cause: H-Hour Targets

Tunnel at Quarry Heights. The formal order would come the following day. The deployment cycle—C-day/H-hour in military terms—would begin officially at 1:00 A.M. on Monday, 18 December.

Kelly called Stiner, who was at home. "It is a go," reported Kelly. "You got your forty-eight hours."

The two agreed that H-Hour would be 1:00 A.M., 20 December. Three reasons determined the time. The assault on Torrijos/Tocumen would include seizing the international air terminal there. There was just one late flight scheduled, and Stiner figured he could work around that. The second was the tide, which in Panama fluctuates by as much as fourteen feet. In the harbors, the mud flats can extend for more than a mile at low tide. SEAL assaults would have to attack at or near high tide. Third, Stiner wanted about four hours of darkness in which to fight.

Monday and Tuesday were extremely busy. Soldiers were called in to their units, breaking Christmas plans short. The 2d Battalion, 75th Ranger Regiment, had just returned to their home post of Fort Lewis, Washington, when they were told to turn around and head south to their staging areas. The Air Force was assembling an armada of 285 aircraft to transport, escort, and refuel the deployment from the United States. In Panama, commanders reviewed their plans and prepared their men.

The combat operations plan, 90-2, was still called by the code name of *Blue Spoon*. In the Pentagon, Gen. James Lindsay, head of U.S. Special Operations Command, mused that soldiers would cringe when they told their children and grandchildren about their roles in an operation with such a silly name. Thus, Blue Spoon became *Operation Just Cause*.

Stiner spent the daylight hours of Monday at Fort Bragg, checking everything with 82d Airborne commander Maj. Gen. Jim Johnson. Thurman had summoned him to Panama, and Stiner wanted all his top troop leaders and his staff to be there that night. Under the cover of darkness, Stiner and key XVIII Airborne Corps staff flew to Howard Air Force Base in an Army C-20. To maintain as much security as possible, they wore civilian clothes, mostly knit tennis shirts and slacks. "The invasion of the yuppies," joked Lt. Col. Tim McMahon.

Operational security was now the overriding concern. Assembling the aircraft and the soldiers of the assault force was a massive undertaking, and there was grave concern about a leak to the press. Cable News Network, which broadcasts faster than the military can react, had learned the ways of the 82d Airborne, and knew to watch Pope Air Force Base—the airfield adjacent to Fort Bragg—for signs of increased activity.

The Bush administration needed to prepare the country for the coming action, though. In its dealings with the press, the administration argued that the Paz shooting was part of a pattern of aggression by the Noriega regime. The *New York Times*'s Thomas Friedman quoted sources as saying the confrontation was the most serious between Panamanian and American soldiers in twenty-five years.

"We are extremely concerned that a climate of aggression has been developing that puts American lives at risk," said State Department spokeswoman Margaret Tutwiler. In separate remarks, Secretary Cheney summed up the administration's recent thinking: "We've seen General Noriega brutalize the people of Panama, crack down on his own civilians and military alike after the latest coup attempt, designate himself the leader of the country, and declare a state of war with the United States. These actions have created an atmosphere in which Panama Defense Forces feel free to fire on unarmed Americans."

A more obvious clue to what the Pentagon was planning came when Tutwiler was asked if she would rule out a military response. "We don't discuss contingency plans or options. We never rule anything in or out," she replied.

As the huge strike force was assembled, reporters began putting the pieces together. In the 20 December issue of the *New York Times,* reporter Elaine Sciolino came close to cracking the code: "The United States added to its forces in Panama today in what officials hinted was the first step toward taking military action against the government of the Panamanian strongman, General Manuel Antonio Noriega." Sciolino reported that American troop transport planes, apparently carrying members of the 82d Airborne, landed in Panama. Pentagon officials confirmed that the 82d was conducting maneuvers. Fort Bragg described the activity as a emergency deployment readiness exercise, a regular event. Pentagon spokesman Pete Williams also confirmed that elements of the XVIII Airborne Corps were on a deployment exercise.

By the time the earliest editions of the paper were rolling through the *Times*'s presses, bullets were slicing the air in Panama.

7

Battles Before the War

Though Stiner and his planners had designed Operation Just Cause as a swift strike that would overwhelm the PDF, the opening salvos in the fight would not be these sledgehammer blows. The first moves would be more stealthy, conducted by an assortment of U.S. special operations forces spread widely across the isthmus.

In all, more than one thousand U.S. Army, Navy, and Air Force special operations troops took part in the operation, and most went into action well before the 1:00 A.M. start scheduled for Just Cause on 20 December. These units assaulted critical PDF garrisons, airports, and key media and transportation facilities. But the primary target was Noriega himself, the idea being in the words of Col. Jake Jacobelly, commander of all U.S. special forces in Latin America, "to decapitate the snake." The Americans wanted to cut Noriega off from controlling his troops and directing resistance as he had during the October coup.

In the weeks prior to the invasion, SOUTHCOM maintained a round-the-clock "Noriega watch," a six-person intelligence team, supplemented by experts from the National Security Agency and the Central Intelligence Agency in Washington, reporting directly to Thurman on Noriega's daily activities and routes.[1] This cell of watchers monitored radio and telephone communications and directed a network of surveillance teams, including Panamanians dispatched to track Noriega wherever he went, a demanding effort as the wily dictator, a former intelligence officer himself, was quite clever at foiling his followers. Hanging on the wall in the SOUTH-

COM intelligence operations center was a map used to pinpoint Noriega's exact whereabouts.

At 6:00 P.M. on 19 December, the eve of Just Cause, the map showed Noriega in Colon, at the Atlantic end of the Panama Canal. Shortly thereafter, Noriega left Colon in a convoy of cars and buses headed toward Panama City.

Noriega then disappeared.

Noriega was cunning. His rise to power within the regime of Omar Torrijos was founded on his ability to use intelligence and psychology to his advantage. In 1969, the young Noriega was rewarded for his loyalty in the failed coup with command of the G-2, the military intelligence organization. From this powerful position, Noriega built the Guardia Nacional's intelligence arm into one of the most ruthless agencies in Central America; his talents won him contacts with CIA officials in Panama and Washington.

Noriega was a respected master in the art of deception, and he was able to fool the SOUTHCOM team just prior to and during the invasion with false messages and decoy convoys. In the weeks before the operation, he moved to different locations an average of five times each night.

From the early morning hours of 20 to 24 December, U.S. special forces conducted more than forty operations across Panama aimed at snatching General Noriega, failing in each attempt. At most of the targets, including a number of foreign embassies, the U.S. troops found nothing. At some, they found PDF soldiers, but no matter how quickly they overcame the resistance, special forces teams would be told that Noriega had left minutes earlier. And at other targets, they thought they were getting close to nabbing Noriega: at one luxurious seaside villa on the Pacific Ocean, a team found lit cigarettes and warm coffee cups.

Yet they never could quite catch up to Noriega, because Noriega was not moving. Eventually, U.S. forces figured that out; when the deposed Panamanian military strongman sneaked into the papal nunciature four days after the massive U.S. attack, special forces teams were no more than one hour behind. By seeking asylum with the papal nuncio, the sly Noriega selected his only escape. He had no other options.

Even as they failed to nail Noriega, his pursuers were satisfied that he was running too hard to direct any resistance to the conventional operations of Just Cause.

Yet the failure highlighted a sore point with military special operators: they are prevented from conducting their own undercover surveillance missions. These are conducted by civilian intelligence agencies, and often the information is not passed to the units conducting the actual operations in a timely manner. This problem plagued Operation Just Cause. As Army Gen. James Lindsay, commander of U.S. Special Operations Command, listened to special operations radio nets as they searched for Noriega, his frustration grew. "I didn't feel real good that night," he says. His men did not know where to focus their efforts. In his mind was the specter of the failed Desert One raid in Iran in 1979. "The whole issue goes back to Desert One," says Lindsay. "I'm plagued by the duck theory. We quack and we waddle, so we're a duck. If we act like spies, then we're spies."

In choosing targets during the planning for Just Cause, planners went to great lengths to cover possible hiding places for Noriega. When the operation began, a special task force was quickly formed to strike or stake out buildings in Panama City suspected of holding Noriega and his top aides.

But they missed one. The papal nunciature was not put on the list for a simple reason: Noriega was no Catholic. He *was* a dabbler in witchcraft, frequently visiting one of two witch houses in Panama in which he kept women who practiced Brazilian Santeria. "He was the anti-Christ," pleads one top planner. "I can tell you that [in] the collective wisdom—and there was a lot of collective wisdom gathered in Panama at that time—it did not occur to them. But it's easy to say that in hindsight." Says another: Noriega's request for asylum to the Vatican must have been "a perverse stroke of genius."

By the 1:00 A.M. H-hour for conventional units, U.S. special forces already had hit numerous targets in search of the elusive Noriega.

Special operations teams, consisting of Delta Force commandos, escorted by the aviators of the secret Task Force 160, and SEAL Team 6, frantically searched for the former Panamanian leader now on the run. Reports and Noriega sightings were flooding into the SOUTHCOM intelligence network, and analysts were trying to separate truth from falsehood, and trying to keep Thurman, Stiner, and Downing updated on the dictator's whereabouts.

The last sure report put Noriega in a house in Colon at 6:00 P.M. on 19 December. Shortly thereafter, he left the Atlantic side of Panama and headed south on the Boyd-Roosevelt Highway, the main artery along the canal. When the convoy was halfway to Panama City, the column split, a move that temporarily disoriented the Noriega Watch team, just long enough for them to lose Noriega.

Noriega may not have realized that he was being tracked by U.S. teams; the split of the convoy was a favorite tactic. Part of the convoy turned off the highway toward Tocumen and Torrijos airfields. The other half headed straight toward La Comandancia. At that time, Joint Special Operations Command headquarters received a report that Noriega was on the way to his office in La Comandancia, but JSOC officials discounted the report as false. "We were watching La Comandancia, so we could tell," says one top U.S. commander.

PDF troops guarding La Comandancia played their part, however, by performing an honor guard ceremony for the Panamanian military chief. Eventually, a vehicle showed up at the front door of the PDF headquarters, and an unidentified man got out and went inside. JSOC officials still did not believe Noriega would walk into the downtown area with the increased U.S. military activity in Panama after the Paz killing. But though JSOC was certain that Noriega was not at La Comandancia, they did not know where he was.

Reports compiled from the whereabouts of Noriega's personal belongings and extensive interviews with Panamanian officials traveling with Noriega the night of 19 December and morning of 20 December show that Noriega was in the first part of the convoy that split off the Boyd-Roosevelt Highway. He went to a PDF club in Panama City.

Noriega next made his way to an appointment with a prostitute, procured for him by Capt. Ivan Castillo, at the Ceremi Recreation Center, a PDF rest area just east of Tocumen military airfield. Despite the clear evidence of increasing U.S. military activity in Panama, aides could not convince him the United States would invade. Noriega spent some hours at the recreation center, remaining there well into the night. His pleasures were interrupted only at 1:03

A.M., when more than seven hundred Army Rangers parachuted into Tocumen military airfield.

By then, intelligence officials had realized what had happened to the convoy and suspected the Panamanian leader had driven to the recreation center. While they were flying down to Panama, the Rangers were told to consider the center an "on-call" target. The Ceremi center, dubbed Objective Hawk, was to be assaulted after Rangers had secured the three primary targets—the 2d Rifle Company barracks, the Panamanian Air Force headquarters, and the Tocumen terminal. When Noriega spotted the Rangers leaping from huge transport aircraft sailing over Tocumen, he hesitated for a moment, then ordered his aides to start the cars. In two small hatchback cars, Noriega and his close aides headed for the airport, beginning their days on the run.

By the time Noriega had reached the airfield, B Company of the 1st Battalion, 75th Ranger Regiment, had assembled on the runway and established a rudimentary roadblock across the entrance road to the military airfield. B Company's task was to provide security along the perimeter as the other companies assaulted the Tocumen targets.

The two cars, driving with their headlights off, came out of nowhere. The Rangers turned and fired at the convoy, but hit only the lead vehicle, which came to a screeching halt. The second vehicle, carrying Noriega, got away. When the Rangers stormed into the Ceremi Recreation Center, they found Noriega's military uniform and shoes. PDF soldiers captured at the Ceremi Recreation Center told the Rangers that the Panamanian boss left in his red underwear. The prostitute was nowhere to found.

After the scare at Tocumen airfield, Noriega did not stop running. "When we didn't get him that first night, JSOC and SEAL Team 6 started hitting every possible place that he could be," says one special operations officer. Noriega kept one step ahead. His personal bodyguard, Capt. Ivan Castillo, who would later surrender to U.S. authorities and provide information on Noriega's location, told investigators following Just Cause that the Panamanian dictator moved every four hours, slipping from house to house in and around Panama City. Driving in a blue, four-door Range Rover with tinted glass, Noriega's band numbered three: Castillo, Capt. Asunción Eliecer Gayton, and Marcela Tason, his loyal secretary.

Noriega was frightened and was exercising no control over the PDF. Castillo later said that Noriega feared his own men might turn against him for bringing on the U.S. attack. But what Noriega feared most was being hounded by American forces. Close behind was the fear of being extradited to the United States.

The Delta Force commandos and SEAL Team 6 spared no efforts to apprehend their quarry. Zipping through the air, ground, and sea, with the highest priority for air routes and ground passage, special operations teams responded to JSOC headquarters, conventional U.S. units, and Panamanians to track down the multiplying leads.

The hounds were in eager pursuit of the fox, often crossing paths with conventional units and then disappearing as quickly as they had come. On 23 December, three days after the initial assaults, D Company of the 3d Battalion, 504th Infantry Regiment (Airborne), part of the 82d Airborne Division, was securing the area around the Madden Dam. The paratroopers received reports from Panamanian civilians that Noriega was hiding in the town of Aguas Buenas, in a house with a painted white wheel in front.

Battalion commander Lt. Col. Lynn Moore reported the sighting but never got a response until he paid D Company a visit. Moore was based at Fort Sherman, but tried to visit at least one company each day by using an OH-58 scout helicopter. On 23 December he rode out to see a platoon of D Company, commanded by Capt. John Campbell, that was securing the southern side of the dam.

As the two officers watched the operation, Moore spotted an AC-130 gunship and a Black Hawk hovering in the distance. Curious about the operation, Moore told his pilot to head toward the two special forces aircraft.

Suddenly, three different Black Hawks crossed directly in front of the much smaller OH-58. Moore, recognizing the helicopters as belonging to Task Force 160, told the pilot to turn east away from the action. The Black Hawks headed them off again. Moore told the pilot to go back to Sherman. It was time to get out of the area. As the OH-58 passed over Madden Dam, the choppers, painted an eerie black, passed in front again.

"They obviously don't even want us in the air. 'Return to the dam and land,'" Moore ordered.

When the tiny scout helicopter landed, Moore could only spot three of the four Black Hawks.

"All of a sudden, Hurricane Hugo hit," Moore recalls. The bulky Black Hawk landed virtually on top of the tiny OH-58, nearly blowing the aircraft on its side. The Delta Force commandos, believing Noriega was trying to escape in a helicopter pilfered from U.S. forces, leapt out, and surrounded the chopper in a flash.

Moore thought: "Okay, I know who they are, I understand."

He threw his hands in the air, pointing to his cavalry patch on his uniform to show he was American. Campbell, fifty yards away, spotted the commandos and lifted his hands.

The rest of D Company, however, did not know who the commandos were. "All they saw was these guys in ninja outfits that had their company commander and battalion commander at bay," says Moore. The airborne troops had been well briefed prior to the operation, but the instructors told them that those in black outfits were likely to be members of the UESAT, Noriega's special forces.

The airborne reacted to the threat on their leaders, firing two warning shots. One passed high and right of the scout chopper. But the other entered the cockpit, ricocheted off the instrument panel and zipped past Moore's head. He heard the crack of the bullet through his earphones.

Moore had had enough. He jumped out and told D Company to cease fire. "It was the closest I came to getting killed," says Moore.

The chase for Noriega was a frantic effort from the moment the invasion began. Fearing Noriega was hiding right under their noses in Panama City, on 23 December JSOC hastily created a task force with Delta Force commandos and infantry troops.

The unit, equipped with M113 armored personnel carriers and Marine Corps LAVs, would be a quick response team, reacting to any spottings of Noriega in the downtown area. In the days following the assault, the task force hit numerous targets. It also cordoned off a number of foreign embassies, including the Nicaraguan and Cuban buildings, to prevent the hounded Noriega from seeking asylum.

Special forces teams got closer and closer to Noriega as they rounded up people on the classified "black list" of 120 Noriega loyalists and high officers in the PDF. Even as the wily dictator eluded them, the trackers were closing the gap. Finally, one house in the city yielded Noriega's briefcase and wallet. Special forces were no more than one hour behind their primary target.

Aides close to Noriega began to peel away from him as the end neared. Early on 24 December, Castillo, the bodyguard, left to search for the next place to hide. He told Noriega that if he did not return by 7:00 A.M. that Noriega was to move without him.

But Castillo had given up. He was tired of running and was ready to betray his Maximum Leader in return for his own safety. He reckoned Maj. Gen. Cisneros, the Spanish-speaking commander of U.S. Army South, was his only hope. If Cisneros would protect Castillo and his family, in return he would show U.S. forces where his former leader was hiding.

Castillo went to look for an American. At 6:30 A.M., Castillo ran into a unit from the 7th Infantry Division. He tried to explain who we was, but none of the soldiers spoke Spanish, and Castillo was taken into custody as a prisoner of war. Cisneros did not get word that Castillo was searching for him until 10:30 A.M..

"General, if I could have gotten word to you when I wanted to, I could have found you Noriega," Castillo told Cisneros.

"Well, where could he be?" Cisneros wanted to know what options were left for Noriega.

Castillo handed the U.S. Army South commander a list of potential hiding spots. Although it was hours past the 7:00 A.M. rendezvous time, and Noriega was likely to be long gone from the house on Alto de Golf, Castillo said he probably left his baggage behind. And he might return to the house. Castillo recommended that Cisneros go there. If he was lucky, U.S. forces would find the daughter of Marcela Tason, Noriega's secretary, and the secretary would probably still be with him.

Quickly, Cisneros formed a team led by Sgt. Anthony Bonilla of the 29th Military Intelligence Battalion and Amadis Jimenez, commander of the PDF naval infantry, who had surrendered to U.S. forces in a tense battle in Coco Solo. Cisneros had adopted Jimenez to help convince other PDF units to surrender.

Cisneros gave the team explicit instructions. They were not to capture Noriega; that was a task for the special operations forces.

The team was just to search for anything that might pinpoint where Noriega had gone. If the team did not see signs of Noriega, they were to enter the house and talk to the people and search Noriega's baggage. But if they spotted the blue Range Rover, they were to call for Cisneros.

When the team arrived, there were no signs of Noriega. In the window, Jimenez saw a lady and a young child. He guessed the lady was Tason's daughter.

The team broke in and searched the house. The bags were gone.

Bonilla and Jimenez thought they would have to go back to Cisneros empty-handed. Then the phone rang. It was Noriega's secretary. She wanted to talk to her daughter.

Jimenez and Bonilla looked at each other, stunned. Jimenez told the lady who answered the phone, suspected to be the housekeeper, to tell Marcela Tason that her daughter was in the bathroom. They needed time to devise a strategy. Marcela Tason said she would call back.

The agreement was that when the daughter was put on the phone to speak to her mother, she would warn her mother that she was in danger. The daughter would convince her mother to turn herself in, along with Noriega. When the phone rang, the daughter took the receiver, and immediately broke down. Crying, she warned her mother in a different way.

"Mama, the gringos are here."

Marcela Tason threw down the phone.

Minutes later, a driver for Monseigneur José Sebastián Laboa, the papal nuncio to Panama, met Noriega at a Panama City Dairy Queen. The exhausted Noriega jumped into the car, hiding himself behind the seat as the driver sped to the nunciature.

Laboa had been trying to reach Cisneros by telephone for hours to tell him that Noriega was seeking asylum. Finally, his call got through to the general.

Laboa whispered: "He just walked in."

Gen. Manuel Antonio Noriega crept into the Vatican Embassy wearing only running shorts and a t-shirt. Over his shoulder were two AK-47 rifles that were never used. He had run out of places to hide. Cisneros called Thurman and Stiner immediately. The fox had gone to ground.

*   *   *

Although the search for Noriega was the top priority for U.S. special operations forces in Just Cause, it was far from their only mission. Indeed, Stiner, with his extensive background in special operations, conceived of Just Cause as something of a giant special operations raid.

Stiner placed the entire special operations effort under the command of Maj. Gen. Wayne Downing, who reported directly to Stiner throughout the operation. And there was a special operations component to nearly every action in Just Cause. Small strike teams performed surveillance missions of conventional force targets, secured vital communication facilities, and halted a convoy of PDF armored assault vehicles at the Pacora River Bridge. Just prior to the 1:00 A.M. H-hour, commandos from the Delta Force, an elite counterterrorist unit, performed a daring rescue of the American radio operator incarcerated in a downtown Panama City prison.

The total number of special operations forces, a term that lumps Army Rangers with SEAL commandos, Army Green Berets, and Air Force special forces, reached 4,150 troops. Special forces accounted for nearly 50 percent of the total American casualties in Just Cause. Of the more than 4,000 total, 11 were killed and nearly 150 were wounded. Of the remaining 23,000 American soldiers 12 were killed and just over 150 were wounded in the whole operation. Special operations forces got some of the toughest assignments. None was more costly than a mission given the SEALs to secure a small civilian airfield in Panama City.

The Navy SEALs were organized into a separate element called Task Force White. The SEALs involved in Just Cause, primarily responsible for maritime missions, were from SEAL Team 4, one of the three teams of Naval Special Warfare Group 2, based in Little Creek, Virginia. Also in Panama were some forty Navy special warfare personnel from SEAL Team 6, the Navy's crack hostage rescue unit, as part of the larger team called upon to strike targets throughout Panama to find General Noriega.

The SEALs, some of the most skilled, best trained men in the U.S. military, live a shadowy existence, carefully shielded from the public eye. They are often tasked to perform "sneak and peek" missions, including secret infiltration into enemy territory to perform clandestine reconnaissance. Additional roles include amphibious sabotage and underwater demolition.

SEAL missions, however, often do not require troops to engage the enemy. Rather, the commandos are deployed to watch enemy movements, to provide target information to another assault force, or to call in naval gunfire. In most cases, the priority of the mission demands that the SEALs avoid all contact. It was with that hope that U.S. military planners sent forty-eight SEALs to block the runway at Punta Paitilla airfield.

Paitilla, formally known as Marcos A. Gelabert airport, is a civilian airfield located in one of the most luxurious areas in Panama City, two and a half miles up the shoreline from the slums of El Chorrillo. Jutting out off the southeast coast of Panama, the airfield, with a single short runway, services domestic airlines and light aircraft.

It also is the location of Noriega's private Learjet, an executive plane he commonly used for his travels within the country and in South America. This fact, and the location of the airfield in Panama City, made Paitilla an automatic target for U.S. planners intent on keeping Noriega from fleeing the country. And during the October coup, Noriega and loyal PDF soldiers used the the airfield to quickly bring reinforcements to La Comandancia. The main runway would have to be blocked.

The SEAL mission at Paitilla was a fairly simple one. A force of forty-eight SEALs, divided into three platoons and augmented by a seven-member command team including an Air Force officer to communicate with air support, would land on shore by patrol boats. These boats, permanently stationed at Rodman U.S. Naval Station in Panama, are made of rubber and equipped with muffled motors, specially designed to slip commando teams ashore without being noticed.

Landing from the south on the seaward end of the airport, the SEALs would slowly move up the 3500-foot runway toward Noriega's hangar, located on the northern part of the airfield. Once surrounding the hangar, the mission was to disable the Learjet by shooting out or slashing its tires. At the same time, SEALs were to drag some undamaged planes onto the runway to prevent other planes from taking off or landing.

Little opposition was expected, and the SEALs would carry only small arms, machine guns, AT-4 light antitank weapons, and a mortar. In briefings prior to the operation, the SEAL team was told that the only resistance it might find on the airport would be lightly armed, and probably untrained, security personnel. As a precaution, the SEALs were instructed to "neutralize" these forces if they presented a hostile threat. The assault team was warned that it would encounter civilian employees, despite the 1:00 A.M. H-hour, and carried bullhorns to convince civilians to surrender or remain calm.

SEAL Team 4 rehearsed the seizure of Paitilla airfield in Florida on 14 December. The exercise, conducted at Eglin Air Force Base in the Florida panhandle, was deemed a dramatic success by Commander Thomas McGrath, who led the assault team ashore in the mock assault. SEALs disabled but did not destroy the aircraft standing in as Noriega's jet, and blocked the runway without a hitch.

But later that night, as they reviewed the rehearsal, the SEALs made a critical decision that would eventually curse the Paitilla operation. Capt. John Sandoz, then commander of Naval Special Warfare Group 2, ordered Lt. Cmdr. Patrick Toohey to lead the assault force; McGrath would remain in one of the boats. From that vantage point, Sandoz believed, McGrath could remain in constant communication with Toohey, the AC-130 Spectre gunship flying above, as well as other SEAL operations going on simultaneously in Panama.

The boats carrying the assault team left Rodman at approximately 9:00 P.M. on 19 December. The SEALs opted to sail from Rodman because it would prove to be a quieter approach than assaulting by helicopter. Paitilla was too close to downtown to be making a lot of noise.

The team came ashore on schedule, at about 12:30 A.M., and the SEALs slowly began walking up the shore toward the runway. Two platoons each started moving up one side of the runway, while a third platoon, tasked to secure the southern area of the airfield and provide the southern point of the triangle surrounding Noriega's hangar, proceeded along the grass beside the runway. Fences lining the runway prevented the team from sneaking behind the hangars on the left side of the airfield. Toohey walked behind the lead platoon.

While they moved up the runway, the SEAL team received a radio transmission relaying a report that a helicopter had just taken off from Colon, worrying Just Cause commanders that Noriega was in the aircraft. If Noriega were coming to Panama City, the helicopter would have to land at Paitilla, at the northern section of the runway.

In response, the SEALs picked up their step. "I was thinking to myself, Jesus, I hope we get there before he gets there," recalls a special forces commander who overheard the broadcast.

Seconds later, McGrath and Toohey received a second transmission. This one was not so clear. The message, from Stiner's headquarters, was sent to all the U.S. fighting units just prior to H-hour to reinforce the rules of engagement: minimize both collateral damage and casualties. Although the broadcast was directed at Army Rangers confronted with a civilian airliner on the ground at Torrijos International Airport and a possible hostage situation, the SEALs somehow interpreted the message as a change in mission. They were not to destroy, but disable the Learjet. To the SEALs, their mission was growing more confusing by the minute.

By five minutes past the 1:00 A.M. H-hour, the SEALs had reached their assault positions. One squad of nine commandos was lying down on the tarmac facing the hangar. This squad was supposed to disable the aircraft. The nose of the jet was sticking out of the front of the open hangar, and the SEALs could see it quite clearly despite the very dark night.

Another squad was positioned just to the north of the first unit, providing cover and observing the northern side of the airfield, carefully searching for the helicopter that may be carrying Noriega.

The command element dug in just to the south, in front of another hangar. Toohey established his command post on the far side of the runway opposite the third squad.

A third transmission then came across the radio.

Three PDF armored cars, U.S.-built V-300s armed with 90mm guns that were far more powerful than anything the SEALs carried, were reported to be racing down the road that circles the far northern end of the Paitilla airfield. Quickly, Toohey decided his best defense was to ambush the armored cars, to get them before they could disrupt the entire SEAL operation.

Toohey ordered the squad positioned to the north, led by Lt. John Connors, to move to the road and either ensure the cars proceeded past the airfield without incident or, if necessary, engage and destroy the vehicles. Connors told his men to get up and proceed to the road.

When the SEAL squad stood up, one soldier spotted a Panamanian holding an AK-47 rifle in the hangar to the north of Noriega's jet. The SEAL got the first shot in, but missed; a split second later, the gunman, with nine American soldiers lined up abreast of each other in his sights, fired a five-second burst that ripped through the American unit. Two SEALs dropped to the runway, killed instantly. Other bullets, some of which richoceted off the tarmac, struck six more SEALs as they dove for cover in a drainage ditch.

The first SEAL squad tried to cover its comrades, and blasted return fire at the hangar, which now seemed to hold two Panamanians. But the squad could not provide support because their view was obstructed by two small aircraft parked in front of the hangar. Toohey then ordered the third squad positioned to the south to move forward to attack the hangar. The SEALs wanted revenge.

As they attacked, the third squad let loose into the hangar with a torrent of gunfire lasting about forty-five seconds. The hangar was riddled with bullet holes, two other light aircraft were damaged, and the Panamanians were killed. But not before one more SEAL, trying to fire a rocket at Noriega's jet, was shot dead. Two more SEALS suffered severe wounds; another wounded in the second battle would later die from loss of blood.

In less than five minutes, Lt. Connors and three other SEALs—Chief Enginneman Donald McFaul, Torpedoman's Mate 2d Class Isaac Rodriquez, and Boatswain's Mate 1st Class Christopher Tilghman—were dead and eight more wounded. Toohey furiously radioed for help, screaming that his team had suffered numerous casualties. But he could not get a medical evacuation helicopter, which was grounded at Howard Air Force Base because of the constant flow of air traffic. The chopper did not arrive at Paitilla until 2:00 A.M., forty minutes after the first SEALs were shot. By then, Panamanian ambulances had arrived and whisked some of the wounded SEALs to the hospital.

Despite the fearsome cost, the SEALs accomplished the mission (see figure 7–1). The Learjet was disabled; antiarmor rockets punched holes in the cockpit and undercarriage and cooked the interior. SEALs also flattened the tires with gunfire.

But the helicopter thought to be carrying Noriega never showed

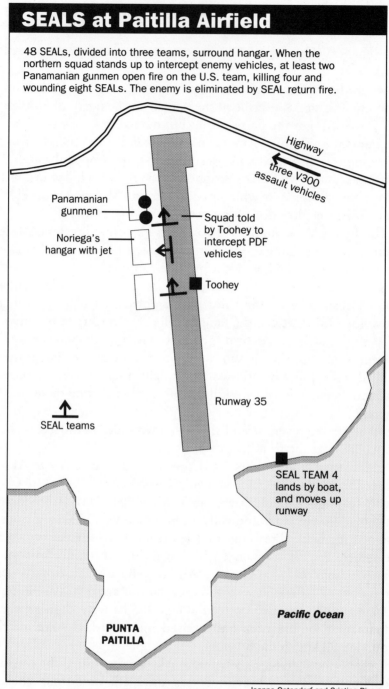

SEALS at Paitilla Airfield

48 SEALs, divided into three teams, surround hangar. When the northern squad stands up to intercept enemy vehicles, at least two Panamanian gunmen open fire on the U.S. team, killing four and wounding eight SEALs. The enemy is eliminated by SEAL return fire.

Highway

three V300 assault vehicles

Panamanian gunmen

Squad told by Toohey to intercept PDF vehicles

Noriega's hangar with jet

Toohey

SEAL teams

Runway 35

SEAL TEAM 4 lands by boat, and moves up runway

Pacific Ocean

PUNTA PAITILLA

Joanne Ostendorf and Cristina Rivero

FIGURE 7–1
SEALs at Paitilla Airfield

up; the V-300s passed by Paitilla unnoticed. The SEALs paid a heavy price for their haste in what was supposed to be an easy six-hour mission. Of the dozens of actions of Just Cause, the Paitilla mission may be the most controversial among the military.

Although Downing as well as SEALs refused to be interviewed for this book, top U.S. military officials have offered a number of reasons for the disaster. One may be that the SEALs could not react to the change in H-hour, forcing the assault team to walk into a trap. The Panamanians could have easily heard the shooting that erupted at La Comandancia or at Albrook Air Station at 12:30 A.M., and just waited for the American forces to arrive at Paitilla.

A complicating factor centers on whether the SEALs could communicate with the two AC-130 Spectre gunships circling above, and whether the aircraft could have helped the situation. Shortly after Just Cause, U.S. Navy officials told *Jane's Defence Weekly,* a defense trade magazine, that the SEALs at Paitilla could not communicate with the Spectres.[2] Some SEALs say the AC-130s could have located the Panamanians in the hangar and eliminated the resistance before the SEAL troop fired on the hangar.

However, one senior special forces commander who has studied the issue denies there were communication problems between the AC-130 and ground forces. He suggests that the SEALs' frustration may have caused them to frantically search for clear frequencies, causing the two to miss each other.

Further, it is far from clear that the gunships would have saved SEAL lives. In fact, the proximity of the SEALs to the hangar may just as easily have resulted in friendly casualties. "A gunship can't see through the roof of a hangar, and as far as the Spectre being able to put fire on the enemy, it was too damn close," the special forces leader says.

Still other controversies surrounding the seizure of Paitilla are whether the mission was proper for SEALs and whether the order was changed just prior to the firefight. Some military officials have alleged that the size of the mission required artillery not carried by SEAL teams or a larger occupation force, such as Rangers. Indeed, special forces leaders questioned the use of SEALs for the Paitilla mission during the early stages of Just Cause planning. The mission was approved for the SEALs because it called for the assault force to block the runway, which was along the water. It did not require the "seizure" of the airfield. Lindsay and Stiner, who went on to replace Lindsay at U.S. Special Operations Command, claim the Paitilla mission was a reasonable one for SEALs.

Further allegations suggest that the second radio transmission received by the SEALs as they moved toward the target changed the mission from the simple need to destroy the aircraft to a more demanding one to disable it without destroying it. This is adamantly denied by Joint Task Force commanders, including Thurman. "If somebody says they changed my mission, I would have to say then show me the documents associated with that because I gave the guidelines many weeks ahead of time," he says. "If you ask me about the tactical formations used, I wasn't there. I know what the aftermath was. The SEALs got caught in a hail of fire that lasted maybe about fifteen seconds, and unfortunately and unhappily, people were both killed and wounded. I'm regretful about that." [But] did Thurman issue an order to change the mission? "The answer is, I did not issue an order to change the mission."

In the end, the official explanation, and perhaps the most plausible reason, for the bloodletting at Paitilla airfield is a simple tactical blunder, in other words, the fog of war. After exhaustive after-action reviews by the Joint Chiefs of Staff and the U.S. Special Operations Command, it was determined that the unit led by Connors stood up on an open tarmac, exposing the squad to an unknown enemy. "The SEALs were not really spread out the way they should have been to fight," laments one top special forces commander. "Even well-trained units make some tactical mistakes every once in a while."

Connors and his SEALs paid for their tactical mistake with their lives.

Task Force White's other missions came off more successfully. In another attempt to cut off potential escape routes for Noriega, two-man SEAL teams equipped with sophisticated scuba gear silently approached Balboa harbor near Fort Amador to disable two fast patrol boats used by the PDF to guard the canal.

The patrol boats are armed with powerful automatic cannons. If the PDF were able to get even a single vessel into the ocean, they would threaten U.S. assaults at Fort Amador and the Bridge of the Americas as well as the SEAL mission at Paitilla. Stiner had limited resources to strike so many targets, and U.S. patrol boats and the ubiquitous AC-130 gunships were dedicated to other missions. U.S. commanders also wanted to prevent senior PDF officers, including Noriega, from using the boats to leave Panama. "We might as well disable them while they are stationary," said Lt. Col. Bill Bennett, chief of contingency planning at SOUTHCOM.

On the night before D-day, the SEALs made their assault, timed for high tide. All went smoothly, despite the fact that this would be the first time since World War II that SEALs had destroyed surface vessels with underwater mines. The SEAL demolition teams placed high-explosive mines on the propeller shafts of the two boats, and set the timers precisely for 1:00 A.M. The explosion at Balboa Harbor rocked the downtown area, which was already starting to light up with the effects of war. The explosion boosted the confidence of U.S. forces trying to break their way through the PDF gauntlet toward La Comandancia in Panama City.

The morning after, SEALs secured the Balboa pier and a yacht club there to grab senior PDF officers on the "black list," the 120 Panamanians who were either close associates of Noriega or loyal to him. Another mission required SEAL scuba teams to swim in the Panama Canal underneath the Bridge of the Americas to prevent the PDF from using the canal as an escape route. Acting jointly with Marines from Task Force Semper Fi, who secured the bridge from above, U.S. forces formed a two-tier wall cutting off the canal from any PDF soldiers trying to escape the U.S. onslaught.

Some of the most important special operations tasks were reconnaissance missions. Task Force Black, consisting of Army Special Forces from the 3d Battalion, 7th Special Forces Group, was responsible for securing four separate targets, primarily outside the canal area. The task of the Green Berets was to keep their eyes open—to search for any activity that would indicate Noriega was moving to another location or trying to exit the country. In addition, the special forces battalion would strike a number of command and control nodes in operations aimed at isolating the general staff of the PDF.

The 7th Special Forces Group, which is responsible for special forces military operations in Latin America, is a brigade-size organization with three battalions. The group is headquartered at Fort

Bragg, with the 3d Battalion permanently stationed in Panama, at Fort Davis on the Atlantic side.

Each battalion contains eighteen teams, which form the nucleus of the group's combat power. The A team, with twelve men, is the fighting force. Task Force Black was commanded by Jacobelly. Since Special Operations Command–South was the planning headquarters for Task Force Black, Jacobelly became one of the few commanders deeply involved in the last-minute planning prior to the launching of Operation Just Cause. By October 1989, he and his staff were working six-day weeks with little sleep.

From 17 to 19 December, Jacobelly's missions changed several times as D-day grew closer. Originally, the 3d Battalion was responsible for thirteen targets, ranging from television and radio transmission towers to the homes of loyal Noriega supporters.

By the evening of the nineteenth, the number of targets had been cut to seven, three of which were friendly: Guillermo Endara, future president of Panama, and Billy Ford and Ricardo Arias Calderón, his two vice presidents. Jacobelly, part strategist and part warrior, did not like the sound of the mission. It required Green Berets to search the downtown area of Panama City in the middle of what would be a raging firefight. Jacobelly decided it would be safer if Thurman invited the three leaders to dinner, and simply refused to let them leave. Stiner approved the idea.

That left four targets on the morning of 20 December: the Pacora River Bridge, Fort Cimarron, Tinajitas, and a television tower owned by the local television station Channel 2 on Cerro Azul, slated to be used by U.S. psychological operations forces to broadcast information to the Panamanian citizenry. The three other targets required only surveillance teams to approach the target and watch; the missions did not require special forces teams to engage the enemy.

Jacobelly established the command post for Task Force Black in one of the hangars at Albrook Air Station, no more than five hundred yards from his peacetime office. Albrook, once home to the 228th Aviation Regiment and a U.S. military-run school for helicopter mechanics, is now little more than a housing area for some Air Force personnel who work at Howard Air Force Base. Many sections of the air station, lumped in between Fort Clayton and Panama City, are used to store ammunition and other supplies for U.S. forces stationed in Panama. The last vestige of military activity on Albrook may well be the Special Operations Command-South headquarters.

The first team from Task Force Black left Albrook Air Station at 6:00 P.M. because they had a long hike to Tinajitas, in eastern Panama City. From the back gate of the air station, the team would slither like snakes into the darkness of the Panamanian jungle.

The decision was to walk to Tinajitas rather than assault by helicopter because of fear that the pre–H-hour activity would compromise other parts of the operation, especially those in nearby downtown Panama City. Tinajitas, home to the PDF 1st Infantry Company and a known location of enemy mortars, was just ten miles from Albrook, but the team made slow going through the dense jungle and unforgiving terrain. "We did not realize how rugged the terrain was between [Albrook] and Tinajitas," Jacobelly says. "They had maps, but it was pitch black." As it became clear that the company was not going to reach Tinajitas before 12:30 A.M., Jacobelly instructed the team to slow down, and proceed with caution.

The official mission at Tinajitas was to observe the reaction of the 1st Infantry Company to the U.S. attack on La Comandancia and see if it moved to reinforce the PDF command center. But there was another reason that made the small hill a vital target. The mortars at Tinajitas could range the U.S. facilities at Fort Clayton. If the PDF moved the mortars more than two hundred yards down the mountain to the Baha'i Temple, built on a small plateau, the enemy could wreak havoc on the U.S. Army South headquarters. Intelligence photos showed that the PDF often used mortars near the temple to drill their gunners. If the PDF moved there, the Special Forces team would have to take them out.

Once gunfire erupted at La Comandancia and Balboa, Jacobelly asked the team to describe what they saw. The team reported that it saw no movement, but did not have a good view of the entire PDF compound. As the team slowly moved closer for a better look, they heard two mortars fire. The team radioed the report to Jacobelly.

Seconds later, Jacobelly cringed as two mortar rounds landed just outside the Fort Clayton gate. He ordered the team to locate the PDF mortar position, but it was gone. The 1st Infantry Company, like most PDF units, had mounted their mortars on the back of pick-up trucks. By the time the special forces had reached a clear observation point, the mortars had been carried away. The team remained in position for two days, later watching as 82d Airborne troops assaulted into Tinajitas the next day.

Special Forces' clandestine missions are often subject to rapid change, and Just Cause was no exception. Until the night 3d Battalion officers received their orders, the operation at Pacora River Bridge called for a four-man team to drop near the bridge and report on the movement, if any, of Battalion 2000 from Fort Cimarron. When A Company landed at 12:45 A.M. on 20 December, twenty-four Green Berets were confronted with a convoy of PDF assault vehicles. The convoy was heading straight toward them.

At midnight, Panama City and Albrook Air Station were fairly quiet. Task Force Black had successfully deployed the first of four teams toward Tinajitas, and although the team was running late, Jacobelly had no reason to believe they were in imminent danger.

The next team, A Company, was scheduled to lift off from the Albrook helicopter pad at about 12:10 A.M. The unit, led by Maj. Kevin Higgins, would fly to the Pacora River Bridge in three helicopters, one UH-60 Black Hawk and two MH-60 helicopters, which are aircraft with Black Hawk airframes modified for special operations.

A Company originally expected to fly to Pacora in two helicopters, and discovered just fifteen minutes before lift-off that a third helicopter would be used. Despite the momentary confusion, Higgins decided that the additional helicopter would provide a more comfortable seating arrangement, making it easier to get off the choppers once they landed at the target. It also allowed the team to grab eight more soldiers to bring on the mission.

A Company's gear, which had been brought down from Fort Davis, had been loaded onto the helicopters the previous day to avoid chaos later. On the evening of D-day, at 7:00 P.M., the team received its last intelligence briefing, which included a recently shot infrared video of Fort Cimarron and the Pacora Bridge; each soldier made a mental picture of the target. By 12:05 A.M., the Pacora Bridge mission looked like it was destined for success. Preparation had gone smoothly, and one UH-60 was cranking away on the helipad. The two MH-60s could be seen flying in from Howard, descending to land right on schedule. A Company soldiers crouched down at the hangar entrance, in position to board the helicopters.

Then PDF gunfire started to pepper the hangar.

A busload of Panamanian soldiers were racing through Albrook, past the helicopter pad, the Panamanians firing their AK-47 machine guns wildly toward the hangar. Green Berets dove for cover as a squad responsible for security around the perimeter returned fire.

One bullet ripped through Jacobelly's briefing board, tipping the rig over onto the Task Force Black commander. The board probably saved his life as one second later a .50 caliber round parted his hair. Two Task Force Black soldiers were hit, but were not killed by the sudden burst of fire. One soldier who suffered a flesh wound refused to report his injury.

At the same time, an even more serious attack threatened, as members of the Dignity Battalion armed with rocket-propelled grenade launchers lined the Albrook perimeter fence. But the Digbats, no more than 660 feet away, never fired on the helicopters or the hangar. U.S. intelligence units had intercepted a radio call ordering a Dignity Battalion unit to hit the helicopters, but apparently the message was never received.

Amid the gunfire, Lt. Col. David Wilderman, the special forces operations officer, informed A Company that he had bad news: H-hour had been advanced by fifteen minutes. He told Higgins. Worse, a column of vehicles had left Fort Cimarron and were heading toward Panama City.

How many vehicles?

Wilderman said he did not know. He told Higgins that "it was imperative" that his team get to Pacora to cut the column off.

One minute later, at 12:14 A.M., A Company raced toward the waiting helicopters.

Despite the PDF attack, the two MH-60 helicopters had landed. They were taking numerous hits, but none at the time were catastrophic. In seconds, Higgins told Chief Warrant Officer John Estep, the pilot of the lead aircraft, that the H-hour had been changed. The pilot agreed that it was time to leave, but Estep said there was another problem.

Estep, after studying the terrain map, had determined that he could not land the three helicopters on the planned landing zone, on the northeast side of the bridge. Electrical wires, the slope of the terrain surrounding the bridge, and the small size of the landing area made a three-ship assault impossible. Estep recommended that the team land on the southwest side of the bridge exactly opposite the planned landing zone.

Higgins hesitated. He was reluctant to change such an important element of the plan just prior to its execution. But he went with Estep's recommendation because it would be easier to adapt to the shift in the landing zone than try to recover from a slow, unsafe landing with a column of PDF vehicles bearing down on the bridge.

As the choppers lifted into the sky over Panama, Estep decided to make another change. Making a mental calculation on takeoff, he realized that the team could not be expected to reach the Pacora River Bridge by 12:45 A.M., the new H-hour. If the helicopters flew the planned flight path, it would take about twenty-five minutes to get to the target.

It was already close to 12:30 A.M. Estep knew the team's success, and lives, depended on reaching the bridge before the PDF column. Without approval he changed the flight route to shave off valuable minutes. It was a decision fraught with risk: dozens of helicopters were flying over Panama around 1:00 A.M., and each flight path was carefully orchestrated to avoid a midair collision. Most of the helicopters would be flying "blacked-out" to remain undiscovered. Pilots flew with burdensome night vision goggles.

Higgins had to laugh; this was becoming a snakebite mission.

The mission for the Pacora River Bridge had changed dramatically in the twenty-four hours preceding the assault. Under the original operations order, a four-man team would air assault to the bridge and provide information to headquarters on the movement of PDF forces originating from the Fort Cimarron compound. The bridge was a vital checkpoint because any PDF troops from Fort Cimarron could influence Ranger and 82d Airborne operations at the Tocumen and Torrijos airfields. The Pacora River Bridge was between both objectives. If required, the special forces team would be instructed to either blow the bridge up or call in an AC-130 gunship to halt the PDF troops.

But with a PDF convoy from Fort Cimarron bearing down, Higgins needed more firepower. A Company was to seize and deny use of the bridge. Although the team had to grab whatever antitank weapons it could find just before boarding the helicopters, the specifics of the existing plan remained essentially intact.

After landing near the bridge, A Company would break into five teams, designated by the last five letters in the alphabet.

Team X, consisting of ten men, would be the primary ambush team. The group carried six AT-4 anti-armor rockets, three British-built Light Antiarmor Weapons (LAW 80), and two light machine guns.

Team Y, just three soldiers, would provide security on the right side of the landing zone. Also, this team, with an Air Force technical assistant, would provide target information to the AC-130 gunship, which would provide the main firepower against the PDF vehicles.

Team Z, with four men, would quickly run across the bridge to establish an observation post and establish a barrier with concertina wire to prevent civilian traffic from moving into the area. Team U, with four men, would initially cover Team Z as they moved across the bridge, and then would fall back to provide rear security. The mission of the three-man Team W was command and control.

As the three helicopters carrying A Company approached the Pacora River, dense fog and darkness made it virtually impossible to locate the Pacora highway and bridge. On the final approach, the helicopters, just one hundred feet off the ground, flew right over the approaching column, performing a button-hook to land.

The Green Berets stared down at the PDF's headlights. There were between six and nine vehicles, at fifty-meter intervals, but it was difficult to determine whether they were tanks or trucks. If the oncoming vehicles were equipped with large guns, the PDF would have no problem blowing the chopper formation out of the sky at such close range.

"We're going in, we're going in!" yelled Estep, stilling any thoughts of aborting the mission.

The lead pilot relied on instinct and the headlights of the enemy vehicles to put his aircraft down precisely at the planned landing zone. The helicopters touched ground, the troops rolled out, and the transport was gone. Higgins looked up.

The first PDF vehicle had just hit the bridge.

The Pacora River Bridge is about five hundred feet long. The PDF convoy was far too close for comfort, and Higgins ordered the ambush team up the thirty-five-foot embankment, but his men, despite being laden with heavy antiarmor weapons, were already scrambling up the hill.

The sound of an engine rumbling brought Higgins up short: Although it would later turn out to be a PDF two-and-a-half-ton truck with an out-of-tune engine, he believed he'd heard an M113 armored personnel carrier idling. Higgins had spent one year in a mechanized infantry unit, and he knew the tracked vehicles, armed with .50 caliber machine guns, were lethal weapons. "We were waiting for a .50 cal to blow us off the side of the hill," he recalls.

Higgins knew his unit would have to tackle the vehicles on the bridge alone. The enemy was too close to call in an AC-130.

S Sgt. Samuel McDonald, a radio operator, was the first soldier up the hill. He threw his rucksack to the ground, pulled out a LAW, and hurriedly moved to the center of the road.

Looking directly into the headlights of the lead PDF vehicle, McDonald fired. The LAW shot toward the vehicle, but dipped low and skimmed the pavement, sliding underneath the target.

McDonald laughed. The lead vehicle, still a good 350 feet away, stopped for a second, but then continued forward slowly. Following McDonald's example, the leader of the ambush team moved to the center of the road, and fired a second LAW.

The column stopped.

Unclear whether the LAWs were having any impact on the vehicles, another Green Beret fired an AT-4 at the convoy. That started the firestorm. The ambush team launched a hail of rockets, grenades and machine gun rounds into the PDF column.

Higgins was not sure what was happening. The convoy had temporarily stopped but it was halfway across the bridge. The PDF had not fired back, but he feared they would move forward and mow the company down. The ambush team, meanwhile, was probably wasting its shots.

Higgins turned to his Air Force controller, asking him if the vehicles were too close for the AC-130 gunship, which at that very moment began to loom above the bridge. The controller estimated the distance between the U.S. assault team and the enemy was probably too close for comfort.

But the gunship was the only chance A Company had. Higgins ordered the teams to conceal themselves along the embankment, and asked the AC-130 to "service" the PDF convoy.

Even as the gunship set the PDF column aflame, Higgins feared that the Panamanians would dismount their trucks and try to sneak into the flanks of the U.S. position. The rear of the U.S. team was totally exposed, and a PDF squad could inflict devastating casualties. When the AC-130 reported movements along the riverbed, Higgins's fears grew. He ordered one of his teams to secure the southern flank, and to fire occasional rounds and grenades into the riverline to discourage any PDF attacks.

At 1:30 A.M., the Spectre, still methodically pumping rounds into the PDF column, reported about five cars coming from Panama City toward the bridge. Given the time of the night, and the sounds of war echoing across the countryside, Higgins assumed that the cars contained reinforcement elements for the PDF column from Fort Cimarron.

But he still wanted to give the cars the benefit of the doubt, and ordered Team Z to fire warning shots high and right of the convoy. The aircraft reported that there were three cars, and that personnel were dismounting, and moving into the elephant grass toward the exposed flank of A Company. Team Z launched five hundred rounds of machine-gun fire and thirteen grenades into the grass. There was no reply.

Higgins now thought his company was being attacked on both sides. He asked for a second AC-130.

Luckily, the delay of the 82d Airborne Division assault at Tocumen airfield, due to poor weather at Fort Bragg, had freed up an AC-130. Ten minutes later, it was on station over the bridge. The power of the two gunships eventually forced the PDF in the cars to the west to pull out of the area.

However, the gunships could not do the gritty infantry work of securing the bridge. As Sergeants Dana Bowman and Joshua Roman crept forward to place a Claymore mine on the span, Bowman spotted three PDF soldiers walking towards them. The PDF were in uniform and armed. Bowman wasted no time and fired his M16 at point blank range.

The shots killed one enemy soldier instantly and wounded the others. One PDF soldier threw his grenade launcher to the ground, and jumped off the bridge into the water fifty feet below. He was never seen again. The third man climbed down from the bridge, and suspended himself from a water pipe that ran underneath. Bowman and Roman, not knowing what happened to the third enemy soldier, heard noises in the river below and threw three hand grenades over the bridge. The third man, who lost his grip due to the impact of the grenades, fell thirty-five feet to the riverbank, where he was found in the morning with two broken legs, but alive.

In time, the situation at the Pacora River Bridge stabilized. At 6:00 A.M., an exhausted A Company was relieved.

The spookiest element of Operation Just Cause was Task Force Green.

Task Force Green was made up of the Delta Force, itself a nickname for the Army's counterterrorist Special Operations Detachment. Created in the 1970s, Delta Force was officially activated in January 1981, but only after it had participated in the flawed Iranian hostage rescue attempt in 1979. The unit consists of just over one hundred of the Army's best-trained soldiers and is an integral part of the Joint Special Operations Command, based at Fort Bragg. The Defense Department never comments officially on the unit's activities, structure, or weaponry.

Although their role in Operation Just Cause is murky, the primary mission of Task Force Green was to strike Noriega's suspected hideouts. These spots could be anywhere in the country, and Delta Force teams, escorted by Task Force 160 "Night Stalkers," a highly specialized aviation unit, were kept ready to pounce at a moment's notice. But another, more publicized mission of the top secret task force was the rescue of American civilian Kurt Frederick Muse from the Carcel Modelo, or Model Prison.

Muse, a forty-year-old radio expert from the Virginia suburbs of Washington, D.C., was arrested by a PDF patrol on 5 April 1989 for committing "crimes against the security of the Panamanian state" and "promoting subversion."[3] The charges, which kept Muse imprisoned in Panama from April to the first morning hour of 20 December, alleged that the American citizen used a clandestine radio and television network to promote the cause of Panama's opposition parties. It is also alleged that Muse, as his underground radio broadcasts grew in frequency and popularity, was recruited by the CIA. Muse himself says he does not know the extent of agency involvement. Intelligence agents supplied Muse with sophisticated radio equipment through a Panamanian intermediary. Although he believed the gear originated in Washington, Muse does not believe he worked for the CIA.

Muse was raised in Panama and returned to the Central American nation in the 1970s, where he continued the family business in graphic arts and printing shops. In 1988, Muse started to become increasingly disenchanted with the Panamanian government. Following Noriega's drug indictments in the United States and the increasing revelations of corruption within the Panamanian government, Muse saw his adopted home being torn apart by a rabid dictator.

His radio broadcasts became more varied, with news reports on antigovernment protests and demonstrations. Muse and his network of seven radio operators became the mouthpiece of the Civic Crusade, a nonpartisan group of Panamanian businessmen and officials who led protests against Noriega and the PDF-run regime.

By spring 1989, the PDF wanted to arrest Muse for spying for the United States. On his return from a trip to Miami to purchase new radio equipment, members of the DENI customs police snatched Muse at immigration control at Torrijos Airport. Under constant interrogation made all the more overwhelming by enforced sleep deprivation, Muse eventually succumbed and admitted his involvement in the underground radio operation. The PDF quickly rounded up the equipment stored throughout Panama City, and threw Muse into the Carcel Modelo, one block away from La Comandancia. SOUTHCOM officials attempted to negotiate his release, without success. Muse smuggled out a letter to President Bush in the spine of a book, urging American action.

By fall, Muse's physical condition had deteriorated considerably. After the October coup, about 150 rebels were thrown into the prison, and the PDF would make Muse watch as the prisoners were tortured and beaten. The U.S. failure to intervene militarily drove Muse deeper into his depression, causing nightmares so intense that he would wake up bathed in sweat. As relations between the United

States and Noriega worsened in November, Noriega announced repeatedly that Muse would be killed if the United States made a military move against Panama. "Intelligence sources said he was to be killed in any attack, so he had to be taken out before it began," says one U.S. official who visited Muse just prior to the invasion.

After the Paz shooting, Muse knew from the increased PDF activity that something was up. He had discovered, through the use of hand signals with a fellow inmate, that the PDF had shot and killed a U.S. Marine, and he was certain that Bush would not allow such a mishap to go unpunished. All day he watched out his window, staring at the sandbag fortifications the PDF had set up that day to protect La Comandancia. He drifted off to sleep just before midnight.

At 12:45 A.M., Muse was jolted awake by the sound of machine-gun fire. Seconds later, he heard the tremendous thumping noise of an AC-130 Spectre gunship and explosion as rounds rocked the PDF headquarters. He peered outside. The sandbags had vaporized.

The lights in the Carcel Modelo were out, despite the prison's backup generator. Muse sensed someone was in the prison.

Suddenly, his cell shook with three explosions. In between blasts, Muse heard fire from a submachine gun. At that moment, he thought he saw white laser beams through the smoke in the prison corridor.

Before Muse stood "an apparition."[4] The man was not wearing a normal uniform or helmet, nor was he carrying a typical M16 rifle.

The Delta Force commando reminded Muse of Darth Vader.

The commando grabbed Muse and they raced at lightning speed through the prison to the roof. On the way, Muse saw at least five bodies, including the guard who Muse knew was supposed to kill him if the United States invaded Panama.

The Delta Force commandos had arrived by an M113 armored personnel carrier driven by members of B Company, 4th Battalion, 6th Infantry Regiment, 5th Infantry Division (Mechanized), but planned to make their escape by an AH-6 helicopter that was to meet the team on the roof.

The infantry on the streets below watched with amazement as the helicopter, absorbing repeated hits from PDF sniper fire, landed on the prison roof. 1st Lt. Harold Powers, a platoon leader in B Company, wondered if it would ever get off the roof again.

With a Delta Force commando on either side of him, Muse jumped into the helicopter. The small chopper could not carry the entire Delta team, and three soldiers jumped onto each pod on the outside of the aircraft.

As the "Little Bird" lifted off the building, it was struck again by sniper fire and the controls went dead. Hovering a few feet off the roof, the chopper started to slide down off the building. The right skid just cleared the corner of the building as the chopper fell to the street.

The pilot strained to keep the aircraft from crashing, and it bobbed between ten and thirty feet in the air as he flew it down the street, "went through the intersection, and took a left turn into the parking lot," in the words of one observer.

Riddled yet again by enemy gunfire, the tiny helicopter collapsed onto its left skid, seriously injuring the three commandos on that pod. One sniper round entered a Delta commando's leg and lodged in his chest. Muse was in shock but unhurt.

One of the commandos responsible for Muse grabbed the American and headed for a position behind a Jeep Wagoneer parked next to a building. Suddenly, the soldier went down, suffering a terrifying blow to the head by the rotor blade of the helicopter.

Muse looked down to find the man's face covered with blood. Before Muse could flinch, the soldier opened his eyes and stood up. The soldier was knocked unconscious for a brief second, but the rotor caused only minor lacerations. Muse realized that if he had been first, his head would have been lopped off.

The Delta team had set up a defensive perimeter in the prison courtyard and waited for a rescue. As team members cared for the wounded, one commando held out an infrared strobe light that could be visible to the night vision goggles used by U.S. pilots. A Black Hawk from Task Force 160 soared overhead, banked right, and acknowledged the light by wiggling its fuel pods.

Seconds later, an M113 held in reserve for the Delta Force mission rumbled to the courtyard and picked up the rescue team. The whole operation had taken no more than six minutes.

The mission was accomplished, but it was a close call. Delta

Force suffered four casualties, with one soldier landing in intensive care following the mission. All four soldiers eventually recovered.

With Muse snatched to safety, the stage was set for the centerpiece of Operation Just Cause: the assault on La Comandancia. Mechanized infantry, light infantry, and Rangers would try to drive a stake through the heart of the PDF.

8

The Gauntlet

With two hours to go before the H-hour, 1:00 A.M., Wednesday, 20 December, the men of C Company, 1st Battalion, 508th Infantry (Airborne), huddled in a classroom of the Curundu Elementary School, located near Fort Clayton, the American fortress overlooking the Panama Canal. The soldiers sat mutely as they readied themselves to strike La Comandancia, the center of Manuel Antonio Noriega's power and the headquarters of the Panama Defense Forces.

For almost all of these men, products of the all-volunteer Army of the 1980s, the attack would be the first time in combat, and they had drawn the toughest assignment in all of Operation Just Cause. After a force of mechanized infantry had cordoned off the headquarters, they would secure the complex itself.

Their leaders had told the men to rest, but sleep would not come; most of them wanted to move, nervously packing and repacking rucksacks, trying to fit that extra grenade. Others wrote letters to their loved ones, searching for the phrases that might stand as their final testament if the worst should happen. Still others paced frequent trips to the toilet.

Six two-and-one-half-ton trucks pulled up outside the room, bringing a perfect stillness and silence to the schoolhouse. Everyone knew where these trucks would take them.

Suddenly a young sergeant leapt to his feet, possessed with the urge to read a prayer he had written in haste that evening.

"You are going into combat. You have got to be worried about the hereafter. But you are an American soldier . . ."

The NCO spoke hoarsely and haltingly, in the grip of emotions he could barely master. Embarrassed, he turned to his company commander, Capt. Tim Flynn, to complete the reading. Flynn told him, no, you should be the one to do it, sergeant.

Michael DeBlois continued.

"You might get killed. You might kill another person. That does not go with God in anybody's book. But you are a soldier, and you are called upon to do those things. So that makes it right. That is the way war is."

DeBlois, a twenty-four-year-old infantryman from Dubach, Louisiana, was killed the next morning by a Panamanian grenade that took a bad bounce. The prayer, which he had shoved into his hip pocket, was blasted from his body and could not be found. Flynn tried to recite the words at the memorial service held on the nearby grounds of Fort Amador one month later. He told C Company that the prayer justified what the unit had to do that morning. "It just made things right," Flynn said.

The grenade that killed DeBlois was thrown by a Noriega supporter from one of the high-rise apartment buildings that crowded around La Comandancia. The grenade was not aimed at DeBlois, nor at any particular target. It dropped several stories, caromed off a wall, and rolled into a small building where the C Company's 2d Platoon had established a temporary command post.

Even after a long night of intense heat and fire and close combat in the tight streets of downtown Panama City, the grenade produced a horrifying scene. The casing blew apart, flinging pieces of metal in every direction. The building shook. Pfc. Troy Coats, an eighteen-year-old infantryman from Great Falls, Montana, was killed instantly, his body shredded and mangled by jagged bits of shrapnel. Sgt. James Almeida staggered out of the building and collapsed. He screamed repeatedly for a medic, his hands peppered with blood. Almeida lived, as did another soldier in the command post, escaping with serious wounds. Medics found more than three hundred pieces of shrapnel in Almeida's body; Coats's index finger was pulled from his gall bladder.

DeBlois, too, was filled with fragments of hot metal. His leg was blown off, and he was choking on his own blood. Despite valiant efforts of four medics rushed to save him, beginning their treatment in less than thirty seconds, DeBlois died in intensive care in nearby Gorgas Hospital some two hours later.

Of all the actions of Operation Just Cause, the fight for La Comandancia was the most vicious. Though only four American soldiers lost their lives in three hours of fighting at La Comandancia, and forty more were wounded, dozens of PDF were killed and scores more injured.

The pillars of fire that erupted into the humid Panama night produced the lasting image of the violence of Just Cause; thousands of rounds from weapons of every variety crashed into the stout headquarters complex, and the PDF trapped inside shot back indiscriminately. The surrounding slums were set afire, killing and injuring impoverished Panamanians and driving them from the hovels that were their apartments and houses: in striking at the American forces assaulting the La Comandancia area, members of Noriega's Dignity Battalions put the torch to the El Chorrillo barrio next to the PDF compound. Fanned by the incendiary rounds of AC-130 Spectre gunships and sparked by the rocket-propelled grenades of the PDF, the fire roared through the decrepit structures first built to house immigrant workers brought to Panama to build the canal. To U.S. and PDF soldiers waging a battle for control of Fort Amador across the bay, the flames appeared as high as the sixteen-story blue and white apartment buildings next to PDF headquarters. To those downtown, it was a raging inferno that turned a fierce battle into hellfire on Earth.

Fort Polk is stuck smack in the middle of Louisiana, right next to the middle of nowhere. Despite the Army's attempt to revitalize the post, to the tune of millions of dollars of new construction in the 1980s, Fort Polk could not shake its permanent nickname: "Camp Swampy." Yet by the middle of December, the men of the 4th Battalion, 6th Regiment, 5th Infantry Division (Mechanized), were looking forward to getting back to Polk. They left "Camp Gator," their bivouac near Howard Air Force Base, on the night of 16 December in a holiday mood, having just lit the official battalion Christmas tree. After four months in Panama, they were looking forward to going home.

The battalion deployed from Fort Polk in September to replace the regiment's 5th Battalion, and were living in the cramped quarters of a few permanent buildings and two inflatable gymnasium-size buildings they called "bubbles." The daily routine in Panama was similar to one at Fort Polk, with small-arms training and vehicle maintenance being the primary chores.

But since the October coup, the tension in Panama had risen to new levels. At Camp Gator, at least one mechanized unit was expected to be ready to move in less than an hour, the entire task force in under four hours. Twice a week, the unit would conduct Sand Flea exercises. Though they often sparked a confrontation with the PDF, even the Sand Fleas could not keep the soldiers focused and motivated. The daily harassment of U.S. soldiers by the PDF made matters worse. Some were detained for hours before release; others had shots fired at them.

The American decision to stay out of the 3 October coup did little to ease the frustration. The day of the coup attempt, units from the battalion and the 193d Infantry Brigade watched from observation points as Major Giroldi was persuaded to surrender after hundreds of PDF soldiers rushed to La Comandancia to protect Noriega. The soldiers watched the events as if watching a baseball game from the stands. But the United States would just sit, watch, and wait.

The frustration and disappointment spread to unit commanders who were familiar with the contingency plan. Morale took a nose dive. Troops began to manufacture reasons to return to the United States, and transfer requests became common.

News of the shooting of Lt. Robert Paz hit Camp Gator as units were dispersing following the tree lighting. The rumor mill was running at full speed. "Troops were ready to attack something," says Command Sergeant Major Rupert Ford. "At that time, I felt we were going to attack the PDF. It looked like the American people were behind some kind of action."

As the crisis developed, the battalion's B and D Companies were ordered to come back over the Panama Canal to Fort Clayton, and C Company of the 1/508 moved its troops and equipment over to the Fort Clayton gymnasium. Task Force Gator had been put on high alert before, but each time the crisis had ended without incident. A U.S. soldier had been killed, but decision makers in Washington had two months earlier passed up an opportunity to topple Noriega. Each man knew that this alert could end the same way, a walk back to the barracks, "with our tails between our legs," as one soldier said.

This time they thought it might be different. The flow of C-130 and C-141 transport aircraft into Howard Air Force Base had quadrupled. Planes were landing continually with troops and supplies. Soldiers spotted other U.S. soldiers with unit patches they had never seen before.

Even the PDF seemed to sense something was up. Convoys of PDF buses streamed back and forth across the Bridge of the Americas. Some carried troops, including members of the Battalion 2000, who pointed out the windows as they drove past American installations. But others were empty. The empty ones would turn out to be as dangerous as the ones with soldiers, for they would be used to set up roadblocks throughout the city.

At the Fort Amador Officers' Club, members of U.S. Army South had just finished the main course in the formal dinner highlighting the command's annual holiday dance. Lt. Col. Billy Ray Fitzgerald, commander of the 1st Battalion, 508th Infantry Regiment (Airborne), part of USARSO's central fighting force, was on the phone with his headquarters making sure the night was calm. As his subordinates were confirming that all was still, he felt a tug on his arm: it was Snell, telling him to put his unit on alert. Quietly, the two officers excused themselves, and still dressed in their formal uniforms, rushed over to an observation post on Fort Amador. Details of the Paz shooting were still sketchy, but Snell and Fitzgerald quickly went about the business of the alert.

They returned to the officers' club, only to find the crowd filing out. Amidst the chaos, Fitzgerald rounded up his staff and company commanders. The battalion would be taking up initial positions on Morgan Avenue, which runs from the area surrounding U.S. installations straight into the La Comandancia area. Capt. Tim Flynn's C Company was confused and disoriented as they drove to their positions. After attempting to set up a security perimeter, the company moved back to a parking lot at Fort Clayton, where they would spend the night.

The next day, 17 December, the battalion was told to move back over to Fort Kobbe; apparently, the Paz crisis had passed. The troops and their equipment quietly moved to the other side of the canal. But Flynn stayed behind at Fort Clayton, where he received a detailed briefing from Snell on the plan. The invasion was on.

Snell's first order to his commanders was to make sure the troops were rested. The trucks would slowly infiltrate back to Fort Clayton a truckload at a time so the PDF would not notice the massive buildup occurring at Fort Clayton. He then set about the business of reviewing the plan with his subordinate commanders. The operation itself sounded uncannily familiar to most of the Task Force Gator commanders.

La Comandancia, symbol of Noriega's oppression, was torn down by the new Panamanian government immediately following Just Cause. It was a compound of fifteen buildings surrounded by a ten-foot wall, planted in the middle of the city. The compound stood about six hundred yards south of SOUTHCOM headquarters, covered roughly a two-block area, extending north to the Carcel Modelo and to the south where the PDF 2d Public Order Company had their barracks.

Inside was a small city within Panama City, one that few Panamanian citizens ever saw. One soldier referred to the compound as a typical American street corner, with a grocery, courtyard, theater, nightclub, and chapel. This city housed hundreds of Noriega's most loyal and elite troops, and was the command center for the PDF throughout the country.

La Comandancia was more than a headquarters building; it was an armory as well. Weapons, including Soviet-made rocket-propelled grenades, as well as small arms from all over the world, were kept in a separate building. A number of military vehicles, including U.S.-built V-150 and V-300 armored cars and towed antiaircraft weapons, were parked in the motor pool. The main building itself was a concrete-and-steel-reinforced structure of several stories in which Noriega and his senior commanders had luxurious offices.

Most importantly, La Comandancia was the nerve center of the PDF. The highly centralized PDF did little without explicit orders from headquarters, and though Just Cause planners would plot strikes against dozens of PDF garrisons throughout the country, there would be many they could not reach on D-day. Capturing La Comandancia would be the key to immobilizing resistance in outlying provinces. It was target number one, dubbed "Bravo One."

The mission, at least on paper, was simple. Light and mechanized infantry units from Panama and the United States, augmented by an armor team consisting of M551 Sheridan tanks and Marine Corps LAVs, would surround and cordon off the Comandancia complex, isolating the PDF inside and prohibiting other units from moving into the area to reinforce the headquarters building.

The problem was the PDF knew well before H-hour the Americans were coming, and were well prepared for the onslaught. As the assault force converged on La Comandancia, they ran into roadblocks and barricades formed by cars and bolstered by fifteen-ton garbage trucks. The PDF had established a perimeter around the complex with sandbagged firing positions, some strengthened by the ubiquitous rocket-propelled grenade, or RPG, launchers. Snipers hid among the windows and balconies of the surrounding highrises, attacking U.S. units from behind and in front. This gauntlet of fire almost forced a halt to the operation, the heat from the fire forcing units to reposition command posts to locations more vulnerable to sniper fire. Camouflage rags on the helmets of some members of the 4/6 ignited spontaneously.

The challenge to U.S. forces was to burst through the PDF perimeter. Task Force Gator was not to enter the actual compound until it was determined for certain that Noriega was not inside. If Noriega was inside, then a special forces team would enter the area to locate and capture him; if the PDF leader was not there, Flynn's company would start clearing the buildings.

In addition, Stiner ordered a Ranger company to be available to help the airborne unit clear the Comandancia complex. Task Force Gator, in some plans known as Task Force 4/6, was a subordinate element of Task Force Bayonet, commanded by Snell, head of the 193d Infantry Brigade. The task force consisted primarily of Flynn's men and B and D Companies of the 4th Battalion, 6th Infantry Regiment. The two mechanized companies, each equipped with fourteen M113 armored personnel carriers, were supplemented by four Sheridan tanks and four LAVs to provide fire support from Ancon Hill, which overlooks La Comandancia.

Additional support would come from engineer platoons of A and C Companies from the 4th Battalion, 6th Infantry Regiment; the 59th Engineer Company; and elements of the 5th Battalion, 1st Field Artillery, and the 5th Forward Support Battalion. The task force also included two military police platoons from Fort Benning, Georgia.

Using the M113s in the tight city streets was an unconventional wrinkle for Just Cause planners. These tracked vehicles were designed for the modern mechanized battlefield, for the open plains of central Europe. Panama City was a world away from the Fulda Gap, but the protection from small-arms fire and the firepower of their .50 caliber machine guns had a decisive effect on 20 December. And the run in to La Comandancia would take all the protection and firepower Task Force Gator could muster. With hundreds of PDF in and around La Comandancia, the attack would be bloody.

When 1st Sgt. William John of D Company looked at the plan of attack, he predicted he would lose at least seven tracked vehicles and forty soldiers. Battalion commander Lt. Col. James Reed, head of Task Force Gator, anticipated that his force would lose between thirty and thirty-five men. Once the shooting started, he felt he was wrong. The death toll, he was sure, would be much higher.

The initial attack on La Comandancia would be two-pronged. Two reinforced companies of the 4th Battalion, 6th Infantry Regiment—each with about 150 men mounted in M113s and other vehicles—were to advance on La Comandancia along different routes. When they had secured the neighborhoods surrounding the PDF headquarters, the infantry of C Company, 1/508 Infantry (Airborne), would move against La Comandancia itself.

One prong of the mounted assault fell to D Company, its three platoons strengthed by one from the battalion's C Company. D Company needed help if it was to to cover its six widely dispersed objectives. These were hundreds of yards apart, most on the western side of the La Comandancia compound, but also in the rear. Small teams of four to nine men were expected to occupy each, usually a key intersection.

As they rumbled toward the line of departure on 4th of July Avenue, D Company came under fire from Ancon Hill. Pfc. Darin Marcinkevicius, driver of the third track in the first convoy, spied muzzle flashes coming from the bushes to his left. Although instructed not to fire—a special forces team was positioned there to target PDF snipers—gunners swept the bushes with their .50 caliber machine guns to cover the advance. The mechanized force pressed on until it hit the 4th of July and the roadblock. It was 12:46, one minute after the revised H-hour.

Three cars blocked the road. Several Panamanians, not in uniform, crouched in the cars, firing AK-47s, but the rifle bullets bounced off the M113. The thirteen-ton tracks chugged onward. One M113 headed toward the cars at about thirty miles per hour, its driver thinking the track would push the car out of the road. Instead, the personnel carrier crushed the car like a cardboard box.

Some Panamanians were able to flee the gruesome scene, running toward Ancon Hill. Others were not so lucky. One Panamanian had lost his leg and managed to wiggle his way out of a car. The sedan was trapped underneath an M113 that had thrown a track. As the wounded man tried to run, he was gunned down by a .50 caliber machine gun. Another Panamanian's head was severed as an M113 crushed his car.

It took about ten minutes for D Company to clear the first roadblock, and as the infantry carriers swung down deeper into Panama City, they ran into another barricade, this time a large dump truck. Fortunately, the convoy was able to skirt around the truck, and was not attacked by PDF. As the company now moved alongside Panama Bay, it stopped to reload and prepare for the final run into La Comandancia.

B Company left the back gate of Fort Clayton at about 11:55 P.M., and took just twenty minutes to get to Quarry Heights. They hit their staging area forty-five minutes early, but had not yet been told of the changed H-hour.

The company's mission was to seal off the east side of the La Comandancia compound, its objectives also mostly street intersections. One of their primary targets was the Carcel Modelo prison; the assignment was to eliminate the PDF guards to ease the escape of the Delta Force rescue squad freeing Kurt Muse.

B Company would have little company. No other American units would be in the immediate area, and fire support from Spectres and attack helicopters would be concentrated on La Comandancia rather than the surrounding neighborhood. The PDF headquarters, too, would not be visible. The job was to secure the area, clear it out, and push any PDF toward the sea.

When B Company got word of the advance in H-hour, it raced toward La Comandancia, its M113s barreling down from Quarry

Heights at forty miles per hour, the boxy vehicles silhouetted by the reddening skies over La Comandancia. Repeated thumps from the AC-130s' 40mm cannons accompanied the fiery scene.

The convoy was anticipating roadblocks like the ones that were slowing down D Company. Intelligence reports from earlier in the evening pinpointed a number, but missed one. As B Company took a sharp left turn off 4th of July onto Avenue B, the unit ran right into two fifteen-ton dump trucks. The convoy came to a halt.

For the final leg of the assault, Task Force Gator's attentions would shift from roadblocks to snipers. High-rises hovered over the narrow streets of central Panama City, and the M113s of B and D companies would have little room for maneuver. They were now a battering ram bent on breaking down the walls of the PDF's sanctuary.

Reloaded and regrouped, D Company buttoned up for the charge. As they turned onto 25th Street, fire came from all directions. Panamanian snipers pecked at them from above, two from atop a billboard, at least two more positioned on top of a water tower. But most of the gunfire was coming from the apartment buildings surrounding La Comandancia.

The high-rises offered perfect cover for the snipers. The PDF, and some civilians armed with AK-47s, could fire from windows and balconies without exposing themselves. American machine gunners quickly became air defenders, searching the sky for muzzle flashes.

But the M113s found it all but impossible to defend themselves from the fire from above. Engaging the snipers was supposed to be the job of the special forces gunners from the hill opposite, and the rules of engagement prevented soldiers from firing unless they were certain that the shot would kill the enemy. Although almost defenseless, most infantrymen held their fire. Some, equipped with sophisticated night vision goggles, were able to see the green tracers of AK-47 rifles, and fired into the windows. But then it was hard to tell if the enemy had been hit. "Prior to H-hour, we were told snipers would be taken out. They were supposed to be taken out. Well, we got into it, and somebody was not taking something out," says one Task Force Gator officer.

B Company had it even worse. The barricade of two dump trucks forced the column of M113s to slam on its brakes in a hurry, throwing personnel carriers into each other in a noisy chain of collisions.

The company's 2d Platoon was the first to hit the barricade. Pelted with sniper fire, the first track tried to run straight through the obstacle. The boxy vehicle, with rounds pinging off its aluminum skin, backed up to ram the trucks. But the trucks, nearly as heavy as the M113s, would barely budge, sliding just inches after two attempts to ram them to the side. 2d Lt. Harold Powers, the platoon leader, riding in the first track, ordered some soldiers to dismount and find a way for the column to pass by the obstacle. At the same time, he noticed a small gap between the right side of one of the trucks and the building wall.

Though the ramming had moved the dump trucks only inches, perhaps those inches would be enough to allow the U.S. vehicles to slip by. Powers sent his dismounts through the gap, the track through right after them. The M113 took a large chunk out of the wall, and the concertina wire hung on the side of the vehicle was stripped away. But the bold move pushed the lumbering M113 past the obstacle.

Behind Powell, Cpl. Ivan D. Perez commanded the second track in the convoy. Perez was manning the .50 caliber machine gun, his favorite weapon, when he saw men rushing out of the track in front of him, leaping from the armored personnel carrier's rear door no more than ten feet ahead of him. Perched above his own vehicle's deck through the hatch, Perez looked for a way to provide the dismounted troops some covering fire. Perez's driver, Specialist Floyd J. Tackett, feverishly tried to maneuver the vehicle to the side so Perez could get a better angle to fire.

Perez noticed the heaviest firing was coming from the roof of the Carcel Modelo, about thirty-five yards to the left. He trained his machine gun at the roof and ripped off a powerful burst. The Panamanians responded from every direction. Specialist John J. Garcia, hearing nothing but gunfire, yelled up to him from the belly of the vehicle to be careful.

Perez looked down with a smile. "I'll be all right. I'll be all right," he yelled into the intercom.

Moments later, Tackett's intercom headset went dead. The muzzle of the machine gun swung down into the hatch and knocked at his helmet.

Perez seemed to follow, sliding into the cargo area in the rear of the M113. Perez slumped at the feet of Sergeant Dave Blair, the squad leader. Blair saw a bullet hole in the back of his track commander's helmet, and yelled for Specialist Andrew Quives, a medic.

"My TC's been hit! My TC's been hit!" Blair screamed in to the platoon's radio net. Perez was dead.

There was no answer. Powers could not hear the call. His lead track had made it past the barricade and sped ahead of the rest of the company.

Soon, Powers became worried. His track was alone on Avenue B. His company did not know where he was.

He radioed the column and drove up and down the street, trying to cover two objectives until the rest of the company arrived.

At last B Company started to assume its positions, key intersections about 250 yards apart. The unit was spread thin. Special forces had taken one of Powers's four tracks to form an ad hoc task force to search for Noriega downtown.

Panamanians in civilian clothes were all around them. Powers's men yelled into their radios. "Should we shoot? Should we shoot?" There was a lot of noise coming from La Comandancia. The company could not see the PDF headquarters, but heard the AC-130 firing.

As Powers, Perez, and the men of the mechanized infantry cleared the way, the light infantry of C Company, 1/508 Infantry (Airborne), mounted their trucks at Curundu Elementary School and rode in them toward La Comandancia. Capt. Tim Flynn's company left Fort Clayton on time, at about 11:30 P.M.

The airborne unit rode in the wake of the two tracked convoys by five minutes. As the Spectre gunships marked the passing of H-hour, the sound rippled through the young troops, causing momentary confusion. The commander of the lead platoon stopped, unable to distinguish between the AC-130 cannon fire and what he thought was mortar fire landing on Quarry Heights.

"What are we doing here?!" he radioed to Flynn.

Flynn instructed him to keep moving. The convoy moved on another hundred yards.

The platoon leader decided it would be safer to walk to the line of departure; it was one thing to ride in an armored personnel carrier, riding in a soft-sided truck quite another. Light infantrymen are supposed to prefer to walk, anyway. As his men dismounted from their trucks, others behind leaped from their vehicles and took cover along the side of the road. Once the group was organized, they began to push their way down the steep slope of Ancon Hill to 4th of July Avenue. The sounds of battle grew louder.

Now it was their turn to come under sniper fire, bullets zipping up and down the street in front of them. It seemed a wall of tracers stood between the airborne and their objective, the wall of the PDF compound. Fire was already swallowing El Chorrillo; Panamanians were jumping off balconies because it was their only exit. For a moment, an elderly woman stood with a small child. She threw the child off the balcony, hesitated, and then jumped. The main avenue was a flood of fear, streaming with Panamanians, most of them barefoot and crying. Some carried luggage, some carried weapons. Some carried both.

The company fanned out, concealing itself from the snipers and the enemy on the streets even as it moved forward. A ditch parallel to the avenue provided cover, soldiers scuttling across in the shadows.

Through the streets of El Chorrillo they moved, closing on their target. Hiding in a position against a wall of La Comandancia, waiting only to hear whether Noriega was inside. As his men poured through an alleyway, setting themselves for the last rush on La Comandancia, Flynn heard a noise to his right.

A woman and a child came out of a building.

Flynn turned, his finger pulsing on the trigger of his M16. He held his fire.

Almost all the elements of Task Force Gator were in place. The mechanized infantry had cleared the way for the light infantry. The last piece in the puzzle would come from the tanks, attack helicopters, and gunships that would provide the firepower to reduce La Comandancia.

From the ground, fire support would come from the tanks of Team Armor. Besides pummeling the headquarters, this small force, consisting of four M551 Sheridan tanks from C Company, 3d Battalion, 73d Armor (Airborne), of the 82d Airborne Division, and four Marine LAVs from D Company, 2d Light Armored Infantry Battalion, would have the important task of defending the infantry from the PDF armored cars that had been stationed in La Comandancia. Some of these vehicles mounted 90mm cannons in their turrets, guns that could tear through the thin skins of the M113s.

The tankers of 3/73 Armor (Airborne), smuggled into Panama one month before Just Cause, had been trying to disappear into the woodwork of the mechanized infantry task force. They were outsiders, and could not afford to have the soldiers of the 4/6 Infantry talking aloud about the tanks. The airborne troops shed their berets and sewed 5th Infantry Division patches on their uniforms. Bumper numbers on the company's jeeps also were changed, a move that fooled even the Army: after Just Cause a soldier supervising redeployment of equipment to the United States ordered the jeeps sent back to Fort Polk.

The advance in H-hour put Team Armor behind schedule. It didn't start moving toward La Comandancia until 12:50 A.M. The tanks linked up with the Marine LAVs out of Rodman Naval Station just before 1:00 A.M., moving up to Quarry Heights. Team Armor then split up into two groups. Two Sheridans and two LAVs took the high road up Ancon Hill to a position called Bull 1. There, engineers set demolition charges to clear trees blocking the first group's view of La Comandancia. One Sheridan and two LAVs moved to a lower position, Bull 2, which had a clear view of the target.

By the time Team Armor had assumed its positions at about 1:30 A.M., La Comandancia had become a raging inferno. Both positions were obscured by smoke and flames from the burning buildings. With detailed maps that had each building in La Comandancia numbered, the Sheridan crews were able to discern the location of most of the targets. But the smoke prevented the crews from being certain their fire would not hit a U.S. position. They would not fire that evening.

Other fire support plans went awry. At H-hour, Chief Warrant Officer Fred Horsley and Capt. George Kunkel, flying the lead of two AH-6 "Little Bird" special operations helicopters assigned to assault La Comandancia, skimmed the top of Ancon Hill and drew a bead on the PDF headquarters building, preparing to engage it with TOW antitank missiles and rockets. As the AH-6 came over the hill, it began to receive heavy fire from snipers. Wary of using the powerful TOWs or rockets to kill individual snipers, the choppers fired back with machine guns.

As they approached La Comandancia, Kunkel had trouble pulling the aircraft nose up. Horsley grabbed the stick to help, but it was no use. The aircraft did not respond, continuing its dive. The pilots were able to gain some control, but only enough to pick where they would crash.

As the tiny helicopter slammed into the ground, it slid across a courtyard and crashed into a concrete pillar. As the chopper slid, it caught fire.

Once it stopped, Kunkel jumped out and limped to safety. Co-pilot Horsley could not get out because the AH-6 was jammed up against a concrete wall. Twisted metal prevented him from wrestling free of his flight vest, but he struggled out of the aircraft and joined Kunkel. The two aviators suddenly found themselves in the middle of a ground battle. Their stomachs sank when they realized they were inside La Comandancia.

The pilots' greatest fear was being hit by the Spectre gunship when it opened fire on La Comandancia. The AC-130 is accurate, and equipped with sophisticated targeting gear, but from the air, the pilots knew, friend and foe look alike. And all around them, the Spectres were raining cannon fire on the PDF complex.

While the Spectres ripped La Comandancia from above, the infantry began to tighten the noose around the PDF on the ground. Most of the Panamanians had been assured by their officers that the Americans would never attack, but now the officers were deserting their posts and the rank and file of the PDF was losing motivation, too. Many chose to try to slip through the lines into the streets of Panama City while the Americans advanced.

The fight for La Comandancia itself was joined. The mechanized infantry now dismounted squads from their tracks to help work in close, the three platoons of D Company advancing toward the compound. The 1st Platoon took up a position, Objective Golf, at an intersection just to the north of of La Comandancia, and task force commander Reed moved his command post there.

Reed could see some soldiers firing from La Comandancia itself, but believed most of the troops had fanned out to establish the outer perimeter, which his troops had broken. He moved the rest of D Company in to complete his hammerlock on La Comandancia. In ten minutes, 3d Platoon had taken its two objectives alongside the complex. Then things began to go wrong.

The 2d Platoon found itself on the sharp end of the spear. Their mission was to breach the southeastern corner of La Comandancia by breaking through a wire fence, attacking across a courtyard, and blowing a hole in the compound wall. An M113 would then be pulled up to the breach, and would bull its way inside, firing its machine gun on the PDF barracks.

This was a tough assignment. As they moved towards a baseball field just behind the PDF compound, snipers on the high-rise shot and wounded American soldiers. Still the platoon pressed ahead into the courtyard, but it turned out to be bigger than it appeared on the satellite reconnaissance photos.

The personnel carriers rumbled forward. The first through the fence pivoted to give the second vehicle space to move. The second, carrying the forty-pound dynamite charge that would be used to blow a hole in the wall, got stuck just as it entered the courtyard. The third M113 managed to park in its pre-planned position.

Manning the machine gun was Pfc. Darin Marcinkevicius, who had led the company across its line of departure. In his covering role, he was to hose down the PDF complex to permit the men on foot to prepare the breach. As he dropped from his hatch into the track's cargo area for more ammunition, he saw flashes of light hitting the ground where the unit had dismounted. He knew something was wrong outside.

Two flashes hit in front of his track. Marcinkevicius told himself that the fire must be coming from rocket-propelled grenades. The shots were getting closer, and he knew the gunners would soon find the range on his vehicle. He quickly dropped the ammunition and got into his seat to pull back. It was then Marcinkevicius saw his shadow on the track's inside wall.

The back end of the track, including the fuel tank, was on fire.

It wasn't RPGs, it was the Spectres!

Cannon rounds had just zipped through the cargo hatch and set the entire vehicle ablaze. Marcinkevicius tried to jump out the front hatch, but did not know where the enemy was. He left his weapon, and bolted out the back of the vehicle. He hit the ground.

When he looked up, he could not believe what he saw.

Most of his platoon was down on the ground. And there were other troops running for cover. Each time they ran in one direction, the same sparks fired from the sky would cut them off. The soldiers would then change direction, only to be headed off again.

It took Marcinkevicius a minute to regain his senses; then he realized there were casualties. A number of his platoon members had been hit. When the gunfire stopped momentarily, soldiers ran to the wounded, throwing them on the lone M113 that still worked.

Marcinkevicius sprinted to one of the wounded and tried to apply first aid. But the soldier screamed every time he touched the wound. Marcinkevicius gave up trying to treat the wound and pulled the man to the M113.

He also saw that Pfc. Michael Heyne was badly hit and barely conscious. The platoon leader, 2d Lt. Doug Rubin, pleaded with Heyne to get aboard.

"Heyne," Rubin yelled, "if you don't get on the track, you are going to die."

Within minutes, the Spectre was back, again wreaking havoc on U.S. forces. Half of the 2d Platoon was wounded, but higher commanders did not understand what was happening.

Capt. Michael Etheridge, the D Company commander, was not with the 2d Platoon; he radioed Lt. Col. Reed to tell him his unit was taking indirect fire, but they didn't know what it was or where it was coming from. Reed figured it was PDF mortars, and told his mortar-finding radars to search for targets, targets they never found.

The Spectres fired again. The second burst exacted an even greater toll.

Twenty-one of the twenty-six members of D Company's 2d Platoon were hit. Sgt. Matthew Pickett's leg was ripped apart. When he was evacuated to the battalion aid station, he ran into the battalion command sergeant major, Rupert Ford. Pickett told him that the rest of his squad was in a burning track, and pointed toward La Comandancia. Wincing in pain, he said they were all probably dead by now. Ford could not see much of the wounds in the dark, but thought he saw Pickett's leg dangling from the knee. There was a lot of blood.

While the men of D Company are convinced it was AC-130 fire that decimated their ranks, other officials contend it was mortar fire, and their citations for bravery mention only "indirect fire." Reed says, "Twenty-one soldiers walked down there by the sea wall and were wounded by indirect fire, and that is all we can say. The only thing we can say that is accurate is that we don't know for sure what caused it. I believe there was mortar fire. It is possible it could have come from an AC-130, but there was other indirect fire into that area." Spectre pilots later said that the smoke and fire from La Comandancia may have obscured their targeting systems, but dismissed claims they engaged American troops.

On the other side of La Comandancia, C Company, 1/508 Infantry (Airborne), hugged the wall, waiting for word to move. If Noriega was in the compound, a special forces team would infiltrate to capture him. Flynn's airborne unit, well trained in urban operations, would clear the rest of the complex room by room. If Noriega was not there, or if intelligence could not determine his whereabouts, then the company would slowly enter the compound and clear it.

As Flynn puts it, the mission was to "give them the chance to surrender. When they failed to surrender . . . blow the living heck out of them with the AC-130, and then go in and pick up the pieces. Our mission was not to get killed."

But the wait turned out to be deadly. As they hid from snipers under awnings or in the darkness of alleys, the PDF troops in the surrounding apartment buildings were pelting U.S. troops with everything at hand, including glass, furniture, and even toys.

The Americans traded shots with snipers. When a Panamanian fired, three men would step out of the darkness. Two would provide covering fire, while the third man launched a grenade into the window. But it was a losing exchange. Grenades and glass, explosives and coffee tables were being dumped on U.S. soldiers, who had little cover besides thin awnings.

Flynn had been given an engineer squad with an M113. The track was expected to back up to the wall, and place a forty-pound charge at the base. At about 3:00 A.M., a breach was blown in the compound wall, and Flynn radioed that C Company was heading inside. The covering force was in position, and the lead platoon was ready to enter the complex.

Reed quickly told them to hold in place. While they sat, the PDF took pot shots at them.

Twice, the Panamanians got lucky with grenades. Each time, several soldiers were hit, and the second grenade killed Sgt. DeBlois and Pfc. Coats. Flynn became increasingly frustrated. Repeatedly he radioed Reed, saying standing still was costing him lives. Says Flynn: "We're here to do a job, and there is no place to go to. There is no place to be. You do what you can with what you've got. I had several discussions on that fact with the battalion commander. The answer is that he is the battalion commander. I'm the company commander, and you do what he tells you."

While Task Force Gator worked to secure La Comandancia, Task Force Wildcat cordoned off the residential areas surrounding Quarry Heights and Albrook Air Station. A subordinate element of Task Force Bayonet, the Wildcat team consisted of a single mechanized company from the 4th Battalion, 6th Infantry Regiment, and three infantry companies from the 5th Battalion, 87th Infantry Regiment, part of the 193d Infantry Brigade permanently stationed in Panama. Its targets were the PDF Engineer Compound, two military police (DENI) stations, and a Department of Traffic and Transportation (DNTT) headquarters. Two additional targets—the PDF dog compound and Balboa harbor—were secured by a platoon from the 519th MP Battalion.

The mission, at least at first, did not require Task Force Wildcat to attack the targets. Instead, Snell specifically instructed the force to surround each objective and begin a series of prerecorded loudspeaker announcements in Spanish. The reason for the restraint was the multitude of residential homes near the targets. The United States could not risk causing civilian casualties nor allowing the PDF to take hostages. The message was made clear: This is not a training exercise, this is an invasion. It also carried a warning. If the PDF did not surrender, the U.S. forces would fire demonstration shots into the targets.

"We got into position without any firefights, and then we began to execute our strategy," Snell says. "We did not want to kill unnecessarily a lot of soldiers because we knew many PDF were there to put bread on the table, and many, we suspected, were not strong supporters of Noriega." However, the tactic was not as successful as Task Force Wildcat would have liked.

By 1:30 A.M., 30 minutes after H-hour, only the MPs had secured their objectives. There was a brief skirmish at the PDF dog kennel, and Capt. Linda Bray, commander of an MP company, made history. After taking fire from PDF who refused to surrender, Bray ordered her assault team to attack the compound. She slammed her HMMWV through the gate of the kennel, hoping to dissuade the PDF from blocking the assault. But the enemy had fled, leaving behind 121 T-65 assault rifles, 31 AK-47 machine guns, 21 9mm pistols, three shotguns, and several cases of fragmentation grenades. As news of the assault spred, Bray quickly earned the distinction of being the first female soldier to lead U.S. forces into battle. After seizing their objectives, the MPs fanned out to provide rear security in the Curundu and Curundu Heights area, and guard the Balboa harbor.

It had become clear that the PDF in the Ancon and Balboa DENIs would not surrender despite the U.S. ultimatums. At the Balboa DENI, U.S. infantry soldiers had surrounded the building, issued the warning and fired demonstration rounds. The assault team had gunned down three PDF officers who had tried to escape out a side door, but the company could not enter the structure because communication with one squad had been lost. The isolated unit was behind a large hedge, and the darkness of the morning hours made it impossible to determine their exact location. The risk of friendly fire was too high.

But Snell, perched on nearby Sosa Hill to oversee the movement of the other teams in Task Force Bayonet, decided he had waited long enough. The brigade commander darted toward the hedge, and had moved about ten feet when he heard three shots zip past his head. Snell jumped out of sight, and spotted a U.S. soldier pointing a gun at him. Snell was furious. He grabbed the platoon sergeant, slammed him up against the wall, and began stuttering angrily. "I didn't know whether to chew his ass for shooting at me or missing me," Snell would later say, laughing about the incident. "He should never have missed at the range he fired."

The Balboa and Ancon DENIs were clear by 3:30 A.M. The Balboa station was leveled by a combination of small arms fire, grenades and help from an AC-130 gunship hovering above. In a testament to the precision of U.S. firepower, the YMCA next door, a landmark of the old canal zone, was left untouched. Similarly, the Ancon DENI met little resistance. But later in the morning before daybreak, the death of a U.S. soldier would dampen the spirits of the victorious Task Force Wildcat. Pfc. Kenneth Douglas Scott, a soldier in A Company of the 4th Battalion, 6th Infantry Regiment, was killed by a sniper while manning a roadblock. Nobody saw the shot.

The Ancon DNTT posed the biggest challenge. Seven PDF soldiers inside the building refused to surrender, and the station "was the one place where we had to go in and really root them out one by one," says one soldier who claims one dead PDF. When the assault team entered the station, they found enemy soldiers hiding in the rafters and under desks. The seven soldiers put up a fight, but were quickly eliminated. The Ancon DNTT, the last of Task Force Wildcat's objectives, was declared secure at 7:00 A.M.

By daybreak on 20 December, La Comandancia was far from secure. Task Force Gator had broken through an unexpectedly tough PDF defense and established a perimeter around the complex. The headquarters building had been pounded mercilessly with munitions of all kinds, but still was not in U.S. hands.

At 7:00 A.M., the smoke began to clear over La Comandancia, giving Task Force Gator a chance to regroup and assess how things stood. Medics were busy picking up U.S. soldiers and bagging dead PDF. On Ancon Hill, the Sheridan tankers of the 3d Battalion, 73d Armor, were finally able to see La Comandancia buildings clearly and begin to fire. At Bull 1, S.Sgt. Kevin Hamilton and his gunner, Sgt. Gregory Krumme, spotted a PDF soldier with a RPG inside the western side of La Comandancia. Task force commander Reed gave them permission to fire, and the crew let loose with four 152mm high-explosive rounds into that end of the building.

The rest of the morning was spent in figuring how to clear the headquarters building. Resistance was ebbing, and by early afternoon, the area was fairly quiet, but reports of PDF holdouts still circulated. There might be nearly thirty PDF troops still hiding in the Carcel Modelo prison, and that many in La Comandancia as well. The time had come to see who was left in the gutted headquarters complex.

Reed, on orders from Stiner, decided it was time to clear the compound to eliminate any remaining PDF forces, and end this portion of Just Cause. Reed called on C Company, 3d Battalion, 75th Rangers, which had just completed a mission at Torrijos International Airport. In the original Panama contingency planning, the

Rangers were assigned the La Comandancia mission; now they had it back.

This ad hoc mission was quickly scrambled, the Rangers moving over from the airport east of Panama City. The plan called for the Rangers to clear Carcel Modelo prison, then assault the front of La Comandancia while C Company, 1/508 Infantry (Airborne) would clear the fourteen buildings behind the main building in the walled compound.

The Rangers of C Company, 3/75 Rangers, had just completed an unexpectedly strenuous mission securing the main terminal at Omar Torrijos International Airport when they got word that they had another tough task to complete. The company was heading toward the sanctuary of Howard Air Force Base in two choppers when the mission came. They had been monitoring radio traffic, and there had not been a single positive report from Task Force Gator. They knew the battle for La Comandancia was brutal. The word was that the downtown area was a meat grinder.

"There was a helicopter that was shot down. There were two tracks blown up. It sounded like a madhouse," says Ranger company commander Capt. Al Dochnal. "I told the company what was going on, and a lot of rumors started flowing. That's when I really felt we were going to lose a lot of people. The whole unit got real quiet, real depressed. The troops started to get nervous."

While the Rangers and the men of the 1/508 prepared for the assault, a last intensive barrage was to hit the central headquarters building. On Ancon Hill, engineers received permission to begin clearing trees for the three firing positions for the tanks. The Sheridans engaged the La Comandancia building just before 3:00 P.M., firing ten 152mm rounds into it. To the tank crews, it appeared the rounds caused extensive damage to the ten-inch thick reinforced-concrete walls. A round hitting the building would have a devastating effect on anyone inside, blasting through the wall, causing shrapnel to disperse like cluster bombs in a confined area.

The second phase of the clearing plan called for two AH-64 Apache attack helicopters to fire laser-guided Hellfire missiles and 2.75-inch rockets into La Comandancia. But the choppers were late. The Rangers and 1/508, frustrated over the delay, complained that the momentum was being lost. To ward off PDF snipers, one of the LAVs on Ancon Hill fired more than one hundred 25mm rounds into the windows of La Comandancia. Despite the night long bombardment, PDF were roaming the halls of La Comandancia.

The Apaches arrived at 3:45, hovering over the bay about two miles away from La Comandancia. The two attack helicopters launched Hellfire missiles and 2.75-inch rockets at the building's rear. At least one Hellfire missile scorched the second floor of the concrete building. But two 2.75-inch rockets missed their targets, slamming into nearby buildings and starting fires. The effect of one stray rocket stripped the skin off the back of one of the soldiers of the mechanized infantry.

Sgt. Manuel Campos, the communications specialist in D Company, and fluent in Spanish, was escorting a PDF prisoner who had emerged from La Comandancia back to the company command post. As Campos approached the soldier, he heard an explosion behind him. Campos grabbed the PDF prisoner, and dragged him to the ground underneath him. A 2.75-inch rocket fired by the Apache had gone astray, and darted straight into the side of a building over the D Company position. Shrapnel from the explosion tore at Campos's back; the PDF soldier was unhurt. Apache pilots say they had spotted a PDF V-300 armored car moving behind La Comandancia.

C Company, 1/508, was finally going to complete the mission it was assigned. The airborne unit had waited patiently throughout the night for the mechanized troops to cordon off the area. Flynn had moved the troops back to a position underneath one of the high-rise apartment buildings, only to watch the El Chorrillo barrio burn to the ground. Looters broke into stores that survived the blaze, stealing televisions, liquor, food, and whatever goods they could get their hands on. One group of thieves smashed the window of a store no more than thirty yards away from the U.S. soldiers, running off with cases of beer.

The airborne unit knew their plan well. Once the Apache had completed its firing sequence, the unit would breach a spot on the wall with a violent blast. The wall already had a gaping hole, but another breach was made for the psychological effect. Once inside, the platoons would split up and start the tedious process of clearing each building. Clearing the rooms was made particularly difficult by the principle of minimum casualties. A soldier could not turn a corner and indiscrimately fire an M16 round.

"We had to see the whites of their eyes," one infantry sergeant says.

The Rangers, caught off guard by the assignment, drew up a plan as they ran down Avenue A toward La Comandancia. Not knowing what to expect, the Rangers grabbed grenades, LAWs, and other weapons for a large-scale urban fight. The Rangers were not going to take any chances. In the earlier assault into the Torrijos terminal, C Company, 3/75 Rangers, went in with "weapons tight," meaning a soldier could not fire unless fired upon. In the assault on La Comandancia, the Rangers would go in with "weapons free."

The map detailing the Ranger assault was drawn as the company was running toward Carcel Modelo prison. Dochnal instructed his 1st Platoon to clear the prison while the 2d and 3d Platoons would hook around the block to establish a position from which they would launch into La Comandancia.

The 1st Platoon went in the front door of the prison, and one soldier thought he saw a person run up the stairs to the top floor. A squad chased the suspected PDF, but found nothing but dead bodies. The cell doors were still locked. One squad of the 1st Platoon remained on the roof of the prison to serve as a scout and sniper position for the 2d and 3d Platoons preparing to take down La Comandancia.

The Rangers blew the back door off the gymnasium across the street from La Comandancia. From a small porch in the front of the gym, one squad provided fire support with grenade launchers while one Ranger ran across the street, slid open the gate, and blew the two glass doors off their hinges with an explosive charge.

The Rangers then poured into La Comandancia. The company's 2d Platoon was first in, moving to the left and rear of the building. The 3d Platoon went right. A squad was put on each floor, and the squads began methodically clearing the building.

At the back door of La Comandancia were a number of rifles leaning up against the wall, a sure sign that most PDF soldiers who had been in the building had left. Dochnal noted that the damage to the building was minimal despite the repeated blasts from the Spectres, Sheridans, and Apaches. "The PDF could have had a company in there, and they would not have been hurt," he says. There was some damage to the top floor of the building, but the bottom floor remained intact.

The airborne troops of 1/508 Infantry would take no chances in entering the PDF compound. The company's 2d Platoon led the way, blasting their way in with 90mm recoilless rifles, grenade launchers, and hand grenades. With 2d Platoon guarding the breach, the 1st Platoon moved into the right. They were followed closely by 3d Platoon, which started to seize buildings to the left, and then finally the rest of 1st Platoon. After the rear of the complex was secure, they were to relieve the Rangers clearing Building 1.

The clearing went essentially as planned. Although there were reports of some sniper fire from apartment buildings outside the compound, the company did not find any living PDF soldiers. Instead, the challenge became broken glass and fire. In one instance, a fire had enveloped the arms room of the elite 7th PDF Infantry Company. The room was stacked with weapons and ammunition. In another storage building near the PDF motorpool, a fire had started on the second floor and was causing metal to melt onto propane tanks below. The infantry worked its way rapidly through the buildings.

By early evening, the Rangers had cleared Carcel Modelo and La Comandancia, but were still under orders to clear the PDF intelligence headquarters across the street from La Comandancia. Capt. Flynn reported to Reed that his units had just one more building to clear, but because he had moved so quickly, Flynn was still not confident that each building had been swept clean. He wanted to conduct a thorough search of all fourteen buildings. But Reed responded that he needed to free up the Rangers to move on to the intelligence headquarters.

As he made his way to Reed's command track to negotiate the relief-in-place, Flynn instructed his unit to continue clearing. He was not pleased, and intentionally delayed to give his company time to conduct a sufficient clearing. Then, as he and a Ranger leader walked around the corner to begin an inspection of the area, three shots from an M16 rifle rang from behind them. Flynn needed no cue.

"Is it clear, or is it not clear?" Flynn asked the Ranger commander in disbelief.

"It's clear."

"Yeah, right."

Pfc. Patrick Kubik was on guard inside the Comandancia complex. From the rear of the central courtyard, a naked man wielding a .38 caliber pistol came running out of one of the buildings, heading straight for a Ranger security position. The two Rangers manning the position had their backs turned.

Kubik, standing guard twenty-five meters away, spotted the man when he was no more than five feet from the position. He raised his rifle, and instantaneously fired three shots into the man's chest and neck.

With the death of the naked madman, Noriega's headquarters was secure.

9

On Common Ground

Captain Bill Reagan, commander of A Company, 1st Battalion, 508th Infantry (Airborne), was happy to be assigned to Panama. The weather is warm almost year round, and the living conditions luxurious compared with some Army installations in the United States.

One of the advantages is that the weather is nearly perfect for golf, a sport Bill Reagan had come to love. The Fort Amador "Campo de Golf," an eighteen-hole course, sprawls across a tiny peninsula that juts out into the Pacific at the southern end of the Panama Canal. At first glance, Fort Amador, a military installation shared by American and Panamanian soldiers, seems more like a country club than a military post. An officers' club sits on the southern end of the peninsula, with a movie theater nearby. The officers' club is known informally as the "19th Hole," where American soldiers gossip over drinks after a round on the links. The fairways and greens of the tenth and eighteenth holes divide the U.S. and Panamanian sides of Fort Amador.

Despite rising tensions between the U.S. Southern Command and Noriega throughout 1989, Reagan and his partners, sometimes his Panamanian friends, found time to play, in keeping with his routine of at least weekly golf at Fort Amador. Yet when playing, Reagan and his teammates could not help but keep an eye on the PDF across the greens. Reagan knew from press reports that Panama had become a thorn in the side of the Bush administration. As a company commander, Reagan was not briefed in detail on contingency planning, but he could tell that the planners were up to something. He and his golf buddies could count the comings and goings of recruits and senior Panamanian officers. It was never difficult to record the movement of a Soviet-made ZPU-4 air defense gun or an American-built V-300 light assault vehicle.

Sometimes the need to gather intelligence became more important than the game itself. Reagan would drive the ball away from the hole, at the risk of scoring a double bogey. But once on the far side of the fairway, he would bend down to pick up his ball, and snap a photograph. When he hit the ball astray, Reagan often asked his wife, "Babs," to hit hers in the same direction. She objected, often furiously. He could not tell her what his purpose was. But the portfolio he developed playing golf would come in handy as his battalion planned to wrest Fort Amador from the PDF.

On 16 December, Bill Reagan scored an 84. Four days later, he was playing an entirely different game at Fort Amador, a game for which he considers himself far more talented. Bill Reagan led his company in an air assault to seize Fort Amador and eliminate the 5th Company of the PDF, a rifle unit.

In the early morning of 20 December, A Company jumped from packed UH-60 Black Hawk helicopters onto the eighth fairway. From there, Reagan's company, with B Company of the 1st Battalion, 508th Airborne Infantry, would systematically surround Fort Amador, forming a cordon that could both fend off a PDF assault and slash with devastating force into the PDF side of the installation.

As the airborne unit descended on Fort Amador at H-hour, 1:00 A.M., the installation seemed fairly quiet. But across Panama Bay, fire engulfed the PDF headquarters and the surrounding downtown area. The sound of automatic weapons fire jumped across the water.

U.S. AC-130 Spectre gunships were visible hovering above La Comandancia, pumping cannon and machine-gun fire into Noriega's walled compound.

The gunfire, which started around 12:30, did not at first scare Sharon Gragg, who lived on Amador between fairways, with a clear view of the bay. Watching the Comandancia, which was "just as bright as day," she thought another coup attempt was in progress. Then she saw the Black Hawks moving toward her, so close that she could see the faces of the soldiers inside. After an evacuation exercise the previous summer, Gragg thought the helicopters were coming to remove families from Fort Amador. Others had the same impression; one soldier's wife immediately went to get her bags.

Gragg, who was alone in the house, was upstairs looking for a place to hide in case the situation got more dangerous, when she heard a loud pounding on the front door. "I thought, 'Oh my God, what is happening.'" A soldier was at her door; he warned her to remain inside, lock the doors, lie low, and stay away from the doors and windows.

Her house, one of a row of houses on stilts that bisects the golf course, was within range of PDF guns positioned to fire across the greens. A mortar platoon was sent to instruct the families in those houses to stay low in their homes, away from the side of the house facing the PDF firing positions.

The soldier's message came as a shock to Gragg, who had rarely, if ever, felt afraid in Panama. "He told me it was the real thing, to get behind one wall or two, the safest place I could find." She hid in a closet, taking a portable phone with her. "I was certain I was going to die," she says.

Tracer fire appeared to be spilling over to Fort Amador and into the landing zone. The Black Hawk pilots screamed "Hot LZ! Hot LZ!" They let the skids touch the ground, the infantry disembarked, and the choppers were gone.

A and B Companies rolled out and found themselves in the middle of a war. Looking in awe across the bay, they realized Operation Just Cause had begun, and it had started early. The 1/508 Infantry had to secure Fort Amador, and fast.

Fort Amador was a unique objective: a battleground in the very backyard of U.S. troops. Some soldiers had played volleyball on the lawns of senior SOUTHCOM commanders on the post. Where a volleyball net stood days earlier, an M113 armored personnel carrier or a 105mm artillery cannon now stood, both set to fire into the PDF barracks across the golf course.

The advantage of the familiarity was a comfort to troops in the 1st Battalion. Many deaths in combat result from being disoriented, but the infantrymen were able to avoid that problem. "Somebody could say Building 20, and you didn't have to look down at your map and say, 'Where is Building 20?'" Reagan says. "You knew where it was, even if you didn't play golf here."

The irony was that some troops had to remind themselves of the danger in walking down a street a soldier had marched down countless times. Some troops lost their edge. Then there was the added frustration, particularly for Reagan, of destroying a favorite golf course with the tracked vehicles and gunfire. "Bill's biggest mission was not to fuck up the golf course," says Maj. Robert Pote, the battalion executive officer.

The enemy was no more than a hundred yards away: the length of a football field. That may seem like an advantage to a military tactician, particularly when the friendly side has superior weaponry. But at Fort Amador, it proved a tactical challenge. Facing the PDF barracks was a row of buildings on stilts, the homes of top Army commanders such as Cisneros, USARSO commander. The homes lined a street that cuts the golf course in half. The enemy could not be allowed to take American soldiers or dependents hostage. But they also had to be prevented from leaving Fort Amador to reinforce PDF units defending La Comandancia.

Persistent rumors of PDF plans to take hostages were taken seriously. Later, in the aftermath of Just Cause, SOUTHCOM intelligence experts discovered PDF planning documents, labeled "Genesis" and "Exodus," that outlined step-by-step efforts to kidnap U.S. citizens and bring them into the country's interior if the United States invaded Panama. From the jungle, the remaining PDF would conduct guerrilla warfare to slowly grind away at the morale of U.S. soldiers and public opinion in the United States.

Immediately following the October coup attempt, Capt. Moisés Cortizo, commander of the PDF's 5th Company, had ordered his soldiers to establish two firing positions on either flank of the PDF barracks on Fort Amador. The bunkers, shaped in a triangle, contained Mauser rifles and .50 caliber machine guns. The guns were trained directly on select American houses.

Fort Amador was of strategic value to the PDF, adding to its priority among twenty-seven targets that U.S. forces would strike simultaneously on 20 December. The installation was the closest PDF barracks to La Comandancia, which the 1st Battalion's own C Company would take part in assaulting. During the coup attempt, some members of the 5th Company, learning of Major Giroldi's maneuver, jumped to Noriega's rescue. Cortizo, a notorious coward, never left Fort Amador to aid Noriega, even though he was the highest-ranking PDF officer within range of the headquarters. Once he discovered the coup attempt was over in less than ten minutes, Cortizo called Noriega and asked if he required help. Some 5th Company personnel managed to make their way to La Comandancia, a drive of about five minutes, to celebrate the failure of the attempted overthrow.

Amador also provided a link to the training grounds of Noriega's special operations forces, known by their Spanish acronym UESAT. The forces train on four islands—Flamenco, Perico, Naos, and Culebra—connected to the peninsula by a thin causeway and guarded carefully by the PDF. The UESAT were proclaimed the best-trained of the PDF and were loyal to Noriega, some serving as the dictator's personal guards. Immediately following the coup attempt, the UESAT placed minefields all over the islands, effectively isolating themselves from a potential U.S. attack.

Thus, battalion commander Lt. Col. Billy Ray Fitzgerald not only had to ensure that the PDF did not take hostages, he had to prevent them from reinforcing positions elsewhere.

Because of the presence of American families and a U.S. naval command and Fort Amador's proximity to La Comandancia, the installation always was considered an objective to be seized at H-hour. The defensive centerpiece of the Blue Spoon plan, it remained a constant in contingency preparations from early 1988 to December 1989. The PDF's 5th Company, along with some Panamanian naval infantry troops on Fort Amador, had to be eliminated rapidly and decisively. The element of surprise would be crucial, as would the ability to hit hard and with precision.

On 16 December, Snell ordered two platoons to assume positions on Fort Amador. These forces were moved in for two reasons. Officially, it was a show of force in response to the fatal shooting of Marine 1st Lt. Robert Paz. The true reason was to ensure the safety of the Americans at Fort Amador. As tensions mounted after the Paz killing, concerns about possible PDF hostage-taking began to mount. As a precautionary measure, the 29th Military Intelligence Battalion was instructed to establish three observation and listening posts in and around Fort Amador. Of particular importance were messages from La Comandancia to Cortizo, holed up in the 5th Company headquarters.

Fortunately, the PDF kept to their side of Amador, failing from

16 December to the eve of Just Cause to cross the golf course or man the bunkers.

The battalion assault force was called Task Force Red Devil, a component of Task Force Bayonet. Its plan was simple. Elements of the battalion, augmented by a military police unit and D Battery of the 320th Field Artillery, would secure the entire area around U.S. housing, including the U.S. Navy sector, and neutralize the 5th PDF Company before its members could escape from their barracks. Other troops would block the entrance to the causeway to prevent the UESAT from moving to or from the islands.

The main Red Devil assault force would consist of A and B Companies, which would fly in by helicopter from Howard Air Force Base, dismount on the U.S. side, and quickly ring the peninsula. Reagan's A Company would secure the north end of the PDF compound. B Company, led by Capt. Bob Zebrowski, would seize the southern end. The 320th Field Artillery would provide two towed 105mm howitzers that could be used to coax the PDF company into surrendering or, if it came to it, to blast them out of their barracks.

Other elements would support the assault. The battalion's headquarters company, commanded by Capt. John Hort, would provide snipers, scouts, and antitank missile crews. Hort controlled three specific elements. One was a makeshift combination pulled together by the battalion, consisting of the scout platoon and a platoon equipped with TOW antitank missiles, the result being two scout/antitank platoons. One would guard the causeway, while the other would block the front gate to Fort Amador.

The second element, the headquarters mortar platoon, would also be given an unorthodox assignment: to inform the Americans on post to stay home. The use of indirect fire would be strictly limited under the rules of engagement, which would allow the firing of howitzers directly on a target only with authorization from high-ranking commanders. Those Americans who needed to be evacuated were instructed to flash their house lights, and the mortar platoon would rescue them. Finally, Hort commanded a scout detachment of eight M113s, moved into position on 16 December and kept hidden among the golf carts.

All in all, the battalion was well prepared for the assault. In Sand Flea exercises conducted two or three times a month, the airborne unit had landed by helicopter at the designated landing zones and rehearsed the movement to their objectives. By spending an increasing amount of time on Fort Amador, the battalion was able to answer most of its questions about the mission, such as: How long does it take a fully loaded helicopter to fly from Howard Air Force Base to Fort Amador? How much light is on the peninsula at night? How much illumination do street lights shed on the American houses?

The exercises, along with three U.S. observation posts across the peninsula, also gave U.S. troops good intelligence on the Panamanian soldiers and commanders. Capt. Pedro Nuñez, the battalion intelligence officer, garnered an enormous amount of knowledge about the enemy. From the number of PDF troops in the mess hall to the number of new recruits—obvious from the length of their hair—Nuñez learned the little ways of the PDF 5th Company. He could even judge the unit's morale from how older PDF soldiers and NCOs treated the recruits, and by observing how hard-nosed the PDF commanders were and which officers were in it just for the money.

The central target in the assault would be the 5th Company headquarters, designated on Fort Amador maps as Building 4 in the row of buildings, numbered one through nine, that faced the golf course. The headquarters, situated in the center of the row, resembled a small-town police station inside and out, except for a luxurious office that Noriega frequented. Next door was the mess hall. Both buildings would be targets for demonstration fires meant to discourage PDF resistance and encourage surrender; only then would Zebrowski's B Company begin to clear each building. The idea was to avoid the grim business of fighting in close quarters and to limit casualties on both sides.

The mess hall, Building 5, was agreed on as the obvious choice for the initial demonstration of firepower, as it was unlikely there would be many PDF troops eating there at 1:00 A.M. If that didn't do the trick, the headquarters would be next; that was where the enemy lived.

By noon on 19 December, Fitzgerald received permission to begin briefing his company commanders. All had heard of the Paz killing, and none was surprised at the news. The men, their families and friends had lived in fear of such extremes by the PDF.

As the briefing began, Cisneros strode into the room, an unexpected guest. Cisneros wanted to brief this part of Just Cause himself. He made a point of talking to the battalion's leaders to stress the intent of the operation as Thurman had outlined. It was not the goal of the United States to create carnage and death, he told them. Rather, one of the principles of Just Cause would be to eliminate the PDF with minimum casualties on both sides. Such restraint would exact all the courage and patience that U.S. soldiers could muster. Cisneros then added a personal touch: it was far more important for the United States to lose no soldiers than to cause casualties among the enemy. Cisneros's speech had a galvanizing effect on the officers, focusing their minds on the mission. Hort says he realized "that the word was God, and now it is time to go."

Quickly, the mission was disseminated throughout the battalion. Platoon leaders were informed of the details at 6:00 that evening, and by 9:00 P.M., four hours before H-hour, each soldier in the battalion had been made aware of his responsibility. While they prepared for combat, Fitzgerald and his company commanders made last-minute changes to the plan, making sure of each second and each step; despite the rehearsals and the planning, many things in the tightly choreographed plan could go wrong. Nuñez and his staff tried to provide quick intelligence updates on events at Fort Amador from on-the-spot reports and the observation posts. As Fitzgerald left the battalion command post to go to Fort Amador at 9:30 P.M., Nuñez handed him a slip of paper with his final estimate of enemy strength: 532 PDF soldiers in and around Fort Amador.

Hort already was at Amador, busily readying those troops already in position for the 1:00 A.M. H-hour. At 9:00 P.M., everything was going like clockwork. Hort still had four hours before A and B companies would touch down behind him. His command post was situated between two civilian homes on the U.S. side of the peninsula.

Despite their unfamiliarity with the plan, the scout/attack platoon leaders knew exactly where to establish roadblocks. Their mixed units had become expert at creating effective blockades by using vehicles, concertina wire, and spiked mats to puncture the tires of wheeled vehicles.

The leader of the mechanized platoon had a Top Secret clearance, so he knew the plan. Earlier that morning, Hort and the platoon leader slowly walked the Fort Amador area, picking four positions that would give the M113s a clear field of fire on Building 4 and the PDF housing row. The boxy beasts were oiled up and ready to move, but remained concealed with the golf carts, about a mile from Hort's command post.

Just one problem remained: ammunition. Hort's troops were responsible for transporting the ammo, which included TOW anti-tank missiles for the scout platoons, but the couriers never got a detailed briefing; Hort was busy preparing for the battle at Fort Amador. The concern was the size of the operation; it was too much ammo to hide and it was too late to try to sneak it in piecemeal. There was a good chance PDF guards would notice the movement. At 9:00 P.M., trucks began pouring into Fort Amador from Fort Kobbe, each carrying boxes of machine-gun rounds, grenades, and missiles. Despite the fact that some crates were uncovered as the trucks drove into Fort Amador, the supply line appeared to pass unnoticed. When the trucks arrived, troops quickly unloaded the ammunition. Even so, the last of the TOW missiles did not arrive until 11:30. Hort began to worry. H-hour was getting close.

It fell upon the troops earlier than they expected. At 12:15 A.M., Hort was warned by radio that the invasion might start early. Seconds later, he thought he heard shots coming from the direction of Balboa Harbor, just outside the Amador grounds. Fitzgerald called Hort and told him to be ready to move on a moment's notice.

The first job would fall to the mortar platoon. Not to fire an initial barrage, but rather to alert and evacuate American families living on Fort Amador. Hort's men were also to block Amador's front gate to prevent additional PDF from entering the compound. Hort screamed at his scout platoons, who had just loaded their TOW missiles onto jeeps, to get ready to move to their objectives. Then came the final call on the radio. Hort knew H-hour was going out the window. The first scout platoon, dubbed Team Recon, was on the way to Fort Amador's front gate.

As commander of Task Force Bayonet, Mike Snell was responsible for more than three thousand soldiers, including the 1st Battalion, 508th Airborne Infantry. His three subordinate task forces would attack separate objectives. Snell positioned himself on Sosa Hill, near the Balboa area. From there, he could direct the movements of the units, maintain radio contact with all three task force commanders and, in some cases, see events with his own eyes.

At 12:27 A.M., he spotted a white bus behind the PDF headquarters at Fort Amador, loading or unloading what appeared to be armed PDF soldiers. Apparently, tactical surprise was gone. At best, Cortizo, the PDF company commander, recognized the pending U.S. attack, and was bringing in additional troops to defend Fort Amador. Worse, Snell worried, was that the bus was taking on troops to counterattack the U.S. forces preparing to assault La Comandancia. By now, those troops would be rolling toward the 4th of July Avenue, which runs perpendicular to the PDF stronghold. Some of them would be within striking distance of the PDF at Amador. Neither Snell nor Fitzgerald was willing to take a chance; these guys had to be stopped. Snell called Fitzgerald, then Fitzgerald called Hort. Shut the Amador gate immediately, the battalion commander ordered.

The PDF bus started to move.

At the gate, two American MPs were having trouble subduing the two PDF guards stationed there. One of the MPs was battling one of the guards in an attempt to arrest him. The two PDF guards surrendered only after the scout platoon pulled up at 12:32 A.M., weapons bristling. The guards were bound with tape, and the MPs ordered them to lie on the grass embankment alongside the guardhouse. The scouts began to build their roadblock, laying out barbed wire.

Seconds later, the platoon leader looked up and saw bright headlights heading directly toward his position at high speed. It was the PDF bus. In the darkness, he could see rounds flying out and hear the familiar crack of an AK-47 rifle. Fortunately, the scout platoon had dropped off six soldiers on the way to the front gate. One sniper position was set up at a small guardhouse where the road to the PDF compound veers left toward the Amador entrance. A second position, manned by four snipers, was placed along the road about two hundred yards from the front gate.

The first sniper saw the bus, but because the PDF did not shoot first, he let it go by. But as the bus turned toward the gate, the second set of snipers began to fire. The PDF spotted the position and returned a volley, firing high because the bus windows were not rolled down completely. The Panamanians were hanging their weapons out, firing without looking. The Americans continued to shoot at the bus, which was barreling toward the front gate at sixty miles an hour.

The scout team, hastily trying to finish the roadblock, jumped behind their jeeps and began to fire at the bus as it flew toward the gate. When the bus was barely twelve yards away, Sgt. Stefan Estes fired a shot that hit the driver in the head. The bus lurched to the right, missing the vehicles but hitting a fire hydrant just outside the gate. The bus beheaded the hydrant, causing a fountain of water to explode into the sky. The bus, swerving, rolled another three hundred yards down the road and slammed into a tree. There it stopped.

The scouts could not see the bus, even with night vision goggles, but guessed by the sound of its wheels that it was out of action. An attempt to locate the bus with thermal sights in the TOW missile launchers also was unsuccessful.

Hort was still worried about the bus. He didn't want a big contingent of PDF running around who knows where. He ordered up two Improved TOW Vehicles from Fort Amador toward the Bridge of the Americas. The ITVs would establish a blocking position on the exit ramp to the bridge to prevent the departure of residents in houses along the road to Amador. The homes, once belonging to the Panama Canal Commission, were home to many 5th Company officers serving under Cortizo. Hort's hunch was right: as the ITVs rolled down the road, they began to receive fire from that area.

Soon other PDF tried to run the gauntlet at Amador. Just one minute after the ITVs reached the Bridge of the Americas, a Toyota Corolla came screaming toward the gate from the PDF side, traveling even faster than the bus. This time, the second sniper position hit the car with a full volley. The driver of the sedan was hit and the car, carrying six PDF soldiers, began to career back and forth along the road.

In the minutes since the bus broke through the gate, the scouts had bolstered their roadblock, parking the jeeps in the middle of the road and setting out concertina wire and spikes. The car crashed into a parked Army truck at about forty miles per hour, killing the Panamanian driver instantly. The crash severed one of the passenger's legs, but he was alive.

Although trapped, the Panamanians would not give up. Two PDF soldiers started firing their AK-47s at anything that moved. Two U.S. soldiers who had been crouched inside a vehicle jumped up and fired a burst into the car. The firing inside came to a halt. The shots killed one Panamanian and wounded two others, and the remaining PDF then threw all their weapons from the car. The scout platoon leader yelled at them to get out. The Panamanian with the severed leg tried to get out of the car, but he could not move well and fell forward. An American soldier, thinking he was reaching for his AK-47, pumped three rounds into his back, killing him on the spot.

Back at Howard Air Force Base, A and B Companies were beginning to squeeze into the fourteen Black Hawk helicopters that would ferry them to Fort Amador for their air assault on the main PDF compound. The sound of the rotors deafened the troops as 7th Infantry Division pilots revved up the engines. It would be a short flight from Howard to Fort Amador, but the pilots could not risk taking fire. Each chopper would be packed with troops; if a stray round sneaked past the door, it could ricochet around the cabin, tearing up anyone in its path.

At 12:25 A.M., A and B Companies began loading the helicopters, packing every inch of cargo space. Up to seventeen soldiers jammed each aircraft, which usually carry eleven. Soldiers were crammed into the corners, some with AT-4 and LAW rockets across their laps. They sat, cramped, for more than twenty minutes before the takeoff notice was given. When they landed at Fort Amador, some had to be dragged from the choppers because the crowding had cut off the circulation to their legs.

Fitzgerald, on the Amador grounds, tried to piece together what had happened at the front gate. Snell, still on Sosa Hill, and Cisneros, also at Amador, repeatedly asked for updates. Fitzgerald reported the highlights. Two PDF vehicles had tried to run the gate, but were stopped. Some enemy soldiers may have escaped from the bus, but the sedan had been halted at the gate. Most importantly, there were no American casualties.

But Fitzgerald was concerned. It was still about thirty minutes before H-hour, but the fighting had already begun. He had only four platoons on the Amador grounds, about one hundred men, who might have to go up against more than five hundred PDF soldiers.

Interior of La Comandancia courtyard. Note charred riot control trucks of PDF "Doberman" forces, left, and severed tail rotor of special operations AH-6 "Little Bird" helicopter, which crashed during the night of 20 December, right. Photo by Doug Pensinger.

Front gate of La Comandancia, 4:30 P.M., 20 December, after C Company, 3d Battalion, 75th Ranger Regiment, entered building. Noriega's office is on first floor, left corner. Photo courtesy 75th Ranger Regiment.

Rangers of 2d Platoon, C Company, 3d Battalion, 75th Ranger Regiment, proclaim La Comandancia secure at 5:00 P.M., 20 December. Noriega's office to right rear. Photo courtesy 75th Ranger Regiment.

Inside of hangar where Noriega's Learjet was parked at Punta Paitilla airport shows results of disabling attack. Photo by Margaret Roth.

U.S. soldier stands guard outside Noriega's main residence in Panama City. Photo by Doug Pensinger.

Balboa DENI station after assault by U.S. forces. Station was one of major obstacles to be cleared during assaults near La Comandancia. Photo by Doug Pensinger.

Gutted PDF barracks at Fort Amador. Note large hole in upper right made by 105mm howitzer round. Photo by Doug Pensinger.

Omar Torrijos's mausoleum, foreground, was deliberately spared by U.S. infantrymen who assaulted Fort Amador. PDF barracks in rear. Photo by Margaret Roth.

Exterior of Eastern Airlines terminal at Torrijos International Airport shows damage from Ranger assault on 20 December. Photo courtesy 75th Ranger Regiment.

Interior of airport men's room destroyed during savage fight between members of 3d Platoon, C Company, 3d Battalion, 75th Ranger Regiment, and PDF holdouts at Torrijos airport. Damage caused by grenades. Photo courtesy 75th Ranger Regiment.

Passengers of Brazilian airliner caught in assault on Torrijos International Airport, after rescue by U.S. forces; in foreground, PDF prisoners of war. Flight was late arriving 20 December, and PDF at airport mingled among passengers to hide from assaulting Rangers. Photo courtesy 75th Ranger Regiment.

Tight confines of prison yard at Renacer were biggest challenge in air assault to free the prisoners. Photo courtesy 7th Infantry Division.

Aerial view of PDF naval infantry complex at Coco Solo shows extensive damage from infantry assault, while American houses across the grounds were spared. Photo courtesy 7th Infantry Division.

Sgt. Joseph Legaspi, fire team leader in 3d squad, 2d Platoon, C Company, 4th Battalion, 17th Infantry Regiment. Legaspi's company conducted assault on PDF naval infantry at Coco Solo. Photo courtesy 7th Infantry Division.

PDF noncommissioned officer academy at Rio Hato. Rio Hato complex was a warren of similar low buildings. Photo courtesy 75th Ranger Regiment.

Member of 75th Ranger Regiment stands outside Noriega's Farallon Beach House near Rio Hato. Photo courtesy 75th Ranger Regiment.

Members of 7th Infantry Division airlanded at Rio Hato, then proceeded to secure the city of David and the western provinces of Panama. Photo by Doug Pensinger.

U.S. soldier stands beside captured PDF V-150 armored car. Noriega's forces had a substantial fleet of these American-made vehicles, some mounting large cannons. Photo courtesy 75th Ranger Regiment.

Example of Noriega's huge arms caches, spread throughout Panama. Photo courtesy 75th Ranger Regiment.

Panamanian President Guillermo Endara, flanked by vice presidents Ricardo Arias Calderón (left) and Guillermo "Billy" Ford (right), meets reporters after he is installed in office by Operation Just Cause. Photo by Doug Pensinger.

U.S. soldier rides streets of Panama City after main engagements of Operation Just Cause ended. Stability operations continued for weeks after the combat. Photo by Doug Pensinger.

Destruction in the El Chorrillo barrio of Panama City, resulting from fires spreading from the attack on La Comandancia, left many poor Panamanians homeless. Photo by Doug Pensinger.

To establish security in Panama, the Endara government chose to reconstitute the PDF as the Panama Public Force. While many PDF leaders were forbidden to join the new security force, many others were allowed into the ranks. The new PPF was equipped by American forces. Photo by Doug Pensinger.

Sign erected by Endara government asks Panamanian people to have patience during the rebuilding of El Chorrillo. Photo by Margaret Roth.

A U.S. soldier consoles a Panamanian whose son was killed in Operation Just Cause. Despite extreme efforts to limit casualties, hundreds of Panamanians died. Photo by Doug Pensinger.

The sound of the firefight at the front gate must certainly have alerted the 5th Company. Hort's headquarters company did not have the firepower to take on a possible PDF attack on the U.S. side. Even Hort's eight M113s still were in their hiding positions.

The key was to speed up the air assault. It was the only way the Amador operation would be guaranteed the firepower it needed. Fitzgerald knew A and B Companies were on the helicopters, preparing to leave. Takeoff time was set at 12:47 A.M., but if he could convince the pilots to leave the tarmac earlier, he might save some American lives. At 12:35, he called Snell, asking that the choppers be given approval to leave early.

Even as he made his request, Fitzgerald could hear the echo of gunfire across downtown Panama City, from Albrook Air Station to La Comandancia. Amador would be exposed for precious minutes. Fitzgerald contacted Reagan on the lead helicopter to pass on his request, but the pilot refused to leave before the planned departure time. The point was moot. Snell had called the Joint Task Force–South command center, and was told H-hour was inviolable.

At last, the first wave of helicopters took off at 12:50 A.M., followed immediately by six choppers carrying A Company. Seconds after lift-off, the troops could see the bonfire that had been La Comandancia as they headed out over the waters of Panama Bay. As the first helicopters banked back toward land, tracers zoomed across the sky to their left and right. Some helicopters were hit by stray rounds from La Comandancia, which burned below a sky turned eerily red. It seemed like a war movie to many in the assault force, which looked on as an AC-130 Spectre gunship pumped round after round into the area. Smaller, lighter AH-6 Little Bird helicopters raced across the roofs of high-rise apartment buildings, searching for and firing on PDF snipers.

Spectres turned to support the Amador assault. The stunning effect of the airplane's 105mm rounds reduced the enemy fire just as the Black Hawks made their approach. As the helicopters flew low to the ground on the approach to the golf course, soldiers could see rounds from the downtown area in front of them. Most had not seen such an intense volume of tracer fire, and were amazed. When someone said there were four rounds between each tracer, the troops grew uneasy. As battalion chaplain Capt. Allen Boatright, with the A Company lift, watched the red and green tracer fire glow in the night, a crew chief sitting next to him asked him to say a prayer. The chaplain turned and replied: "Are you kidding? I haven't stopped praying since we got on board this thing!"

In minutes, the assault force was over the landing zone, the Black Hawk pilots screaming "Hot LZ! Hot LZ!" As the choppers' skids touched the ground, the infantry tumbled out onto the eighth fairway. The choppers left as quickly as they had come, away to other missions.

B Company landed behind the row of U.S. housing. After setting up a security perimeter, the company moved toward the southern end of the peninsula to secure the left flank of the PDF housing. The three platoons moved into their objective near the end of the U.S. housing row that faced them. No PDF were found. A Company landed on higher ground, southeast of B Company's landing zone. Reagan and his company disembarked and moved toward the caddy shack behind the clubhouse.

Immediately following the assault helicopters were three AH-1 Cobra attack helicopters that would escort the troop assault. Closely trailing the Cobras was a lone OH-58C scout chopper flown by Capt. Timothy Jones, commander of B Company of the 7th Infantry Division's 1st Battalion, 123d Aviation Regiment. Jones's copilot was Chief Warrant Officer Andy Porter. The air escorts were to cover the air assault, giving reconnaissance and fire support as the troops landed on the golf course. Once the infantry were safely on the ground, two of the Cobras would leave for other assignments.

Jones, ordering a single Cobra gunship to stay nearby, planned to watch the Amador assault force for thirty minutes. Then both the AH-1 and OH-58 would have to refuel and escort the 82d Airborne as they moved from Tocumen airfield toward other targets. As he watched, Jones was told to pinpoint the location, and if necessary coordinate the destruction, of a suspected PDF air defense site that could threaten not only the Amador operation but the attack on La Comandancia.

The target was a ZPU-4 gun hidden behind the PDF barracks closest to the causeway. Nuñez, the staff intelligence officer of the 1st Battalion, had told the aviators about the air defense gun before the assault. Though it had not been moved or fired in days, Fitzgerald wanted to be sure it was eliminated.

Jones took his chopper down to about forty feet. Masked by the gas station and the Amador movie theater, he and Porter spotted the gun and moved in for a closer look. They also saw a PDF armored car just behind the barracks, but the gun appeared deserted. There was no fire coming from Fort Amador.

But as Jones steered the OH-58 north over the canal, Porter screamed that they were taking fire. Jones tried to spot tracers, but could not see any. Going on Porter's information, he cranked his controls to the left and headed south. As he turned, Jones saw fire everywhere. Rounds ricocheted around the cockpit, destroying the controls. The throttle went limp in Jones' hand. He braced for a crash. The OH-58 turned 180 degrees to the right and slammed into the water.

The chopper was upside down. Though dazed by the crash, Jones struggled to free himself and began frantically to search for Porter under water. Jones couldn't find him. The helicopter sank deep into the canal within seconds.

Jones had to come up for air. Fighting to master his fears, he peered into the darkness. He was alive, but where was he? He was still wearing his life-preserver vest, so he had no problems staying afloat. When he got his bearings, he realized he was about 100 yards from the shore of Fort Amador. In the distance he could see the lights of the officers' club, about 250 yards away. His first thought was to swim north along the canal to the yacht club where he knew the U.S. force was beginning to secure the installation. If he went ashore near the causeway, he could find himself in the middle of a firefight. He started to swim, but after fighting the current for ten minutes, found he had made no progress.

At last, Jones reached the coastline. As he started to crawl up on the rocky shore, he heard voices speaking in Spanish.

Terrified, Jones scuttled back toward the safety of the deep water. What to do? Momentarily, he thought of staying in the middle of the canal all night. Just Cause was supposed to end by daylight. He then would wade to shore, knowing American forces were occupying Amador.

But staying in the water was no guarantee. A PDF sentry could easily spot him in the moonlight. The shoreline was his best chance, worth a second shot.

Jones moved about twenty yards south. Adrenaline pulsed

through his body. Again, somebody yelled in Spanish. Jones knew it was directed at him. He froze.

The scout platoon securing the causeway heard splashing in the water. The paratroopers' instructions were to challenge in Spanish. Maj. Robert Pote, the battalion executive officer, yelled in his best gringo Spanish: "Come here, come here. Put your hands up." There was no response. Pote ordered warning shots fired.

Jones dove back into the water, shedding his life preserver as fast as he could.

Pote was growing impatient, and called for a better Spanish speaker. "Tell that motherfucker we are going to kill him," the major said.

Just then, Jones came up for air. He heard the English—and the speaker had no Spanish accent. Jones decided it was now or never. He stood up in the shallow water.

"Don't shoot, I'm American," he yelled.

"What's the password?"

"Flounder." Jones knew he would never forget that word.

"That's the wrong password."

Jones's jaw went slack. He had just been shot from the sky, he was alive, and he knew the password, but some U.S. soldier was standing there on land, telling him he was wrong. Jones started screaming, yelling any word he could think of.

"Don't shoot me, I'm an American. I was just shot down."

Thirty minutes after his helicopter crashed into the canal, Jones was pulled from the water. He was hurt, but felt no pain. On impact, he had sprained his left wrist and both of his thumbs. He was covered with scrapes and bruises. Pote says the pilot was in shock, but noted how calm he was. Jones was carried to the command post of the 1st Battalion, 508th Airborne Infantry, where he received medical attention and spent the night recuperating.

The helicopter was pulled out of the canal two days later. Andy Porter died not from the gunfire, but from drowning after being knocked unconscious on impact, or from the impact itself when the chopper hit the canal at more than forty knots. Porter was the first and only U.S. casualty of the battle for Fort Amador.

Jones received a Bronze Star for Valor when he returned to Fort Ord in February.

The last task prior to the main assault was to secure three PDF houses on the left side of the Fort Amador causeway and ensure that the UESAT could not leave the islands to reinforce Amador. Fitzgerald assigned the job to a scout platoon, which would fill the dual role of an assaulting and blocking force.

The platoon's first mission was to eliminate two PDF guards at the entrance to the causeway. Just before 1:00 A.M., the scouts entered the guard station; the guard there surrendered before any shots were fired. The other guard was not found until daylight, when he popped out of a culvert and surrendered, surprising a U.S. soldier eating breakfast.

The houses on the causeway were worrisome targets. The first of the houses was known as Noriega's "witch house," where he practiced voodoo. Before it was attacked, the scouts hurled concussion grenades inside. As the scouts entered, they found a candle burning and fresh fish laid out on the floor. The fortified house is said to have contained cocaine, a bucket of blood, voodoo artifacts, and a brewery. The scouts found cigarettes still smoldering in ashtrays, but no Panamanians.

The second house, too, was empty. The third house was the home of a former UESAT commander.

Intelligence officer Nuñez had warned the platoon that the commander's wife and young child still lived in the house. Instead of using grenades, the soldiers kicked in the doors. They found the maid and baby in an upstairs bedroom. The commander's wife had gone to a party for the evening.

With the first hundred yards of the causeway secured, the scout platoon settled back into its blocking position. Clearing the islands of Amador would be more safely done later, in daylight and with more forces.

By 2:15 A.M., the entire 1st Battalion assault force was on the ground and in position.

The plan to seize Fort Amador revolved around a demonstration of overwhelming firepower from 105mm cannons and the .50 caliber machine guns mounted on M113s. Throughout the night, as A and B Companies secured the surrounding areas, the Americans broadcast a Spanish recording telling the PDF to come out of the barracks and surrender. A separate live announcement was delivered to each building. There was a countdown. The PDF had six minutes to lay down their arms and surrender, or they would die.

In most cases, there was no response. In fact, many of the PDF had escaped out the back of the buildings, into an alley. Some hid along the rocky bank of the canal. In one case, four PDF ran out the front of Building 4 and fired on the M113 positions. There was no return fire.

Cisneros gave the order for the demonstration fire to begin. Hort's headquarters contingent, with help from the 320th Field Artillery, was to launch two rounds each at the dining hall and the main barracks. After the dust from the 105mm cannon settled, troops began firing the .50 caliber machine guns, peppering the buildings with holes. Finally, soldiers fired AT-4 rockets and their rifles.

Though the fusillades were brief, they were violent, leaving the two PDF buildings pockmarked with holes. Where the 105mm rounds blew through the stucco walls, the effects inside were devastating, a cone of destruction ripping through the drywall and light paneling of the PDF offices.

The American quarters offered better protection, although it proved unnecessary in most cases because very little fire struck the houses. Their solid construction was more a psychological benefit than a physical necessity.

"At least our walls are foot-thick concrete," thought Sharon Gragg, huddled in a hallway closet of her home, as she heard what sounded like a deadly firefight outside.

The cannon was positioned at a house two doors down from hers. From the explosions of gunfire below her, she thought the PDF was putting up a vicious defense. When she heard U.S. soldiers count down the seconds to induce the PDF to surrender—"Uno. Dos. Tres."—she was terrified, until she called a Spanish-speaking neighbor who told her the voices were American.

"I had no idea that the PDF wasn't firing back. I was too frightened to watch," she says. At one point, only the portable phone, her link with other humans, saved her from panic. Her sons, twenty-year-old Jason and eighteen-year-old Torrey, called her from friends' houses, where they had gone to spend the night in a rare break from curfew. The boys and their mother exchanged notes about the progress of the war from their different vantage points on and off Fort Amador.

Gragg could not call anyone outside of the post. The U.S. military had cut the phone lines to isolate the enemy. But she could receive calls. Every fifteen or twenty minutes, a friend would call from within the Canal Zone, using the Panama Canal Commission phone system. Her husband also called, but she didn't know where from. Col. Larry Gragg had disappeared earlier to his job as commander of the military community in Panama, with the mysterious words, "I have a lot of stuff to do. I may not be back."

For the most part, U.S. soldiers accomplished their aim not to damage American houses. One house near Gragg's received a large bullet hole, though. Another house received such violent vibrations from the cannon fire that the windows shattered, one after another. The occupants, including four children, spent the night on the floor beneath mattresses, listening to glass bursting around and on top of them.

During the firing, American troops had only one clear rule to follow: Do not hit Torrijos's tomb. The mausoleum, with a bronze statue of the revered populist general, sat in front of the main PDF barracks. It emerged from the battle with one small nick, but otherwise it was unscathed. "We did walk over it," one officer says.

The impact of the demonstration fire was awesome, and the results swift as the gunners methodically worked their way down the row of buildings. PDF troops began filing from the rear of the buildings into the alley, some walking straight to the prisoner-of-war compound established near the officers' club. Others, following orders from a PDF naval infantry officer, climbed down the rocky canal embankment.

The evacuation of the buildings fit neatly with the U.S. plan. As Hort wrapped up the last demonstration fire at about 6:00 A.M., Zebrowski's B Company moved into position to begin clearing each building. Zebrowski and his team would start with Building 9, at one end of the row, and work their way down. Before the assault, Hort ordered 105mm cannon, .50 cal machine-gun, and AT-4 fire on Building 9, in case any PDF still were inside. As B Company cleared the first structure, Headquarters Company fired on Building

8. When Building 8 was cleared, fire would be directed at 7, and so on. It would be like squeezing toothpaste out of a tube.

Daylight was coming. That made the battalion leaders happy. Zebrowski's men were equipped with night vision goggles, but clearing buildings is a chore they preferred to tackle in daylight.

Clearing the installation, building by building, was to be the last step in securing Fort Amador, but potentially the most dangerous aspect of the entire operation. B Company would be walking into unfamiliar buildings that were a warren of small offices, tight passages and stairways. Behind every door and corner, an enemy soldier might be prepared to launch an ambush.

Building 9 was shaking when B Company moved in just after 6:00 A.M. Hort's heavy weapons had rocked the structure with hundreds of rounds. Men lined up on either side of the front entrance; one threw some concussion grenades inside, and the troops scurried in afterward. The decision to use stun grenades was typical of the rules of engagement designed to limit Panamanian casualties, but the choice made American troops tense. They preferred the deadlier fragmentation grenades, feeling that if they were the ones who had to go in, they would rather have the enemy dead than surprised. It was a tricky principle: shock the enemy, and take him down before he could react, but hope not to kill too many. Before each building assault, a soldier with a hand-held megaphone sent the remaining PDF a message: "Give up. It is futile to resist."

As the infantrymen of B Company worked down the line, clearing Buildings 9, 8, and 7, the job grew easier. The remaining PDF put up no armed resistance. They fled the buildings with their arms in the air before the assault team even entered. In the first entry, the company's 1st Platoon caught one unarmed soldier trying to escape. In Buildings 8 and 7, the platoon entered through the front door with no resistance. It still took hours, however, to secure all the rooms in all the buildings.

The combination of growing success, dwindling resistance and sheer exhaustion took its toll. The assault teams were getting too comfortable. The pace of the operation was both painstakingly slow and more than the undermanned battalion could keep up with. Working through the buildings was slogging work, but prisoners of war were coming out in a flood, arriving at the makeshift POW compound faster than they could be processed.

The 1st Platoon of B Company had given way to 3d Platoon, which was clearing Building 4, the headquarters and most important of the PDF structures. Snell, having come down from Sosa Hill, was with Fitzgerald behind Building 8, examining an abandoned V-300, when an antitank round zipped over their heads. Two PDF soldiers had peeped around the corner from the vicinity of the gymnasium, armed with a rocket launcher. The two American officers saw the rocket coming. It flew over Snell's vehicle and blew up about fifty yards behind the two men.

Fort Amador was far from secure; there was more toothpaste left in the tube.

"Things were pretty calm. And then all of a sudden they started in all over again," says Sharon Gragg. Her son, Jason, had come home by that time and was watching the battle from a window of their house, trying to catch the tail end of the action he had missed. His mother entreated him to get away from the windows.

Panamanian holdouts still held the last buildings in the line. As they walked toward Building 3, a squad from B Company took fire from a group of eight enemy soldiers in the gymnasium, a long, four-story, red-roofed, building on the line between the American homes and the PDF. When they spotted the PDF group, the U.S. squad started walking toward them to accept their surrender. But that was not the PDF's intention. Gunfire poured into the area. Fitzgerald winced, seeing the troops in the open, and thought they would be wounded or killed. The troops hit the ground and crawled to safety as Hort ordered two M113s to blast away at the gymnasium. The enemy fire stopped.

Fitzgerald wanted to finish the operation off. Fort Amador was expected to be cleared by 9:00 A.M. and it was already past 9:30. There wasn't much left to do; only Buildings 1, 2, and 3; the gymnasium; and a medical dispensary needed to be secured. But clearly there were PDF diehards out there, and they were likely to be in one or more of the buildings.

B Company was pulled back and instructed to provide supporting fire. The mission to clear the remaining structures was given to 3d Platoon of A Company, led by 1st Lt. George Rosser. Two

M113s would provide support. A Company's 1st and 2d Platoons stood at the ready.

Just after noon, the final assault began. Hort rained another torrent of fire into the gym and Building 1, while Building 3 was seized. The remaining PDF troops were isolated; there was nowhere to run. At 1:00 P.M., A Company's 3d Platoon shot its way into Building 1. As the assault began, a sniper began to peck at the assault team from one of the top floors. A return burst from rifles and grenade launchers silenced the sniper.

Building 1 posed more challenges during the clearing. It was yet another maze of offices and rooms. The glass-paned doors were locked with deadbolts, which took a long time to break. Rosser's men found weapons stashed everywhere.

Shortly after 1:30, Building 1 was clear, and 2d Platoon passed through 3d Platoon to go clear the gym. That took just an hour; there were no incidents. The Americans, anticipating a run-in with the PDF, were beginning to wonder where the enemy was. The 2d Platoon then cleared Building 2, uncovering a cache of arms and ammunition, but no enemy soldiers.

There were two buildings left: a medical center and a communications building. The communications center was empty; in the medical center, there were four Panamanians. One appeared to be a doctor, the others young PDF recruits with injuries. None was interested in fighting.

At 6:05 P.M. on 20 December, seventeen hours after H-hour, Fort Amador was declared secure. A and B Companies, after rechecking the gym, linked up and reported that each room in each building was clear. Two more PDF soldiers were found quivering in the ceiling of the gymnasium.

They would be the last of some 150 prisoners captured by the airborne unit in the fight for Fort Amador. The operation was nerve-wracking, but it achieved a dramatic success: the PDF 5th Rifle Company had been eliminated, and American citizens were entirely safe. Most important, Fort Amador had not turned into a bloody battlefield. Troops maintained discipline and precision, using force only when necessary.

In the end, the U.S. forces did not encounter the number of PDF troops at Fort Amador that they were expecting. After-action reports revealed that more than four hundred of the PDF soldiers knew about or had predicted the U.S. assault and had left the peninsula by 1:00 A.M. on 20 December.

Except for La Comandancia, this was to be a pattern throughout Just Cause. The PDF had little stomach for a real fight with the gringos, especially one waged on the Americans' terms. Faced with overwhelming odds, most of the PDF would simply empty the magazines of their rifles and bug out.

The mission of Task Force Semper Fidelis, a Marine Corps unit from the 2d Light Armored Infantry Battalion, was to seize control of the Bridge of the Americas, defend the westward approaches to the Panama Canal, and prevent a PDF attack on Howard Air Force Base.

Each operation would be crucial to the success of the U.S. attack. By securing the Bridge of the Americas, the Marines cut off Panama City from any PDF reinforcements stationed in the countryside across the canal. Once the bridge was seized, D Company of the 2d Battalion would fan out into the jungle, seeking to prevent PDF units from taking to the roads that lead to the bridge span. Security at Howard airfield was also of paramount importance. The U.S. Air Force Base would be the primary staging area for U.S. forces during the operation.

The Marines had been residents of the west bank of the Panama Canal for more than eighteen months. Company A of the 2d Battalion was the first unit to deploy to Panama on 12 May as part of Operation Nimrod Dancer. Up until 20 December, four of the battalion's companies would see duty in Panama. Marines frequently traded shots with Panamanian agitators near the Arraijan Tank Farm, a fuel depot about five miles west of downtown Panama City.

When D Company flew into Panama on 24 October to relieve B Company, the departing unit told Capt. Gerald Gaskins, commander of D Company, that the atmosphere was tense. But it was more like war.

Later that month, Gaskins's unit began exercises to familiarize themselves with their area of operations, occasionally in tandem with B Company. One, dubbed Operation Chisum, took B and D Companies toward La Chorrera, where it encountered a hasty roadblock formed with civilian vehicles. Capt. John Dunn, commander of B Company, requested permission to ram through the roadblock, since the obstacle was in violation of provisions of the Carter-Torrijos Treaty allowing U.S. troops free movement. But by the time the reply was received from the Joint Task Force, the situation at the roadblock had grown ugly, and the answer was disappointing: "Turn around, come home."

Less than a month later, D Company became convinced they were going to war. Operation Rough Rider would take the Marines through four major towns: Nuevo Emperador, Nuevo Guarre, Vista Allegre, and, finally, Arraijan. Two minutes out of Nuevo Empera-dor, where they received a warm reception, the Marines ran into a roadblock on Thatcher Highway, which runs to the Rodman Naval Station, a U.S. facility. Gaskins called for help from the Center for Treaty Affairs.

The roadblock had not been detected by an OH-58 scout heli-copter providing the Marines with a forward observer. When officials from the Center for Treaty Affairs approached, the crowd be-gan waving Panamanian flags and hollering anti-American slogans. The crowd grew out of control and the Marines leaped into the safety of their LAVs.

The Panamanians pounded the vehicles with rocks and sticks as the column inched forward to escape the crowd. One Panamanian rammed an LAV with a pickup truck, puncturing the fighting vehi-cle's right front tire. As the LAV limped on, a woman protester threw her body onto the front of the vehicle. She fell backwards, feet in the air, and flipped over one of the roadblock vehicles.

Shocked at the accident, the Panamanians began to beat on the LAVs with flagpoles, other objects, and even their bare hands. The U.S. force slowly made its way down the highway.

Operation Rough Rider would be the last training exercise for the Marine company.

At 8:00 A.M. on 19 December, Col. Charles Richardson, com-mander of Task Force Semper Fi, ordered a maintenance stand-down. Each platoon was to report to base and ensure the LAVs and trucks were in working order. Richardson ordered the Marines to perform the maintenance "as if their lives depended on it."

By 6:00 P.M., the Marines were 100 percent ready for combat. At 7:00 P.M., D Company commanders were told to execute their battle plan, and at 8:00 P.M., the unit's 2d Platoon was detached to

Task Force Bayonet. The 2nd Platoon, with four LAVs, would become part of Team Armor, tasked to blast away at La Comandancia alongside Army Sheridan tanks.

By 11:00 P.M., D Company was assembled and ready. Gaskins had kept his speech to the soldiers short and sweet. He announced that the United States, and the U.S. Marines, were going to overthrow Noriega. The mission of D Company was straightforward, and it had been practiced routinely for two months. The unit, in a column of fourteen LAVs, one five-ton truck, and two light vehicles, would take Thatcher Highway from Rodman Naval Station up to the city of Arraijan, securing key installations and intersections along the ten-mile route. The column would be led by the 3d Platoon, followed by the 1st Platoon and the Headquarters element. The 3d Platoon would break from the column and blast into the DNTT Station Number 2, headquarters of one of the more aggressive units in the National Department of Traffic and Transportation.

As the column approached the DNTT, the lead LAV made a hard left turn into the driveway, breaking through a locked fence without problem. Seconds later, the column was hit with a hail of small-arms fire from the single-story building. Scouts assigned to clear the building dismounted from their vehicles, while the LAVs provided covering fire with machine guns. They were prohibited from using the 25mm cannon on the LAV because it was believed that the DNTT station contained radio equipment that could later be used to monitor PDF traffic.

The scouts raced to the wall of the building and Cpl. Gary Isaak used his grenade launcher to blast open the door.

Isaak led the 3d Platoon into a building full of smoke and darkness, knowing that the soldiers inside were unhurt. He was shot several times by a single rifle as he entered the first room in the building. Issak, a twenty-two-year-old from Greenville, North Carolina, was the only Marine killed in Operation Just Cause.

The voice of the 3d Platoon leader echoed over the radio carried by Gaskins's radio man: "One man: KIA."

The gunfire from the DNTT station forced the column to separate. The 1st Platoon, in LAVs, moved on toward Arraijan. The headquarters element, protected only by the Kevlar lining the side of their jeeps, could not drive through the tracer fire. Prior to leaving Rodman, Gaskins hastily formed a unit that could occupy the

DNTT station so he could drive into Arraijan, a PDF stronghold, with at least two platoons. The occupation element, consisting primarily of cooks, armorers, and mechanics, entered the building as the 3d Platoon was leaving to rejoin the column.

But the fight was not over. A brief firefight broke out just after the column broke up; the cooks took four PDF soldiers prisoner.

After bypassing an oil tanker used as a roadblock, the LAV column rode on toward the Arraijan PDF station, a two-story building surrounded by a six-foot concrete wall.

The station entrance was guarded by a massive iron gate. The LAVs quickly established positions surrounding the building. Then the lead vehicle in the 1st Platoon slowly maneuvered through the gate while dismounted scouts walked concealed behind the vehicle. The PDF began shooting when the scouts entered the station. As the firing continued, Gaskins requested a clearing team be established to complement the scouts. A close quarters battle team from the Fleet Antiterrorism Security Team, or FAST, platoon was attached to D Company and began their assault on the PDF structure. A combination of U.S. grenades and shooting on both sides caused the building to burst into flames before it could be completely cleared.

The next objective in Arraijan was the campaign headquarters of Rigoberto Paredes, a Panamanian legislator who supported Noriega. The building was one floor, but each window was covered with locked iron bars, posing a challenge to the scouts, who once again called on the FAST team to blast the bars open with shotguns. Before entering, a Marine who spoke Spanish called inside, warning the building's occupants that they were under attack. The Marines then lobbed a stun grenade inside and the clearing team quickly followed it into the building.

A Panamanian stumbled out of the door, dazed by the grenade. The FAST team found five more Panamanians inside the Paredes headquarters.

D Company now faced what may have been the most difficult part of the military operation—handling prisoners. The Marines who would normally be tasked to guard prisoners captured during battle were occupying the DNTT station. The job was therefore given to the scouts. As the FAST team secured the area, the unit rounded up eleven more Panamanians. Most of the prisoners were members of Noriega's Dignity Battalions, and some Panamanians told U.S. counterintelligence officials that additional Dignity Battalion members were on the way to Arraijan. As the Marines closely guarded the town and improved the security of their perimeter, only two cars tried to ram through the roadblocks established with LAVs. Both were halted by gunfire.

10

"It Got Real Personal
Real Quick."

At 12:29 A.M. on 20 December, members of the Panamanian Air Force sitting in the control tower at Tocumen military airfield received a frantic radio call from the main headquarters of the PDF twenty miles away in downtown Panama City. An uneventful, if not boring, night in the Tocumen watchtower suddenly turned ugly.

"The Americans are invading Panama! La Comandancia is under attack!"

The report was jumbled, punctuated by gunfire that members of the Panamanian Air Force, or FAP in its Spanish acronym, in the control tower could not recognize. But the call was sufficiently understood. One FAP air controller hastily jotted the information into the control tower journal before dropping his pen.

Most of the 150 members of the small FAP squadron, a combination of pilots and security and maintenance personnel, scrambled to find a way out of the Tocumen area. As word of the invasion spread across the airfield, most of the two hundred PDF soldiers of the 2d Rifle Company, an infantry unit headquartered in barracks about six hundred yards from the airstrip, scattered, some in only their undergarments. Some soldiers grabbed rifles and other weapons in the event they would not be able to leave Tocumen in time.

At 12:59 A.M., thirty minutes after the call from La Comandancia, Tocumen airfield was unusually quiet. Most of the PDF had left, except for those who were members of airport security. They were busier than usual because their commander, Gen. Manuel Antonio Noriega, had come to visit one of several female prostitutes in the

Ceremi Recreation Center, a former hotel revamped into a gymnasium for the 2d Rifle Company and FAP.

Noriega was with the prostitute in the recreation center just east of the airstrip when, without warning, an AC-130 Spectre gunship opened a tremendous burst of cannon fire into the 2d Rifle Company barracks. The thumping sound of 105mm and 40mm cannon fire from the Spectre shocked the remaining PDF soldiers on the airfield, the security personnel, and Noriega.

The Spectre leveled the PDF barracks, while two AH-6 Little Bird helicopters swarmed over the control tower. Gunfire from the Little Birds struck the glass of the tower, yet, unbelievably, did not disable the radar. The choppers, flown by pilots from Task Force 160, also eliminated enemy soldiers at two guard posts on either end of the military airfield. Like hunters stalking their prey, the special operations forces aircraft tracked movement on the airfield, and then quickly blasted the enemy. The AC-130 hit one of the most important targets: a ZPU-4 air defense gun. One unfortunate PDF soldier was hit when he got too close to a round fired by the Spectre's 105mm cannon. The next day, Army Rangers would confront the human element of combat when they surrounded the charred remains of the body. After three minutes the firing had ceased.

At 1:03 A.M., right on schedule, 731 Army Rangers jumped out of 11 huge transport aircraft flying in a straight line over the airfield. For the remaining PDF on the ground, a relatively clear evening sky soon filled with black berets.

The battle would end quickly.

Tocumen military airfield, and the adjacent commercial Omar Torrijos International Airport, were obvious targets for U.S. forces. Since one of the primary missions of the attack was to isolate and capture Noriega, it would be necessary to cut off his escape routes. The day after the invasion, Rangers counted thirty-seven aircraft, both fixed-wing and helicopters, on the ground at Tocumen. None of the aircraft were used, and none of them were destroyed.

Torrijos/Tocumen was also critical because of its vicinity to downtown Panama City. U.S. military planners knew the harshest fighting would be at La Comandancia and wanted to prevent additional PDF forces from using the airfield as a staging base to launch assaults into the city, as the 7th Infantry Company had done during the Giroldi coup.

Perhaps the most important reason to secure the two airfields was the need to have access for follow-on parachute and, especially, air-landed operations. Howard Air Force Base on the west side of the canal was in the line of PDF mortar fire, and PDF snipers could easily position themselves along the outer fence of the installation. It was possible that Howard would become inoperable; aircraft carrying 7th Infantry Division troops would not be able to land safely. Tocumen was the only alternative.

Before his promotion to command of the 75th Ranger Regiment, Col. Buck Kernan had been 1st Battalion commander, and he had planned the assault on Torrijos/Tocumen for Blue Spoon operations. Kernan again gave the job to the 1st Battalion.

On Tocumen, the 1st Battalion could be expected to find as many as 380 enemy soldiers. The FAP totaled about 150 people, and not all would be armed. But Kernan didn't want to take chances, and the FAP barracks became Objective Tiger. The primary target on Tocumen would be the 2d Infantry Company, numbering about 200 soldiers. The plan relied on the AC-130 and Little Bird helicopters to shock and eliminate most of the 2d Company prior to H-hour, but there was little doubt that most of the company would be ready to fight when the Rangers landed. The company barracks became Objective Pig.

In the main airport terminal located in the northern part of Torrijos, the Rangers guessed there would be thirty to forty security personnel, most with sidearms, some with automatic rifles. Kernan then attached C Company, 3d Battalion, and gave them the mission to isolate and secure the international terminal. It was dubbed Objective Bear.

Kernan was not so much concerned with the threat at Tocumen/ Torrijos as he was with the enemy about sixteen miles to the northeast. Fort Cimarron was home to the Battalion 2000, Noriega's personal creation and an elite fighting unit. There were an estimated two hundred soldiers in the Battalion 2000, equipped with nine American-made V-300 light assault vehicles and at least twelve mortars. Each V-300 was armed with a 90mm cannon easily capable of tearing up a Ranger jeep. The Battalion 2000 was only forty-five minutes away. If the PDF troops were able to reinforce the 2d Company at Tocumen, the Rangers stood to lose two-thirds of their force.

Battalion 2000 also had an added incentive to demonstrate their loyalty. The commander of the unit, Maj. Federico Olechea, was fired for his failure to aid Noriega in the initial minutes of the 3 October coup, and the battalion was considered suspect. This time, their lives were on the line. "We assumed they would react this time," Kernan says.

The Tocumen assault would have to be executed quickly, and with as few glitches as possible. The threat posed by Battalion 2000 meant the objectives had to be secured within forty-five minutes. There was another factor that forced the Rangers to move with lightning speed. At 1:45 A.M., more than two thousand paratroopers from the 82d Airborne Division were to drop onto the Torrijos runway. From there, the ready brigade of the 82d Airborne would board helicopters to air assault three objectives in Panama City. It was the task of the Rangers to make sure the 82d Airborne was not attacked while preparing its assault.

The shift in focus away from an incremental buildup of forces toward a rapid, overwhelming strike, like the airborne assault at Torrijos, was one of the most important changes Thurman brought to the Just Cause contingency plan.

U.S. planners confronted three distinct objectives in Panama: Panama Viejo, a known UESAT location in Panama City and home of the PDF 1st Cavalry Squadron; to the north, Tinajitas, home of the PDF 1st Infantry Company; and Fort Cimarron. Prior to October 1989, the contingency plan called for a task force to be on call to strike all three objectives. The force would be airlanded into Torrijos, and then board helicopters for the short flight to each of the other targets. The gradual buildup—the difference between a parachute assault and an airlanded assault—of U.S. forces would be one of the several flaws listed by Thurman as he studied the Blue Spoon plan.

By parachuting a brigade of the 82d Airborne Division from Fort Bragg into Torrijos, more than two thousand soldiers could be introduced into the battle within six hours after the planes took off from the United States. Military planners estimated it would take at least twenty-four hours to land a brigade of the 7th Infantry

Division into one of the Panama airfields. "If you're talking about a rapid buildup of combat power, then you're talking about a drop," says Maj. Gen. James Johnson, commander of the 82d Airborne.

The plan called for a team of Rangers, known as Task Force Red-T, with support from civil affairs and psychological operations troops, to parachute into Tocumen and Torrijos and simultaneously attack three targets. The area of operations was dubbed Condor. The 1st Battalion would be responsible for the northern targets on Tocumen airfield, including the FAP barracks, the 2d Rifle Company barracks, and if necessary, the Ceremi Recreation Center.

A company, 1st Battalion, would assemble farthest to the north and assault Objective Tiger, as well as the FAP aircraft fleet. C Company, 1st Battalion, would secure the center of the airfield, and seize what was left of Objective Pig. This company also would secure the Tocumen control tower, including the luxurious apartment of one of Noriega's girlfriends. In the multi-room apartment, Rangers would find occult paraphernalia and an altar for practicing santeria rituals.

B Company was to secure the perimeter of Condor and establish roadblocks around the airfield. In addition, B Company would prepare the runway for the onslaught of U.S. aircraft carrying troops from the 7th Infantry Division from the west coast of the United States. The aircraft would start landing at 8:00 A.M. On order, B Company also would clear the recreation center, designated Objective Hawk on tactical maps. Ceremi was a suspected arms storage site for Noriega's Dignity Battalions, and a known hideout of Noriega's. Noriega was there the evening of 19 December, but would escape through a hastily formed roadblock before the Rangers had secured their objectives.

C Company, 3d Battalion, would land just south of the Torrijos Airport main terminal on the civilian runway. The four platoons would quickly assemble and within forty-five minutes, move north of Phase Line Apache. Their mission initially was not to enter, but to cordon, the terminal. One of the primary reasons Stiner selected 1:00 A.M. as H-hour was because the last international flight into Torrijos airport was scheduled to arrive between 10:30 and 11:00 P.M. on 19 December. The plan allowed enough time for the passengers to get through customs, pick up their luggage, and leave the airport. Or so U.S. planners thought.

Kernan recognized that there could well be a few people inside the terminal shopping at the twenty-four-hour duty-free shops. As a result, C Company's mission was to choke the terminal off from the rest of the airfield to keep PDF from escaping and to keep civilians inside and outside in control. The mission would quickly change.

The Rangers, according to the plan, dropped precisely at 1:03 A.M. in a massive assault lasting just thirty seconds. Prior to the jump, between 1:00 A.M. exactly and 1:02:30, the AC-130 and Little Bird helicopters launched pre-assault fires at specific targets: two air defense guns, one just north of the FAP barracks and the other at the northern entrance to Torrijos International; the 2d Rifle Company barracks; the control and communications facility; two guard posts; and other threats to the Rangers.

Seconds before the Rangers left the aircraft over Tocumen, the firing came to a halt, and the AC-130 would cover the parachute drop. It would not fire while the drop was occurring, but was prepared to engage the enemy once the Rangers were on the ground. Rules of engagement required precision fire, used only when absolutely necessary, particularly from the powerful Spectre gunship and the Rangers once they were heading toward their objectives.

The principle handed down by the Just Cause commanders to minimize enemy casualties and collateral damage was relentless. "We would carpet bomb the airfield if we could," Kernan says. But the Spectre was only allowed to fire on key military targets that threatened or had the potential to affect the Ranger's mission.

The 82d Airborne Division, according to the plan, would parachute into Torrijos in one enormous wave of C-141 and C-130 transport aircraft at 1:45 A.M. At the same time, these aircraft dropped nearly one hundred different vehicles and crates, ranging from High Mobility Multipurpose Wheeled Vehicles (HMMWV)—the Army's replacement for the Jeep—and M551 Sheridan light tanks to food and ammunition. The 82d Airborne were not to move north of Phase Line Apache, the marker between the two airfields.

They were to follow the Rangers into the Torrijos area, and immediately assemble troops and equipment for the air and ground assaults to the three objectives. Once assembled, General Johnson would assume control over the 1st Ranger Battalion, which would either be sent back to Howard or on to additional missions. The transfer of operational control, however, was dependent on one condition: that Tocumen airfield and the Torrijos International terminal were secure (see figure 10–1).

Sardines. Tiny little fish packed airtight into a tin can. That is how Capt. Al Dochnal, commander of C Company, 3/75 Rangers, felt for more than seven hours as the four C-130 aircraft flew down the eastern coast of the United States toward Panama. C Company was in four transport aircraft; the 1st Battalion was in seven larger C-141 aircraft in front. From the ground, one Ranger thought, the air convoy must look awesome.

More than seventy Rangers were packed into each aircraft and the effect such crowding has on the human body is something the Rangers had not trained for. Normally, the C-130s fly with no more than sixty soldiers. There were interlocking bodies and overlapping rucksacks. The flight, overall, was smooth, even the slight dip when the aircraft tried to swoop under Cuban radar. But the Rangers of Task Force Red-T were in no mood to sit around.

Since Sunday, 17 December, the Rangers had been preparing for combat. Lt. Col. Joe Hunt, commander of the 3d Battalion, and Dochnal were let in on the military operation Sunday night, hours after the president had handed down the order to execute Just Cause. The troops were not informed of the plan, but to many, there was little doubt they were going to war in Panama.

The Rangers had spent all of December rehearsing for a specific mission. In full-scale exercises in Florida, the regiment attacked detailed models of each objective they would find at Rio Hato and Tocumen/Torrijos. The exercises mimicked the assault to each objective to the smallest detail, and also involved fire support from Spectre aircraft and Little Bird helicopters. The last exercise was conducted on 15 December, and it was a dramatic success.

To minimize the signature of the massive airlift operation, C Company had left their headquarters at Fort Benning, Georgia, and moved to Hunter Army Airfield, home of the 1st Battalion near Fort Stewart, Georgia. The seven Air Force aircraft carrying Task Force Red-T were already at Hunter Airfield, in Savannah. Dochnal's company left Fort Benning early in the morning on 18 December in a convoy of buses. Kernan wanted to fly the command team for the Tocumen assault, with Lt. Col. Tony Koren, deputy regimental commander, to Hunter, but the weather would not allow it. So Koren

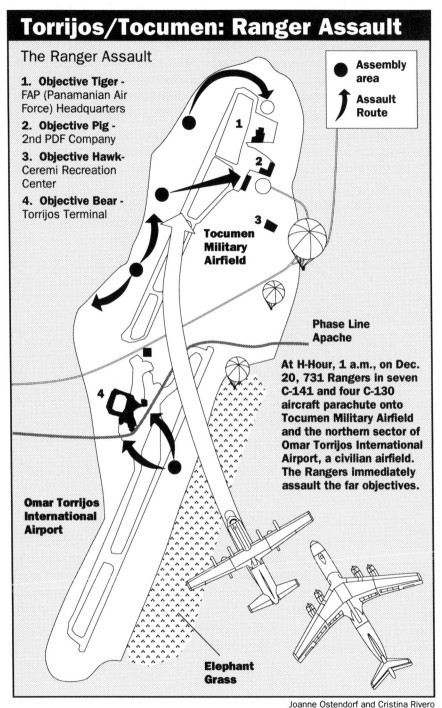

Torrijos/Tocumen: Ranger Assault

The Ranger Assault

1. Objective Tiger - FAP (Panamanian Air Force) Headquarters

2. Objective Pig - 2nd PDF Company

3. Objective Hawk- Ceremi Recreation Center

4. Objective Bear - Torrijos Terminal

● Assembly area

↰ Assault Route

Tocumen Military Airfield

Phase Line Apache

At H-Hour, 1 a.m., on Dec. 20, 731 Rangers in seven C-141 and four C-130 aircraft parachute onto Tocumen Military Airfield and the northern sector of Omar Torrijos International Airport, a civilian airfield. The Rangers immediately assault the far objectives.

Omar Torrijos International Airport

Elephant Grass

Joanne Ostendorf and Cristina Rivero

FIGURE 10–1

Torrijos/Tocumen: Ranger Assault

and C Company boarded the buses for the long six-hour ride to Hunter.

The buses arrived at Hunter at about 8:00 A.M. on 19 December. Once there, Dochnal met up with Lt. Col. Bob Wagner, 1st Battalion commander, to coordinate details of the assault. The troops, told they were preparing for yet another training exercise, sat and waited.

There was little time to rest. Through the morning, Dochnal and Wagner began to inform the platoon leaders that this was not an exercise. Slowly, the platoon leaders briefed each soldier. Dochnal used a technique to brief squad leaders. He gave them a piece of the map detailing their objective, and ordered them to draw their assault plan as the unit leaders thought it should happen. Dochnal was confident that each platoon, and each squad, knew their mission.

The word was that the mission would be just like training. And for the most part, soldiers reacted as if it were an exercise. They knew their objectives, and what they had to do to take them.

But when the Rangers lined up to receive live ammunition, the idea that this mission was just another training exercise faded from their minds. "There was live ammo as far as I could see down the runway," says Specialist Michael Eubanks of C Company, 3d Battalion. Butterflies set in.

"I was nervous, but I didn't want to come across like I was nervous, because my squad has an impression of me," says Sgt. David Reeves.

> I really wasn't worried about it because from the operation order we got, it didn't seem like it was going to be real hot when we jumped in. I was going in thinking I was going to survive.
>
> From the past experiences the United States has been in, you know we're going to overwhelm 'em. We're so much better trained. In fact, it was more of a relief than anything else because I didn't feel like going through the same mission again. Now it's like we're going somewhere. That's the way all my guys were. Finally, we're actually going to do something for real. We're actually going to see whether our training pays off or not.

As the Rangers prepared to load the aircraft for a 7:00 P.M. take-off, fear and tension gave way to misery and cold. The weather in

Georgia on 19 December was miserable. A winter storm had gripped the southeastern United States at the worst possible time, sending rock-hard pellets of ice down on the Fort Bragg area and sparking a Georgia downpour across Hunter Airfield and nearby Fort Stewart. Freezing rain pelted the Rangers all day as they lined up to draw their ammunition on the Hunter tarmac, and prepared their rucksacks for the much warmer climate of Panama.

Prior to boarding aircraft for a parachute assault, the Rangers practiced each step except the jump itself. In the skeleton of a C-130 that sits near the airfield, the troops repeatedly went over jump commands and procedure. What does a soldier do if the aircraft is hit by gunfire and takes a nosedive? What if one jumper gets tangled up in a fellow soldier's parachute?

Troops temporarily forgot they were about to enter combat. They yearned to thaw out in the airfield control tower. Reeves, a two-time visitor to Panama, could only think about the tropical warmth of Panama, and how nice it would be. After the sustained airborne training, the Rangers went inside for their last meal. The troops expected a fine meal as it was the final dinner before they went into combat. It was fried chicken, which was disappointing.

By the time the sixteen aircraft of Task Force Red-T, including five C-141s carrying trucks, jeeps, ammunition, and weaponry, took off the night of 19 December, the Rangers were completely exhausted. Most of the soldiers, some aided by a strong dosage of Dramamine, quickly fell into a sound sleep. There was little discussion in the planes. But there usually isn't much talk, even on training missions, because the soldiers must concentrate on the task at hand. It was war, but the troops knew they would live as long as they stayed with their unit. "There just wasn't time to be scared," one nineteen-year-old Ranger said.

But it wouldn't be long before the flight would get exciting. When the airlift was a little over two hours away from Panama, the command aircraft received a call from the Joint Task Force command center there. The operation had been compromised. The impact of the news was obvious. The element of surprise was destroyed, and the Rangers would have a tougher fight on their hands than they originally believed.

Lieutenant Colonel Koren immediately passed the information across a secure communications net to the other aircraft. The reaction was mixed. To the commanders, most of them veterans of the 1983 invasion of Grenada, the news of the compromise came as no surprise. From the plan, it was known that a brigade of the 82d Airborne had been alerted at the same time as the Rangers. It would be difficult to prepare two thousand troops for war without some leak. As a result, the Ranger leaders predicted the operation would be compromised. In fact, some were surprised they managed to get two hours away from the objective before the call came.

It was another call from Panama, however, that gave Koren the jitters. A Brazilian airliner that was scheduled to land at Omar Torrijos International Airport at 10:45 P.M. had arrived late. The plane was on the ground and empty, meaning its passengers were dispersed throughout the terminal. The good news was that it appeared the airport security personnel in the terminal were unaware of the pending U.S. attack. The bad news was that the Brazilian aircraft was carrying as many as 376 passengers.

Among the soldiers, the news of the compromise was worrisome. In one aircraft, the troops were informed that a Panamanian cargo plane was unloading surface-to-air missiles on the Tocumen airfield. If the operation had indeed been compromised, the PDF could be standing on the roof of the barracks waiting to shoot down the last aircraft to fly over the airfield. But the soldiers could do little about it.

"The troops were saying things like, 'They know we're coming! They know we're coming!'" said one Ranger. "I said, 'Well I sure can't do anything about that now. What am I going to do? Go tell the pilot to turn around?'" Sgt. Reeves said, "I'm sure I could speak for everyone when I say we wanted to get on the ground as quickly as possible."

Almost as threatening to the Rangers in Task Force Red-T as any PDF soldier was the fact they were expected to jump from aircraft flying no more than 500 feet from the ground. Because the injury rate is so high from such a low jump, troops usually jump from at least 750 feet in peacetime training missions. The fact that the PDF could be awaiting the arrival of the U.S. force made it that much worse. "We didn't know if we were more nervous about getting shot on the jump or frapping," says Sgt. Erik Wilson. Frapping is a delicate way of describing when a paratrooper runs out of time to open the chute, and slams into the ground.

Fifteen Rangers suffered torn knee ligaments, broken legs, fractured feet, and other orthopedic injuries on the Tocumen/Torrijos jump. To lessen the hazard of being fired upon before the Rangers could get out of their harnesses, they practiced escaping the chute as the planes neared the objective. "If you're taking fire, just get rid of your canopy, and run like hell."

The pilots of the Rangers' transport planes dropped the Rangers right on time and right on "the money." With the help of a lighted, fully operational runway at Tocumen, the seven C-141 aircraft carrying the 1st Battalion dropped their loads on the concrete runway. The four C-130 aircraft carrying C Company, 3d Battalion, following close behind also flew a straight line, dropping the soldiers onto the tarmac surrounding the Torrijos main terminal.

The fourth aircraft carrying C Company, however, caught a wind shear and shot right. The Rangers, including Dochnal, landed about one hundred yards from the runway in the grass. From the overlays of the Condor area of operations provided by U.S. intelligence agencies, the grass did not appear to be cut. But it also didn't look twelve feet high! As C Company dropped from the C-130s, they could see tracer fire to the north at Tocumen. The battle for the airfield had begun.

When the the 1st Battalion assembled on the military runway and darted toward their objectives, it looked like the war had started— and ended—without them. Three minutes earlier, the AH-6 Little Bird helicopters had shot up the Tocumen terminal and eliminated the PDF personnel occupying the northern guard shack. The AC-130 Spectre aircraft, which now circled overhead like a black guardian angel, had leveled the 2d Rifle Company barracks. The sturdy wood barracks now lay in ruin. The walls had collapsed inward; the roof was soon to follow. The problem was there was nobody in the 2d Company barracks at the time.

The seizure of Tocumen airfield occurred flawlessly. A Company assembled farthest to the north, and hooked around the northern tip of the airfield into the Panamanian Air Force area. The company quickly seized the barracks and a number of fixed-wing aircraft and helicopters belonging to the FAP. Most of the enemy in the FAP area had escaped, and the company quickly overcame the handful of FAP personnel that chose to fight the overwhelming U.S. assault.

C Company of the 1st Battalion gathered in the middle of the runway and launched like a spear into the 2d Rifle Company barracks. The company quickly secured the area, gathering hostages and killing those who stayed to fight. C Company received some rapid sniper fire as they surrounded the control tower. Here, Pfc. James William Markwell, a medic, was shot and killed. Markwell joined the Army in February 1989 to learn to become a doctor. The twenty-one-year-old was scheduled to start a two-week Christmas vacation the day he was shot. The Ranger assault into Tocumen airfield was his first combat mission.

B Company assembled to the south to establish blocking positions along the airfield to provide security for the assault. One roadblock team encountered a two-car convoy trying to escape the airfield minutes after H-hour. The Rangers stopped the first car, but missed the second. Kernan would later find out the second vehicle had contained General Noriega.

The next day, elements of B Company would secure the Ceremi Recreation Center, dubbed Objective Hawk. There, the Rangers found some of Noriega's personal belongings, including his uniform and shoes. After securing the perimeter, B Company began preparing the runway for next morning's airland operation.

By 2:10 A.M., the 1st Battalion had just about eliminated the enemy resistance at Tocumen. The Rangers had suffered a handful of casualties, including one fatality, but the mission was performed with precision. As the Rangers slowly cleared the barracks, they received some unexpected visitors.

The 82d Airborne was supposed to arrive forty-five minutes after H-hour and land on the Torrijos airport runway. Instead, the transport aircraft, disrupted by an ice storm at Pope Air Force Base, arrived in three waves, dumping troops on a diagonal slope that extended from the southern tip of Torrijos to the FAP barracks on Tocumen. One group of airborne soldiers landed in the middle of the remains of the 2d Company barracks while C Company, 1st Battalion, was clearing the area.

Wagner, the Ranger commander, was faced with an immediate and potentially catastrophic problem. There were still minor fire fights going on in the area, and suddenly, paratroopers were everywhere. He quickly ordered his heavy broadcast team, equipped with hand-held megaphones and loudspeakers, to tell the airborne soldiers that they were among U.S. Rangers—in what was now friendly territory. Over the loudspeaker, Wagner gave the visiting troops directions back to Torrijos once they were on the ground. The 82d Airborne did not suffer any casualties during the drop. Less than five minutes later, Wagner and the 1st Battalion declared Tocumen military airfield secure.

Mother Nature hated the 82d Airborne Division. The same weather that had hassled the Rangers as they prepared to board the transport aircraft wreaked havoc on the entire 82d Airborne operation. On the evening of 18 December, the 3d Battalion, 73d Armor Regiment—part of the division's complement of light tanks—began loading up its Sheridans and other support equipment onto the first of twenty-eight mammoth C-141 aircraft sitting on the tarmac at Pope Air Force Base, North Carolina. It was extremely cold, especially for North Carolina. It was clear that there was a storm coming. The weathermen knew it, and they kept telling Johnson and Lieutenant Colonel Jim Grazioplene, the 3/73 Armor commander, that it was coming.

The storm warnings forced the heavy drop fleet to move to Charleston Air Force Base, South Carolina, to complete the loading. But there was a more important reason for the move. The heavy drop aircraft had to make room at Pope Air Force Base for the twenty C-141 aircraft that would carry the 2,176 82d Airborne Division paratroopers into Panama. The planes arrived at Pope without a hitch. Then, on 19 December, just as the airborne troops were boarding the aircraft, the storm hit. And it hit bad.

According to the plan, the 82d Airborne would follow right behind the Rangers, landing onto Torrijos airport at precisely 1:45 A.M. in a steady stream lasting fifty-seven seconds. Ten minutes earlier, the twenty-eight heavy drop aircraft would have unloaded the tanks and equipment along the east side of the Torrijos runway. The heavy drop could not be dumped on the airfield because there was concern that the weight of the tanks might damage the runway. A damaged runway would delay indefinitely the landing of the 7th Infantry Division, slated for the next day. Further, it would take hours for troops to clear a Sheridan off the runway if for some reason one of the parachutes did not open and the tank tumbled to the ground.

As the scheduled takeoff time neared, airmen of the 317th Tactical Airlift Wing and Combat Support Group feverishly tried to remove the ice that accumulated on the wings of the C-141 aircraft as fast as they could scrape it off. Each aircraft was de-iced twice; some were treated three times. When it became clear that the airlift would not leave on time, and in fact, might have to be split into three waves, Johnson called Stiner in Panama.

The airborne commander was in the first of eight aircraft that made it off the ground from Pope. Johnson suggested that the lift-off be delayed so the twenty aircraft, including three resupply aircraft, could arrive in a complete formation. Stiner rejected the plan. "His response was, 'Bring what you got,' and that's what I did," says Johnson. The late arrival of the 82d Airborne Division did not concern Stiner despite the fact that the airborne assaults into Panama Viejo, Tinajitas, and Fort Cimarron would have to be performed in daylight rather than darkness, a fact he knew might result in additional casualties.

The first 82d Airborne soldiers dropped at 2:11 A.M., more than twenty-five minutes later than the planned arrival time. The second wave would arrive at about 3:30 A.M., while the last of the troops finally dropped at 4:30. As the first wave of aircraft approached Torrijos, Johnson could see tracer fire to the north at Tocumen. The shooting did not worry Johnson, despite the extended range of the drop and the five hundred foot altitude. He was confident that the Rangers would spot any PDF shooting at the airlift, and they would in turn hand the target over to the AC-130. "My main concern was to get out, get on the ground, and get out to our objectives."

At the same time, however, he could see the inaccurate location of the heavy drop. Johnson's best guess was that just over 40 percent of the eighty-six tanks, trucks, and artillery cannons had landed on the lowlands close to the runway—on target. That meant that nearly 60 percent landed off target, in the ten-foot-high elephant grass.

Heavy drop aircraft are expected to fly no lower than 1,350 feet to ensure the survival of tanks, trucks, and crates of supplies. It is the suspicion of the 3/73 Armor as well as the Rangers who watched the drop that the heavy drop aircraft were flying lower than that. The aircraft also flew a diagonal, rather than straight, route across the airfields, dumping some tanks in swampland three hundred yards from the runway.

Either way, the first Sheridan was finally located at about 6:00 A.M. One Sheridan was completely destroyed when it hit the ground, and it had to be blown to pieces because the Air Force could not take it on board the aircraft for safety reasons. Another Sheridan was severely damaged, and was never put into combat.

Lt. Randall Hicks, a platoon leader in the 3/73 Armor, dropped with the first eight personnel aircraft, which also dropped their cargo in the high grass to the right. His first task was relatively simple. He would drop in, and as the troopers assembled on the runway, he would find the Sheridans. It took Hicks four hours to reach the runway. It was a tense morning. It was pitch black, and from ten feet away, a close friend looked like the enemy. From the runway, Hicks hijacked a HMMWV to search for the Sheridans.

The 82d Airborne Division did not engage a single PDF troop as they scrambled to assault their objectives, a testament, Johnson says, to the Ranger task force at Tocumen (see figure 10–2).

At the Torrijos terminal, the ten-foot-high grass provided Dochnal and Lt. Brian Pugmire, his fire support officer, a soft landing. But the two had to fight the grass to get to the runway. Pugmire relentlessly pushed his rucksack in front of him to knock down the weeds. Dochnal brought his M16 rifle over his head and threw it down in front of him. He would then take a step. Pugmire and Dochnal worked at it for thirty minutes until they finally reached the edge of the runway. Both soldiers were whipped.

On the radio, Dochnal learned that 90 percent of his company had reached their initial objectives within fifteen minutes, a fine statistic. The last jumpers out of the last aircraft landed in a ditch just north of the tall grass. The operator of a satellite communications radio fell into a tidal pool and wound up buried up to his neck. These soldiers were found later in the morning by members of the 82d Airborne searching for their Sheridan tanks.

By the time Dochnal reached the target, the company platoons had already run into the enemy on both the north and south sides of the terminal. The mission of C Company, 3/75 Rangers, was to secure the buildings surrounding the terminal and systematically surround the main structure.

After the jump, the 3d Platoon assembled to the north of the

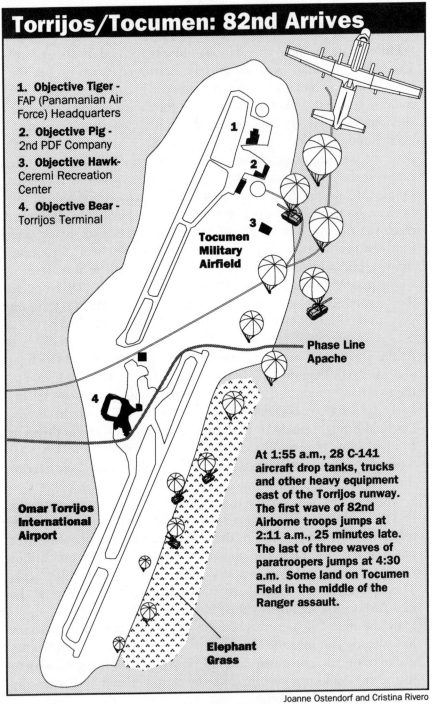

Torrijos/Tocumen: 82nd Arrives

1. Objective Tiger - FAP (Panamanian Air Force) Headquarters

2. Objective Pig - 2nd PDF Company

3. Objective Hawk- Ceremi Recreation Center

4. Objective Bear - Torrijos Terminal

Tocumen Military Airfield

Phase Line Apache

At 1:55 a.m., 28 C-141 aircraft drop tanks, trucks and other heavy equipment east of the Torrijos runway. The first wave of 82nd Airborne troops jumps at 2:11 a.m., 25 minutes late. The last of three waves of paratroopers jumps at 4:30 a.m. Some land on Tocumen Field in the middle of the Ranger assault.

Omar Torrijos International Airport

Elephant Grass

Joanne Ostendorf and Cristina Rivero

FIGURE 10–2

Torrijos/Tocumen: 82d Arrives

terminal, and was assigned the task of clearing a fire station. The 1st and 2d Platoons would assemble south of the terminal. The 2d Platoon was to clear a small cargo area owned by Eastern Airlines, and then establish an overwatch position. On order, the 2d Platoon would lead the assault into the terminal. The 1st Platoon secured the entrance to the Torrijos Airport, and then was to move past the 2d Platoon and clear a restaurant.

The Eastern Airlines baggage handling area was on the right-hand side of the main terminal. As the 2d Platoon approached the building, the platoon leader spotted a Panamanian sticking his head around the corner. Right away, the U.S. troops could tell the curious Panamanian wasn't a PDF soldier. The platoon leader raised his rifle toward the civilian, and he disappeared. One Ranger ran forward and shot the lights out, while one squad pushed their way inside the area. Inside was a storage area; stacks of crates containing soft drinks and beer lined the wall. Quivering in a corner with their hands up were four Panamanians. They were taken prisoner.

The 2d Platoon then formed a half-moon perimeter facing the main terminal.

The 1st Platoon secured the main entrance to Omar Torrijos Airport and immediately headed for a building used as a restaurant. After cutting a chain-link fence, the 1st squad sent an interpreter forward to tell the employees inside to surrender. They did. The restaurant was cleared thoroughly, and the 1st Platoon arrested eighteen Panamanians with no shots fired. After marking the guard house, leveled earlier by an AH-6 helicopter, the 1st Platoon also established a perimeter facing the terminal.

North of the terminal building, the 3d Platoon was moving to secure the fire station when one of the fire trucks sped out of the garage. One of the soldiers pointed his M16 at the truck, and was ready to fire, but the squad leader told him to halt. The soldier was instructed to fire across the front of the truck. The driver, spotting the tracer three feet in front of him, turned the truck around and drove back into the station.

Before the forward squad of the 3d Platoon could get to the building, the Panamanian fireman had run into the rear of the station, where there were a large number of civilians. The Panamanians were screaming obscenities at the American troops, as the squad leader attempted to convince them to surrender. One Ranger sug-

gested throwing in a grenade as a "convincing device." The squad
leader rejected the idea and ordered an interpreter to warn the Panamanians that they ought to surrender. Seconds later, about fifteen
firemen walked out of the station with their hands in the air.

The 3d Platoon then started to make its way to the main terminal.
The terminal itself consists of a large rectangular building with
two spider arms jutting out to the side. At the end of each arm
is a rotunda that houses a number of gates for arrivals and depar-
tures. As the platoon moved into the open of the tarmac, shots
started to ring out from the northern rotunda. The glass windows shattered as a hail of fire descended onto the platoon. The
troops scattered. One team, led by Sgt. Reeves, quickly dived
underneath the concourse and found maintenance stairs going into
the terminal. Specialist Eubanks and Pfc. William Kelly followed
closely behind.

The two PDF soldiers ran into the women's restroom. Since the
PDF soldiers had started the firefight, Reeves did not believe they
would surrender without a battle. So he wanted to end the fight
quickly. Reeves pulled the pin from a grenade, opened the bathroom
door, and stopped. There was another door inside. He had no time
to lose. He tossed the grenade into the middle of the concourse, and
the squad jumped for cover. The grenade exploded, creating a gaping hole in the floor. The blast shattered what terminal windows
remained following the initial firefight. Reeves decided these two
PDF soldiers had to go.

He locked his M16, and pushed open the first door. Reeves had
to be quick. Although Eubanks and Kelly were right behind, only
one person could fit through the door at one time. He pushed open
the second door, and jumped inside. He looked to the right, saw
nothing. As his head turned toward the stalls to his left, he saw
something close out of the corner of his eye. He tried to raise his
rifle. A split second later, Reeves felt a sharp pain in his right shoulder. He winced, and fell to the ground, bleeding.

One PDF soldier was standing on the toilet in the stall closest to
the door. When Reeves entered the bathroom, the soldier opened
the stall door, and with the muzzle of his AK-47 rifle less than three
feet from Reeves's head, fired three shots. The first two shots went
through Reeves's shoulder. The third shot rammed through his
collarbone. The muzzle was so close that powder burns covered his
face.

As Reeves lay on the floor, one of the PDF jumped on top of him and stared him in the face. He told himself it was the end, said goodbye to his life, and closed his eyes. But the enemy soldier disappeared. The two PDF ran to the rear of the bathroom. Reeves opened his eyes and saw blood dripping from his shoulder, but didn't feel too much pain. He had to find a way to defend himself. He spotted his rifle lying on the floor next to him, but he couldn't move his right arm. He used his left arm to reach for a grenade. He knew a grenade explosion in the latrine would kill both PDF instantly.

"At whatever cost, those two guys were going to die. That was all there was to it," Reeves recalls. "That guy was going to be dead because he shot me and I was mad. It got real personal real quick." But he could not move his left arm far enough to reach the grenades in his hip pocket.

Eubanks and Kelly heard the shots and darted into the bathroom. Shots richoceted around the dark latrine as the two crawled toward their team leader on their hands and knees. As they dragged Reeves back toward the lobby, one of the PDF jumped out and fired at Reeves. The shots bounced off Kelly's Kevlar helmet. He didn't even feel the shots, and they weren't discovered until 22 December. Reeves was placed sitting against the wall just outside the bathroom next to a Coke machine, and Eubanks applied what first aid he could. Reeves didn't care; he just wanted the enemy dead. Eubanks and Kelly started to plan their assault.

First, they threw a grenade into the left side of the bathroom. When it exploded, the mirrors shattered, sending pieces of glass in every direction. The grenade was ineffective. The PDF spotted it, and moved to the other side, protected from the blast by the partition. If the enemy was to be eliminated, Kelly and Eubanks would have to do it personally.

Eubanks was the first one in. Kelly stayed close behind to watch the other side of the wall. Eubanks crept along the wall, remaining as concealed and quiet as possible. When he saw the two PDF, he raised his Squad Automatic Weapon to take both troops out. It malfunctioned. The bolt went forward but did not load a round into the chamber. Helpless, Eubanks looked up. One PDF soldier fired three shots at him with a handgun. The bullets went high and left, but Eubanks could hear the rounds whistle past his head. He jumped out of the room.

Eubanks grabbed Reeves's M203 grenade launcher, reloaded it, and took another grenade off his uniform. He pulled it and threw it into the bathroom. It was not his intention to kill the PDF with the grenade, though that would have been an acceptable side effect. Rather, this blast was to stun the enemy as Eubanks and Kelly stormed both sides of the room, firing at everything that moved. Seconds later, the firing stopped, and Eubanks heard the PDF cursing him and the United States in Spanish. There was no leaving the room now.

Eubanks, who speaks some Spanish, told the two troops to throw down their weapons three times. Each time, one of the soldiers would poke his head around the corner and yell at Eubanks: "Fuck off!" Finally, one of the two stuck his head out too far. Eubanks fired a single shot, and it burst through the soldier's neck. The PDF soldier fell to his knees, dropping the gun in front of him.

Eubanks screamed at him to lie face down. But the soldier wasn't listening. He was babbling. Eubanks, with his M203 in one hand, grabbed the man by the back of his shirt and pushed him to the ground. Kelly, standing around the corner providing security, did not see the other PDF soldier behind the stall door. The second soldier lurched for Eubanks's outstretched gun. The soldier on the ground then rolled over and made an attempt to pull his handgun out of his own waistband. In a split second, Eubanks and Kelly kicked the man on the ground out a window and off the ledge to the tarmac. The soldier fell twenty-five feet. He survived the fall, but landed in front of a Ranger M60 machine gun position. He tried to run, but the machine gunner killed him.

The second PDF soldier put both hands on Eubanks's gun, wrestling to free it from his hands. He could have shot Eubanks then, but didn't. He instead tried to take it away. Eubanks was now in a rage. With a second wave of adrenalin, Eubanks pushed the soldier against the urinals, and started kicking him repeatedly. He screamed for Kelly, who bolted around the corner and shot the soldier in the arm. Kelly fired two more shots into the PDF soldier's head, and the man released Eubanks's weapon.

The bathroom fight lasted five minutes. Eubanks carried the blood and the brains of the PDF soldier around with him on his uniform for the next few days, in the heat of Panama.

"He knew he was going to die. He did," Eubanks says. "These

two idiots just holed themselves up in that latrine and thought they were going to take out a whole company of Rangers, and they were going to start with our squad. They knew they were going to lose, and were just going to stay there until they died. I guess they thought their cause was worth dying for."

In May 1990, Kelly and Eubanks were awarded the the Bronze Star for heroism. Reeves was awarded the Army Commendation Medal for maintaining his composure while wounded to describe the disposition of the enemy.

Meanwhile, in the terminal, the 1st Platoon had entered the ground floor through the main airport entrance in order to establish a holding area for prisoners of war. The unit had with them the 18 Panamanians from the restaurant as well as 30 additional detainees from a rental car facility just outside the terminal building. Soldiers in the 1st Platoon found 40 more Panamanians while clearing the ground floor. These civilians were brought to a single area. They had no PDF prisoners yet, but expected some to arrive soon. They were not prepared for the 376 civilians from the Brazilian airline who began to emerge from every corner of the terminal.

The 2d Platoon, still outside the terminal, was tasked to systematically clear the building. The plan called for one squad to be responsible for each floor. As the platoon sat outside waiting for permission from Wagner to enter the terminal up at Tocumen, a mortar shell suddenly dropped about two hundred yards to the unit's left. The round came in on the other side of a Texaco station and an airplane; as a result, the platoon didn't think much of it. A second mortar shell then landed in between the gas station and the aircraft. Dochnal, just arriving on the scene, used the radio to try to locate the origin of the mortars. A third shell dropped too close. The Rangers ran into the terminal.

The 3d squad was the first to encounter PDF gunfire as they climbed the escalators to the second floor, a thin hallway that overlooks the terminal atrium. An estimated five PDF soldiers, seeing the onslaught of American forces in the terminal, retreated into the customs police office, and immediately started burning files. It was thought that the police files contained information linking Noriega and other PDF officers to drug operations. The PDF were as determined to destroy the records as the Rangers were to protect them.

As the squad approached the office, smoke poured out from under the metal door leading into the room. While some DENI officers piled furniture and files into a bonfire, other PDF soldiers fired blindly through the door to ward off the Rangers. Dochnal, still outside the building, was listening to the fire and asked the squad leader to urge the PDF to surrender. The squad leader said they did ask the enemy to surrender, and they were firing through the door. Dochnal gave the 3d squad the answer they wanted. "Well, you have to deal with them now."

A team of Rangers, providing point security for the 3d squad, hosed two magazines of rounds into the door. But the gunfire did not dent the metal. The squad leader then ordered the team to drop a grenade under the door, and the impact bent the bottom of the door up about one foot. The squad rolled a second grenade under the door. It rolled to the middle of the room, and detonated. The blast killed the five PDF soldiers, but added fuel to the already blazing fire. The smoke activated the sprinkler system, and Dochnal ordered the squad to leave the floor immediately. The heat was still intolerable when the C Company commander inspected the room at 9:00 A.M.

The 1st squad, the first unit into the terminal, headed for the third floor. When the squad reached the area, they heard women crying. It sounded like dozens of civilians, and the screams echoed across the terminal. The squad frantically searched for the civilians. Finally, the unit heard a Panamanian with a heavy accent.

"Don't shoot. We're civilians! We're civilians!" The squad looked down. Hundreds of civilians, some obviously American, were on the bottom floor. The squad leader opened a blue chemical light and dropped it to the floor, and yelled at the civilians to gather around the light and lie on the floor. Slowly, the airline passengers came out of hiding, and gathered around the light. The 3d squad, fleeing the fire in the customs police office, reached the first floor and began to escort the civilians outside the terminal to the road crossing the airport entrance.

Suddenly, a woman started to scream. A passenger on the Brazilian airline had given her baby to another woman. The Rangers got nervous. The airport was large and it was on fire. Each squad was busy with a task, and there were not enough Rangers to go around. But a search wasn't necessary. A Panamanian civilian who spoke

English told the 2d squad leader that he had seen a woman and a baby enter a baggage claim area in the corner of the bottom floor. He did not say anything about the nine PDF soldiers who grabbed the civilians as hostages.

The 2d squad sent one team to retrieve the woman and child. The two U.S. soldiers kicked open the door and jumped into the baggage handling area. Equipped with night vision goggles, the team spotted a number of Panamanians holding AK-47 rifles. An American woman and child were being held at gunpoint on the other side of the room. The baby was crying.

The team called the squad leader, who instructed each soldier to stand on either side of the door, and the civilian who brought them to the area to warn the PDF inside to drop their weapons. One PDF soldier responded. They were not going to come out, they had hostages, and they were staying right where they were. The Ranger team leader believed the incident was above his level of authority and the soldiers headed back to the terminal entrance. The squad leader called Dochnal.

The situation in the Torrijos terminal was quickly getting out of control. Dochnal was dismayed about the increasing number of civilians throughout the airport. "I ran downstairs, and I'm getting more reports. 'Hey sir, we just found another 50 [civilians] in this area' and all of a sudden it's 150, 200, then it's 300. And I'm going upstairs, saying holy shit. We're taking people out from behind the baggage counter and all over the airport. There were no reports of any civilians getting killed, but they were scattered to the four winds." The hostage situation added to the Rangers' frustration.

While Koren in the Ranger command post at Tocumen worked to form a surgical strike team to end the hostage situation, the 2d squad isolated the baggage claim area. The area consisted of a number of rooms separated by mirrored windows, which confused the Rangers as they tried to keep an eye on the PDF soldiers inside. U.S. civil affairs and Heavy Broadcast teams tried repeatedly to convince the PDF to surrender, but nothing was breaking the stalemate. One Ranger heard the female hostage scream: "Don't do anything, just go away. They're going to kill us if you try to do anything."

But the Rangers were not going to leave. The PDF colonel who headed Panamanian security quickly changed sides, and began speaking to the PDF in the baggage claim area. Dochnal noticed that he spoke to one of the PDF inside by name. Sgt. Santos, first sergeant of the 2d Rifle Company, was the senior PDF soldier inside. This was a high-stakes game. As negotiations continued, one Ranger team broke into a room next door to get closer to the PDF, and perhaps establish a sniper position. As Specialist Michael Smith jumped over a conveyor belt, he landed on top of a PDF soldier. With his weapon at the ready, Smith pointed the gun at the enemy troop's head, and the PDF soldier dropped his rifle. The remaining PDF soldiers then opened a hail of fire into the room.

The rounds flew high over Smith's head, but Dochnal had seen enough. He went to the door, and got the PDF soldiers' attention. "If you don't come out, I'm just going to kill you. You've got five minutes to come out or I'm just going to kill you." Three minutes later, the door opened and the PDF came out, dropped their weapons and lay on the floor. The American woman then came out, holding the baby.

Santos then came out with his hands up. The remaining enemy soldiers followed suit. When U.S. soldiers searched the enemy, they found one man carrying a Cuban diplomat identification card. The American woman would later tell Dochnal that the Cuban was giving the PDF soldiers instructions.

At 5:00 A.M., the hostage situation was declared resolved. As American soldiers fed and comforted the aircraft passengers and guarded some thirty PDF prisoners found in the Torrijos terminal, Dochnal walked leaders of the 82d Airborne Division through the building, retracing each confrontation. At 7:00 A.M., Major General Johnson, the division commander, assumed responsibility for the terminal.

Dochnal was glad to be rid of it.

The first aircraft carrying the 7th Infantry Division (Light) from Fort Ord, California, landed at Tocumen airfield at 8:00 A.M. There was no enemy resistance because the Rangers had eliminated the 2d Rifle Company and the FAP. All told, the assault into Tocumen and Torrijos airfields went precisely as planned.

One Ranger, Pfc. Markwell, lost his life. Amazingly, only eight Rangers were injured; some, like Sgt. Reeves, concede that they really should be dead. The number of Rangers wounded in the assault fell short of the number of troops injured on the jump itself. By the latest count, thirteen PDF soldiers were killed, but it is still unclear how many enemy soldiers were wounded. Task Force Red-T captured a total of 54 PDF as prisoners, and later freed 376 civilians.

The only bad news was that the Rangers missed Noriega.

In Broad Daylight

The core of the PDF was shattered, but there remained the threat of the enemy reinforcements from PDF units within Panama City, at Panama Viejo and Cerro Tinajitas, and from Fort Cimarron, northeast of the capital.

It was Task Force Pacific's job to eliminate this threat. In the original plans for air assaults on the three PDF installations, taking out Battalion 2000 at Fort Cimarron came first, followed by an attack on the PDF's 1st Infantry Company at Cerro Tinajitas, then the garrison at Panama Viejo. The list of air assaults was first drawn up in October, briefed to Thurman later that month and rehearsed at Fort Bragg in November.

Battalion 2000, by coming to Noriega's aid in the botched 3 October coup, had proven a critical element of the PDF. Then Noriega decided to move the UESAT, his antiterrorist special operations force, to Panama Viejo after the coup attempt. Until October, the UESAT had been stationed at Flamenco Island, at the southern end of the causeway through Fort Amador.

The UESAT was a more potent force than even Battalion 2000, a battalion of which Noriega also moved to Panama Viejo. Suddenly the bayside garrison became a major threat to the U.S. operation, and senior war planners moved it to the top of their list of targets for the 82d Airborne soldiers who would arrive in Panama shortly after H-hour.

Just before 2:00 A.M., the first airborne units parachuted into Torrijos Airport. But because of the ice storm in North Carolina, the three-battalion task force, under the command of 1st Brigade, did not assemble until 4:30 A.M. Two of the three battalions—the 1st and 2d Battalions of the 504th Parachute Infantry Regiment—were intrinsic to the brigade. Because the 3d Battalion had been in Panama since 10 December and had missions well north of Panama City, the 4th Battalion of the division's 325th Parachute Infantry Regiment became the third battalion in the air-assault task force.

Stiner decided not to scrub the assaults when he learned the paratroopers would be arriving late, but to proceed as quickly as possible, relying on the heavy firepower of the attack helicopters to even the odds. The assaults would also have limited armored strength. A convoy of HMMWVs, escorted by M551 Sheridans from the 82d Airborne's 3d Battalion, 73d Armor Regiment, was to move from Tocumen Airfield to each target to support the assault troops and provide the tracks and HMMWVs they would need after knocking down the PDF (see figure 11–1).

It was painfully obvious to the soldiers as they assembled at Tocumen that with daylight approaching, the odds were mounting against them. They could only hope to get the job done quickly, and grew impatient for lift-off. They had plenty of time to contemplate the odds. Because of the strenuous demands on airlift, they did not start loading until about 6:00 A.M.

Capt. Timothy Jones, commander of 7th Division attack aviators who were to provide escort for the air assaults, was alarmed to learn around 7:00 A.M. that his colleagues were just beginning the assaults. Just five hours after his own helicopter had been shot out of the sky at Fort Amador, Jones was at Task Force Aviation tactical operations center at Fort Kobbe, eager to hear a final report on the missions.

"I thought the whole thing was over," Jones says. "So how did it go? How did we do?" he asked others in the Ops center. "The answer I got surprised me: they were just now starting."

The mission of dismantling the PDF at Panama Viejo fell to the 2d Battalion, 504th Parachute Infantry Regiment. The intent of the air assault was to surround the garrison, which sat on the shore of the Bay of Panama, and demand the PDF surrender. About 250 soldiers lived in the barracks, Southern Command estimated, including 70

82nd Airborne Air Assaults

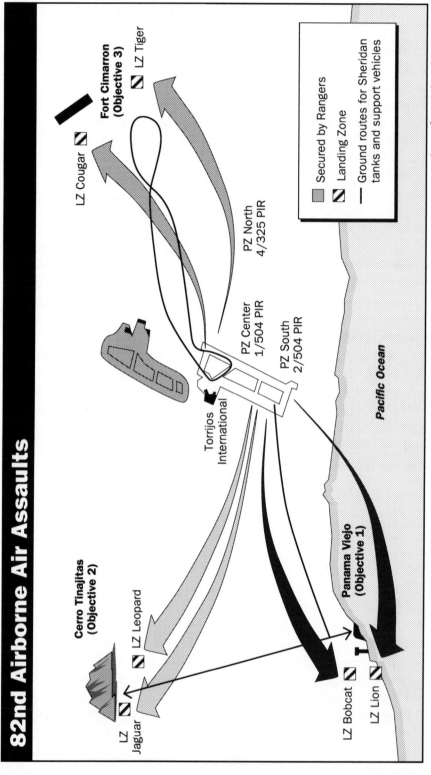

Joanne Ostendorf and Cristina Rivero

FIGURE 11–1
82d Airborne Air Assaults

from the UESAT and 180 from the 1st Cavalry Squadron, a largely ceremonial unit also responsible for guarding Noriega's home. The squadron kept 48 horses in a nearby stables.

After cordoning off the garrison, loudspeaker teams from the 4th Psychological Operations Group would offer the PDF a choice: surrender or fight for your lives. The troops would come into Panama Viejo at two landing zones: LZ Bobcat, an area of eight-foot-high elephant grass 220 yards north of the garrison, and LZ Lion, to the south of the garrison along the shoreline. LZ Bobcat, situated next to a seventeenth-century stone ruin, was a strip of grass between the bay and the garrison. "It was extremely narrow," says Capt. Tom Muir, commander of A Company, 3d Battalion, 123d Aviation, one of the assault companies that provided lift for the three targets.

The aviators did not realize until they arrived at Panama Viejo just how narrow the landing zone was. They had done most of their reconnaissance of the area with night-vision goggles. Muir said they had been offered an opportunity to scout out the garrison in civilian clothes during the day, but could not find the time before they got their orders. It didn't seem that important to see the target during the day. "We were told this would not be done during the day," Muir says.

Twenty-one UH-60 Black Hawks from Task Force Hawk were to provide the battalion's airlift, with escort from four Cobras and surveillance by two Apaches and an OH-58 Kiowa. An additional Black Hawk provided command and control (see figure 11–2).

As the first lift touched down on each landing zone around 7:00 A.M., the soldiers were met with automatic-weapons fire from PDF troops in the barracks and adjacent civilian houses. LZ Lion proved to be more treacherous than Bobcat. Some of the Black Hawks, flying in at the edge of LZ Lion, slipped and shifted. The soldiers found themselves waist deep in mud. What had looked like solid ground from the air, the troops were aghast to find, was not-so-solid mud.

Loaded down with combat gear, they struggled helplessly to gain a foothold on solid ground as they tried to stay clear of persistent enemy fire. A few sank to their armpits, unable to move. At least one Black Hawk hovered precariously just a few feet from the ground, the pilot careful to maintain engine power, while the crew

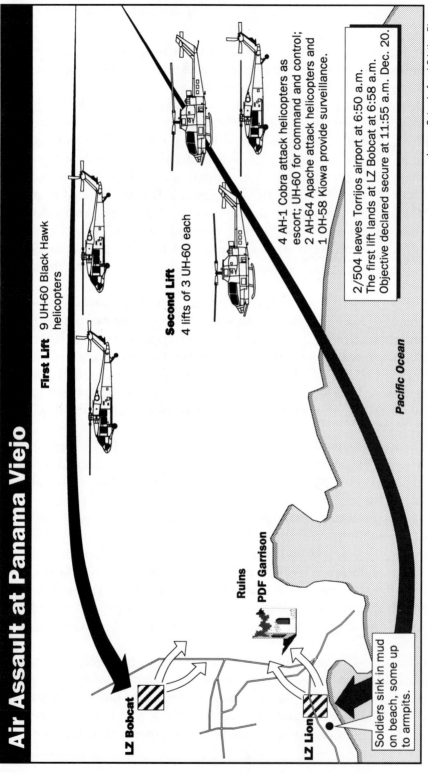

Air Assault at Panama Viejo

First Lift 9 UH-60 Black Hawk helicopters

Second Lift 4 lifts of 3 UH-60 each

4 AH-1 Cobra attack helicopters as escort; UH-60 for command and control; 2 AH-64 Apache attack helicopters and 1 OH-58 Kiowa provide surveillance.

2/504 leaves Torrijos airport at 6:50 a.m. The first lift lands at LZ Bobcat at 6:58 a.m. Objective declared secure at 11:55 a.m. Dec. 20.

Pacific Ocean

Ruins

PDF Garrison

LZ Bobcat

LZ Lion

Soldiers sink in mud on beach, some up to armpits.

Joanne Ostendorf and Cristina Rivero

FIGURE 11–2
Air Assault at Panama Viejo

chief and door gunner reached down to pull the soldiers out by their rucksacks. None were hit during the struggle to find firm ground.

The mishap was a direct result of the paratroopers' delayed arrival. One of the reasons 1:00 A.M. was designated H-hour for Just Cause, according to Stiner, was because the tide would be high at Panama Viejo and Paitilla Airport. But at 7:00 A.M., when the assault troops finally arrived, the tide was out, exposing a long stretch of mud flats.

From the crowd gathering to watch the helicopters, the scene did not look like a military attack. "It was a combat assault, but there were a lot of civilians that were just standing there watching, like it was a show, an air show," says Jones.

The attack pilots were severely constrained in their ability to return fire because of the large number of civilians gathered below them. But the civilians also proved to be lifesavers when they formed a human chain at the shoreline, despite PDF fire, and extended ropes to the paratroopers to help pull them from the muck.

LZ Bobcat presented the opposite problem. Instead of being too exposed, it was blanketed in eight-foot elephant grass, completely obscuring the pilots' view as they landed. In the tall grass, the soldiers were disoriented, unable to find each other, much less locate the source of the automatic-weapons fire flying at them.

Three UH-60s were hit as they left the drop zone after delivering the second lift. All managed to land at Tocumen, out of action for the day. Chief Warrant Officer Anthony Montano of Muir's company had no indication his aircraft had taken three rounds until, after shutting down the engines at Tocumen while he waited for the next lift, he found the generator did not work.

In one of the less celebrated incidents of women under fire in Panama, another Black Hawk, flown by Chief Warrant Officer Deborah Mann of the same company, also took three rounds in the tail rotor. Another pilot alerted her to an oil leak from the rear gear box as she was returning to Tocumen.

After the difficult drop into Panama Viejo, it was a pleasant surprise to find that the military force the soldiers were up against was not 250 Panamanian troops, or even 200, but only about 20. The PDF garrison was known to be heavily armed, but the Panamanian troops put up only a fleeting defense.

"There was initial resistance, stiff resistance—stiffer than we thought—but it faded very quickly," says Maj. Gen. James Johnson, commander of the 82d Airborne Division. "Essentially, the leaders didn't show. The troops were deserted." Johnson later learned that, in his words, the Panama Viejo garrison commander called his men from his home in Panama City and said, "Issue the weapons. . . . See ya' later."

Sgt. Michael Alexander, of C Company, 2d Battalion, 504th Infantry (Airborne), found the PDF arms room. Its inventory was impressive: Uzi submachine guns with night sights, antitank rockets, sniper rifles, an automatic grenade launcher and state-of-the-art body armor. One room of the barracks contained explosives. A .50 caliber machine gun was mounted on top of the building. A ZPU-4, a four-barrelled antiaircraft gun, was positioned near the shoreline to fire out over the water. Loaded with ammunition, the gun was in a position to fire on the air assault helicopters and create a bloodbath, Johnson says, but the gunner never fired a shot. He fled as one of the Cobras swooped down towards him.

Still under fire himself, Alexander called for a grenade launcher and fired several rounds at the enemy, following them with machine-gun fire. The tactic succeeded, allowing his unit to move off the landing zone. The sergeant later received the Bronze Star for Valor.

Those PDF who were not surrounded fled the barracks for nearby civilian buildings, leaving breakfasts half-eaten and the arms room a shambles. Some of the Panamanian soldiers assigned to Panama Viejo did not find out about the invasion until they went to work that morning, only to be detained as they arrived at the garrison.

Jones, glued to the radio in the task force tactical operations center, was relieved to learn at 7:50 A.M. that the air assault had been completed. The worst was yet to come.

The next assault, on Cerro Tinajitas, was to become one of the most-celebrated "if only" stories to emerge from Operation Just Cause (see figure 11–3).

If only there hadn't been an ice storm back at Pope Air Force Base, the paratroopers from the 82d Airborne's 1st Battalion, 504th Parachute Infantry Regiment, would have been able to attack Tinajitas at night, as planned. If only the landing zone hadn't been so

Air Assault at Tinajitas

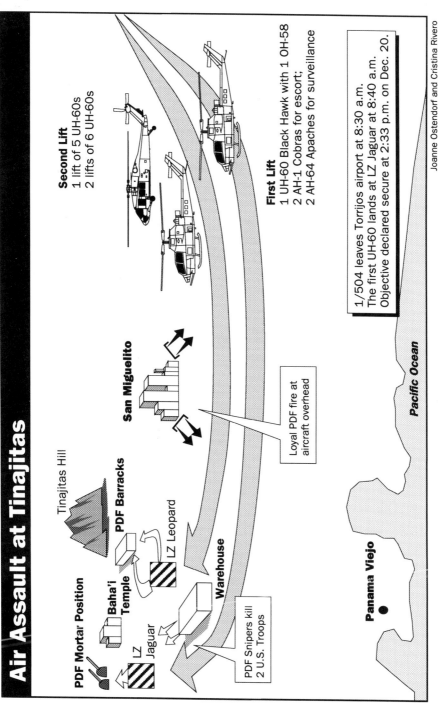

PDF Mortar Position

Tinajitas Hill

Baha'i Temple

PDF Barracks

LZ Leopard

LZ Jaguar

San Miguelito

Warehouse

Loyal PDF fire at aircraft overhead

PDF Snipers kill 2 U.S. Troops

Second Lift
1 lift of 5 UH-60s
2 lifts of 6 UH-60s

First Lift
1 UH-60 Black Hawk with 1 OH-58
2 AH-1 Cobras for escort;
2 AH-64 Apaches for surveillance

1/504 leaves Torrijos airport at 8:30 a.m.
The first UH-60 lands at LZ Jaguar at 8:40 a.m.
Objective declared secure at 2:33 p.m. on Dec. 20.

Panama Viejo

Pacific Ocean

Joanne Ostendorf and Cristina Rivero

FIGURE 11–3
Air Assault at Tinajitas

tight, they might have had an easier time evading ground fire. Maybe they wouldn't have taken so many casualties, or the helicopters so many hits.

It was shortly after 8:00 A.M. when the first of eighteen Black Hawks, preceded by two Apaches hugging the treetops and escorted by two low-flying Cobras and an OH-58, approached the sprawling concrete barracks of the PDF's 1st Infantry Company. True to its name, the "Tiger" company garrison was flanked by life-size concrete tigers.

The U.S. command knew Tinajitas would be a tough mission. Intelligence reports said the garrison was defended by dozens of 81mm and 120mm mortars. "We were concerned about them putting effective fire onto Howard Air Force Base," Johnson says. As a defense against the mortars, two Q-36 mortar-finding radars were set up at Howard.

These PDF infantrymen also were known to be aggressive. Reconnoitering the target from a helicopter, the 82d Airborne's brigade commanders had seen the PDF infantrymen rush to defensive positions as soon as the helicopters approached the garrison.

As if the odds weren't bad enough, now the troops were flying into Tinajitas in broad daylight in the first of two lifts from Tocumen. The PDF could see them coming for miles. "As pilots, we all realized we were going to go in at day and it made us all nervous," says 1st Lt. Robert Healy, a Black Hawk pilot assigned to ferry troops into Tinajitas. Only two pilots in his unit, the 3d Battalion, 123d Aviation Regiment, had flown in combat before.

"It was a very hairy situation," says Johnson. The 82d Airborne commander would have liked to have special forces surveillance teams placed at all three targets before the air assaults. He had requested them, but special forces troops already were spread thin, and he got only a "maybe." In addition to the many demands on his men, Maj. Gen. Wayne Downing, commander of all special operating forces in Panama, felt that to insert special forces troops at assault targets before the invasion might tip off the PDF, Johnson says.

Preparatory fire also was ruled out because of the populated neighborhoods surrounding Tinajitas. Normally, the first stage in an air assault would be to "prep" the target, or lay fire on it from attack helicopters, artillery, and fixed-wing aircraft to suppress enemy defenses. "We put our soldiers at risk in order to minimize casualties and damage to the Panamanian people and their country," Johnson says.

The soldiers' mission was to gain control of the high ground and neutralize the PDF and its weaponry.

Most of the Black Hawks flew into LZ Leopard, a ravine alongside a road leading to Tinajitas, about 750 yards from the PDF installation. One helicopter flew into LZ Jaguar near the Baha'i Temple, a suspected PDF mortar position, on a 4,900-foot hill just west of the enemy garrison. Landing Zone Jaguar was not visible from the Tinajitas garrison. Johnson says the site was selected because it provided maximum shelter from PDF fire.

A mortar team inserted into the landing zone by the Black Hawk positioned a .50 caliber machine gun next to the temple to give fire support to the soldiers assaulting Cerro Tinajitas. From talking to 82d Airborne Apache pilots flying about fifteen minutes ahead of the airlift, "We knew very early on that we would be taking fire at Tinajitas," says Muir, the flight lead and Healy's company commander.

Ground fire started as soon as the helicopters appeared over San Miguelito, an impoverished community near Tinajitas with strong loyalty to Noriega. It was mostly small-arms fire, but amazingly precise, a change from the erratic defense the PDF and DigBats had mustered so far. For the first time, the Panamanians had time and daylight on their side. Both escorting Cobras came under ground fire, while the Apaches hovered close above to provide additional air support. The Black Hawks, flying in three flights of six each, took numerous hits on their two trips into the landing zone.

Muir warned the paratroopers in the back of his Black Hawk that they were flying into a hot landing zone.

Healy was flying behind Muir in the second group of six Black Hawks when he heard the captain talking to his passengers on the radio. The lieutenant was thinking about whether to fly over or under several power lines hanging just about two hundred feet over the ground near the garrison, and how to deal with the elephant grass on the small LZ. Flying over them, as he decided to do, would require a steep, almost vertical ascent during departure. "It was not really a smooth area to land in," Healy says.

To complicate the situation, the pilots had trouble pinpointing enemy fire positions and so, in many cases, could not order return fire. In those cases where there were no civilians around the enemy weapons positions, the Cobras returned fire. "It was pretty difficult to locate the targets, because it was a populated area," says pilot Chief Warrant Officer Jeffrey Harris.

The decision to fire belonged to Lt. Col. Howard Borum, commander of Task Force Hawk. He considered pilots' information on the radio,then gave orders to fire: "capone left" or "capone right." Door gunners in the helicopters would see a Panamanian pointing an AK-47 at the assault birds, but the enemy snipers would duck back in the crowd as soon as they fired their shots, making retaliation impossible.

The casualties began even before the first lift touched the ground. A few soldiers were struck by bullets that flew up through the floor of the Black Hawks.

Not being able to fire back put the door gunners on edge. "That was so difficult," says Pfc. Bryant Clark, a combat crew chief in Muir's company.

Healy heard Borum give an order to fire on the radio, and relayed the message to his door gunner. No response. "He couldn't talk. We didn't know why," Healy says. The gunner's microphone cord had been shot through by ground fire. The gunner, from the 7th Division's B Company, 4th Battalion, 17th Infantry Regiment, also took a round in his left arm as he held the microphone.

Healy then learned his commanding officer had been shot and was in much worse shape. Just minutes before, Muir had taken a 7.62mm AK-47 round in his head through the window on his left. The impact of the round threw him back, then he slumped forward, bleeding profusely. Muir's copilot, Chief Warrant Officer Neal VandenHoovel, took over the controls of the Black Hawk. He still had to carry twenty-six soldiers into the landing zone.

"Going into Tinajitas, I heard Mr. VandenHoovel yelling that Capt. Muir got hit, and I heard everybody else yelling, 'We're taking hits.' And all this time I kept hearing this clicking noise," says Chief Warrant Officer John Petraroi. The clicking was AK-47 fire hitting Petraroi's helicopter. He had never heard a helicopter taking gunshots before.

VandenHoovel reached the landing zone. Some paratroopers left the Black Hawk without all their gear. As he waited for them to gather their equipment, a bullet shattered the controls, sending metal flying into his face. Yet he managed to lift off with only minor injuries. Muir says he wanted to continue flying to pick up the next lift as scheduled, but he was losing too much blood. VandenHoovel broke left and flew to Howard to get medical help for Muir, while the other Black Hawks continued to Tocumen for the second lift.

From VandenHoovel's description, the pilots thought Muir was a goner, Healy says. "We were all thinking, 'Capt. Muir is dead. Who else is going to get it?'"

The helicopters took more fire on the second lift, but without injury to any of the aviators. The Cobras' farewell to Tinajitas, as the helicopters made their way back to Tocumen, was to fire half a dozen 2.75-inch rockets up the hillside as the Black Hawks departed. The attack birds managed to suppress automatic-weapons fire from the garrison.

The paratroopers, however, had not yet seen the worst of it. They were four to five hundred meters from their target.

As they maneuvered east toward the PDF garrison, the assault force came under heavy automatic-weapons and mortar fire from a warehouse to the north, across from the landing zone. The fire continued as they maneuvered, raining down on them from the top of Cerro Tinajitas and from the surrounding barrio. Tall grass obscured the Panamanian firing positions, preventing the soldiers below from getting a fix on the enemy. The paratroopers knew they would survive only if they kept moving up the hill, forcing the PDF to continually adjust their mortar fire.

Two paratroopers died in the assault. Pfc. Martin Denson of the battalion's B Company was struck by gunfire as he got off the helicopter. He suffered another hit from mortar fragments and later died, according to 82d Airborne casualty reports. Pfc. Jerry Scott Daves of B Company was shot in the head by a sniper as he pulled himself up the hill. As a medic attended to him, a mortar round exploded nearby, killing Daves and wounding the medic.

If enemy fire made the soldiers' movements difficult, it made landing impossible for rescue helicopters. Incoming medical evacuation helicopters were waved off because of the heavy mortar fire.

The heat of the sun was almost unbearable, overwhelming a number of the heavily laden soldiers, who just twelve hours before had been shivering in icy cold at Pope Air Force Base. At least a half-dozen of the seventeen infantrymen wounded during the assault were casualties of heat exhaustion or heat stroke, aggravated by the inability of rescue helicopters to evacuate them.

Almost every helicopter carrying troops took some hits during the assault, although all returned to Howard Air Force Base that afternoon under their own power. At least three aircraft, including a Cobra, had been shot out of service. Two paratroopers died and seventeen were wounded, along with Muir.

When the paratroopers reached the 1st Infantry Company garrison, they found few PDF troops but a number of artillery tubes with rounds still in them. An unknown number of PDF soldiers had abandoned the garrison, taking the two-wheeled mortars with them in vans. The enemy continued to harass U.S. troops occupying Tinajitas with mortar fire for the next two days. Blending in with the surrounding community, PDF and Dignity Battalion troops fired and moved, fired and moved.

The paratroopers, meanwhile, dug in for the long haul.

The Sheridan convoy to Panama Viejo that morning was no less treacherous. No one had yet traveled the road between Tocumen and Panama City. For U.S. troops, it was a dangerous no-man's-land.

The convoy consisted of two Sheridans, two HMMWVs, and two airport baggage trucks mounted with .50 caliber machine guns. D Company of the 2d Battalion, 504th Infantry (Airborne) was assigned to travel with them.

It was about 10:00 A.M. when the convoy, moving in tight formation with the HMMWVs sandwiched in ones and twos between Sheridans, ran into one of what proved to be trademark Panamanian obstacles. The enemy used anything it could find to build roadblocks: cars, propane bottles, dump trucks, fuel trucks, refrigerators, and concertina wire. Often, Panamanians crouched on the other side to shoot at approaching U.S. forces. The soldiers, moving southwest to Panama Viejo, encountered such an obstacle on a bridge less than a mile from the airport. It was fashioned mainly from trucks and propane bottles, with more of the same to the convoy's left.

The tankers had orders to fire over any roadblocks before dismantling or rolling over them. As a Sheridan moved up to the roadblock, the convoy took fire from nearby buildings. The paratroopers dismounted and moved up to clear the obstacle themselves with grenades. The lead Sheridan fired five rounds, three of them over buildings from which the convoy was taking fire.

The shooting stopped, but a U.S. soldier was dead: Specialist Alejandro Manrique-Lozano, nicknamed "Alphabet" by his comrades because of his long name. Manrique-Lozano was a member of D Company, of the 2d Battalion, 504th Infantry (Airborne).

It was too dangerous to continue. About a mile farther down the road, the convoy mission was called off.

Back at Fort Kobbe, the pilots returning from Tinajitas to refuel and load more ammunition wondered how Muir was. They also wondered why no one had planned for the possibility that the air assaults would be pushed back into daylight.

Healy suggested the assault on Cimarron be put off until after dark. After Muir's experience, "The company realized it was deadly serious," Healy says. His proposal was shot down.

Muir lived. The machine-gun round penetrated his nose, breaking it and requiring ninety-five stitches. The round also knocked his helmet down against his face, breaking his cheekbone.

The pilots and their crews accepted cold Cokes from the ground crews and took stock of the aircraft.

They were pleased to see how well the Black Hawks had come through. Those that had been hit were still able to fly. But because their staying power was questionable, the command decided to go into Cimarron with six Black Hawks, including one for command and control, two Cobras and an OH-58 for escort, and two Apaches flying ahead for surveillance (see figure 11–4).

In less than five minutes, the helicopters were on their way to Fort Cimarron with the soldiers of the 4th Battalion, 325th Infantry (Airborne). An AC-130 provided air cover. The paratroopers had rehearsed the assault in November at Fort Bragg's Holland Drop Zone, using HMMWVs modified to resemble the armored cars of Battalion 2000 and antiarmor weapons to defeat the enemy.

Fort Cimarron was more sophisticated than the average PDF installation, with a large airfield and concrete runway. Battalion 2000 was known to have a dozen V-300 light assault vehicles. The assault force found four at Fort Cimarron when it arrived, including one

Air Assault at Fort Cimarron

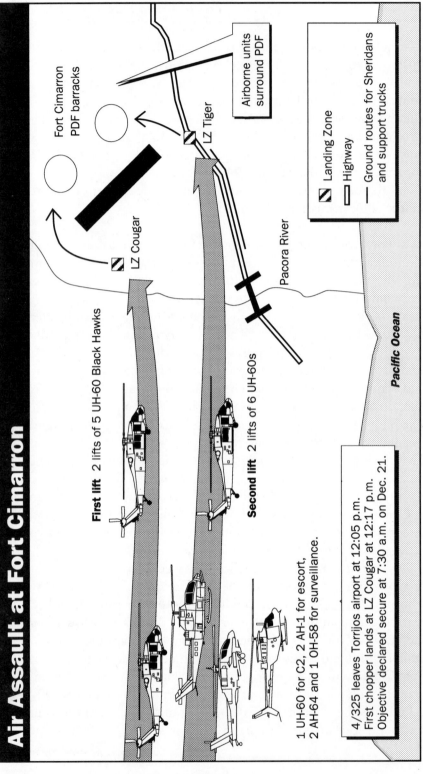

Fort Cimarron
PDF barracks

Airborne units
surround PDF

LZ Tiger

LZ Cougar

Pacora River

First lift 2 lifts of 5 UH-60 Black Hawks

Second lift 2 lifts of 6 UH-60s

Pacific Ocean

◪ Landing Zone
▭ Highway
— Ground routes for Sheridans
and support trucks

1 UH-60 for C2, 2 AH-1 for escort,
2 AH-64 and 1 OH-58 for surveillance.

4/325 leaves Torrijos airport at 12:05 p.m.
First chopper lands at LZ Cougar at 12:17 p.m.
Objective declared secure at 7:30 a.m. on Dec. 21.

Joanne Ostendorf and Cristina Rivero

FIGURE 11–4
Air Assault at Fort Cimarron

with the engine running. The soldiers also were worried about two ZPU-4s the PDF was believed to have at Cimarron.

The landing zone was out of direct range of the Battalion 2000 headquarters.

The assault force confronted no serious firepower, as it turned out. Much of Battalion 2000 had fled. Although the lead helicopter took several hits, "Cimarron really went off without a hitch," Healy says. After the helicopters landed, a support element moved to the west of the cuartel, about 1,500 yards away from the battalion headquarters complex of several buildings. A special forces team blocked the bridge over the Pacora River, keeping the enemy from fleeing west.

The assault force maneuvered north toward the complex and isolated the remnants of the battalion and the road west to Panama City. Meeting only token resistance, the assault troops took little time to isolate the remaining PDF.

Infantrymen and psychological operations teams with bullhorns moved into the compound, going building to building and asking Panamanian holdouts to surrender. It took a show of force from the AC-130, infantrymen, and mortars to convince the Panamanians to give up.

The Sheridan convoy assigned to the mission, carrying D Company of the airborne battalion, was held back from the cuartel overnight because of the firing between U.S. forces and Battalion 2000 holdouts. The convoy itself had come under fire twice on the way to Fort Cimarron, both times from buildings along the road. The Sheridans did not return any fire because of their limited field of vision. All night, the paratroopers watched tracers fly from outside the fire zone.

The next morning the infantrymen cleared the battalion headquarters, firing a few rounds from one of the Sheridans to help flush out stragglers. Some members of Battalion 2000 who had drifted into the surrounding areas surrendered later in groups of two or three. Others just disappeared. No one knew where they went.

The danger did not end with the take-over of the garrisons. While U.S. troops dug in among the grassy ruins of Panama Viejo, protected by four-foot-thick stone walls with parachute canopies draped overhead, Dignity Battalion members and PDF soldiers in civilian clothes continued to harass the 2d Battalion all day with intermittent fire and drive-by shootings. PDF forces also fired three mortars, but hit no one.

The members of the 2d Battalion stopped or destroyed nine such vehicles with weapons fire. In one case, an AT-4 antitank rocket stopped a PDF V-300 armored car. Three other V-300s were destroyed by 82d Airborne Apache helicopters. Also that day, the paratroopers discovered two V-300 armored cars and several two-and-a-half-ton trucks in a junkyard within three hundred meters of Panama Viejo. Both V-300s were destroyed by Hellfire missiles, and the trucks with 30mm and 2.75mm rockets.

As soon as the harassment subsided, the battalion received another, unexpected mission: to rescue American hostages.

Dozens of Americans, mostly airline workers and journalists, were in the Caesar Park Marriott hotel shortly after H-hour when men wearing civilian clothes and carrying assault rifles forced about eighty hotel employees and guests into the lobby.[1] The armed men ordered the group to lie facedown on the floor with their hands on their heads, according to an Associated Press report.

A luxury hotel and tourist mecca, the Marriott sits on the shore of Panama Bay in the affluent San Francisco area, two miles west of Panama Viejo. It was an obvious target for Panamanian forces loyal to Noriega. Not only is it a large hotel, with 391 rooms, but it is four miles from the nearest U.S. military installation. So removed was the hotel from the military community, in fact, that one Eastern Airlines flight attendant staying there thought the flares streaking through the sky early on the morning of the invasion were fireworks. She went back to sleep, only to learn at dawn that the city was under siege.

Downstairs in the lobby, a man who appeared to lead the intruders announced: "We're being invaded, so we're taking hostages."

Joe Clark, a Miami businessman, describing the Panamanian captors as "goon squads," said they went to the eleventh floor, where most of the Americans were. Clark told the Associated Press he jumped from his room to the fire escape, where he hid all morning until a Marriott security official found him a safer room in which to hide. Clark crouched behind a door while the security employee told the intruders no Americans were in the room.

Other Americans hid in the hotel basement. A number of Eastern Airlines flight attendants took refuge inside industrial-size washing machines.

The men assembled a group of about a dozen captives and held them in a private home near the hotel for about four hours. At 4:00 A.M. the hostages were loaded onto two vans. One group was released on the street, while the other vanished from sight.

Around 9:00 A.M., armed men calling themselves members of the Dignity Battalions returned to the hotel and grabbed three foreigners, whom they forced to lie facedown in the bed of a pickup truck. Two were journalists—news producer Jon Meyersohn of CBS and Robert Campos of ABC. The third was Daniel Sarria, the hotel's resident manager. They were released that afternoon.

As they left, the armed Panamanians demanded that the hotel staff produce a guest list and master key. They promised to return.

At about eight that evening, B Company of the 2d Battalion, 504th Infantry (Airborne), defending the captured garrison at Panama Viejo, got orders to rescue the American civilians at the Marriott. "We were notified there were U.S. citizens, media personnel, airline crews, and third-country nationals trapped," says 82d Airborne commander Johnson. "Some said they were hostages." Whatever their description, PDF troops were harassing them. "They couldn't get out, and they desired to be rescued and evacuated."

Special forces troops, busy trying to pin down Noriega, "did not have time to deal with a mess like that. Thurman felt U.S. forces had too many missions elsewhere in the city—dismantling the PDF, restoring public order, and protecting vital services—to be given the additional job of defending the Marriott.

Initial military reports on the situation said there were twenty-nine people being held against their will inside the hotel, which was about half-full. Lt. Col. Harry Axson, the battalion commander, and his command group led B Company to the Marriott. An engineer squad and the 1st Brigade surgeon joined in the mission. An AC-130 Spectre gunship provided air cover, which proved to be badly needed.

It took the troops three hours to make the two-mile trip. They had moved only 150 meters down the road when four PDF soldiers ambushed them. The four enemy soldiers were killed. None of the paratroopers was injured, but the force took heavy sniper fire along the route, even with the fire-suppressing efforts of the Spectre.

Another 150 meters down the road, a large truck appeared from nowhere, bursting into the road. Three machine guns and two AK-47s fired from inside the truck peppered the area with bullets as the truck careered along the troop column. When the truck sped up, a passenger inside fired a pistol and a grenade soared out of the cab, flying over the paratroopers' heads and landing in the bay.

Two soldiers suffered minor injuries in the attack. A makeshift ambulance, actually a van, itself was ambushed on the way back to Panama Viejo with wounded soldiers. Enemy fire shattered the windshield, injuring the driver's assistant. Specialist Richard Lucas, a radio operator with 2d Battalion, continued to drive the van back and forth along the route until he was ordered to stop because of the danger.

Responding to the attack, paratroopers riddled the truck with fire until it started to burn. The truck was still moving at about thirty-five miles per hour when Specialist James Smith of 3d Platoon, hearing the commotion behind him, stepped directly into its path and let loose with his M203 grenade launcher. The round exploded on the passenger side of the truck, which continued to bear down on Smith's platoon.

Still standing in the road, he loaded a second grenade and fired. The grenade hit the mark, exploding on the windshield in front of the driver, who veered off the road and crashed the truck into a building. Smith received the Bronze Star for Valor.

A Black Hawk helicopter from 1st Battalion, 228th Aviation Regiment, landed on the roof of the Marriott to fly about thirty hotel guests to safety. Eventually, all of the people snatched from the Marriott by the armed Panamanians were released unharmed. Meyersohn and GTE Corporation executive Doug Mullen were among the last to be released, three days later.

A group of Smithsonian Institution scientists also became pawns in the D-day struggle for control of Panama.[2] About thirty Panamanian soldiers, in a bid to strengthen Noriega's hand, forcibly removed eleven scientists and research assistants, along with the four-year-old daughter of one of the biologists, from a tropical research center in the San Blas Islands in the Caribbean. The group included five Panamanians, a Venezuelan, and five Americans.

The soldiers, believed to be members of the PDF, held the scientists for two days, moving from the island to a rain forest on the mainland.

As he walked in front of his captors into the forest, research assistant Steve Travers braced himself to die. "Everybody thought they were going to shoot us," Travers later told reporters.

The researchers managed to take with them three two-way radios, which they used surreptitiously to make contact with Smithsonian officials in Panama City on 20 and 21 December. Despite this clearheaded move, they were terrified when they called Ira Rubinoff, director of the research institute, based in Panama City. Rubinoff alerted the military.

On Thursday, 21 December, the Panamanian captors left the group at a schoolhouse in a remote Indian village in the jungle. They asked the scientists to describe the incident to U.S. authorities later as protective custody, not an abduction, according to press accounts.

The first rescue attempt failed when two U.S. helicopters could not find the group that night. The helicopters, running low on fuel, returned to Howard Air Force Base. On the second try, the helicopters found the scientists. "That was a fantastic moment, seeing the helicopters come," Travers said.

Not all the Americans in Panama were so lucky.

Raymond Dragseth, a computer science teacher at the Defense Department's Panama Canal College and the husband of a Panamanian, was kidnapped and shot to death. Dragseth, forty-seven, was one of three U.S. civilian casualties from Operation Just Cause.

His wife, Vicky, and daughter, Carolyn, said armed men in civilian clothes forced their way into the family's apartment at Punta Paitilla around 3:00 A.M., shortly after the invasion began.[3] Identifying themselves as members of the PDF, the four men said they were looking for Americans. They threatened to kill Dragseth on the spot if he did not go along with them. Dragseth left with the Panamanians.

Carolyn Dragseth said her family reported him missing immediately, calling everyone they thought could help: the American embassy, the military police, the provost marshal. "The assistance that was given to us was absolutely minimal," Carolyn Dragseth later told the Cable News Network. "We called for five days in a desperate attempt" to mobilize U.S. forces in the search for her father.

Dragseth's family never saw him again. His body was recovered on 28 December in a shallow grave near Fort Clayton, one of twenty-eight shallow graves dug in which bodies had been buried a few days before for sanitary reasons. He had been shot in the back of the head. Anel Beliz, Dragseth's brother-in-law and a close associate of Endara, identified the body.

Earlier that night, Gertrude Helin, a teacher in Defense Department secondary schools in Panama, was trying to get home safely before the invasion began when she was fatally shot. Steve Helin, her husband, was driving them home from a party when he encountered an armed Panamanian in camouflage pants and T-shirt, who was waving them down near the main gate to Albrook Air Station. Helin slowed down until he saw the Panamanian had a gun. As he sped away from the man, the Panamanian fired, striking his wife in the abdomen. She died later at a first aid station in the nearby neighborhood of Corozal, just minutes from her Los Rios home.[4]

In a tragic twist, Vicky Dragseth's nephew also was killed just as the invasion began. Richard Paul, twenty-two, was shot by American troops when he tried to run a U.S. roadblock shortly after midnight. He and a friend had just left a party in the Cardenas housing area near Fort Clayton, although the group had received a call from a parent, warning them to stay inside because U.S. forces were about to attack Panama. Paul had almost reached his home in La Boca, a Panama Canal Commission housing area outside Fort Amador, when he was fatally shot.

The deaths of Dragseth, Helin, and Paul soon were eclipsed by the greater loss of life and livelihood among Panamanian civilians, perhaps because the potential for harm to U.S. civilians was far greater than actually occurred. But the failure of U.S. troops to protect civilians at H-hour tarnished the triumph of the invasion.

"The U.S. was lucky, very lucky," Beliz says. "They didn't get protection to their people."

In a city of 1.2 million, U.S. troops engaged in a shooting war simply were not able to protect every American, much less shield stores and businesses from looters. Soldiers were assigned to protect military housing areas and other American neighborhoods in the canal zone, but Americans downtown were on their own. So were Panamanian merchants.

"Not to downplay anyone's loss," Thurman says, but "we had to make a choice given the manpower we had. We made a choice to protect high-value targets: the utilities, the television facilities, power, water pumping, food warehouses, and telecommunications, not the local 7-Eleven."

12

Sweeping the North

The first taste of combat came too early for the troops of 4th Battalion, 17th Infantry Regiment.

The rifle battalion had the job of dismantling the PDF in and around Colon and protecting Americans living along the canal north of Panama City.

Col. Keith Kellogg, commander of Task Force Atlantic, had forces arrayed against nine H-hour targets. Nowhere in Panama were U.S. forces as fragmented at H-hour as in Kellogg's area of operations. Stretched from Paraiso, just seven miles from SOUTH-COM headquarters, to Colon, fifty miles distant, Task Force Atlantic waged assaults over an area of 1,800 square kilometers, including five PDF installations and the Madden Dam, a strategically vital target.

In all, the task force had fifteen simultaneous missions. Its assigned targets were diverse, ranging from a company of naval infantrymen at Coco Solo to the less threatening force of forest police at Gamboa. In the north, the four companies of the 4th Battalion, 17th Infantry Regiment were to take down the PDF at Coco Solo and Fort Espinar, both shared by U.S. troops and the PDF, and seal off the entrance to Colon and the highway connecting it with Panama. In the southern half of Kellogg's area of operations, four companies from the 82d Airborne Division's 3d Battalion, 504th Parachute Infantry Regiment, were to take control of Gamboa, where three PDF units were stationed and ninety-five Americans lived; Renacer Prison, where the PDF had an estimated forty to sixty guards and uncounted prisoners, including unsuccessful plotters against Noriega; Cerro Tigre, the PDF's central supply center; and Madden Dam, a hydroelectric plant critical to the operation of the canal.

Task Force Atlantic also had to protect Americans and U.S. property, including bases, housing, and schools, most of these located cheek-by-jowl with Panamanian facilities. Only one of four schools in Kellogg's sector, for instance, was safely on U.S. territory. The most daunting responsibility for Kellogg was to ensure the survival of more than one thousand Americans living on joint U.S.–Panamanian military installations or in housing for employees of the Panama Canal Commission.

The message from Thurman was loud and clear, Kellogg says: "If you lose an American—a civilian—I don't care how good you've done, you've lost the battle, guys."

Task Force Atlantic's strategy mirrored the approach worked out by Joint Task Force Panama: hit the PDF hard and fast and hope thereby to end the fight quickly. For Kellogg's troops the hammerhead strike was even more important. His forces and the enemy were in a one-to-one ratio, so he couldn't afford to let the enemy get away. He had no reserves to call on. To make matters worse, he had evidence that the PDF was expecting the U.S. to strike.

At about midnight, Kellogg says, a U.S. counterintelligence unit intercepted a call from a desk sergeant at Fort Espinar to Military Zone 2 headquarters in Colon. The caller said, according to Kellogg, "The party's on for one o'clock. Get out of the area." But the attack plan of Task Force Atlantic remained largely the same in spite of the tipoff (see figure 13–1).

For years, the PDF had been hard on Americans. Now Kellogg was ready to give it back to the PDF. "We were going to be very hard on them," he says. "Our intent was to use overwhelming firepower to break their backs." But, as Thurman had warned in briefing his senior war planners, the battle would not go exactly as planned. It was to be a night of surprises.

The mission started on time. At eighteen minutes to midnight 19 December, Maj. Tom Ryan, 4th battalion operations officer, called in "Jets 4" to Kellogg's tactical operations center at Fort Sherman. "Jets 4" was the code word meaning all units were in their attack positions or assembly areas and ready for combat.

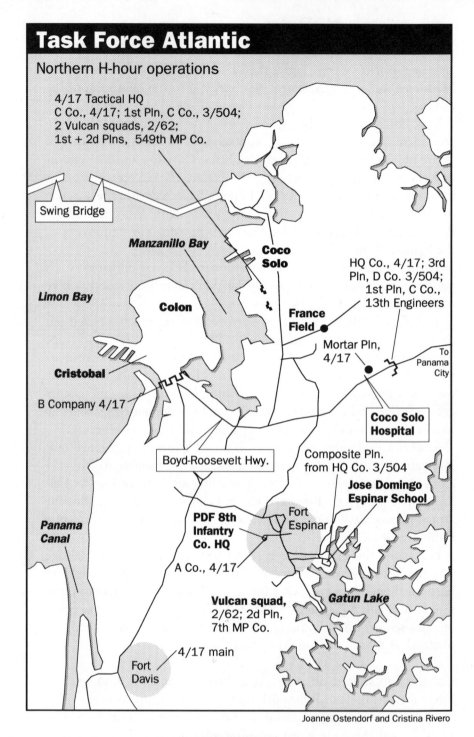

Task Force Atlantic

Northern H-hour operations

4/17 Tactical HQ
C Co., 4/17; 1st Pln, C Co., 3/504;
2 Vulcan squads, 2/62;
1st + 2d Plns, 549th MP Co.

Swing Bridge

Manzanillo Bay

Coco Solo

Limon Bay

Colon

HQ Co., 4/17; 3rd
Pln, D Co. 3/504;
1st Pln, C Co.,
13th Engineers

France Field

Mortar Pln,
4/17

To
Panama
City

Cristobal

B Company 4/17

Coco Solo Hospital

Boyd-Roosevelt Hwy.

Composite Pln.
from HQ Co. 3/504

Jose Domingo Espinar School

Panama Canal

PDF 8th Infantry Co. HQ

Fort Espinar

A Co., 4/17

Vulcan squad, 2/62; 2d Pln, 7th MP Co.

Gatun Lake

4/17 main

Fort Davis

Joanne Ostendorf and Cristina Rivero

FIGURE 12–1

Task Force Atlantic: Northern H-Hour Operations

At 1:00 A.M., 20 December, the battalion's A Company would assault the PDF's 8th Infantry Company at Fort Espinar, also known by its pre-treaty name of Fort Gulick. B Company would block the bottleneck, the narrow base of the peninsula on which Colon is built, and thereby close off the city.

Headquarters Company would block the Boyd-Roosevelt Highway, the route to Panama City. The company was supported by an understrength platoon of 7th Division engineers, a mortar platoon, and a platoon of paratroopers from D Company of the 3d Battalion/504th Infantry (Airborne). The company had the added mission of guarding Coco Solo Hospital, the medical headquarters for Task Force Coco.

C Company would assault the PDF naval infantry headquarters at Coco Solo, across Manzanillo Bay from Colon, and capture nine PDF boats. A Vulcan 20mm antiaircraft cannon and various light antitank weapons would blast the headquarters if necessary.

A platoon of 7th Division scouts and a 7th Division antitank platoon would block France Field, Colon's domestic airport at Coco Solo, and destroy all multi-engine aircraft. Their mission was to block any attempt by Noriega or the PDF to flee Panama or fly in reinforcements.

Supporting the infantry companies would be military police from the 549th MP Company, based at Fort Davis. The MPs—one platoon from the 7th Infantry Division and one from 549th MP Company—would seal off the installations at Coco Solo and Espinar. Heavily armed with M16s, M203 grenade launchers, 9mm pistols, and grenades, the MPs deployed in three-man teams to establish blocking positions.

Coco Solo Hospital, a four-story building, formed the core of Kellogg's medical support. Although it hadn't functioned as a full-service hospital since the Panama Canal Commission operated it, the hospital was the best the area had to offer Task Force Coco. "Early on in Colon, it became apparent there was no medical capability there," said Lt. Col. Robert Stephen Bausch, 7th Infantry Division Surgeon.

Only the first floor of the hospital, where the emergency room was, served any medical purpose. The second floor consisted of administrative offices, while the two upper floors were vacant. At least half the Panamanian doctors who worked in the hospital lived in

Panama City. They weren't expected to make it to work after the shooting began, Bausch says. U.S. doctors assigned to Fort Sherman moved to Coco Solo to manage the medical effort there.

Most of the elements of Task Force Coco were in their assembly areas when Kellogg told his commanders at 6:35 P.M., 19 December, that they were going into combat. Standing by for their missions on this clear, balmy night, the soldiers thought they would be the ones to control the fire. They had counted on the element of surprise. But what happened took them by surprise and cost the life of a twenty-two-year-old father-to-be.

The evening would be a dicey lesson in rules of engagement. During the earlier missions that proved to be rehearsals for Just Cause, "Everybody was very well versed on what they were and were not supposed to do," says S.Sgt. James Kusinski, a squad leader with B Company, 4th Battalion. The rules of engagement were to kill only in self-defense against an identified enemy, including anyone carrying a weapon. The first test of those rules came even before H-hour.

Sfc. Charlie Gray, the platoon sergeant of 3d Platoon, 549th MP Company, was to lead a team of four MPs at 12:30A.M. to seal off an entrance to the naval infantry installation. The entrance was next to a patch of woods where drug users were believed to party. Gray, a Vietnam veteran, approached his position with the MPs and found a group of men in the woods. He says the men were watching the movement of U.S. troops and had a radio. "What they were doing was giving away our positions," Gray says.

He radioed this information to his platoon leader, 1st Lt. Mark Ferraro, who was at the battalion command post in front of Cristobal High School, located next to the naval infantry complex. "The order came down that I was to take that position and silence that radio at all costs," Gray says.

Here, as in many respects, Gray's account of what happened differs from that of the battalion staff. "He didn't have an order. He didn't have a mission to take anything down, simply to block," Ryan says. "He was sent there with his team to seal off the area, make sure nobody got in or out," says Ferraro.

The incident later was the subject of an Army criminal investigation, but no charges were brought against Gray. According to him, his MPs, three hidden in the underbrush and one in a

HMMWV, were prepared to fire if necessary. They were armed with M16s, and one had a grenade launcher. Gray says he confronted a man wearing a PDF uniform, who held a Motorola radio. The man was in a guard shack at the entrance Gray was assigned to block.

"Maybe I can talk some sense into this shithead," Gray recalls thinking. No one in Gray's team witnessed his encounter with the PDF guard. The other U.S. forces were positioned too far away to see what happened. The guard stood his ground, Gray says. "He looked at me, one of those looks like, 'Go to hell, asshole,'" Gray says. "I told him, 'This is an invasion and you are now a prisoner of war. I want you to give your people the order to surrender or they're going to die.'" He says the PDF guard jumped him, and the two fought hand-to-hand. With a flack vest, helmet, and two bandoliers of ammunition, Gray felt heavy and awkward.

"He reached up with his left hand and grabbed my rifle," set on semiautomatic, Gray says. At the same time, the guard reached for his own .38 caliber revolver, pulling back the hammer as he lifted the weapon from its holster. Gray put his rifle to the guard's chest and pulled the trigger. The men Gray had spotted in the woods came out with their hands up, he says.

Pfc. John R. Van Cleef, operating the radio for Ferraro, heard the shot, followed by a frantic call over the radio. "We had just stopped the vehicle and I heard it ring through the air as clear as anything I've ever heard," Van Cleef says. "And then Sergeant Gray came over the radio and said, 'We have one down, We have one down.' The only thing I could think of was that one of our guys got shot." While Gray tried to administer first aid to the PDF guard, another member of his team radioed Van Cleef that the casualty was PDF, not American.

Accounts differ also as to when the shot actually was fired. Ryan says he looked at his Rolex and recorded the time as H minus 26 minutes, or 12:34 A.M., in his operations journal. Members of the MP company, including Gray, put the time at closer to 12:45 A.M. In either case, the shooting occurred after 12:30 A.M., when the rules of engagement took effect allowing use of deadly force against an armed enemy.

The Army's Criminal Investigation Command looked into Gray's actions that night, but never referred the case for charges because of a lack of evidence. The guard's gun and identification were lost during his evacuation to the rear. Gray retired from the Army seven months later, as he had planned before the invasion.

The shot registered clearly across the Coco Solo installation. U.S. troops shared the installation, a narrow strip of land about a mile and a half long, with the PDF naval infantry company. At the northern end was a U.S. housing area along Manzanillo Bay.

A Vulcan from 7th Division's 2d Battalion, 62d Air Defense Artillery Regiment, was positioned at the housing area to fire on any PDF attempting to escape in one of the boats, which were moored about 185 meters behind the naval infantry headquarters. The air defense battalion set up another Vulcan, aimed at the headquarters, in a U.S. housing area at the southern end of the installation. The housing area, with about twenty-five homes, was largely vacant at the time of the invasion. The Vulcan was placed about forty-five meters from the naval infantry headquarters.

Between the two housing areas lay the core of the installation, consisting of two, almost identical C-shaped complexes of gray cement. The three-story buildings had three wings running northwest to southeast, with the middle one set back towards the bay. The complex to the north belonged to the United States. The southern one was partially occupied by the PDF. A textile factory filled the north and south wings, while the PDF had offices and barracks in the middle wing. A single street separated the U.S. forces from the PDF.

Until the May 1989 Panamanian elections erupted in violence, the complex to the north was Cristobal High School. But after President Bush recommended that military dependents return to the United States, one-fifth of the students moved out. The soldiers assigned to protect Coco Solo during Operation Nimrod Dancer—most recently C Company, 4th Battalion, 17th Infantry Regiment, moved into the southern wing of the high school, sleeping on Army bunk beds in the classrooms.

Billeted since 18 November right next to the PDF naval infantry, C Company had had two months to observe the enemy: their activities, their belligerence toward U.S. troops, and their reaction to the gringos massing with weapons on the installation. The naval infantry unit, the single largest company in the PDF, had subjected its American neighbors to a steady barrage of obscene gestures and verbal abuse.

Just after midnight, soldiers evacuated the eight families living in the southern housing area, then cordoned off the housing area and moved the Vulcans into place. The soldiers had positioned the Vulcans in the same places each night for the past several months. They hoped the naval infantrymen would think the troop movements were just another night exercise, but Kellogg did not expect an easy takedown.

"We thought this would be one of our tough fights because the naval infantry company had been openly aggressive during the entire time we were down there," Kellogg says. The naval infantrymen, for instance, liked to point their weapons at U.S. soldiers. For that reason, the battalion established its command center in the courtyard of the high school.

The battalion's plan for the naval infantry, barring an immediate surrender, was to fire the Vulcan at the headquarters building for two minutes, then request a surrender. If the Panamanians refused to back down, the two hundred U.S. soldiers at Coco Solo would up the ante. The Vulcan would fire again, followed by a second chance for surrender, the alternative being complete destruction.

LAW and AT-4 antitank weapon systems were positioned to suppress fire from the naval infantry headquarters. C Company's 3d Platoon took up a blocking position at the south end of the southern housing area.

"Once the Vulcan fired, everything else was to go into motion," says Capt. Chris Rizzo, commander of C Company. The loud boom was to be the signal for C Company's 1st Platoon to seize the PDF docks, where two large patrol boats and seven smaller craft were moored, and cover the bayside entrance to the PDF barracks. The platoon was positioned behind the high school, in a parking lot belonging to a refurbishing plant for Soviet-made Lada cars.

While an assault force from the platoon maneuvered south to capture the PDF boats, a support force was to seize a one-story aluminum barracks, housing about thirty PDF, next to the car lot. From the northern end of the PDF complex, 2d Platoon would enter the complex and be prepared to disarm the naval infantry in the middle wing. (see figure 12–2).

When Gray fired his M16 into the PDF guard, the plan collapsed like a row of dominoes.

Assault on PDF Naval Infantry

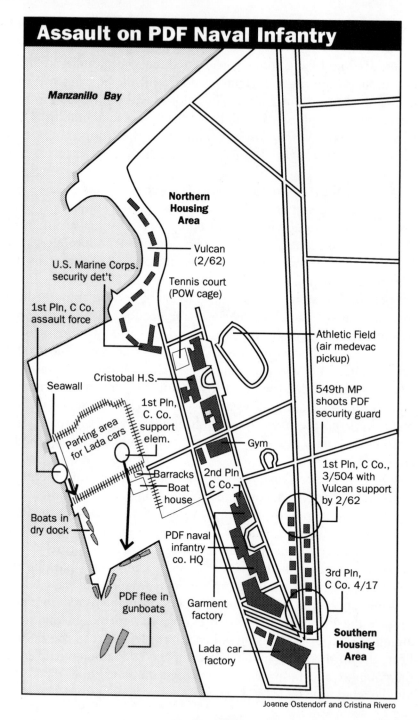

Manzanillo Bay

Northern Housing Area

Vulcan (2/62)

U.S. Marine Corps. security det't

Tennis court (POW cage)

1st Pln, C Co. assault force

Athletic Field (air medevac pickup)

Cristobal H.S.

Seawall

1st Pln, C. Co. support elem.

549th MP shoots PDF security guard

Parking area for Lada cars

Gym

Barracks

2nd Pln C Co.

1st Pln, C Co., 3/504 with Vulcan support by 2/62

Boat house

Boats in dry dock

PDF naval infantry co. HQ

3rd Pln, C Co. 4/17

PDF flee in gunboats

Garment factory

Southern Housing Area

Lada car factory

Joanne Ostendorf and Cristina Rivero

FIGURE 12–2

Assault on PDF Naval Infantry

Battalion commander Lt. Col. Johnny Brooks and his staff were monitoring the brigade and battalion radio nets. Operations chief Ryan, sitting in a jeep in the central courtyard of the high school, had one ear tuned into the battalion radio and the other to Kellogg's tactical operations center at Fort Sherman. Rizzo was on the radio simultaneously to Ryan and to the company's 1st Platoon leader, 1st Lt. Walter Burke.

Ryan and Rizzo talked for about two minutes about the shooting of the PDF guard. Suddenly Burke radioed that a dozen or more PDF troops were running toward the boats. "Chris requested permission to engage," Ryan says.

There was little time to decide. "I distinctly remember taking a good fifteen-second assessment of what this was going to mean," he says. "We had B Company moving. We had A Company probably not all the way into their position." Headquarters Company, he figured, probably was in position at Coco Solo Hospital, southeast of the naval infantry headquarters. A Company was maneuvering through the woods at Fort Espinar, and B Company was on its way from Espinar to the bottleneck.

Ryan turned to Brooks. "We kind of nodded. There wasn't really any words exchanged," Ryan says. This was it. The major called Colonel Kellogg, knowing he would give his okay to turn on the heat. Kellogg did so immediately at eighteen minutes to one, from a helicopter flying over Renacer Prison, where 7th Division helicopter pilots were preparing to land paratroopers from the 3d Battalion, 504th Infantry (Airborne) for their assault.

The eighteen-man assault team of 1st Platoon was maneuvering along a twelve-inch-wide seawall between the car lot and the bay when they heard the growl of PDF gunboat engines starting. The parking lot was completely fenced in, the chain-link fence rising from the seawall. The soldiers moved single-file in a duck crawl.

Sgt. Rick Mowatt, leading the assault, worried about running into one of the PDF's regular two-man patrols when he reached the end of the wall. He was about seventy-five meters from the end of the wall when he heard the boat engines start up. With the rest of the force right behind him, the sergeant moved to the end of the wall and swung himself around the chain-link fence, which extended a short distance into the water. He crept to a small pile of junk metal that he could crouch behind and observe the PDF. "We waited there for approximately four to five minutes" while the assault element's radio operator alerted Rizzo that members of the PDF were fleeing, says Mowatt, 1st squad leader.

Platoon leader Burke told his men to hold their fire until everyone in the assault force had swung around the end of the fence. When everyone had cleared the wall, Mowatt moved forward. The fleeing naval infantrymen spotted the soldiers immediately and opened fire, balancing their weapons against their hips as they ran.

"As soon as I turned the corner, they opened up," Mowatt says. "They were firing from every boat." With a burst of M60 and AK-47 fire, the war was on for Task Force Coco. Rizzo, positioned with the Vulcan and a heavily armed rifle platoon of the Airborne's 3d Battalion, gave the order to fire.

Zulema Hutchinson was discussing civic activities with some friends in a Colon park when the sky lit up. Sitting in her car just off Paseo Gorgas, they were at the shoreline of Manzanillo Bay, across the water from Coco Solo. It was the kind of place that is perfect for watching fireworks, which was Hutchinson's first impression of the combat across the bay.

"It looked like fireworks," says Hutchinson, a 26-year-old business manager. Then she thought the naval infantrymen were conducting an exercise. It took a few minutes to realize the truth. "We were telling each other, 'No, that's not the way they practice,'" Hutchinson says. Then she thought of something her friends had told her earlier that evening. U.S. soldiers were stopping all cars at a favorite parking spot by Gatun Locks, south of Colon, and ordering Panamanians to leave the area.

Also curious about the noise, residents of Colon started to fill the streets as soon as the shooting started.

The sound of the Vulcan, coming fifteen minutes before it was expected, struck a tense chord in the men of 2d Platoon. It was their signal to breach the naval infantry headquarters. But the platoon was still in the high school gym, psyching themselves up for war. Some had applied camouflage paint as if it were armor, smearing it from their foreheads to their shoulders.

"You hear these little potshots, then you hear the [M]60s, and then the Vulcan. Boom," says Sgt. Joseph Legaspi, a fire team leader on 3d squad. The troops had no time to be afraid, he says. Rizzo had told them, if the operation was compromised, to go for it. They rushed outside into a cacophony of fire and a rainbow of tracer bullets—red, orange, and blue. "It was so loud and noisy. It was just like a light show out there," says Legaspi, a recent graduate of the Ranger School who had just joined the unit. "Tracers everywhere, all kinds of colors. We couldn't hear each other."

The platoon entered the naval infantry building through an open door leading directly to a staircase. Two squads began climbing the stairs while the third remained outside to cover their movement. Once inside, the soldiers began moving south toward the enemy.

Captain Amadis Jimenez, commander of the PDF naval infantry company, had been in command for only three days. While the PDF was expecting retaliation for the killing of U.S. Marine lieutenant Paz, the all-out invasion came as a shock, he says.

"We did not know anything about the invasion," says Jimenez, who later played a key role in persuading other PDF commanders to surrender and was hired as a Panamanian liaison for USARSO. "Our orders were to avoid any type of contact that would cause any greater conflict," Jimenez says through an interpreter. "It was perceived that there would be major implications. Nobody really knew how or when. There was a point in time where people believed there was going to be only intimidation."

When he took command, he was alarmed to see U.S. artillery pointed at his company headquarters from 6:00 P.M. to 6:00 A.M. Apparently the psychology of confrontation had worked on the PDF, because other officers told Jimenez not to worry, that the guns had been there for fifteen or twenty days and were not a real threat. Shortly before H-hour, the Vulcans officially became a threat. Jimenez got a call from his immediate superior, a PDF lieutenant colonel, who told him to reinforce security around the naval infantry complex because a U.S. operation was about to go down.

"That's all he told me," Jimenez says. "He did not explain to me what was going to happen." Jimenez weighed his options. His car was the only land transportation available to the company. If the naval infantrymen were to flee on foot, they would have to be lightly armed. He asked his staff what plans existed for a mobilization. The answer was none, because the company had been without a commander for some time.

"So I decided to use one of the basic principles of war, which is dispersion." He assigned one platoon to engage U.S. forces at the front of the headquarters, and another to man the patrol boats. The ultimate goal was to escape to Colon, two nautical miles away. As surprised as C Company was when fighting started at Coco Solo, the "shooting caught us by surprise," says Jimenez.

The naval infantry company was under assault from north and east, but on the west, the Panamanians had 1st Platoon in a difficult position. Stealthy as they were, the assault team was exposed once they had emerged from behind the seawall onto the lighted docks. Their only cover consisted of the dry dock, formed of railroad ties, that extended 150 meters south from the seawall.

The support element of 1st Platoon blew a hole in the fence around the aluminum barracks. The soldiers tossed hand grenades at the metal building. No response. As it turned out, no one was inside, but two naval infantrymen had taken cover beneath two trucks parked inside the fence. A brief firefight ensued when the PDF men refused to come out from under the trucks.

Two other PDF troops burned to death when soldiers in the support element tossed hand grenades into a tin-roofed concrete boathouse on the dock to clear it, setting off a butane gas explosion and fire.

The largest craft in the PDF fleet—a Vosper and a so-called swift ship, each about sixty-five feet long and with .50 caliber machine gun mounts in the stern—were moving south into the bay, out of the assault team's range of fire. If the two gunships had moved directly west into the bay, the U.S. troops could have stopped them, Rizzo says.

Seven smaller boats with cabins and machine-gun mounts remained to be captured. Mowatt ducked for cover behind a dry-docked landing craft and prepared his LAW hoping that if he fired it at the nearest PDF boat, he could give himself more room to maneuver. "We could see the flashes coming up from the ground," he says. He could see firing around the aluminum barracks, too. What he saw was firing by the men under the trucks.

What worried Mowatt most, though, was that the Panamanians would mount the guns on their boats. He would have to hit them hard enough that they didn't have time to do that.

Sgt. James Daniel, leader of a Dragon antitank missile team, was positioned behind the fence to take out any boats fleeing northward. When the Vosper and swift ship moved south, he moved forward, taking a LAW. Pfc. Rudolf Ubersezig followed, and then Sgt. Joseph Hein. With Mowatt, the soldiers formed two, two-man teams, about twelve meters apart. One team would fire at the PDF boats, about seventy meters away, while the other gave cover with M60 and squad automatic weapon fire. Then they would switch roles.

Mowatt was prepared to fire his LAW immediately after Daniel. There was a barrage of fire, and Mowatt heard the other three men scream: first Daniel, then Ubersezig, then Hein, who was Mowatt's partner. Daniel was yelling, "My leg's blown off," Mowatt says. Ubersezig was yelling, "My hand is shot off." The blast from Daniel's LAW had attracted the attention of the PDF, who showered the men's position with automatic weapons fire, sending a round through Daniel's thigh and a round through Ubersezig's hand and ankle. Hein yelled: "We've got men hit."

Fearful that the yelling would betray their vulnerability, Mowatt told his partners to shut up and yelled for a medic. Then he moved forward to cover them against a PDF assault, firing four antitank rockets at the boats. In a volley of fire, Mowatt saw one PDF soldier collapse in his perch on the bow of a boat. Another, struck by a tracer bullet, fell next to the boathouse. Daniel's LAW apparently had knocked over the mast of the first boat. Two teams from 1st Platoon moved forward to clear the boat while Mowatt gave them cover.

Another surprise awaited 2d Platoon as it entered the second floor of the PDF complex. In the northern wing of the naval infantry building, on the second floor, were sewing machines, part of the textile factory that occupied much of the building. Below them were an area advertised as a daycare center, which later turned out to be a weapons storehouse—and a Chinese restaurant, both closed at this late hour.

Starting on the second floor, the soldiers maneuvered carefully back toward the PDF wing, consisting of an open bay with 120 bunks and a hallway flanked by rooms. The soldiers knew they would encounter enemy soldiers in the building, says Sgt. Chance

Brooks, leader of the platoon's 2d squad, the first to enter the building. "We were supposed to take them if necessary. We didn't know what to expect," Brooks said.

They certainly didn't expect a family to be living there. One soldier saw a shadow and fired a few shots across it. But as the soldiers moved into the darkness they saw seventeen Chinese people looking at them in horror. A woman approaching the door to see who was there came face to face with Pfc. Jeffrey Secor, his face blanketed with camouflage paint. She fainted.

The soldiers weren't sure how to react. "Everybody was kind of afraid to fire," Brooks says. Then the troops saw that the Chinese, living in three furnished rooms, were not armed. At the same time, the Chinese hit the floor. "They just automatically got down," Brooks says. The soldiers told the family to stay down; if they ran, they would be shot.

Legaspi's squad, the next to enter the building, shepherded the Chinese family into one room, keeping guard and escorting members of the family to the bathroom. Brooks kept watch on the movement of 1st squad, now maneuvering toward the building.

Incessant gunfire on both sides of the building told the soldiers of 2d Platoon there would be no quick surrender. They would have to find and flush out the enemy themselves. Brooks had only been squad leader for two weeks. What next, he wondered. "You've got a hundred possible things that could happen."

Led by Sgt. David Rainer, 1st squad climbed to the third floor to start methodically backing the PDF into a corner. Another round exploded from the Vulcan. Still no surrender. The third floor of the PDF wing was an empty expanse of darkness, a gym with a basketball court. Getting in there would not be easy. The entrance was a locked steel door, against which were stacked bolts of fabric.

The soldiers set up C-4 plastic explosive against the door and took cover along the front wall of the textile factory. Platoon leader 2d Lt. Dan Kirk, who could see the firing in front of the building through grillwork in the wall, radioed to Rizzo to stop suppressive fire long enough for his men to detonate the explosive. The door popped off the hinges, and the textiles caught fire. While the door was being blown, Rizzo stopped the Vulcan fire on the front of the building. His men laid machine-gun fire on the second floor to push the PDF backward.

Rainer's squad jumped immediately through the flames, while Brooks and one of his team leaders used hand-held fire extinguishers left in the building to suppress the flames.

Clearing the third floor took about two minutes. The PDF were all below on the second and first floors. Soldiers from 3d Squad stayed behind to continue fighting the fire, but the flames were gaining on them. Rainer's squad, positioned at the top of front and back stairways leading down to the PDF, proceeded to squeeze the enemy.

Pfc. Sidney Goffney and Pfc. Michael Hardy threw hand grenades down the stairs. The squad moved down to the second-story hallway. Kirk's plan was to corner the PDF on the first floor, at the back of the building, and the plan seemed to be working. The PDF was retreating. Specialist James D. Davis, Jr., 2d Platoon radio operator, could decipher a burst of obscenities in Spanish, warning the American soldiers not to come back toward the naval infantrymen's quarters. Goffney and Hardy responded by tossing more grenades down the hall.

Again, Panamanians yelled to the gringos above them not to move closer, or at least that was what the soldiers thought.

Jimenez says he started to surrender, only to be attacked with grenades.

The sounds of battle were deafening. Jimenez and his men had to shout to make themselves heard. After a period of heavy fire, apparently before 1st and 2d platoons entered the building, Jimenez shouted at his men to be quiet. Then he waited for U.S. assault troops to ask for a surrender through a loudspeaker.

The company had only AK-47s to defend itself: no rocket-propelled grenade launchers or antitank weapons. "We had none of that sophisticated equipment," he says. Jimenez knew his men were no match for the heavy fire coming into the roof of the naval infantry headquarters. He was ready to call off the fight. "But I never heard any loudspeakers," he says. "I started yelling, 'Stop fire' in English and that we were surrendering. But nobody paid attention to us."

Fifteen minutes later, he heard U.S. troops talking on the floor above him. "They were very nervous," he says. "We started to yell again that we would surrender. They were so nervous that they started throwing grenades from the upper floor down to where we were." The grenades wounded three soldiers in the room with Jimenez.

"That's when I was most nervous," Jimenez says, growing somber. "There was a lot of yelling in Spanish," with U.S. and Panamanian troops screaming at each other. After clearing the barracks area on the second floor, U.S. soldiers threw hand grenades through the windows to let the PDF know their rear exit was unsafe.

While one group of soldiers covered the stairwell, others clambered down the front staircase to the first floor. Jimenez, cornered with about twenty of his men in a first-floor back room where they had sought cover from the frontal attack, yelled again for surrender. Kirk didn't respond until he was sure he had the PDF surrounded. His troops checked all the rooms behind them to rule out any chance of ambush. With Davis acting as interpreter, Kirk shouted down a hallway leading to the back of the building.

Jimenez says that Davis, after determining that he was the PDF commander, asked him to lead the way out a back door into the light to begin the surrender process. As they stepped outside, Jimenez heard the sound of a grenade fired in his direction and darted back inside for cover. The grenade exploded, hitting one of his men in the eye. His men asked Jimenez to stay in the building and not expose himself further. They were convinced U.S. troops just wanted to kill them, he says.

Jimenez didn't think so. He wanted to continue negotiations for a surrender. Yelling down the hall, he complained in Spanish to Davis. "Why do you ask me to surrender and then throw grenades at me?" he asked. "The soldier apologized and said his men were nervous," says Jimenez, who gradually persuaded his men that they would not die if they stopped fighting. He won assurances from Davis that there would be no booby traps.

Jimenez was the first one to walk out of the large empty room where the company had taken shelter. He told the U.S. troops not to shoot and asked to speak to an intelligence officer.

It was about 5:00 A.M. when Kirk accepted the naval infantrymen's surrender. Kirk told Jimenez to have his men stack their arms inside the room and come out of the building, one by one, on all fours. The situation was tense, according to Jimenez. One soldier told him to stand against the wall, while another ordered him to hit the ground. A third told him to face toward the wall. "I didn't know what to do," Jimenez says.

Out on the docks, the hostilities also ceased. Mowatt told Specialist Ruben Rodriguez, who speaks Spanish, to tell the PDF they had thirty seconds to surrender.

To the soldiers' surprise and relief, they did. Following Rodriguez's orders, twelve PDF emerged from the shadows of the boats, climbed on the dock with their hands up and crawled on all fours into the light. They were made to lie flat on the dock, arms stretched out, until soldiers tied their hands. A trail of blood led across the docks to the boats, but none of the fleeing PDF had lost their lives. All in all, about twenty-five PDF had taken part in the fight—several times as many as the soldiers were told to expect.

"We were surprised because our reconnaissance told us there were about six personnel total down there," says Mowatt. Considering all the elements working against his platoon and the little mistakes he remembers making, Mowatt says he felt lucky that the platoon won the battle.

He received a Bronze Star with "V" for valor for his actions on the dock that night. Many heroic actions went unrecognized, Mowatt says, because of the Army's sensitivity to criticism that it gave out awards like candy canes after the invasion of Grenada. "I thought of myself as being stupid when it was over. It could have worked out wrong," Mowatt says.

"It came down to the PDF running out of ammunition," Rizzo says. The battle had taken only about an hour, but it took several hours to clear the area completely. U.S. soldiers tied the Panamanians' hands behind their backs and marched them into a prisoner-of-war cage, actually a high school tennis court reinforced with concertina wire and manned by cooks from Headquarters Company of the 4th Battalion.

Soldiers from 1st Platoon, C Company, 3d Battalion, 504th Airborne Infantry, who made up Rizzo's support element, were given the mission to bring the fire under control, but it was impossible. The blaze was consuming the third floor. Soldiers evacuated the Chinese family and moved them into the high school gym, where they had food and water and wrestling mats to sleep on.

Around 7:00 A.M., intelligence specialists arrived to interrogate the prisoners. So did a fire engine from the Mount Hope fire department, just south of Colon. But the firefighters' efforts could not keep all three wings of the building from burning to a shell, or the roof from collapsing. The Chinese family recovered some of their belongings, but lost their home.

Two PDF troops were dead and many wounded. All in all, C Company captured twenty-seven of the enemy. Given the limitations of his defensive force, Jimenez expected at least twice as many of his troops to die.

Major Ryan had guessed right about his battalion's B Company. The company was just passing Fort Espinar, about two miles short of its blocking position, when Coco Solo erupted in gunfire ahead of schedule.

"You could hear the Vulcan and the AT-4s going off," says Capt. Doug Thorp, B Company commander. Thorp's troops, traveling in HMMWVs, five-ton trucks, and school buses, knew they had lost partial control of the battle when they heard the guns register. No one in the company except two senior noncommissioned officers who served in Vietnam had been in combat before.

Moreover, B Company was the only element of the battalion that had not rehearsed its assault before H-hour. Even Thorp had had little chance to reconnoiter, flying over the bottleneck once in an OH-58 helicopter, a twenty-minute trip.

Thorp had known about the operation for about five weeks. He was briefed shortly after the battalion began its rotation at the Jungle Operations Training Center at Fort Sherman. But the NCOs of B Company had not seen the area they would have to defend at H-hour. Their first time in combat would also be the first time they walked their targets.

Task Force Coco's other blocking element, Headquarters and Headquarters Company of 4/17, had better knowledge of its target. The company had twice conducted patrols along the Boyd-Roosevelt Highway, where the troops would establish a roadblock at H-hour. Headquarters Company was in position at H-hour to block the road with four school buses and to turn away traffic. A team of 7th Division engineers constructed a barrier of concertina wire and fifty-five-gallon drums to complete the roadblock.

Shortly after the initial roadblock was in place, a white van approached and engaged the soldiers with small arms. The occupants of the van were killed.

B Company's preparation for the bottleneck mission consisted of an exercise one day on a pier five hundred meters west of the bottleneck, and a walk-through in the sand at the Fort Davis sniper range on 16 December after Paz was killed. Thorp told his men the exercise was a dress rehearsal for an unspecified "mission" that would take place if hostilities broke out between the United States and the PDF. That was the same day Thorp briefed his platoon leaders on the purpose of the "mission." He could not declassify that information for the squad leaders until 9:00 P.M. on 19 December, but they were smart enough to figure out what they were practicing for.

Thorp was not only new to combat. He was new to the command. He thought to himself, "I've been in command two weeks, and we're talking about this already?"

B Company had three objectives: 1st Platoon would block the entrance to Colon at the Boyd-Roosevelt Highway and secure the east flank of the bottleneck; 2d Platoon was to cut through fences and secure a railroad roundhouse, using its position to keep an eye on the roadblock, the road south to Mount Hope, and a Texaco station just inside Colon; and 3d Platoon would secure the Panama Canal Commission's oil pollution control building on the shore of French Canal and protect the west flank of the bottleneck, keeping an eye on Limon Bay to the west and the Cristobal shipping yard to the northwest. The pollution control building was seventy-five meters from the western edge of 2d Platoon's area of operations.

A sniper team and mortar team would give B Company added firepower. An advanced trauma life support team was available to treat casualties. Line medics were to move casualties away from the bottleneck to a specified point where the trauma team picked them up and moved them back another eighty meters for treatment.

The only picture the company had of its objectives was a map used during the mission briefing. The map introduced them to the fences they would have to breach, the elephant grass they would have to penetrate. "We knew where we were going—more or less," says Pfc. Anthony Threadgill of 2d Platoon.

Three of the four school buses, borrowed from Fort Davis, that had carried fire teams to the bottleneck were parked end-to-end across the road to the rear of the troops. The fourth was positioned across the Boyd-Roosevelt Highway. Under intermittent fire, a squad of 7th Division engineers placed the bus, eleven-strand concertina wire, and pickets in a roadblock across the bottleneck. Chains and railroad ties formed a barrier across the railroad tracks. At 1:15 A.M., the city of Colon was closed off, theoretically trapping sixty thousand civilian residents and an unknown number of PDF and Dignity Battalion forces.

Anyone trying to run the roadblock would come under fire from a 549th MP Company platoon in HMMWVs mounted with M60 machine guns and a "deuce and a half" mounted with a .50caliber machine gun. One team was positioned on Boyd-Roosevelt Highway, the other farther back, on the road to Mount Hope.

Riding toward their target, the soldiers grew increasingly nervous as they listened to the firing in the background. "The briefings said we were going to have the element of surprise. But you could hear firing in the background," Threadgill says.

"People were thinking, worrying, saying their prayers," says Cpl. Kenneth Thruman, an M60 gunner in 1st Platoon. "That just intensified things, hearing the firing." So much for surprise, he thought. Instead the soldiers would encounter—what? "I didn't know if it was going to be chaos, confusion. I didn't have any idea what to expect," Thruman says.

He had just returned to duty after breaking his right ankle. Because of his injury he had missed the one exercise carried out to prepare B Company. He prepared himself by expecting the worst. So preoccupied was Thruman that when the five-ton truck he was riding in made the first of two stops, he mistakenly got off and had to jump back on quickly.

Already pumped up with adrenalin, Threadgill says the reality of combat hit him with a jolt when the five-ton truck he was in bounced over the railroad tracks on the way to the roundhouse. This was it.

The troops could hear no movement outside as they reached the bottleneck. At the roundhouse, Threadgill could not even see the roadblock, about seventy-five meters away, because of the tall grass. The silence was shattered immediately by a hail of gunfire. "Basically, when we hit the ground we were receiving fire," says S.Sgt. James Kusinski, leader of 3d Platoon's 2d squad. Tracers flew between the soldiers and their targets.

A squad each from 2d and 3d Platoons, including Kusinski's, teamed up to construct the roadblock. Kusinski and his squad were unloading concertina wire from the school buses when Specialist William Gibbs was shot down on the west side of the road. Gibbs also was in 3d Platoon, in a squad assigned to secure the pollution control building. Kusinski heard the shots. He sprinted to Gibbs's area in about ten seconds and found him in bad shape.

Three bullets, later surmised to have been fired from a range of less than one hundred meters, had pierced Gibbs's flack vest and lodged in his chest and neck. Two minutes later, William Delaney Gibbs was dead in Kusinski's arms. He left behind his wife, Kimberley, pregnant with their first child. In the eight months since Gibbs had joined the squad, he and Kusinski had become close friends and sports buddies, ready to take on anyone in volleyball.

Gibbs, who was promoted posthumously to sergeant, was the only soldier in his battalion to be killed in action that night. Another soldier, Specialist John Velotta, was struck in the shoulder with two bullets. One tracer round lodged beneath his Kevlar flack vest and burned his shoulder, while the second bullet knocked his right shoulder pad off, grazing his skin. He was evacuated to the rear but refused to be evacuated back to the United States, preferring to return to the fight four days later.

"That was the first time we really realized that you can get killed," says Kusinski. "You also realize you've got to keep going. You didn't really worry about when the next meal was coming."

The firing continued, subsiding in the first hour but never stopping. The light from within the city and the dense vegetation on both sides of the bottleneck worked to the enemy's advantage. Kusinski's squad was helpless to return fire as the men wormed their way through eight-foot-high elephant grass to link up with the rest of 3d Platoon. "We kept running into AK-47 fire," Kusinski says. "You couldn't do anything because you couldn't tell which way anybody was."

It took his squad an hour and a half to cover the thousand meters to the pollution control building. They linked up with the rest of the platoon, which had just secured the building.

Trained to fight at night with night vision goggles, the soldiers of B Company did not fare as well under the glow of city streetlights. The light was betraying their movements to the enemy. Once the firing lifted from inside the city, Captain Thorp's soldiers started shooting out streetlights to recapture the night.

Although the firefights had subsided, the lines of battle grew no clearer as the night wore on. Around 2:30 A.M., a Panamanian bus tried to run the roadblock at the bottleneck. The bus driver sat, with the headlights out, about four hundred meters north of the barrier. Then the bus roared up toward the roadblock, and the headlights went on.

"Everybody assumed it was a PDF vehicle," Kusinski says. But no one knew. Unsure how to react, Kusinski ordered his squad to shoot out the tires. In doing do, he chose the calculated risk over the sure hit. If the bus was carrying PDF intent on getting away, the soldiers could count on a messy firefight.

Pfc. Augustus Tutu, a member of Kusinski's squad, shot at the bus tires with his squad automatic weapon, a machine gun. Kusinski fired a buckshot round from an M203 automatic grenade launcher. "That dropped the front end of the bus," he says. At Kusinski's orders, the occupants of the bus stepped slowly into the road. A far cry from hardened PDF troops, they were about twenty civilians, many of them infants and children. It was a close call, but happened to be the right one. "I consider myself lucky," Kusinski says, that the squad obeyed orders not to shoot to kill.

On the eastern flank, the soldiers of 1st Platoon could hear the rumble of diesel engines several hundred meters out in the water of Manzanillo Bay. "They came in close and they just seemed to idle," Thorp says. Unsure what the boats were, he ordered his men not to shoot.

As the boats lumbered toward shore, their size, shape, and guns took shape against the dark water. In communication with the battalion command post at Coco Solo, Thorp confirmed they were the PDF naval infantry gunships that had escaped C Company's assault force. No one knew where they had gone until they appeared at the bottleneck.

Sgt. Henry Howard, Cpl. Jeffrey Mason, and Sgt. Anthony Martinez, all of 1st Platoon's 2d squad, fired AT-4 rockets and a LAW, killing one man on each boat. No one knows if there were other naval infantrymen on the gunships. It is possible some jumped overboard and swam for safety.

B Company's position was secure enough by now that Thorp could gain an upper hand. He ordered an artillery illumination to expose enemy snipers. B Battery of 7th Battalion, 15th Field Artillery, a 7th Division regiment, fired illumination over the Texaco station just inside the city. The station was believed to be a staging area for snipers.

"After messing around with these guys for three or four hours, I was tired of it," Thorp says. "We put three rounds over that and sent a very clear message." It was Task Force Atlantic's only use of artillery during H-hour.

Twelve PDF troops were killed or wounded at the bottleneck that night. A member of B Company was killed in action, and another wounded. Uncounted Panamanian civilians were wounded. Many of the first casualties were Panamanians fleeing Colon who fell or were shot along the way, says Pfc. Victor Walton, a 7th Division medic who was part of the advanced trauma life support team attached to B Company. "We pulled people out of the street," says Walton, who was struck by the strangeness of his surroundings. "I can't believe I'm here," he thought.

Though the bottleneck was firmly in U.S. control by 5:00 A.M. on D-day, the area just to the north remained hostile territory. Enemy pressure would continue for the next three days.

The battle at Fort Espinar, contrary to General Thurman's warning, went remarkably as planned.

For two months A Company, 4th Battalion, 17th Infantry Regiment had played mind games with the 8th Infantry Company, the PDF military police unit headquartered at Fort Espinar. The post, formerly known as Fort Gulick, had been jointly occupied by U.S. and Panamanian troops since the 1977 canal treaties took effect. But the United States no longer had military offices there—only a housing area, school, commissary, and other services.

Two platoons of A Company were housed in Building 217, just a block and a half away from the PDF company headquarters. Using binoculars and sometimes night sights, the men of 2d and 3d Platoons would watch Panamanian troops through the windows of the building. The soldiers taped the PDF's movements with a video camera.

Every night for weeks before the invasion, a team of soldiers from the division's 2d Battalion, 62d Air Defense Artillery, would set up a Vulcan on a baseball field in plain view of the PDF company headquarters. "They would make no bones about it," says 1st Lt. Dan Evans, the executive officer of A Company. "It was just a mind game."

The men of A Company and attached paratroopers from the 3d Battalion, 504th Airborne Infantry had unwittingly rehearsed their roles in the invasion many times. The company, under the command of Capt. Mike Beech, always had at least a fire team of four or five men patrolling somewhere in the U.S. housing area on Espinar, an attractive post with rolling hills shaded by palm trees. Sometimes A Company ran checkpoints in front of the commissary or Fort Gulick Elementary School, checking identification cards and searching cars. Sometimes they patrolled the thick tropical forest around the housing areas. Remote ground sensors, monitored by 7th Division military intelligence personnel, were laid throughout the jungle to detect intruders.

The soldiers thought they were protecting the 429 Americans on Fort Espinar from thieves and terrorists. But they were also learning the terrain they would have to seize at 1:00 A.M., 20 December.

Under the canal treaties, U.S. forces were permitted to maneuver on Panamanian territory, but only to move between two points under U.S. control. That allowed A Company, fully armed, to conduct road marches across Fort Espinar. Gradually, they took greater advantage of their limited rights of movement to escalate the U.S. campaign of intimidation. Instead of daytime marches, they maneuvered at night.

Through a wiretap on the infantry headquarters, U.S. personnel listened for the Panamanians' reaction. To Kellogg's delight, the Panamanian reaction was typically, "The Americans are at it again. They're doing this just to harass us." Around Thanksgiving, when Joint Task Force Panama pushed its rehearsals into high gear, A

Company started reconnoitering the actual route they would follow to assault Buildings 212 and 213, which housed the PDF infantry company.

The soldiers didn't know it, but their platoon leaders were using the exercise to scout for the best fence to breach into the headquarters compound, Evans says. The company's mission at H-hour was to disarm the PDF infantry company.

A composite platoon of about twenty-nine men from the airborne battalion, mostly from Headquarters Company, had a separate mission at the opposite end of Fort Espinar: to take control of the Jose Domingo Espinar School, the PDF's academy for noncommissioned officers. The students at the school, known as the School of the Americas when it was under U.S. control, were believed to comprise a platoon-sized force. A guard stood watch around the clock at the neck of the peninsula.

Being senior NCOs for the most part, the students were thought to present a possible threat to the Americans living on Fort Espinar. They could easily grab weapons from the school's arms room and join the fight. "They could become a force," says Capt. Matthew Halder, commander of the Headquarters Company. "They could easily get a hostage situation going." U.S. troops had to keep the students not only from reinforcing the PDF 8th Infantry Company, but also from taking Americans hostage.

The paratroopers were to seize the guard shack at the Espinar School. That would seal off the three buildings on the peninsula: the school itself, a school barracks, and the bachelors' quarters. At the 8th Infantry Company, the 2d and 3d platoons of A Company, 4th Battalion, 17th Infantry would assault Buildings 212 and 213, while 1st Platoon provided fire support from alongside Building 215, next to a U.S. post office. The air defense element would stand ready, on a steep rise up the street between Buildings 218 and 219, to fire the Vulcan and antitank weapons at the 8th Company headquarters and a guard shack between the headquarters buildings.

Second Platoon of 7th Division's 7th MP Company was to seal off the main entrance to Fort Espinar. The 549th MP Company, based at Fort Davis, originally was picked to lead the MP mission at Fort Espinar, but the MPs were considered too close for comfort to the Panamanians they would have to fight. At Fort Espinar, they patrolled together with PDF troops.

A mutual disdain developed between the 549th MP Company and the 7th MPs, who had operational control of them before and during the invasion. The 549th MPs were concerned about doing their day-to-day job of law enforcement—keeping the peace and controlling traffic—while the 7th MPs focused on preparations for war.

The soldiers of Task Force Espinar were briefed at 9:00 P.M. 19 December at the U.S. officers' club, on a steep hill just up the street from the Espinar School. They were nervous, but psyched. Finally they had the chance to do something about the PDF. "We knew we could take them," says Sgt. William Smith of 1st Platoon.

"I was nervous when I first heard about the mission," says Specialist Jim Johnson, also of 1st Platoon. "We were going to carry live rounds, and people could shoot at us."

The 1st Platoon was the first to move out from the officers' club, operating as if it were conducting an ordinary patrol. The three platoons assembled in the basement of Building 217 to wait for H-hour. Preparatory exercises showed it would take the assault force about two hours to maneuver from Building 217 through the woods to the assault positions by 8th Company headquarters. Moving the Vulcan from the officers' club to its firing position would take seven minutes.

Originally, the platoon of paratroopers, driving in from Fort Sherman, was to assemble in Building 217 before moving to the peninsula. Beech decided it would be less risky to assemble the platoon at the officers' club, closer to the school, about two hours before the invasion was to begin. The paratroopers waited in the darkness inside the club, surrounded by triple-strand concertina wire, for the mission to begin. At about twenty minutes to one, the platoon crossed over the concertina wire and proceeded down a set of concrete stairs to the housing areas. It was slow going. The soldiers carried a .50 caliber machine gun and tripod.

What seemed like a simple mission—to block the peninsula on which the school was located—became more complicated when the firing started at Coco Solo. Halder had just reached a tennis court at the bottom of the steps and was making sure all his soldiers cleared the steps when he heard the Vulcan open up.

"I figured out this was going to wake up everybody on my side of the world," he says. "My surprise was going to be very limited. So we launched our attack." The platoon darted along the housing area, through the grass to Gulick Lodge, a rambling, three-story U.S. guest quarters across the street from the Espinar School barracks.

Halder sent one squad and a .50 caliber machine-gun team into position to fire on the barracks. His other two squads moved with him into positions around the corner, "basically just to provide a block, allow no soldiers to go outside." But as the machine-gun team approached its position, a soldier opened fire on the barracks. The Panamanian NCOs fought back, and a ten-minute firefight ensued.

The two assault platoons were trudging through the tropical forest to the PDF headquarters when they heard shots from the direction of the school. It was 12:42 A.M.. The soldiers wondered what had gone wrong, but tried to remain confident. At about five minutes to H-hour, the 1st Platoon moved into its support position next door to the post office. At the same time, the soldiers of A Company could hear the pounding of the Vulcan at Coco Solo.

"This is for real," thought Cpl. Larry Franks of 3d Platoon's 3d squad as he heard the gunfire in the background. "We couldn't really believe it, that we were ready to go. I didn't really know what to expect . . . the worst."

The sounds of battle were a relief to many. "We were just like, 'This is too good to be true, they're going to call it off,'" says Sgt. Vincent Schreiber of 2d Platoon, who had grown tired of the patrols, the road marches, the constant face-offs with the PDF. "This was something happening," he says.

The assault team sprinted through the jungle toward their positions, abandoning their quiet stealth. With 1st Platoon moving into position, they were afraid the Vulcan would open fire before they reached their assault positions. The darkness made maneuvering more difficult than usual in the thick vegetation. "It was a pain in the ass to travel in," says Schreiber. "It was real dark. We had to stay, like, right behind the guy in front of us just so you could know where you're going."

In fact, the soldiers were not sure where they were, because they emerged from the woods at least one hundred meters short of the exit they had rehearsed. Seeing that the support element had not yet opened fire, they worked their way back into the jungle and waited a few minutes until 1:00 A.M. so as not to rush the assault. Evans, positioned by the Vulcan, ordered the gunner not to fire until 1:00.

At the appointed hour, the assault force emerged southwest of the PDF headquarters building, which stood on a small rise. The lights were out in Buildings 212 and 213—more evidence that U.S. troops had lost the element of surprise. When the attack began, Maj. Luis Guardia, commander of the 8th Infantry Company, had already fled to downtown Colon.

The two headquarters buildings were surrounded by an eight-foot fence of chain link set in a knee-high concrete wall. Concertina wire was strung along the top. Building 212, the larger and closer of the two, was 3d Platoon's to assault; 2d Platoon would handle Building 213.

The first rounds from the Vulcan burst through the darkness across the baseball field, hitting the guard shack inside the head-quarters complex and sweeping along Building 213, then Building 212 behind it. For Johnson, the thunder of the Vulcan firing was an odd relief. It cleared his mind and set him in motion. "You knew what to do," Johnson says. "You just got down and did your job."

PDF infantrymen responded a minute later with a hail of small-arms fire across the 200 to 250 meters between their headquarters and 1st Platoon's position. But the Panamanians inflicted only one U.S. casualty: Sgt. Moli Sapatu, wounded when a rocket-propelled grenade exploded right next to him. "There was this loud crunch and I felt a wave of heat come off of it," says Specialist Darrel Miller, a rifleman with 1st Platoon's 1st squad who was standing about five meters to Sapatu's right.

Sapatu, a pillar of muscle inaptly nicknamed Sgt. Sap, was evac-uated to the rear and from there back to the States. Aside from the pain, Sapatu was angry that he was out of the fight. "When we got the mission, I was thinking I was going to bust somebody up. All the plan I had in my mind never happened," Sapatu says.

The firing continued. Miller says it seemed like quite a while, but was actually only a couple of minutes, before the assault force pen-etrated the fence around 8th Infantry Company headquarters. When the Vulcan started firing, says Smith of 1st Platoon, "My whole platoon, we just started firing into the building. It looked like Swiss cheese." Most of the supporting fire was aimed at the second floor of the PDF company headquarters, where the barracks and communications center were.

While 1st Platoon provided supporting fires, soldiers from 2d Platoon laid a bangalore torpedo along the fence and blew a hole several meters in diameter. "Their effective small-arms fire was pretty short," Evans says. "It was really, really dark. I don't think the Panamanian guys could see what they were shooting at at all, because anything that was shot back was way out of line. We pretty much suppressed them right away." The firefight lasted only five or 10 minutes, Evans says. All told, the air-defense unit fired 500 rounds from the Vulcan after the initial volley; 1st Platoon fired 40 to 50 antitank rockets at the headquarters, in addition to rocket-propelled grenades and machine-gun fire.

The company issued its invitation to the PDF to surrender. No further prompting was necessary, Evans says. About 40 soldiers inside the company headquarters gave themselves up. "A lot of guys came out, they were crying and they'd urinated on themselves." he says. "We'd been very intimidating to these guys and it worked." By 2 A.M., the fight against the infantry company was all but complete. It happened so fast, in fact, that some soldiers never had a chance to carry out their missions.

"By the time we got ready to assault, they were calling for the PDF to surrender," says Franks of 3d Platoon, 3d Squad.

It remained for 2d and 3d Platoons to clear the two buildings, a task that took about three hours. Few stragglers remained in the buildings, and they put up little resistance. What the soldiers found was the makings of a bloodbath that the PDF had decided, for whatever reasons, not to inflict. "We found a lot of weapons with magazines discarded and ready to go," Evans says. "It looked like they were ready to fight but they changed their minds. For 150 people in the 8th Company, I'm guessing they had 500 weapons in there and a lot of ammunition." The arsenal included AK-47s, M16A1 rifles, shotguns, a couple of Uzis and T-65s, a Taiwanese copy of the M16, Evans says.

A Company survived their most hazardous mission of the night with only one casualty, only to suffer a half-dozen more casualties at the Espinar School.

The paratroopers, after bringing their AT-4 and light antitank weapons to bear, had secured the surrender of about 35 NCOs at the school within an hour of their assault. Two of the Panamanians and at least one paratrooper had been wounded in the exchange of fire. Light was creeping up on the horizon when 2d and 3d Platoons finished clearing the PDF infantry headquarters and moved across post to clear the school buildings, along with soldiers from 1st Platoon.

Most of the Panamanian NCOs were now locked inside the temporary prison of the tennis court, but A Company had reports of possible holdouts inside the school barracks. "No one was firing from inside. We didn't know if there was anybody in there," says Schreiber of 2d Squad, 2d Platoon. After firing a LAW rocket and several rounds from an M203 grenade launcher into the windows of the barracks, Schreiber's squad went inside.

The mission was classic MOUT, or military operations in urban terrain, a situation the 7th Division soldiers had practiced repeatedly at Fort Ord, Calif., their home base. Working in groups of three, soldiers conducting MOUT operations move carefully from room to room, using grenades if necessary to flush out any opposition while they take cover from the blast and possible enemy fire.

Two mistakes combined to put six soldiers in the hospital and injure several others. First, nine soldiers gathered in one room, three times as many as MOUT procedure dictates; and second, one of them threw a grenade into a small room, in the mistaken belief that it led to a larger room. The grenade bounced off a wall and came back to the soldiers, exploding among them. No one escaped injury. "I knew I wasn't going to die, but I didn't feel much like living, either," says Schreiber, who took shrapnel in the legs, hand, arm and his buttocks. He was evacuated to the United States that afternoon.

Schreiber has not run since the accident at Fort Espinar. He got a medical discharge from the Army, after only six years of service. Despite the swiftness of the battle that night and the injuries he received, Schreiber is thankful he saw combat. "It's something you train for, you want to do it."

At 5 A.M., Beech informed battalion commander Brooks that Fort Espinar was secure and sent soldiers into the housing areas to check on the American residents, who had stayed inside throughout the operation. The soldiers of A Company awaited their next mission.

At 6:30 A.M., Hutchinson awoke at her home in Colon and noticed how quiet it was. The explosions from Coco Solo had ceased. But the silence would be short-lived. As looters and Dignity Battalion troops spread mayhem through their city, residents of Colon waited for U.S. troops to rescue them. No soldiers came.

13

The Great Divide

As far as Capt. Derek Johnson was concerned, he had already been in combat in Panama. The unit he commanded, C Company of the 3d Battalion, 504th Airborne Infantry, was on its way to what promised to be one of the nastiest missions of any in Task Force Atlantic's southern area of operations.

C Company was to seize Renacer Prison, where Noriega had imprisoned two Americans and uncounted plotters in the unsuccessful 3 October coup attempt, and liberate the prisoners. The prison guard force of twenty to twenty-five PDF troops was expected to put up a fight. They had made C Company's one dress rehearsal difficult, and Johnson had no reason to believe they would roll over for the raid he was to conduct.

Neither Johnson, nor the commanders of A, B, and D Companies of the 3d Battalion, heard the battle begin at Coco Solo that night. They were too far away, spread among four targets in a seventy-five-square-mile area.

Johnson stayed behind at 3d Brigade's operations center on Fort Sherman to receive a 7:00 P.M. mission briefing while his soldiers loaded onto Landing Craft Marine (LCM), the landing craft they had used to rehearse their assault on the prison five days before. The captain approached them somberly around nine to tell them they were not embarking on another exercise, as they thought. They were going to war. In fact, the troopers' departure for their "exercise" had been calculated to place them at Renacer at H-hour (see figure 13–1).

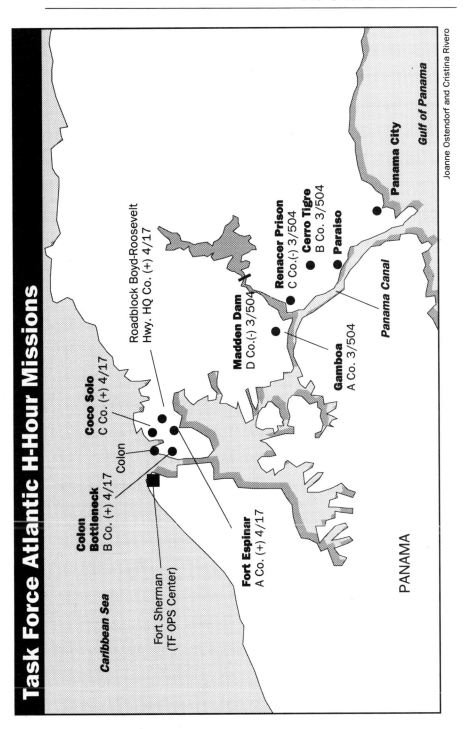

FIGURE 13–1

Task Force Atlantic: H-Hour Missions

"The soldiers exhibited a calm that they did not exhibit on the Sand Flea," Johnson later recalled in a post-invasion briefing for Col. Keith Kellogg, commander of 3d Brigade. "There was no reaction. There was no fidgeting around or scurrying for cover or Hail Marys or anything. There was a job to do and they were going to do it."

For Johnson's company, the crisis response exercise known as a Sand Flea, in which they marched through the Renacer Prison grounds, had been a close brush with war. But Johnson came away thinking that although it did not allow his soldiers access to the inside of the prison, the Sand Flea was invaluable in acquainting C Company with the layout of the prison compound.

No one knew just how many prisoners were inside Renacer, located about halfway between Panama City and Colon across the Chagres River from the town of Gamboa. Navy SEALs and infantry scouts had conducted surveillance of the prison, but never saw the prisoners come outside. What they did learn was the location of the guard quarters, the guards' apparent level of training, the construction of the buildings, and the physical obstacles standing between U.S. forces and the prisoners.

C Company would have to secure the prisoners immediately. "It was always our intent to make sure the prisoners were secured first," says Lt. Col. Lynn Moore, commander of 3d Battalion, 504th Infantry. "We didn't want a hostage-barricade situation to develop."

The most difficult part of the mission would not be the strength of the PDF's weapons. The guards were believed to have only small arms at their disposal, mainly AK-47s and T-65s. The difficulties lay in the number of guards and the close confines in which C Company would be operating. The prison was hemmed in on three sides by water—to the north, the Chagres River and to the south and west, the Panama Canal—and by a jungle ridge to the east.

Of all the Sand Fleas in Task Force Atlantic's area of operations, C Company's had provoked the strongest reaction from the enemy. "The response was very severe," Moore says. As soon as the soldiers disembarked from their LCMs at Omaha Beach, as they called the landing site on the canal shore, the prison guards rushed from their quarters, weapons locked and loaded, to confront Johnson. The PDF guard in charge told Johnson the prison was off limits to U.S.

troops without consent in advance from the Panamanian government. In treaty parlance, Renacer was a "red" zone.

As PDF and U.S. troops faced off, pointing their weapons at each other, Moore says the PDF guard told Captain Johnson, "You're not allowed to come here without prior coordination."

"Derek Johnson looked at him and said, 'Okay, I'm coordinating it right now. We're going through here in five minutes.' They went crazy," Moore says. After consultation with his men, the PDF guard proposed to let the troops through in fifteen minutes. Johnson agreed and his company proceeded through the complex, splitting into two parts to see as much as possible of the layout.

One platoon walked northwest along the railroad tracks that cross the Chagres into Gamboa, while the remaining two platoons walked through the compound to the front gate of the prison and out to Gaillard Highway, where the company reassembled. All three platoons were prepared for a fight, their weapons ready with live ammunition.

Watching the incident were two teams of Navy SEALs positioned on high ground north and south of the prison complex the day before to gather as much intelligence as possible. Scouts also watched from the Gamboa Bridge, a railroad crossing and one-lane bridge. The SEALs produced valuable details of the compound, including ground-level photographs to supplement the aerial shots 3d Brigade had obtained—but no information on the number of prisoners, who never had left the prison buildings. Nonetheless, Johnson said later, "A company commander couldn't ask for anything better except the names of the prison guards."

The soldiers had seen their target. They had practiced loading and unloading helicopters, not knowing what kind of transportation would be available if they were called on for combat. Squad and team leaders had conducted numerous equipment inspections. "Every soldier, down to the last private, knew what was going on with his mission," Johnson said. But they had not practiced air-assaulting into Renacer because the prison was controlled by the PDF.

It would be a tight fit. The four-sided, oblong prison yard where two Hueys were to land with the initial assault force was no more than forty by seventy meters. Surrounding it was a twelve-foot chain-link fence.

C Company launched the LCMs from Fort Sherman at about midnight. Shortly after 12:30 A.M., an AH-1 Cobra attack helicopter and two OH-58s flew south over the canal for a final look at Renacer, Gamboa, and Cerro Tigre, three of Moore's four company objectives. Warrant Officer William Parsons, a helicopter pilot assigned to B Company of 7th Division's 1st Battalion, 123d Aviation Regiment, didn't relish the idea of flying over the H-hour targets before H-hour. Neither did his fellow 7th Division pilots.

Parsons was to be the copilot under 1st Lt. Bruce Beck, the aviation mission commander for Renacer, of an OH-58 Kiowa helicopter that would help immobilize a prison guard tower in the northwest corner of the compound so Johnson's men could come ashore safely. The tower overlooked the canal, providing a front-row seat for C Company's amphibious landing. The two pilots, with 7th Division's 2d Squadron, 9th Reconnaissance Regiment, were attached to B Company, of the 1st Battalion, 123d Aviation Regiment while in Panama.

Chief Warrant Officer Bob Stacy, a Cobra pilot also with the reconnaissance regiment but attached to B Company, and copilot Warrant Officer John Marsh of B Company, would barrage the guard quarters, prison headquarters, and an office building with 20mm cannon fire so the two Hueys could land inside the prison compound. Stacy voiced strong doubts about the mission Moore described in his briefing. The pilots felt the rumble of helicopters overhead would alert the PDF guards to the movement of troops, while Moore theorized that the overflight would have exactly the opposite effect: to lull the PDF into thinking U.S. troops were just conducting another exercise.

"It was a foolish idea, especially once we had an idea that the plan had been compromised," says Capt. Timothy Jones, commander of B Company of the aviation regiment. Jones was flying a reconnaissance mission at Fort Amador at the time his fellow 7th Division pilots were planning the final pass down the canal. "A desensitizing pass immediately prior to firing isn't going to do anything except wake people up," Jones says. But in the end, Moore outranked all four pilots. He was particularly irked by Stacy's vehement resistance.

"I tried to tell him he was going to fly the mission the way it was briefed, or I'd find somebody else to fly it," Moore says. "We had some guys on the LCM who were hanging it out a lot more than he was." There could be no change in the landing zones at Renacer, either, despite the fact that the PDF had been tipped off to the invasion. "We could not change the LZs and still feel like we could get into the prison in time" to protect the prisoners, Moore said in the after-action briefing.

The pilots clung to the southern edge of the canal, as far away from the targets as possible, until H-hour, although the normal helicopter route down the canal passed right over the prison. Moore checked to see that the LCMs were on schedule as he flew back north in the other OH-58, a helicopter from 1st Battalion, 228th Aviation Regiment, which he was using for command and control. C Company was nearing the shore as planned.

At about fifteen seconds to go, the three helicopters pulled abreast of Renacer prison. A sniper in C Company, positioned in the back of Parsons' Kiowa, fired on the guard tower.

The first two of three Hueys to fly into Renacer flew south down the Chagres and across the canal and made a 180-degree turn to fly into the prison compound. The pilots had to fly high to avoid hitting the railroad bridge, which stood a hundred feet above the river, then swoop down over the high fence into the prison yard, called Landing Zone Hawk. "They had to come in at a very high angle and then shoot straight down," Moore says.

As the Hueys emerged from over the Chagres, the first LCM approached the dock chosen for the landing, rammed it, shifted direction and docked. The Hueys, from the 228th Aviation Regiment, were taking fire from the prison quarters as they headed southeast into Renacer. Again, no one was hit. Once the Hueys had passed the railroad bridge, door gunners, squad automatic weapons gunners and a soldier with a grenade launcher returned fire out the right side of the choppers. No fire was directed out the left side for fear of hitting prisoners.

Stacy parked his Cobra, hovering over the canal, and let loose with 20mm Gatling cannon fire on the guard quarters, which occupied high ground. The first Huey was descending on the prison. The cannon fire did the trick, stopping the PDF in their tracks while the Hueys landed. A gunner in Moore's command and control helicopter, hovering opposite the main prison compound, also laid small-arms fire on the quarters.

It fell to Parsons, with a C Company sniper in the back of his OH-58, to take out the guard tower, which sat on high ground on the northwest corner of the prison compound. "We were shooting and constantly moving," Parsons says. Moore watched the fire slice through the air. "It looked like the Fourth of July," he says.

"I honestly don't think they saw us. They were just shootin' everywhere," Parsons says. No one in the helicopters was hit. The bright lights over the prison went out about thirty seconds after the assault began, possibly because of a short-circuit caused by gunfire hitting overhead electrical lines.

Each of the two Hueys carried eleven paratroopers, together comprising Team Oswald, after 2d Lt. Chris Oswald, leader of 2d Platoon. Their mission was to break through the fence and seize the enclosed prison compound, consisting of prison quarters, a chapel, and a recreation building. Armed with automatic weapons and about a dozen AT-4s, they were to defend their objective until the rest of C Company relieved them. The third Huey touched down at LZ Owl, north of the prison courtyard, with ten scouts who were to seize a guard shack at the main entrance to Renacer and block any PDF reinforcements from entering the compound. The total prison guard force was believed to comprise three platoons, or about seventy-five personnel. The scouts' mission was uneventful.

The assault force had to cut their way into the central prison compound, which was reinforced by a ten-foot fence. The fence was impervious to grenades and Claymore mines. Two paratroopers crawled forward and hacked a hole in it with bayonets. "It was really heavy-gauge wire," Moore says.

When the LCMs landed, carrying most of 3d Platoon and the rest of 2d Platoon, a reinforced squad of soldiers moved northwest of the guard quarters to seal off the guards inside. Others went inside the prison yard to defend it. "They started suppressive fire on all the buildings that were outside the wire," Moore says. The troops were armed with M60 machine guns and about a dozen AT-4s, to be used against buildings and vehicles.

Once inside the prison yard, 2d Platoon's 1st squad blew a hole in the main prison building. One soldier was hit in the arm. The platoon's 3d squad crossed the breach to see to the prisoners' safety, while 2d squad secured the recreation building. The prisoners were lying on the floor. They had covered themselves with mattresses.

Under the protective watch of the fire support element, now in position with five machine guns, 3d Platoon moved up from the LCM to clear the office building and prison headquarters from the inside out. An M60 gunner in Team Broadus, as it was called after 2d Lt. Chuck Broadus, 3d Platoon leader, shot and killed two PDF soldiers as they ran between the buildings.

The prisoners were secure, but the night was far from over. Clearing the prison complex would keep the soldiers busy for another few hours.

Sgt. Kevin Schleben was leading 3d Platoon's 3d squad into the dark headquarters building to clear it when the soldiers walked into a cloud of tear gas. The squad went outside to don protective masks and returned to finish the job. As Schleben was walking down a hallway, he noticed a trail of blood. He told his men to stay inside and secure the building, then pursued the red path. Following it outside, he saw two PDF soldiers next to the building, just a few feet away from other paratroopers who were unaware of their presence.

The PDF troops spun around to face him, their weapons pointed at him. Schleben opened fire, killing them both. For his quick reaction to protect other troops, he received a Bronze Star with "V" device for valor. "It could have been a really bad situation," Moore says. In all, five PDF guards were killed as the paratroopers flushed out the remaining enemy, building by building.

Johnson was relieved his company had not lost any men. Perhaps his biggest worry throughout the night was that his own soldiers would shoot each other in the dark confines of the prison. "It was completely black," Moore says. Further obscuring the scene was a fog that settled on the prison at about 2:00 A.M. To avoid hitting the assault force or the prisoners, the area between Team Oswald and the prison compound was declared a no-fire zone for 2d and 3d platoons, unless the target was clearly a PDF guard. "We had troops all out to their front," Johnson said. "The likelihood of hitting friendly targets was just too great."

But the amphibious-assault troops had to prevent anyone firing on Team Oswald from the buildings outside the fence. They were permitted to fire on any enemy north of the railroad tracks, which cut through the prison complex. "We had no friendlies across this railroad tracks," Johnson said.

Five minutes after the assault began, Team Oswald secured the prisoners. At that point, the no-fire zone grew to encompass everything inside the fence. Likewise, once 3d Platoon had crossed the railroad tracks to begin clearing the prison, the support element had to cease fire altogether.

A PDF lieutenant, his wife, and child escaped being shot during C Company's clearing operations. As 3d Platoon's 1st squad moved up to the jungle to finish clearing the prison complex, the soldiers encountered the family in one half of a duplex. They had just cleared the other half when the woman cried out, "Don't shoot!" The soldiers held their fire and discovered the three Panamanians waiting to surrender. They were taken prisoner but not harmed.

The last of the PDF to give up the fight were fourteen guards in their quarters. The several teams Johnson sent to seal off the quarters were fired on sporadically early in the assault. After Johnson's men laid on light antitank weapons and AT-4s the PDF ceased fire, but did not surrender. When soldiers entered the quarters later that morning to clear it, they found the guards had taken cover under beds and wanted to give up the fight. The walls outside bore the smallpox of persistent fire. "They were willing to fight, I think, until the AT-4 made the big hole in the side of the building," Moore said later.

By 4:30 A.M., the prison complex was silent. Five PDF guards lay dead and seventeen others had switched roles with their former captives. Now they were prisoners of U.S. forces, while the sixty-four Noriega had incarcerated at Renacer were free.

Across the Chagres River, Capt. Pete Boylan was contemplating the things that could have gone wrong in the battle, but didn't.

Gamboa was the only one of the 3d Battalion's targets where the safety of an entire American community was at stake. The intent of the mission was to secure U.S. lives and property in the town, where four PDF units were based. The units consisted of two platoons' worth of police, three platoons of forest police, and a company of female counterintelligence soldiers, known by the unit's acronym FUFEM, or Fuerzas Femininas.

Boylan's troopers counted 167 Americans living in Gamboa. Most were employees of the Panama Canal Commission and teachers working in Defense Department schools for military children in

Panama. The command made it clear that not one of the Americans in Gamboa was to be hurt, nor their houses damaged. Moore had impressed on Boylan, commander of his A Company, that this was one absolute in an otherwise uncertain situation. "The colonel said, 'Pete, if one American dies, then you have really screwed the pooch.'"

"If he damaged their houses or killed or injured an American, then everything else we did in the entire task force was for naught," Moore says. To complicate matters, the forest police headquarters was a mere twenty meters from four American homes.

The Sand Flea that A Company conducted at Gamboa on 14 December had ended on a nasty note.

The company flew into Gamboa in four CH-47 Chinook helicopters, landing at a golf course on the western shore of the Chagres River. Most of the town was designated a "red" zone. Under the terms of the canal treaties, that meant U.S. forces were not supposed to enter without arranging it in advance with the Panamanians. But by this time, U.S. troops in Panama were under instructions to ignore such treaty procedures during Sand Fleas. The command wanted to see how the PDF would react.

Boylan designed a route that would allow his men to reconnoiter all four objectives in his contingency plan: Ranger, the forest police headquarters; FEM, the FUFEM headquarters; Cop, the police station; and Iron, the Gamboa Bridge across the Chagres. Renacer Prison lay at the other end of the bridge, to the southeast. The company marched west from the golf course, splitting at an intersection into two elements.

The 3d Platoon moved southwest to get a look at the FUFEM headquarters. Then the platoon marched along Gaillard Highway, which runs parallel to Gatun Lake and the canal, to a building that once housed a Defense Department school. Being a Defense Department facility, the school was within the soldiers' proper territory. Boylan, with his 1st and 2d Platoons and mortars, headed southeast toward the forest police headquarters. Here the Sand Flea proved itself useful in yet another detail, as Boylan discovered the building he thought was to be his target was in fact a home occupied by Americans.

The actual target was two doors down. Boylan walked by it, noting the construction and surrounding terrain, and split the unit again. He sent 2d Platoon to reconnoiter the police station, a block from the shore of Lake Gatun, while 1st Platoon took a cursory tour of all the housing areas.

The company reunited at the school, located behind the police station. So far, so good, thought Boylan. "We really didn't run into any problem," he says, "until all of a sudden."

As soon as the soldiers stepped onto Gaillard Highway south of the school, about eight Panamanian police cars came flying over the Gamboa Bridge and stopped on the road. The troops were moving toward a dock at a Panama Canal Commission dredging facility, where they were going to load onto LCMs for the trip back to Fort Sherman, when the Panamanian police blocked their path. Boylan saw weapons in some of the Panamanians' hands, but nothing impressive.

"We just walked right by them," he says. His soldiers took pleasure in scowling at a baby-faced PDF soldier who sat on the south side of the road with an AK-47. "Everybody who walked by him . . . looked right at the kid and just pointed their weapon right at him. We just walked around all the police cars. We kept on going."

The company was ready for combat when the word came down 19 December that Just Cause was about to happen. Boylan was briefed on the mission just before 7:30 P.M. He briefed his men at nine. Like C Company commander Johnson's troops, "My guys got very serious. They were ready," Boylan says. "When I briefed my guys, I got an awesome feeling of strength."

The mission would not go exactly as planned. The phone conversation intercepted around 11:00 P.M., warning, "The party is on for one o'clock," forced Boylan's company to make some last-minute changes in the assault plan. The original notion of landing at two spots, LZ Duck at the FUFEM headquarters and LZ Vulture, a soccer field just west of the forest police headquarters, was scrapped. It was too risky to send soldiers, packed sixty to a helicopter, into a potentially hot landing zone. The chances of a bloodbath were too great. The battalion planners decided to fly all three helicopters into LZ Vulture, officially called McGrath Field. The company could secure it more rapidly.

At quarter past midnight on D-day, the soldiers started to load two CH-47 Chinooks and one UH-1 Huey. At twenty minutes to one, the helicopters took off with the Huey in the lead, carrying the

3d Platoon leader, his radio operator, and three gunnery teams, each consisting of an M60 gunner, an assistant gunner, and a squad leader carrying an M203 grenade launcher. Following thirty seconds behind the Huey were the two Chinooks, carrying 1st Platoon, 2d Platoon, and the remainder of 3d Platoon. Boylan traveled on the second Chinook with his company headquarters, mortars, and 1st Platoon.

In the intellectual pursuit of a better battle plan, Boylan had never fully grasped the reality of combat. The son of an infantry division commander, he had spent his whole life in the Army, steeped in the language of tactics, maneuvers, contingencies. Yet, he says, "It never really hit me that the operation was going to happen." When he passed over Renacer prison, he understood. From the gunner's window, he saw the Cobra open fire. "I'll never forget that point," he says. "All of a sudden I can see the rockets open up on the Cobra. That is the point, in my life, anyway, when I said, 'Holy shit, this is definitely for real.'"

Flying down the Chagres, the helicopters turned right over the golf course and landed at McGrath Field.

The Huey landed first with eleven people. The three M60 machine gun teams took up positions so that an M60 was pointed at each of the three PDF units: FUFEM to the west, the police station to the south, and the forest police headquarters immediately to the east. The Chinooks touched down a minute later. Boylan set up his command post in a building abutting Objective Ranger, the forest police station, which was his greatest concern in the Gamboa mission.

He assigned 1st Platoon to secure it, telling the men to fire as far away from the American houses as possible. "We had to do a very surgical takedown of the objective," Boylan later said in a briefing. No LAWs or AT-4s could be fired on the forest police headquarters. "We stuck strictly with small-arms fire and M203s to make the initial breach. And then, once inside the building, it was all small arms with a couple of grenades." It did not surprise him that this objective was the last to be secured.

The first was Objective Cop, secured within an hour of landing by 2d Platoon, the only one of Boylan's platoons to suffer any casualties. Sgt. Christopher Thompson was shot in the thigh, apparently from the roof of the police station, just as the Chinooks landed. He was evacuated to the rear, where he refused to return to the United States but instead spent the next three days trying to find a way back to Gamboa to continue the fight.

As they maneuvered around the police station, the troops eyed a Shell gasoline station right next door. "They had to be very selective" in choosing their targets, Boylan says. Four soldiers were shot while clearing the building. "That's where the majority of the fire came," Boylan says. Inside, the troops found a large arsenal of weapons in footlockers: T-65s, bayonets, shotguns, and .38 caliber pistols.

The forest police fled out the back of the building and escaped into the jungle. Boylan's company found no casualties inside, although he later learned that a couple of the PDF troops had been wounded. Once Objective Cop was secured, two teams from 2d Platoon moved southeast to establish a roadblock on the Gamboa Bridge, Objective Iron. At 2:30 A.M. the roadblock was in place. Objective FEM was next to go.

A brief firefight broke out between the women troops and the men of 3d Platoon. FUFEM troops who later turned themselves in to U.S. forces said that several had been hit but managed to escape out the back, crawling along a drainage ditch into the jungle. The platoon began systematically clearing the two buildings on the objective and secured the target by 3:00 A.M.

Inside their homes, the Americans living in Gamboa were relieved to hear the firing stop—as relieved as many of them had been to hear the firing start at 1:00 A.M. One of them "started hearing machine-gun fire and was pretty happy," Boylan says. "The U.S. was finally going to do something."

A staff sergeant made the rounds of the American homes, asking people to stay inside and await further instructions. Boylan walked around Gamboa after daybreak and saw that the Americans whose lives had been placed in his hands were alive and unscathed. None of the American houses was even nicked.

Although he had taken no PDF prisoners, Boylan considered the mission a success. "We were real pleased with the fact that it was a real accurate attack."

Cerro Tigre, the largest of the targets assigned to the 3d Battalion, 504th Infantry, also presented the greatest theoretical danger in terms of sheer enemy strength. Yet the threat was perhaps more ambiguous than at any of the battalion's other targets. The installation was the heart of the PDF's resupply operations, a central storage point for food and equipment. It was also believed to be one of the most heavily defended PDF installations, in large part because of the explosives ordnance school just north of the logistics facility.

Dyer expected to have to go one-on-one with the enemy: his company against three platoons of infantry at Cerro Tigre. But he lacked any clues as to how tough they would be.

B Company saw the target, but no enemy, during a 12 December Sand Flea. The information Dyer's men gathered on Cerro Tigre was strictly from the exterior. There was no possibility of marching as close to the installation as C Company had around Renacer. Cerro Tigre, covering one-and-a-quarter square miles, lay outside the canal zone. Soldiers had no treaty rights whatsoever on the fenced-in logistics base. Instead, the company's mission for the Sand Flea was to secure an antenna and electrical substation immediately southwest of Cerro Tigre, within the canal zone. It was billed as a purely defensive mission.

As if their jungle training at Fort Sherman hadn't taught them enough, the Sand Flea was yet another lesson in the difficulties of operating in tropical forests. Approaching Cerro Tigre in LCMs, B Company made several attempts to land on the steep banks of the canal before successfully landing, albeit at a point where the shore rose perpendicular from the water.

The company split up, each platoon assigned a different objective. One secured the antenna site, another set up a blocking position, and the third secured a point at the power station, which also happened to provide a clear view of the entrance to Cerro Tigre. Dyer and a couple of his NCOs walked along a railroad track separating a golf course from the southern edge of Cerro Tigre, studying the fence around the installation to find the best place to insert the troops.

That was the most valuable part of the Sand Flea, Dyer later said in a briefing on the battalion's H-hour missions. But B Company encountered no PDF troops during the entire nighttime exercise. "There were no guards, just lights," Dyer says. "We didn't see anyone moving around."

With the Sand Flea mission accomplished, the soldiers moved to the golf course south of Cerro Tigre, where they planned to load onto helicopters but wound up returning to Fort Sherman by truck. They left behind a gouge in the ground to mark the spot where they would break into Cerro Tigre.

Before D-day, B Company also rehearsed the various positions in the assault using a landing strip at Fort Sherman, so the soldiers in each squad would know where they stood on the battlefield. By a stroke of sheer luck, Dyer found that several buildings on Fort Sherman closely resembled buildings at Cerro Tigre.

But Dyer and his men still were unsure how much of a fight they were facing. On the evening of 19 December, Dyer learned that the mission was a go. He knew all he was going to know about Cerro Tigre without forcing his way in.

At nine, he briefed his company on the plan, walking his platoon leaders through the mission one more time. The soldiers had been expecting this briefing for several days, since the shooting of Marine Lieutenant Paz. The air had pulsated all day with the beat of helicopter rotors. "The soldiers wanted to go that Saturday night," Dyer says. "It was obvious to most everybody that something was coming." But their reaction to the news that they would have their chance to get back at the PDF was not jubilation. It was a sober resolve. "They didn't cheer or anything," he says. The company seemed to take a quiet, determined approach to what lay ahead. "They knew what they were going to do and they were ready to do it," Dyer says.

While the platoon leaders back-briefed their commander, the NCOs took charge of final inspections. The company moved to the pick-up zone at midnight and started loading the two UH-1 Hueys and two CH-47 Chinooks in which they would conduct their air assault.

At the last minute, the plans changed when U.S. intelligence officials got reports that the PDF knew the invasion was coming. Instead of landing in front of the infantry company barracks at Cerro Tigre as planned, Dyer's company would land on the golf course south of Cerro Tigre. The Hueys would land first at 1:00 A.M., followed thirty seconds later by the Chinooks. An AH-1 Cobra, flying on an east-west line along the railroad tracks, would pelt the perimeter of Cerro Tigre with cannon fire to suppress enemy automatic-weapons fire on the landing zone.

The mission suffered another setback when one of the Chinooks broke down after loading. A replacement Chinook was available, but the lead pilot was unfamiliar with the route to Cerro Tigre. After leaving Fort Sherman with the Hueys at 12:30 A.M., 20 December, the two Chinooks got lost and flew all the way to Panama City, where the Comandancia was under bombardment.

As they approached the golf course, the two Hueys came under small-arms fire. The Cobra responded immediately, silencing the enemy fire. Gunners in each Huey joined in the fire, spraying the enemy position through the right-hand door. The Chinooks arrived at the golf course ten minutes later. "I had a platoon on the ground for five minutes by themselves," Dyer says.

The soldiers wondered what else could go wrong. Many things could, but few did. The company did not even have to break into Cerro Tigre. As 1st Platoon approached the fence to breach it, the soldiers saw a PDF guard patrolling the area. Dyer told his men to hold fire.

"We felt we weren't in a position to engage," he said later. "We let him continue moving." The support element assigned to help 1st Platoon conduct the breach was not yet in place, Dyer said. "At that point we thought we were going to have to fight to get into the facility." But the guard fled.

In watching the guard patrol, the soldiers spotted an open gate. "We didn't have to blow the wire or make an explosive breach," Dyer said. The company simply walked into Cerro Tigre. The 3d Platoon moved to the western edge of the installation, while 2d Platoon stayed back as a reserve force. After clearing a guard shack at the western edge of Cerro Tigre, 3d Platoon continued north toward another guard shack, a mess hall, and motor pool police office. To the southeast, 1st Platoon was clearing another group of buildings, starting with a maintenance shed.

The soldiers spotted enemy activity in the guard headquarters. They moved an AT-4 into position and fired it at the building. The PDF troops scattered, heading north and east toward the jungle, and left their headquarters to the U.S. troops. The platoon closed in on the building to clear it.

Once the guard headquarters was secured, 3d Platoon conducted its clearing operations to the northwest. The soldiers in 1st Platoon suspended their operations until 3d Platoon had moved into place.

Then 1st Platoon was free to fire to the west if necessary. The platoon started clearing a perishable-goods warehouse between the maintenance shed and guard headquarters.

First Lieutenant Clarence Briggs, B Company executive officer, and Sfc. Thomas Crittenden followed 1st Platoon to a corner of the warehouse. "We were crouched at the corner of the warehouse when suddenly gunfire and the scream of tracers seemed to surround us," Briggs writes in his account of the invasion.[1]

The two soldiers hit the ground, then scurried to the guard headquarters, where they spotted movement in the shadows to the left. "Someone was firing on the building," Briggs writes. He laid his grenades in front of him and switched his weapon off safe in preparation for a fire fight. "I drew a bead and was about to fire when I heard, 'Hurry up, get across the fucking road!'" He put his weapon back on safe and breathed a sigh of relief.

"It was 3d Platoon, taking out the guardhouse," Briggs writes. "Evidently, when they fired on the guardhouse, the bullets richocheted and flew over the berm that was supposed to be the restrictive fire line between 3d and 1st platoons."

Dyer called in 2d Platoon to clear the remaining buildings immediately east of the guard headquarters. They consisted of a warehouse for nonperishable goods and another dining facility. PDF troops continued to flee as the soldiers cleared the buildings. "We didn't chase them. They were running right into machine-gun fire," Dyer says. No PDF soldiers were killed. Nor were any enemy wounded found later.

Two of Dyer's men were wounded while clearing buildings, according to Briggs. One took grenade fragments in his leg when he mistakenly fired a high-explosive round from his M203 grenade launcher. The other took an M203 fragment in the eye.

By 6:00 A.M., B Company was in full control of Cerro Tigre, having cleared all buildings on the installation. The PDF had abandoned Cerro Tigre. But the mission was not yet accomplished. The explosives ordnance school, about three-quarters of a mile north of the warehouse area, remained untouched. The company regrouped at 7:00 A.M. to clear the school and its bunkers.

Using trucks captured from Cerro Tigre, the troops rode up Madden Road most of the way to the explosives school, then hopped off the trucks to trek the rest of the way through the jungle. They walked right into a trap.[2] An explosion shook the air, and a soldier started to scream: "I'm hit! I'm hit!" Briggs writes. "For a moment, we were so astonished that no one reacted or fired a shot."

When the soldiers finally moved forward to seek cover, they came under fire from a guardhouse less than fifty meters away on the left side of the road. The guard apparently had detonated the booby trap.

"The men began to fire at the guardhouse, but their shots had little effect. . . . Most of the rounds went high," Briggs writes. Unnerved by the wounded man's screaming, Briggs yelled at the medic to come out of the hole where he was scrunched down in fear and take care of the soldier.

The soldier had taken some shrapnel in the arm. His wounds were not as serious as he originally feared, but he later was evacuated to the rear.

Cpl. Mark Ruiz pushed back whatever fear he might have felt and ran forward from his squad's position on the left side of the road. Darting across open terrain, he took up a position at a berm right in front of the guard house, Briggs writes. The rest of the squad followed Ruiz's unspoken command and rushed forward into a position where they could annihilate the guard station. "Steel and concrete flew everywhere," the lieutenant writes. The guard fled. The soldiers slowly advanced, and then stopped. Briggs looked at an M203 gunner frozen in place and saw what was wrong.

"He turned his head slowly, looked me directly in the eye, and pointed to the ground. 'Sir, be careful. This whole area is rigged with booby traps.'" The lieutenant looked down at his feet and saw that explosive detonating cord ran between his legs to the road, where it was wound around a 4.2-inch mortar round. A chorus of obscenities ensued, Briggs writes, as soldiers realized their deadly position.

The soldiers inched forward, eyeing the ground for booby traps before every step. Finally, they reached the first barracks building. A grenadier blasted the barracks, first with an M203 grenade launcher and then, moving in closer, with his shotgun, shifting his fire at the last minute as the clearing team assaulted, Briggs writes.

It took about a half-hour to clear the school complex, except for the arms room, which proved impervious to AT-4s. The soldiers crawled in through a window and handed the weapons out to be carted off in trucks.

Dyer asked for engineers to clear the booby traps. B Company was finished with Cerro Tigre. At about 7:30 A.M., Dyer and his men were summoned to Fort Sherman for a raid on the DENI police station in Colon.

There was no question this time of what to expect. As home base for a brigade of PDF military troops, the "Sovereignty" unit of the Dignity Battalions and the company of police at Cristobal, Colon seethed with firepower. B Company braced for a real fight.

What scared Capt. John Campbell, D Company, 3/504 Infantry (Airborne), the most was not getting into a firefight at his objective, Madden Dam, although one of his men would later be tried for killing a Panamanian there. His greatest fear, as he prepared for H-hour, was getting into a firefight before he and his men reached the dam.

Campbell, commander of D Company, an antitank unit, had the mission of securing the dam and power plant at H-hour. The dam is the primary power source for the U.S. military installations to the south, which comprise the very heart of SOUTHCOM. That made the dam Task Force Atlantic's only strategically significant objective, the others being enemy positions or areas where American civilians were in danger.

In addition to being an electrical generating site, the dam held back enough water to submerge completely the town of Gamboa. If a saboteur were to destroy the dam, Gamboa would virtually disappear, and with it all the water in Madden Lake. To drain the lake would cripple the electrical generating plant. It might take years for Madden Lake to fill up again.

Campbell knew that getting to the dam would be one of the hardest parts of his mission. His unit would have to drive the fifty miles from Fort Davis, its staging area, to Madden Dam without air cover, passing three PDF stations on the way. All the helicopters available to Task Force Atlantic had been committed to other targets. He also would be operating without his entire company. D Company's 3d Platoon was assigned to provide antitank support to a roadblock of Boyd-Roosevelt Highway, south of Coco Solo. His

H-hour force would be augmented, however, by two squads of engineers, a mortar section from C Company of 3d Battalion and two MP teams from the 549th MP Company.

Campbell's primary mission after installing his troops at Madden Dam was to establish a roadblock just north of it, where Madden Road intersected Boyd-Roosevelt Highway. D Company had rehearsed the mission in a Sand Flea exercise on 11 December, the day after the company arrived in Panama for four weeks of training at the Jungle Operations Training Center on Fort Sherman. It was the first Sand Flea for the battalion.

The company deployed in two military police HMMWVs and three two-and-a-half-ton trucks. One of the trucks, mounted with a .50-caliber machine gun, provided firepower while the others carried personnel. Ironically, D Company was provided air cover for the Sand Flea, though not for the D-day mission.

Campbell and Moore had driven the route earlier that day with a lieutenant from the 549th MPs, based at Fort Davis. They wanted to locate the road leading from Boyd-Roosevelt Highway to the dam. The lieutenant missed it, and on the way back toward the dam took a wrong turn through a water treatment plant just south of the dam. A guard ran out and started to close a gate to keep them out, but they kept moving and went on their way.

D Company was prepared in the Sand Flea to establish a roadblock at Boyd-Roosevelt Highway north of the dam if the PDF blocked the highway to the south, where Madden Road splits off and goes over the dam. "If the PDF blocked the road, as they had done before, and sent all traffic across Madden Dam, I was to block the road and send them back," Campbell says.

To make its scheduled 1:00 A.M. arrival time, the company crossed the canal at Gatun Locks to assemble at Fort Davis. The convoy left Fort Davis at about 11:30 P.M., planning to arrive at the dam at one. "I fully expected to be stopped somewhere, either at Sabanita or Buena Vista," Campbell says. "We were never stopped. I was surprised." Sabanita, eleven miles northeast of Fort Davis, was about one third of the way to Madden Dam. Buena Vista is seven and a half miles northwest of the dam.

The road march also took the troops by a PDF customs station just north of the dam. No one attempted to stop Campbell's troops there, either. "The night of the Sand Flea, nothing much happened,"

Campbell says. "The operation went off with no problems." The troops returned to Fort Sherman shortly before dawn.

That was D Company's one rehearsal for H-hour. Campbell also flew over the dam to survey the terrain. His men got additional training in searching live prisoners of war, a skill that would be more important to their mission than any of them imagined.

Despite the uncertainties of their planned road march to the dam, Campbell's men were jubilant when they learned in their 9:00 P.M. mission briefing that they were going to war. "I actually thought we were back in the Civil War, getting ready for First Manassas," Campbell says. "Everybody was cheering, they were stomping. I thought, 'Well, Jesus, I hope we're this happy when it gets through. I hope we all come back.'"

Campbell was more worried than ever about the ride to Madden Dam. In Kellogg's briefing to the battalion and company commanders, the colonel made it clear that Campbell was not to engage the enemy under any circumstances on the way to Madden Dam. "Col. Kellogg said, 'Who is going to Madden Dam?' I said I was," Campbell recalls. "He said, 'You will not make contact. You cannot make contact.'" Campbell's cover, if stopped, was that he and his men were heading back to Howard Air Force Base to return to the States the next day. If necessary, he would tell the PDF he was lost. "That's all we want to do, is just go home," he was to say.

At 10:00 P.M., the company loaded the trucks, departing shortly thereafter for Fort Davis, their staging point. Again, D Company sailed by the PDF stations. In fact, they practically flew. Campbell had planned to leave Fort Davis around 11:30 P.M. and travel to Madden Dam at about thirty-five miles an hour, placing them on their objective at H-hour, as planned. The two MP teams assigned to Campbell from the 549th were new to him. The MP lieutenant in charge told Campbell his plan was too dangerous.

"He said, 'Sir, that won't work. There's only one speed, that's hauling ass. That's the only safe way to go.'" Campbell says he spent the next hour and a half trying to catch up with the lieutenant's HMMWV, pulling up behind him just northwest of the dam. The company was twenty minutes early.

Moore came on the radio and told Campbell not to take the objective. The captain pulled over just past the PDF customs station at the intersection of Boyd-Roosevelt Highway and the road leading to the dam. At five minutes to one, he could not wait any longer. "I'm not going to just sit here," he said, and moved forward to seize his objective.

The 4th Platoon, with two .50 caliber machine guns, established a roadblock at an intersection to the south, while Campbell and the engineers moved on the dam itself. He knew he would have to deal with an armed Panama Canal Commission guard outside the electrical plant. "We knew he was friendly," Campbell says. "The hardest part was trying to talk him out of his weapon without him shooting at us." But the guard willingly surrendered his gun and his position. "We had no problem," Campbell says. "We had the dam secured within, say, fifteen minutes."

The captain put a platoon on top of the electrical station. The engineers occupied part of the dam and part of the power station. Campbell, who knew little about either dams or power plants, simply told the engineers, "Make sure nothing happens."

The mortar section from C Company, with two 60mm mortars, took up a position at the southern end of the dam to deal with any threat from a sizable PDF station in Chilibre, four miles to the south. One platoon established a roadblock north of the dam, where Madden Road intersects Boyd-Roosevelt Highway.

At 2:10 A.M., D Company was asked for intelligence reports on activity along Boyd-Roosevelt Highway. Campbell positioned a team of scouts at the water purification plant south of Madden Dam, between Boyd-Roosevelt and Madden Road. Feeling his troops were secure in their positions, at 3:45 A.M. Campbell prepared to move on the DENI customs station to the north. Driving by on their way to the dam, his men had seen guards at the station.

Campbell did not expect the DENI men to be as cooperative as the canal commission guard. He took part of 1st Platoon back to the customs house. The takedown was a cinch, with eight U.S. troops against only two guards. "We assaulted the building and they surrendered," Campbell says. "Not a shot was fired." The soldiers searched the building, removing a number of small arms along with the DENI officials, locked it, and returned to the dam.

Positioned south of the dam, 4th Platoon spotted two men carrying AK-47s, who turned and fled when they saw the U.S. soldiers. The close encounter was unnerving.

The next intruder, a wizened, toothless old man looking for food, did not get away. He was arrested as he foraged for yucca leaves. "Fourth Platoon, after those guys got away, weren't going to let anybody else get away," Campbell says. "They brought him to me and said, 'Hey, sir, we got a POW.' And I started laughing: What the hell are we going to do with this man? He just wanted something to eat." Campbell told his men to give the barefooted old man some food and send him home. "We just gave him MREs, told him to go home and not come back," Campbell says.

The night passed without further incident, Objective Dam having been completely secured. At daybreak, Campbell says lightheartedly, "I was growing kind of bored." Knowing there were at least two PDF stations within a four-mile radius, Campbell considered what else he could accomplish with a force of sixty men. Shortly after dawn, he took ten of his men in two MP vehicles to the smaller of the two PDF stations, outside of Buenos Aires. It consisted of one building with about six rooms, surrounded by a chain-link fence.

As the soldiers approached the PDF station, they saw a number of men who clearly carried weapons, but around them was also a group of children. Campbell told his men to hold their fire. The visit sent the PDF fleeing out the back of the station into the dense tropical forest. Campbell's men tried to follow them but they disappeared. They seized a few guns and grenades from the PDF station and returned to Madden Dam.

Campbell and his soldiers saw no more action that day. He could not foresee that by the time he and his company left Madden Dam, they would feel utterly besieged.

14

The Ceding of Colon

The battle was nearly over, but the men of B Battery, 7th Battalion, 15th Field Artillery, had yet to fire a shot. They got their chance Friday, 22 December, when Stiner gave the go-ahead for an assault force massed just outside Colon to move in and take control.

Soldiers continued to take fire at the bottleneck. Snipers already had claimed the lives of three soldiers on D-day, one from 4th Battalion, 17th Infantry, and two from Task Force 160 when their AH-6 was hit. The command wanted the gunfire silenced, but not at the expense of more lives.

The potential for mass destruction in the city was considerable. Colonel Kellogg and his war planners expected hard-core resistance inside the city, both in numbers and in weapons. The PDF's top guns in Colon had surrendered, but even before D-day, the city was a seedy, unwelcoming place. Although traces of grandeur endure in Colon, with its broad verandas and pillared homes, the city has become a warren of crowded homes and dark alleys. Not only could this impoverished city explode in violence, but a tracer bullet could start a blaze that would engulf Colon.

The assault phase of Just Cause was about to end, and a new phase begin that would prove far less familiar to U.S. troops and in some ways more taxing. Noriega had fled the invaders and was running out of options. The PDF was collapsing, and with it law and order. The U.S. military was charged with laying the groundwork across Panama, from the crowded inner-city neighborhoods to the isolated rain forests, for a new government built on democratic principles.

By the time the last assault in Just Cause began, Sgt. Antonio Ramos and his fellow soldiers in B Battery could recite their mission backwards. Twice they had been briefed—to fire their 105mm howitzers at the Cristobal police station in Colon—only to learn that the assault was postponed.

The police station, run by the hated DENI, was believed to be a bastion of hard-core PDF troops. It was too far away from the bottleneck—about 750 meters—to observe or fire at, but Kellogg and his subordinate commanders suspected that forces in the DENI station had a hand in the continuous sniping at U.S. soldiers.

Poised to enter Colon through the bottleneck, the battery waited two days for their cue. Across Manzanillo Bay in Coco Solo, the men of A Company, 4th Battalion, 17th Infantry also were anxious to complete the taking of Colon. They had received orders at 2:30 P.M on D-day to launch an amphibious assault on the city, but other events intervened to delay the mission twice.

In the two days since the invasion began, Colon had become a looters' free-for-all. Thugs and thieves broke into every store and house they could penetrate, starting with the supermarkets. But the delays were also a measure of success: negotiations were under way for key PDF units to surrender with their weapons.

The commander of operations in and around Colon would have liked to seize the city immediately. "We wanted to go in the night of D-day, because we'd finally powered up enough forces by securing all the objectives. I could reorganize and move in there," says Kellogg. But the danger was too great, said General Cisneros. About 5:00 A.M. on D-day, he received a report that the roadblocks were in place in Colon and Task Force Atlantic was preparing to storm the PDF garrison inside the city.

"I called them up and told them to put a hold on that until I got there," Cisneros says. "Colon is a ghetto area and we were going to have a lot of burning." Sobered by the death of three soldiers at the bottleneck and the persistence of the sniper fire, Cisneros opted to try to talk the resistance down, rather than incur more casualties by storming the city. A Panamanian woman and child had died on D-day in a high-rise apartment building in Colon. A Cobra helicopter gunship, hit by what was thought to be 7.62-mm sniper fire from the high-rise, fired back, blowing a large hole in the side of the building.

Cisneros went to Fort Davis, where Task Force Atlantic had set up a holding facility for prisoners of war, segregated those prisoners who had been jailed for participating in the 3 October coup attempt and identified the most senior of the prisoners: Jimenez, the former commander of naval infantry forces at Coco Solo. Jimenez agreed to help Cisneros talk the regional commanders of the PDF into surrendering, including Lt. Col. Anibal Maylin, commander of Military Zone 2 headquarters in Colon. Cisneros ordered Kellogg to wait (see figure 14–1).

So B Battery waited, at once fearful and eager. "We got the word it was postponed," Ramos says, and the artillerymen groaned. 2d Lt. Robert C. Kleinhample, the battery executive officer, could feel the frustration grow each time the mission was scrubbed. "They're in a war, you know, and these guys are highly motivated. They wanted to crank some Joes down range," Kleinhample says. "They really wanted to fire some rounds." While the artillerymen waited, all they could do was to check and recheck their perimeter security at the bottleneck.

B Company of the 4th Battalion, dispatched at H-hour to seal off Colon at the bottleneck, reported widespread shooting downtown. The company itself was still receiving sporadic but persistent sniper fire. Navy SEALs were firing back from atop the Panama Canal Commission's pollution control building.

The city was in a state of panic, made worse by the release of shiny yellow tear gas, possibly taken from the PDF's Military Zone 2 headquarters in Colon when the complex was ransacked. B Company's men urged residents through loudspeakers to stay in their homes, but an estimated two hundred civilians fled Colon, a city of sixty thousand.

The business district of southwest Colon was being stripped of everything from radios to running shoes by enterprising thieves who stole forklifts from the shipping yards at Cristobal, the port district of Colon, and used them to break into stores. The iron screens supposedly protecting many stores were no match for the forklifts. The container yard at Cristobal was pillaged. Using light antitank weapons taken from the ransacked PDF military headquarters in Colon, looters blew open shipping containers and stole crates of Jim Beam whiskey, Nike athletic shoes, and whatever else looked promising.

On a peninsula southwest of France Field in Coco Solo, the warehouses stocked with goods for Colon's duty-free shopping district

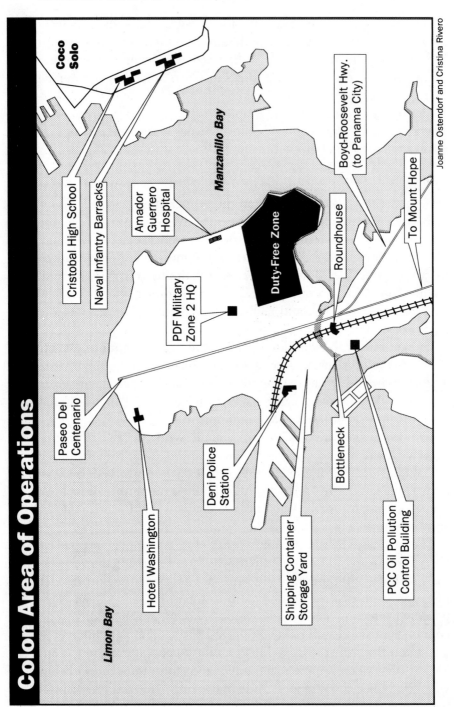

Joanne Ostendorf and Cristina Rivero

FIGURE 14–1
Colon Area of Operations

also were open to looters from all sides. MPs and infantrymen assigned to block the airfield spent much of D-day chasing away looters from one point, only to find that the looters created another "Ho Chi Minh trail" into the storage area. At least one Panamanian sniper in the warehouse area was killed.

Two days into the invasion, the rules of engagement in Colon still allowed soldiers to shoot anyone armed. "The guidance was simple," says Maj. Tom Ryan, the operations officer for the 4th Battalion. "It was, 'If you see anybody with a weapon, they are dead.'" In fact, many soldiers were reluctant to shoot unless they felt they were in danger. They had been briefed on the need to keep destruction to a minimum.

On the concrete outside Cristobal High School at Coco Solo, Ryan, battalion commander Lt. Col. Johnny Brooks and battalion Command Sergeant Major Larry Dunlap hammered out the plan for the final assault on Colon.

The battalion's A and C Companies would conduct the amphibious assault in LCM-8 landing craft with fire support from a Navy patrol boat and AC-130. Navy SEALs would swim from the boats to the beachhead and mark it with infrared chemical lights. The assault force then would raid the PDF's Military Zone 2 headquarters in Colon, striking hard and then withdrawing. At the same time, B Company of the infantry battalion, and the 82d Airborne's B Company would attack the DENI police station at Cristobal. B Battery, 7th Battalion, 15th Field Artillery would blast the building with 105mm howitzer fire. The operation was to go off at 3:00 A.M. on 21 December, giving U.S. troops the cover of darkness.

For the moment, however, B Company of the 4th Battalion was in a state of siege itself. The first prisoners of war and countless frightened civilians were leaving Colon. Every person and every vehicle coming through the bottleneck had to be searched for drugs, weapons, and contraband. Long lines of cars formed, some waiting five or six hours to leave the city. "It was pretty hectic," recalls Pfc. Anthony Threadgill of B Company's 2d Platoon. "You had to search everybody, and a lot of us could not speak Spanish."

Capt. Doug Thorp, the company commander, listened to the continuing sniper fire and wondered if this was the right time for an assault on Colon. Even with 154 combat soldiers at his disposal, "I didn't know if I had the manpower to go another six to eight blocks under heavy fire," Thorp says.

At 6:00 P.M. on D-day, Brooks called a meeting at Cristobal High School in Coco Solo to issue orders for the two-pronged attack on Colon. Three hours later, A Company of the infantry battalion, guarded by a platoon from a home unit, arrived at Coco Solo to prepare for the amphibious assault. B Company, of the airborne battalion, had moved that morning from Cerro Tigre back to Fort Sherman to prepare for the raid on Military Zone 2 headquarters.

At 9:30 P.M., the operation was called off. No time was set for its execution. Brooks learned at 3:30 P.M. the next day that Cisneros and Jimenez had personally called the headquarters to encourage a surrender and arrange for the PDF's orderly exit from Colon. Another sought-after PDF officer was Military Zone 2 commander Maj. Mario del Cid, the virtual emperor of Colon with command of all the PDF within the city, where the PDF wielded considerable power.

Throughout that evening and the next day, a steady stream of Red Cross vans, loaded with dozens of PDF personnel and weapons, flowed through U.S. lines at the bottleneck. Just to the north, the airborne troops, were waiting at the Panama Canal Commission pollution control building for the assault on the Cristobal DENI station.

With the core of the resistance leaving Colon, the mission changed from a raid to an all-out assault, after which U.S. troops would remain in Colon to restore law and order. C Company of 2d Battalion, 27th Infantry Regiment, a 7th Division unit, was added to the assault roster, making it the eighth maneuver element under the command of the 4th battalion. At 6:30 P.M., the company started arriving at Coco Solo for the amphibious assault, which was to take place at 3:00 A.M. the next morning.

But the surrenders were still in progress. For the second time, the mission was scrubbed. As 21 December drew to a close, 127 PDF had given themselves up at the entrance to Colon, with another 100 to follow. The six five-ton trucks that delivered soldiers in B Company, 4th Battalion, to trap the PDF in Colon now carried Panamanian troops out of the city.

The surrenders lasted into the morning of Friday, 22 December.

Finally, as MPs and infantrymen continued to chase looters at France Field, U.S. soldiers accepted the surrenders of Maylin and del Cid, dressed in civilian clothes. Also surrendering were two bus-loads of PDF, many of whom initially had abandoned their posts, shed their uniforms, and taken refuge in the civilian community. Maylin was out of the picture now. So was del Cid. The PDF had abandoned the city.

Thorp's company relaxed slightly. "Believe me, it was a good feel-ing when I saw all those people come out with their hands up," says Sgt. Henry Howard of 1st Platoon, B Company, 4th Battalion. It remained to subdue the Colon police and looters, and the looters were heading for the Free Zone, the city's economic heart and soul.

A shopper's paradise, the heavily guarded Free Zone is ninety-four acres of duty-free warehouse outlets, selling everything from gold to golf clubs. Faced with the prospect of economic ruin in Co-lon, Kellogg decided to scuttle the original plan for a two-pronged night assault and launch the amphibious assault immediately, de-spite the added risk of a daytime mission. The Free Zone's chief of security had called the 3d Brigade tactical operations center at Fort Sherman to ask for help in fending off looters.

After waiting for two days to move on Colon, the soldiers got about a half-hour's notice that the mission was on. Ryan had to rush to photocopy the final assault plan, using the copying machine in the Cristobal High School principal's office, while the infantry soldiers assembled on the docks to cross Manzanillo Bay.

Maj. Greg Gardner, 3d Brigade operations officer, arranged for A Company to meet a civilian security guard at the Free Zone, at the southern shore of Colon. C Company of the 4th Battalion and C Company, 2/27th Infantry, would follow in landing craft to the eastern side of the city. C Company of the 27th Infantry had arrived in Coco Solo the previous evening for the amphibious assault.

The word from the command was that Colon was awash in weapons. "We thought it was going to be some kind of D-day or something," says Sgt. William Smith of A Company's 1st Platoon. Escorted by a Navy patrol boat, A Company stopped just off the shoreline—"kind of a garbage pile," one officer calls it—to wait for the chief security guard, who was to wave a white flag. He never arrived. The company moved on shore, maneuvering two blocks through a weird symphony of chanting—"USA, USA"—and sniper fire from a rooftop. "Everyone got down and popped smoke," says company commander Capt. Mike Beech. No one was injured.

After the somber warning about what to expect in Colon, the soldiers were stunned by the welcome they received.

"It surprised us," says Smith. "As soon as we moved in, there's all these people on rooftoops cheering. Then there was people firing at us." Smith's platoon was the first to enter the Free Zone. Seeing a large number of armed men inside the main gate of the Free Zone, the soldiers yelled for everyone to hit the ground.

"I probably saw a hundred guys, stomachs on the ground, hands out. They had weapons in front of them," says company executive officer 1st Lt. Dan Evans, who followed 1st Platoon into the Free Zone. As it turned out, "they were shopkeepers and security guards," Evans says. Many of them had taken weapons from the Military Zone 2 headquarters.

At 1:15 P.M. Beech's company had a foothold in the Free Zone. Ryan located the security chief and arranged with him to arm the Free Zone security force against looters. Kellogg was wary of the idea, but the security guards received assault rifles and six-shot Colt pistols to defend the Free Zone. By 3:00 P.M., the Free Zone was under control.

The rest of Colon was another matter. The infantry and paratroop companies at the bottleneck maintained control there, but soldiers were badly needed to calm the city. As scheduled, the two companies of infantrymen made the amphibious assault from Coco Solo to 11th Street in eastern Colon to seize Military Zone 2 headquarters, by then believed to be totally evacuated.

The troops, packed shoulder-to-shoulder like matchsticks in the wells of the two landing craft, were apprehensive about moving across the water in broad daylight. It was midafternoon when they landed on the beach. But the buzz of friendly attack helicopters over Colon reassured them. "We had all kinds of support: Navy SEAL snipers looking out from LCMs with .50 caliber machine guns off the sides. We could also see white flags in the windows [along the shoreline]," says Sgt. Joseph Legaspi of C Company, 4th Battalion, 17th Infantry.

Indeed, after the nerve-wracking assault at Coco Solo, Legaspi couldn't believe his eyes. The soldiers had no plan for a guide to lead them into Colon. But there, at the beachhead, stood a Panamanian in tidy civilian clothes, wearing a white armband and white headband, with a megaphone in his hand. He introduced himself as Renato and offered to help the Americans secure the city.

"I'm here to help you. We don't want anyone killed," he told Brooks, who had crossed the bay in the lead LCM. The battalion commander sized up Renato as a man of means who sincerely wanted to stop the destruction of his city. "He met us with a bullhorn, so I put him ahead of our troops, telling everyone to get inside and throw out their weapons," Brooks says. As Renato led the line of soldiers down 11th Street, residents showed their approval of the troops by flying white flags and cheering. Many laid weapons down in the street.

The troops, ready for another battle in their face paint and ragtop helmets, didn't know how to react to this unimaginable welcome. "We were getting applause. It was incredible," Legaspi says. "What do you do? You don't want to smile."

Reaching the military headquarters at 4:30 P.M., C Company of the 2/27 Infantry started systematically clearing the complex. The headquarters was a cluster of several buildings covering a square block. Surrounding it was a forbidding masonry wall topped with spikes. A PDF holdout was shot and killed in the armory as he attempted to fire at a clearing team. Otherwise, the complex was there for the taking.

Then a frantic call came over the brigade net: the headquarters was wired to explode by remote detonator, according to a tip called into the 3d Brigade operations center by civilians in Colon. Kellogg, who had met the landing party at the PDF headquarters, and the assault troops raced from the complex, and an explosives team moved in to inspect the area. No explosives were found. Brooks learned later that Maylin, the headquarters commander, had driven a pickup truck full of explosives to the front gate of the complex the day before and left the truck there with a time fuze wired to it. But citizens in Colon had driven it away.

With the military headquarters vacated and under U.S. guard and the Free Zone cleared of looters, all that remained of any organized opposition was the DENI station in Cristobal, about 750 meters from the bottleneck and a few blocks from the canal. By 4:00 P.M., the surrender operation at the bottleneck had ceased, although the two infantry companies there were still receiving sporadic fire from the Cristobal area.

Maj. Jim Coggin, executive officer of the 4/17 Infantry, did not expect a warm welcome in Colon. Intelligence reports warned of a threat from armed civilians along the route into the city. But the assault on the DENI station could not wait any longer. Finally, the long-awaited attack was on.

Starting just before sunset, a platoon from B Company, 4/17, moved into the city to cut a path through fences into the Cristobal container yard and reconnoiter the area so the paratroopers could follow and take up assault positions around the DENI station. B Company would provide flank security for the mission, blocking the route against the threat of armed civilians. B Company, 3/504, crossed through the wire at the bottleneck at 6:30 P.M. and crept through the container shipping area.

By now feeling secure again in their own city, residents of Colon came out to watch the advance. The onlookers' attention was drawn, for the most part, to B Company, 4/17, to the east of the paratroopers. "It was like one humongous party," says company commander Capt. Doug Thorp. "You'd see hundreds of American flags." White flags also flew from apartment windows.

While the gathering raised fears of possible civilian casualties if firing broke out, it had an unexpected advantage. "The 504th got in basically undetected, and the howitzers, too," Thorp says. When the artillery forces followed the infantry into Colon at 7:30 P.M., most of the civilian onlookers had gathered around Thorp's company, two blocks away from the DENI station and out of the line of fire.

But the artillery battery did not entirely escape attention. "Going into Colon, there were maybe 100 or 150 civilians, cheering as we was going in," says S.Sgt. Edward Kreeger of B Battery, 7th Battalion, 15th Field Artillery, who did not know what to make of the crowd.

It made battery commander Capt. Dwight Watkins nervous. "The frightening part is not knowing who can actually pull a piece out and fire it," Watkins says. "So you really had to be cautious. There could be some twelve-year-old kid out there, clapping his hands and cheering and stuff, and all of a sudden another twelve-year-old kid pops some rounds."

B Battery established a position to the east of the white cement DENI station. Capt. Bryan Dyer, commander of B Company, 3/504 Infantry, sent his fire support platoon to the southern end of the building, where intelligence reports said PDF forces were preparing defensive positions. Once the platoon was in place, the other two platoons maneuvered to the west for the assault. Lastly, Dyer called for two artillery tubes. When they were in position, he moved to the east side of the building to the fire-support position. Then he gave the signal to start firing.

The howitzers were a mere twenty to thirty feet away from the building, by Dyer's estimate.

No sooner had Watkins's battery set up the howitzer than the men got the order to fire. The holdouts in the DENI station had had long enough to surrender; Kellogg was prepared to crush them. "I said, 'We're not going to take any fire from these guys.' I told them to use direct-fire artillery on the building. I just didn't want to have any more collateral damage."

Watkins gave the signal, and Specialist Ed Holman pulled the first lanyard on the howitzer. When firing began, most of the curious civilians scurried away.

Boom. The first time Holman had executed direct fire in combat. "It was loud," he says. In training, he was used to firing over a distance one hundred times what he encountered at the PDF police station. The boom of the howitzers was followed by the incessant staccato of M16, machine-gun, and squad automatic weapons fire.

Kreeger didn't even look at the building after the first round. "After we started firing, about the second or third round, then the infantry, they started firing theirs. So you had gunfire going off all over the place," he says. The sound of gunfire was so powerful that Cpl. Kenneth Thruman, a gunner in B Company, 4/17 Infantry, at first thought the squad was being fired upon. For twenty minutes, the battery fired, expending a total of eighteen rounds while infantrymen from the 3/504 riddled the DENI station with machine-gun fire.

There were no casualties on either side, but the barrage of fire burned the roof off and speckled the walls on the southern end of the building. The northern end, housing the Panama Canal Commission's Atlantic headquarters, was virtually unscathed, its smooth white facade left intact.

"It didn't take very long, but you could feel the vibration. You could see the lights flashing all over the place," says Howard of B Company, 4/17 Infantry, a squad leader assigned to block access from two blocks away. But again, the show of force worked. "When the fires started with the howitzers, the white flag went up," Kellogg says. Panamanians could be seen fleeing out the back door of the DENI station. One of the three PDF soldiers B Company, 3/504, captured inside the DENI station confirmed that the howitzer had convinced his compatriots to flee. "He said they left right after the booms," Dyer said later in an after-action briefing. "All he could say was BOOM."

Dyer's fire-support moved in on the DENI station, laying a blanket of fire on the southern corner of the building. Once the bullets had blown out the windows, the company closed in and cleared the building. The PDF put up minimal resistance, but uncontrolled fire from U.S. forces was a major problem, according to Dyer. "We had a significant problem with the MP platoon" attached to B Company, 3/504, Dyer said. "We're lucky no one was injured."

The task given to the MP platoon, part of the 549th MP Company, was to escort B Battery into position. "That was their only mission," Dyer said. But the MP platoon joined in the assault. Despite numerous briefings on the mission, the MPs started firing after the howitzer fire had ceased and the paratroopers began to close in for their assault. The MP fire cut off one of Dyer's squads, forcing it to move into the assault teams' line of fire. "Luckily they were bad shots," Dyer said. Major Coggin, executive officer of 4/17, managed to enforce a cease-fire on the MPs.

The artillery battery didn't stick around to watch their job completed. They were withdrawn to Fort Davis after firing the howitzers, never to see what they had accomplished in the battle. But they heard nothing but hurrahs as they rode out of Colon. The crowd of cheering Panamanians had swelled to five hundred or more. It was a good omen.

But it was not the end of the fight for Colon, despite Thurman's rosy remarks to Ted Koppel that night. Colonel Kellogg stopped by his operations center at Fort Sherman about 11:00 P.M. to make sure all operations were on schedule in Task Force Atlantic. He decided to take a break and catch the latest television news. Ted Koppel was just about to begin the evening's *Nightline* show. Thurman was on live. "He said, 'Well, I've got some good news to report. We now control the city of Colon.'"

Kellogg winced, feeling the eyes of the world upon him. In fact, his soldiers had yet to clear major portions of Colon. "I picked up the radio, and I called Johnny Brooks," Kellogg says gamely. "I said, 'Johnny, whatever you do, get me Colon by six in the morning and for God's sake, don't get in a firefight as you do it, because General Thurman just told the entire world we own the city of Colon.'"

One more contingency would delay the establishment of peace in Colon. At about 2:00 A.M. the next morning, a SEAL team, assisted by infantrymen from A Company, 4/17, assaulted the Washington Hotel in pursuit of Noriega and a report of American hostages. He wasn't there. Nor did the SEAL team find hostages.

Kellogg's forces resumed the task of methodically securing Colon. When dawn broke on Saturday, 23 December, the weary city was poised to pick up the pieces under the leadership of the U.S. military.

"When we initially went in, basically the whole city was armed," says Captain Beech, commander of A Company, 4/17. "It was quite obvious they weren't hostile. Because if they were hostile, they could have engaged us with a lot more firepower than we had." Most people, he says, put their weapons down and their hands up.

Five rifle companies fanned out to patrol the streets. Soldiers gathered weapons and rounded up criminals, DigBats, and simple thugs. Brooks established a command post in the fire station next to Military Zone 2 headquarters. The fire station became the city's ad hoc administrative center until a new city and provincial government could be installed.

For the soldiers of the 4/17 Infantry, at least, the war appeared to be over. The battalion staff began to contemplate how much bloodier the battle could have been. Ryan wondered why, for example, the PDF hadn't seized the Panama Canal Commission headquarters and taken hostages. "It was a relief when we went into Colon, because that was the major obstacle in our way," says Brooks. "I wasn't sure we were going to go into Colon."

Even more relieved was the business community of Colon, many of whose members had despaired that the United States would step in to protect their livelihood from complete destruction. Eduardo Cattan, manager of a fabric store chain called Textilindo, had to wait three days after the invasion to travel from his home in Panama City to Colon. The two-lane road connecting the two largest cities in Panama was closed. He arrived at his store that Saturday to find his livelihood a shambles. Fluorescent lights had been ripped from the ceiling, mirrors shattered, and the display floor left bare. Even the rug had been stolen. All told, looters· robbed him of some $200,000 worth of property.

Hundreds of merchants had similar stories, and worse. The troops could see there was much to be done to get Colon—the city and the province—back on their feet. Looters continued to run through the streets with weapons, undeterred by the arrival of U.S. forces. Panama City was in similar shape. But as far as the soldiers in Colon were concerned, Panama City didn't exist. There was no phone communication between the cities.

With the consent of Leopoldo Benedetti, who at Cisneros's request temporarily assumed the post of Colon's provincial governor, a curfew was established from 6:30 P.M. to 6:30 A.M. Despite the warm welcome its residents extended to the Americans, Colon still was not considered safe at night, although Panama City maintained a more liberal curfew of 11:00 P.M. to 5:00 A.M. U.S. forces, in consultation with Benedetti, used three Colon radio stations to broadcast appeals for order and discipline. "Basically we used them for psychological operations," Brooks says.

In their patrols, the soldiers were awed by the poverty and squalor of Colon. No sooner had the city's residents gotten used to the presence of U.S. forces than they started to approach the soldiers for help in solving myriad problems, from abusive husbands to busted pipes. "Every little thing that went wrong, they was continuously grabbing us," says Sergeant Henry Howard of B Company, 4/17. "For me it was a very hard switch, because we train every day for certain actions, and being a policeman is not one of them."

On the positive side, the soldiers could feel a sense of control creeping back into Colon. "You could feel it inside the city," Howard says. "Most of the people who were PDF or had weapons, people would tell us who they were."

Security duty was no less a strain than patrolling the city's streets. Soldiers would get tired of defending one site, so they would ask to be assigned to patrols. But that, too, was not their line of work.

"Constantly patrolling: it was the same thing every day, every night," says Cpl. Larry Franks of A Company, 4/17.

South of Colon, A and B Companies of the 3/504 had completed their combat missions and were reassigned to secure the areas of Sabanita, Cativa, and Buena Vista. The battalion's complement of eight hundred was scattered even farther than they had been at H-hour. D Company of the 3/504 remained at Madden Dam operating checkpoints on the highway between Panama City and Colon. The battalion's other three objectives presented little resistance. C Company, which had freed the prisoners at Renacer, defended Gamboa and Cerro Tigre.

Perhaps the hardest part of the security mission was not knowing how long it would last. After ten days of what commanders in Washington euphemistically called mop-up operations, the soldiers couldn't wait to leave Colon. Colonel Kellogg insisted the soldiers in Task Force Atlantic remain in full battle dress—camouflage, ragtop helmets, flak vests, the works—whenever they were in contact with Panamanians, even if they were just passing through. "It was real hot," Franks says.

Even the heartwarming gratitude the Panamanians lavished on their liberators could not erase the physical and mental discomfort that the infantrymen felt. "It got old after a while," Franks says. Weary of chasing after potshots, searching cars, collecting weapons, and picking up trash, they longed for the familiar, well-defined tasks of combat. And the Army as a whole came to realize the tremendous scope of its post-invasion responsibilities.

"We stayed there two weeks in the civil-military mode, which was kind of long," Lieutenant Colonel Brooks says. "I couldn't wait to get off the streets of Colon. I knew it was very dangerous for the soldiers. I was always waiting for a guy to drive down a road and throw a hand grenade into four or five of my kids. That's probably the most amazing thing about the whole operation, that we went into Colon and didn't shoot anybody. The kids were really disciplined."

In Panama City, the paratroopers of 1st Brigade, 82d Airborne also were learning a new mission: peacekeeping operations. That meant securing the water processing plants, electricity, radio stations, and food stores, and maintaining control through twenty-four-hour street patrols.

The paratroopers, assigned to restore public order in a ten-square-miles section of Panama City, had a seemingly endless checklist of sites to secure: supermarkets, warehouses, utilities, radio and television stations and embassies providing shelter to Noriega and his cronies. Prisoners had to be searched and refugees settled. Soldiers also received orders to secure key facilities that were critical either to the new government of Guillermo Endara or enemy forces who might be looking for refuge. "At one point we had seventy-four sites we had to secure," says Major General James Johnson, 82d Airborne commander.

Defending the PDF targets they had seized was the least of the soldiers' worries, as the PDF's armed resistance had all but evaporated by the end of Thursday, 21 December. Some of the soldiers who assaulted the targets remained there to ship off captured enemy weapons and equipment, while others were reassigned to patrol the streets of Panama City. Elements of the 2/504 Parachute Infantry, for example, became more useful as peacekeepers in Panama City than they were as guards of captured enemy weapons at Panama Viejo, where they had seized a PDF garrison.

Even at Tinajitas, the most difficult of the air-assault targets seized the previous day, the PDF installation was securely in American hands. The adjacent community of San Miguelito was anything but secure, however. While the PDF had given up its opposition, Dignity Battalions terrorized the area, firing at will.[2] Vandals and looters joined in the melee, setting fire to a supermarket warehouse and overturning cars.

Civil affairs personnel from Ft. Bragg started arriving late that day to help the infantrymen restore basic services.

"This we had not exactly trained for," says Johnson. He had not expected his troops to be so deeply involved in the peacekeeping mission, but there was much ground to cover and not enough civil-affairs personnel or military police. Most of the military's civil-affairs capability was in the reserves, and the call-up was just beginning. "There had been a lot of looting, and we wanted to restore confidence in the people that the new government was in charge," Johnson says.

The general took most of the 4/325 Parachute Infantry out of Cimarron, where they had squashed the remnants of Noriega's elite Battalion 2000, and put them at Paitilla to relieve the Rangers there. Johnson left only a platoon of B Company at Fort Cimarron.

Most of the soldiers who would lose their lives in the invasion had died in the first day of the invasion, but the danger was still considerable. Pvt. James Allen Tabor, Jr., eighteen, of Headquarters Company, 4/325, died as his unit moved toward Panama City to patrol.[3]

Johnson left a Ranger battalion at Tocumen to deny enemy forces entry and exit. Also at the airport, held in reserve, was Company A of the 3d Battalion, 505th Parachute Infantry Regiment. The 193d Infantry Brigade and the 82d's 1st Brigade divided Panama City into sectors, freeing the Rangers to control Tocumen and branch out into more remote Panamanian cities where the joint task force feared PDF forces loyal to Noriega were digging in for a war.

The mission of sweeping the remaining enemy from Panama gradually sucked in more and more U.S. forces. Reinforcements arrived 22 December: the 9th Infantry Regiment, or Manchu Brigade, of the 7th Infantry Division from Fort Ord, California. The brigade, consisting of three battalions, came under the 82d Airborne's command. The new arrivals spread out into Panama City systematically, to secure sectors arranged like squares on a checkerboard.

Groups of fifteen soldiers—such as a squad and fire team—were posted at the ministries of the new government, the ministers' homes, the Cuban embassy, and the residence of the Cuban ambassador, to name a few.

The residence of the Nicaraguan ambassador to Panama, Antenor Ferrey, was one of the targets on the list. Acting on a tip about weapons supplies to the PDF and Dignity Battalions, the U.S. soldiers assigned to search it apparently were unaware of who lived there, and proceeded to violate the ambassador's diplomatic immunity by insisting on entering and searching the house. In the furor that followed, wildly conflicting stories emerged as to what they found.[1] While Nicaraguan diplomats said the soldiers ransacked the house and reporters who went in afterward saw clothes and belongings tossed on the floor, the soldiers who conducted the search said the tip appeared to be genuine. Sgt. Ronald Blenker of the 7th Division's A Company, 2d Battalion, 9th Infantry, saw weapons throughout the house: in upstairs closets, under beds, on counters, in the kitchen.

"We found a house full of weapons before we got the order that we weren't supposed to be in there," Blenker says. "We found an arsenal." This arsenal included fifteen to twenty AK-47s, rocket-propelled grenades and launchers, two pistols, automatic weapons, ten Uzis, a couple of grenades, and various kinds of ammunition. The soldiers had loaded them on a truck when they got the order to put the weapons back. Before they left, they made a point of straightening up the rooms they had searched, Blenker says. What he saw on the television news that night was a totally different scene. Only two pistols were shown. In addition, the ambassador said five rifles had been confiscated but returned. "I guess they hid the weapons before the news media came—they put them back upstairs," Blenker says. And the house was a shambles, with tables and chairs overturned and suitcases tossed around.

Once the paratroopers had established calm in the streets, they would pass off the task to military police working in conjunction with the new Panamanian police force assembled by the Endara government. Eventually U.S. forces divided the city into precincts, establishing an MP company in each with a magistrate in charge. The MPs started joint peacekeeping operations with former PDF troops who had been cleared to join the new Panamanian police force.

The country was in the hands of junior NCOs, who conducted house-to-house searches asking if the enemy had been there and if anyone was harassing the residents. The approach, Johnson says, was "Just want to let you know we're in the neighborhood." Roadblocks were set up to stop and search cars.

The atmosphere on military posts was one of intense relief, coupled with pride and a community spirit revived after a months-long depression. Service members' families emerged from their hiding places inside locked homes to show troops their gratitude. Messages painted on bedsheets proclaimed a "job well done" to troops passing by. The anger some felt at not having been evacuated before the invasion began to dissipate.

"If the results had been anything but what they were, I, too, might feel angered," said Janet Thompson, wife of Gorgas Army Hospital's pharmacy chief, several months later.[4] Thompson spent the night of the invasion with her six-year-old daughter, Katie, wrapped in blankets inside a storage closet. "Yet the fact remains that we were protected by our forces and we were safe."

On-post stores remained closed for the first two or three days after the invasion, until U.S. forces had suppressed enemy snipers and silenced mortar positions to secure the installations. Fort Clayton, for example, was shelled intermittently for several hours before dawn on 20 December, with no casualties. The nearby community of Los Rios took three mortar hits that night, while small-arms fire erupted briefly at Albrook Air Station.[5] By and large, the fire was ineffectual, but it sharply curtailed normal routines. Families that ran out of food borrowed from others who had, by luck or forethought, stocked up before the fighting began.

When the shoppettes reopened, family members mobilized to run the cash registers. Lines formed by eight in the morning to get into the stores. An informal rationing system took shape, in which no single purchaser was permitted to buy too much of any one item. Family members also took over the running of post exchanges, commissaries, post offices, gas stations, and dining halls until the Panamanians who formed a large part of the workforce could return to their jobs safely. Spouses and children administered first aid to injured soldiers, washed their clothes, cooked them hot meals, and cared for refugees.

"They're pretty much unsung heroes in this whole operation," says Air Force Col. Edward L. La Fountaine, Howard Air Force Base deputy commander for operations during Just Cause.

Most of the really hard-core criminals had fled the city, if not the country, or taken refuge in one of the embassies friendly to Noriega. The Dignity Battalions, however, remained a threat. Working in groups of a dozen or fewer, they kept fighting weeks after the PDF had given up. Their tactics bordered on the suicidal, and in fact cost them their lives in many cases. They would pile into a car, sometimes a half-dozen packed into a Volkswagen, all of them carrying AK-47s, according to Major General Johnson. Sometimes they would charge a roadblock, as they did at least once at the Pacora

River Bridge and innumerable times in Panama City. All wore civilian clothes, so it was impossible to tell if any were PDF.

The fierceness of the Dignity Battalions surprised the U.S. military command. "We didn't expect that," Johnson says. Although their military training obviously wasn't sophisticated, "They gave us a real hard time."

The mission of securing the area between Colon and Panama City went smoothly, with one notable exception that would cast a shadow on the invasion for months to come.

The sixty-man complement of D Company, 3/504 Parachute Infantry, in charge of maintaining security at the strategically vital Madden Dam was stretched to the breaking point. The company's position attracted Panamanians' attention like a magnet, says company commander Capt. John Campbell. Not only did Panamanians bring in endless reports of enemy activity, many of which proved to be exaggerated or untrue, but the roadblocks that the paratroopers set up to search passing cars were a target for hostile Panamanians, who tried to run them.

"Delta Company at Madden Dam was the most isolated force, in my mind, in the entire canal," says battalion commander Lt. Col. Lynn Moore. "Everybody would come to me and say, 'Hey, I got this, or I got that,'" Campbell says. The company sorted through the reports of weapons and Dignity Battalions, sending out soldiers to investigate the more credible leads.

On Saturday, 23 December, Campbell and his first sergeant, M. Sgt. Roberto Bryan, were waiting for some prisoners to arrive at the dam. A local civic leader had arranged the surrender of about thirty prisoners, Campbell says. At about 1:00 P.M. a car drove up to a roadblock near the dam.

Soldiers got the five occupants out of the car and began a systematic search. As they were searching the car, Campbell says, they found tear gas grenades and AK-47 rifle magazines and made the Panamanians lie on the ground. "As one guy was getting down, he was kind of a pain in the ass about it. He threw a grenade," Campbell says. The grenade exploded at a soldier's feet, tossing him into the air. At least ten soldiers were injured in the blast, according to later accounts. After the explosion, the soldiers opened fire on the

Panamanians for about one minute. Four of the five Panamanians were dead.

"They were pretty much waxed," Campbell says.

Bryan later told the Associated Press he heard the grenade explode, came running and ordered his men to cease firing.[6] "It was chaos," he said. The soldiers thought the dam was about to be attacked. "There were thirty to thirty-five Panamanians 150 meters away. We didn't know if they were a Dignity Battalion or not."

Bryan learned that one of the Panamanians was still alive. Turning toward him, "I saw the man make an arm movement, like he was reaching for something," Bryan told AP. "It was a possibility this guy was going for a grenade. I fired six to eight rounds. When I opened up, everybody else opened fire in that direction again."

In April, Bryan was charged with unpremeditated murder, which caused considerable dissension within the 82d Airborne Division.[7] Col. Jack Nix, commander of 1st Brigade, protested through internal channels that the case against Bryan was incomplete, lacking physical evidence that bullets from Bryan's gun killed the Panamanian. The charges nonetheless were referred for trial.

After two days of deliberation, a court-martial acquitted Bryan on 31 August 1990.[8]

With the approach of Christmas all but forgotten, Christmas Eve brought U.S. soldiers some early gifts.

Private First Class Threadgill and his buddies in B Company, 4/17 Infantry, got their first shower and shave—"much, much overdue," Threadgill says—at a pumping station near the Colon bottleneck. Soldiers found showers where they could: in a Colon high school, a gas station, the Panama Canal Commission pollution control building. Panamanian citizens opened their homes and businesses to soldiers throughout the country, feeding them, washing their clothes, and bringing them hot coffee every morning.

Fifty miles away in Panama City, having concluded that his chance of regaining power was nil, Noriega arrived unnoticed at the Vatican's embassy to Panama and asked for political asylum. When his private car drove up around 3:30 P.M., the battle changed direction for the United States.

Soldiers of the 7th Division's 9th Regiment, on their second day in Panama, were on a mission to patrol Panama City streets and search door-to-door for enemy holdouts and weapons when the city erupted in jubilation at the news Noriega had given up the fight. It was about 11:00 P.M., time for all cooperative Panamanians to get off the streets. S.Sgt. Ronald Blenker of the regiment's A Company, 2d Battalion, had no idea what was happening as he patrolled the well-to-do San Francisco district, but the commotion had all the earmarks of Mardi Gras.

In the pitch-black dark, "I heard firecrackers going off, pots and pans banging," he says. Caravans of cars streamed through the streets, honking their horns and flying Panamanian and U.S. flags. A Panamanian woman ran up and hugged Blenker, her excitement spilling over in a torrent of Spanish, which Blenker could not understand. It was obvious to another Panamanian woman, who spoke English, that the soldiers were ignorant of Noriega's fate. She broke the news about his surrender.

Blenker called back to his platoon leader, who called off the patrol. Revelry ruled the streets of Panama. The jubilation was beyond the power, or desire, of U.S. forces to control. Not permitted to join the celebration, the sergeant instead pulled guard duty that night at his patrol base, a General Mills plant.

At the other end of the country, the same cacophony filled the streets of David. U.S. soldiers heard Panamanians "screamin', hollerin', any way they could make noise and celebrate," says CW2 Bryan Turner, assigned to an intelligence control and analysis group under 2d Brigade. "It was just mass hysteria and a great party," Turner says. "The curfew just sort of went out the window." While the soldiers couldn't join the party, they basked in the feeling of liberation. "You felt like a conquering hero," Turner says.

When Noriega went into hiding, he took with him a large measure of the threat to U.S. Forces. They still were vulnerable to sniper fire, but "the perception that we had was that any type of increase in hostilities was unlikely," says Capt. Steven Collins, commander of C Company, 2d Battalion, 9th Regiment.

Not all soldiers could afford to feel gleeful at the news of Noriega's giving up. C Company, 1/9 Infantry, spent much of that evening trying to pin down a sniper in the Panama City community of Hollywood, an ironic nickname for this impoverished shantytown community located outside Albrook Air Station. The company was "first in the barrel" as the 1/9 moved into southwest Panama City to secure the area. AK-47 and automatic-weapons fire were coming from a hilltop by a high-rise apartment complex in Hollywood, officially known as Curundu.

The sniper or snipers—the soldiers didn't know how many they were dealing with—would shoot and move, then shoot and move again, says S.Sgt. Steve Siddle of C Company. "They were in civilian clothes, so it was hard to tell who they belonged to," he says. It took most of the night—to Siddle, it seemed like forever—but the company's sniper team, armed with M24 sniper rifles, located and killed at least one of the enemy and wounded another.

Late that evening at Albrook, Maj. Harry Tomlin, 7th Division chief of plans, stepped outside the division headquarters in the officers' club to clear his mind. The division staff had just finished their daily briefing for Maj. Gen. Carmen Cavezza, commanding general of the 7th.

An AC-130 droned over the city, its lights flicking on and off periodically, while inside the club, soldiers sang "Silent Night." Strange medley, Tomlin thought, but serene: a Christmas he would surely remember.

Like many first-time visitors to Panama, the invading forces soon learned that their first impressions were deceiving. The stark contrast between the flimsy shacks of Curundu, overgrown by weeds, and the cool luxury of San Francisco, with its many banks casting a neon glow over the central business district, belied the almost universal welcome they would receive after Noriega relinquished power.

During their first week in Panama, the soldiers did not know what to expect as they drove through the city. "There was people out partying and waving U.S. flags and cheering for us. And then we would turn a corner and start heading down another way, and all of a sudden we'd start getting shot at," says Sgt. Joseph Ruzic of Headquarters Company, 1st Battalion, 9th Regiment.

Poverty, trash, and graffiti were Pfc. Ronald Schow's first glimpses of Panama. Schow, of Headquarters Company, 2/9 Infantry, had only been in the Army four months when he arrived in Panama. "At first I was actually kind of scared," says Schow. "My head was spinning. You're just all of a sudden thrown into all this." Schow took heart from the spirit of professional soldiering he sensed among the senior NCOs. "They made it seem like it was more a job, that it wasn't such a dramatic thing," he says.

Later he would feel almost a pampered guest among Panamanian citizens who cooked dinner for his platoon and treated the soldiers to free phone calls home.

"The visual part was nothing compared to the reception that we got," says S.Sgt. Thomas Sans of B Company, 2/9 Infantry. Coming across the Bridge of the Americas into the slums of El Chorrillo, Sans remembers walls and sidewalks peppered with anti-American slogans—but no people. The city seemed to wear a veil of desolation. "But once you got into the areas where there was people around, everybody out there was cheering and clapping and waving," Sans says. "And all through our tour, people kept coming up to us and telling us how they were mistreated by Noriega." The Americans heard tales of torture, harassment, and the theft of entire businesses.

By no means everyone welcomed the Americans, however. Those assigned to bring quiet to the poorer communities encountered an abiding mistrust, although it was not universal. Women and children generally were more receptive to the presence of U.S. soldiers than the men, says Capt. Tom McCool, who commanded Headquarters Company, 1/9.

The soldiers' practice of marching through neighborhoods, heavily armed and camouflaged, was a double-edged sword. "There's something to be said for seeing thirty guys with camouflage walk into your neighborhood," McCool says. "We provided security." At the same time, those who had something to hide from the gringos had plenty of time to hide it.

In the poorer neighborhoods people congregated on the streets and balconies, where people watched the soldiers as they went from door to door, asking about bad guys, drugs, and weapons. It was a welcome break from the heat and monotony. As a result, "Everybody knew what was going on," says Sergeant Ruzic. "And the people who had the stuff, it gave them a chance to get rid of it before we got to them."

Lt. Col. Lynn Moore, commander of the 3/504 Infantry, was eager to close the book on peacekeeping operations. The battalion had been in Panama since 10 December, and the soldiers were growing impatient for the two weeks of leave that they had been promised to make Christmas away from home more palatable.

Moore was eager to finish clearing his original area of operations, from Gamboa east to Madden Dam and south to Paraiso so he could declare his mission accomplished and go home. "When things started to calm down, the troops were starting to get antsy, because the fight was over," Moore says. "Everyone was spread all to hell." His area of operations had expanded to cover more than three hundred square miles. "I really had in mind that if I could say that my area of operations was clear, that we could still make our redeployment schedule on the sixth of January, so block leave could start the tenth."

Kellogg agreed to let Moore return to his battalion, taking A Company with him. No sooner did he start the process of wrapping up his area of operations than all hell broke loose at Madden Dam in the 23 December fracas that left almost a dozen of his soldiers wounded and five Panamanians dead. Moore pulled his C Company from Coco Solo and assigned them to reinforce D Company at the dam.

After several days of negotiating, Moore succeeded in freeing B Company from the mission of patrolling Colon. A Company already had moved back to Gamboa. Finally, by New Year's Day, Moore had reunited his task force. With headquarters in Gamboa, he went about the remaining security missions in his area.

With Colon and Panama City subdued, Joint Task Force Panama turned its attention to the other nine-tenths of the country. The canal zone, with 40 percent of the country's population, was well in hand and the PDF shattered. But no one knew what lay beyond. As he grew increasingly hostile to Americans, Noriega had restricted travel outside the canal zone over the past two years. Only a handful of Americans stationed in Panama had ever been to David, three hundred miles away, although it is Panama's third largest city.

David was among the list of PDF strongholds that U.S. forces would have to seize if they were to forestall a protracted guerrilla war. It was home base for Lt. Col. Luis del Cid, a member of Noriega's SEM, the war council that he packed with cronies. Like Noriega, del Cid was under federal indictment for drug trafficking.

Virtually no one in the invading force had traveled to Panama's easternmost and least inhabited province, Darien, on the border with Colombia.

So unprepared was the U.S. military for what lay ahead that the 7th Division's 2d Brigade arrived in Panama on 20 December to find themselves without a specific mission. One of its three battalions, the 2d Battalion, 27th Infantry Regiment, had been on the ground since October, having deployed for Operation Nimrod Dancer. But for the first twenty-four hours after the balance of the 2d arrived at Tocumen Airfield, the brigade task force, two thousand strong, simply defended the airfield. The mission belonged to the 82d Airborne's 1st Brigade, but the brigade was "putting out fires" throughout the canal zone.

"They had their three battalions spread out all over hell's half-acre," says 2d Brigade commander Col. Linwood E. Burney. Another element of the 82d was still trying to assemble at Tocumen. It had missed the drop zone and landed in the tall grass of the airfield. The only force defending Tocumen was 1st Battalion, 75th Ranger Regiment. "We assumed defense of Tocumen airfield, an implied responsibility," Burney says.

It was 7th Infantry Division commander Major General Cavezza, visiting 2d Brigade at Tocumen the night of 20 December, who decided the brigade was most needed in the hinterlands of Panama, where the joint task force was unsure of the strength and intentions of the PDF. As Cavezza briefed the brigade on its new role, David became just one target on a long list.

The immediate targets were those immediately to the west. They included Coclecito, a favorite refuge of Gen. Omar Torrijos and a possible hideout for Noriega. Coclecito was thought to be a possible command post for Noriega. The brigade's first job would be to relieve the Rangers at Coclecito and Rio Hato, where PDF resistance continued to simmer, and then to develop a long-range plan for securing and stabilizing the rest of Panama.

Soldiers would have to get control of Penonome, headquarters for one of the PDF military districts and reputed to be a stronghold of support for Noriega. Penonome was the seat of government for the province of Cocle. Also on the list of targets was Chitre, the seat of government for the province of Herrera and another military headquarters.

The next phase of operations would include David; Changuinola, home to a Panamanian jungle training center; and Coiba Island, a penal colony for some of the most hardened criminals in Panama and some of the plotters in the failed 3 October coup against Noriega. Burney's staff set to work gathering intelligence on all the targets and developing plans for the immediate assaults.

As the list of targets grew, Burney also listed the obstacles in such far-flung operations. For starters, there was the supply problem. David, capital of the far-western province of Chiriqui, is at least a six-hour drive from Panama City and was at or beyond the fuel range of the transport and attack helicopters Burney would need to support his operations.

Burney, known for devising some of the most grueling exercise regimens ever seen in the 7th Division, relished the assignment. He chose to make Rio Hato his eastern logistics base and expand from there to David, which became his western base. He considered working entirely out of David, but that would leave a large swath of Panama untouched and stretch the already strained airlift to the breaking point.

The brigade got an immediate taste of the supply problem when it landed at Tocumen. The supplies that would be needed for the first offensive—food, water, fuel, ammunition—not only were constrained because of the perennial lack of airlift, but wound up elsewhere in spite of detailed plans for two delivery points at Tocumen. Some of the pallets of equipment wound up in Texas. Others ended up at Howard Air Force Base after planes were diverted from Tocumen. Some of them arrived at Tocumen several days later, after the brigade had left for the interior.

So much for a resupply in twenty-four hours, Burney's staff thought. "It was, in fact, five days before we got a resupply," says Maj. Jim Moon, the brigade's planning chief during Just Cause. In the meantime, not knowing when more supplies would arrive, the brigade had a crash course in urban foraging. Two battalions were preparing to move out to unfamiliar terrain, where they could not be sure of rapid resupply, and provisions were short.

Being in a developed area, the soldiers did not have to go far to get food and water, although they had to find it. And enemy pressure was negligible, since the airfield already was secured, so it was possible to conserve ammunition. "Fortunately there was no sustained heavy fighting that burned up our basic load," says Maj. Rob Yanichko, who as the brigade's logistics chief had confronted the puzzle of gathering supplies.

Water was a major concern. The division's soldiers are trained and equipped to survive for three days on what they carry, but they would need water in case of an extended operation without immediate resupply. "Another thing that we did not have is fuel," Yanichko says. "That was a real problem for us, right off the bat." The 82d was having the same problem, because of the paratroopers' difficulty in assembling at Tocumen. "A lot of their logistics was still out in the drop zone," Yanichko says.

Since 2d Brigade was under operational control of the 82d for the defense of Tocumen, Yanichko approached the division headquarters for supplies, only to find the 82d was hoping to tap into the 7th for supplies. "It was two have-nots," Yanichko says.

Both units found a fuel source: a Texaco gas station. Using a small hand pump, the troops lined up their jeeps, HMMWVs five-ton trucks, and even Sheridans, two or three at a time, and drained the station dry. It was a primitive solution, but it worked. The soldiers would take turns, standing on the pump and operating it with both hands. "That's what we did for approximately eleven straight hours, until it was gone," Yanichko says. The brigade was able to put sufficient gas in its vehicles to venture out into the interior, but with no reserve.

With only two MREs remaining for each soldier, the brigade ate airline food while it remained at Tocumen. It was vegetarian fare: canned baby corn, canned asparagus, canned potatoes. Gallon jugs of spring water, taken from nearby Air Force supplies, replaced water the soldiers had drunk on the flight into hot, humid Panama. "It was really a catch-as-catch-can operation, putting that together," says Yanichko. But it allowed the brigade to distribute its scarce food and water where it was most needed.

Almost as critical as the shortage of food and water was the lack of maps. "When we were lucky enough to get a 1:50,000, we would Xerox it," Burney said. For much of Darien province, no maps existed. The Indians in Darien measured distance by so many days' walk. It was readily apparent that logistics would be a problem.

Airlift continued to be in short supply. While 2d Brigade prepared for the clean-up phase of the invasion, all the helicopters the Army had in Panama were busy with the last assaults, including the brigade's own air assault into Coclecito. The division was designed to have at least one lift company for logistical purposes, but there simply were no helicopters available to transport food, fuel, water, or ammunition.

On Thursday, 21 December, one of 2d Brigade's battalions, the 5th Battalion, 21st Infantry Regiment, conducted an air assault by helicopter into Coclecito, on the the northern border of Cocle province.

Colonel Burney, his brigade headquarters and the brigade's 2d Battalion, 27th Infantry, flew out in about twenty-five sorties on C-130s to Rio Hato, taking as many vehicles as could fit on a C-130. The 3d Battalion, 27th Infantry Regiment, followed in C-130s the next day.

The 5/21, in convoys and aircraft, spent all of Friday, 22 December, moving from Coclecito to link up with the troops at Rio Hato.

With the soldiers went medical units and supplies, assets that would prove to have value far beyond patching wounds and treating disease as the troops went about pacifying the country, town by town and hamlet by hamlet.

There were not enough C-130s to transport all the brigade's heavy equipment to Rio Hato, particularly the five-ton trucks, Q-36 radars, and howitzers. Those that could not fit, about seventy-two vehicles, formed a convoy to move over land through Panama City to Rio Hato. No one had traveled from Tocumen across the canal since a company from the 82d, trying to secure the route in Sheridans and HMMWVs with machine guns the day before, had lost a soldier to sniper fire.

Lt. Col. Bob Phillips, executive officer of 2d Brigade, had stayed behind at Tocumen to bring the remaining forces through by land. He was dismayed to find that not only would he need armed escort, but that a four-kilometer stretch of the road was undefended. The 193d Infantry Brigade covered the road from Fort Clayton eastward, and the 82d covered the section between Tocumen and the infamous San Miguelito overpass, a staging area for snipers.

Between the two areas of operation lay the grim prospect of more casualties, Phillips thought. "I'll be durned if I know why that gap existed," he says. "I suspect the 193d was busy with other things at the time, and the 82d was busy. And they just never had a reason, really, to close that."

"There were big gaps in there during the initial days because we didn't have enough forces to put in there," Cisneros says.

Starting out from Tocumen at midnight, the 2d Brigade had darkness on their side. They also had firepower. As arranged and rehearsed at Tocumen, tanks led the convoy, and an AC-130 provided air cover. "With the AC-130 overhead, I knew everything that was moving, both sides of the road, down the road. We didn't have to fire on anybody," Phillips says. The vehicles, armored and sandbagged, encountered only two minor shooting incidents.

In one, a sniper shot an AK-47 round into a tire of one of the MPs' HMMWVs. It just kept rolling. The driver didn't discover the bullet until a couple of days later, Phillips says. In the other, a sniper fired a burst into the air and fled.

A third mishap, although not a sniping incident, would test the mettle of two women in combat. A five-ton truck blew a tire just as it approached the overpass. The driver was a woman who, along with another female driver, had asked Phillips at Tocumen to be excused from the convoy. "They asked not to be included in the convoy, a normal reaction," Phillips says. "And I basically told them no, everybody's going, and that ended it." The driver, panicking, made a wrong turn toward an area where soldiers from the 82d were engaged in a firefight. She stopped, petrified, until Lt. Col. Rick Brown, the battalion officer leading the division troops in the convoy, calmed her down.

Phillips and Burney dismissed the incident as a normal case of nerves for someone under fire for the first time. Once she got over her panic, she and the other woman soldier who had asked to stay behind at Tocumen "did an incredible job," Phillips says.

The first air assault by the 5/21 Infantry marked an undramatic beginning for what the brigade labeled "our western campaign," a six-week series of missions whose drama lay more in their novelty than in guns fired or men killed. The battalion task force, consisting of about 550 men and artillery, gained control of the installation at Coclecito with no resistance.

They found radios, but no Noriega. Neither the PDF forces there nor the weapons were impressive. About twenty-five soldiers surrendered, each with his personal weapon. It was hardly a "cache" of the kind SOUTHCOM expected to uncover.

Likewise, at Rio Hato the 5/21 encountered sporadic mortar and machine-gun fire as the first of their planes approached the airfield, but the battalion took no casualties. They turned their attention to scouring Rio Hato for weapons and routing the last of the PDF. The soldiers discovered two ZPU-4s, the PDF's strongest antiaircraft gun, in a warehouse on the east side of Rio Hato. The troops dismantled what they could, and took a sledgehammer to the rest.

Over the next three days, the Macho de Monte who had eluded the Ranger assault continued to snipe at U.S. forces. Mortar fire also was a threat. A number of PDF elite had fled their compound on D-day in a white van with a mortar in the back, although they did not take enough ammunition for a prolonged battle. Nonetheless, the "Mountain Men" were reported to be massing for a counterattack.

Two Panamanians were shot and killed when they tried to run a roadblock at Rio Hato. The Americans continued to receive sporadic mortar fire. But by 25 December, it had ended. Christmas night, Task Force Red ordered all-night mortar illumination in hopes of flushing out the Machos. The 6th Battalion, 8th Field Artillery, registered its 105mm howitzers over the Gulf of Panama, with the desired result: the next morning, the holdouts started to surrender.

"At 10:00, ten Machos surrender; at 1300, fifteen Machos surrender," reads the war journal of Capt. Rich Burklund, intelligence officer for the 5/21 Infantry and then 2d Brigade. Thousands of weapons were removed from Rio Hato. One helicopter pilot counted twenty-one semitrailer loads full of arms confiscated from the Machos de Monte.

"The general gist of talking to them was that they decided once we had this constant flow of planes coming in there, began to police up several of their local caches and people were mentioning things to us, and then the artillery registering and the illum going off all night, that we were serious and it would be fruitless for them to carry out their counterattack," Burklund says.

The mission at Rio Hato went a lot faster than the "light fighters" had planned. On 26 December, the soldiers of 2d Brigade moved on to new targets. The assaults on Coclecito and Rio Hato were well-defined missions with narrow objectives, to subdue and disarm the PDF and DigBats. But what lay ahead was a potential minefield of uncertainty. "There were really no firm plans for anything beyond the, 'Take this target down,'" says Burney. "It was left pretty much to all of us to see what role we should play."

A Vietnam veteran, Burney knew what he did not want to do. "Some of us who had been in Vietnam remembered the torching of villages and so forth, and realized that was not the way to go," he says wryly. The skeleton of a plan began to emerge: to dissuade, disarm, destroy if necessary and then draw back. The intent, Burney says, was to make as few enemies as possible. As soon as the soldiers had done their job, they would be withdrawn from the area so that "the tendency to overpopulate an area, the tendency to make prostitutes out of women, that's eliminated," Burney says.

"The whole attitude of the brigade was not to kill people. The best way of winning was to have the other side surrender," Phillips says. "We did that from the largest operation to the smallest." Disarming the enemy became a small part of the mission for 2d Brigade. The rest of the mission would be to install a new Panamanian regime—from the bottom up.

15

Bulldog!

Sunday, 17 December, was a day of reunion for Staff Sgt. Wayne Newberry and his wife, Rebecca. Newberry, a fire support NCO with A Company, 3d Battalion, 75th Ranger Regiment, had just returned to Fort Benning, Georgia, from an extended and exhausting exercise. The young couple, anticipating their first wedding anniversary on the twenty-third, had spent a fun day Christmas shopping. In the afternoon, they returned home and began a night flopped on their couch, relaxing before the television and talking. When a call came in from the company headquarters, Newberry's easygoing demeanor suddenly switched, Rebecca remembers. It was a side of his personality she had never seen before: coolly professional.

"I got alerted and I got to go in," was all he said. In the pit of his stomach, he felt this was the one. He would be going into combat.

Rebecca felt it too. Quickly and quietly, Wayne began gathering his gear together and in a few minutes was headed for the door. Rebecca looked at him and said, "You're not coming back in five or six hours. It's not going to be go in and do the road march and come home."

"I don't think so."

Large, warm tears collected in the corners of her eyes. Gently they fell down her cheeks. Wayne hugged her and kissed her deeply, then was gone.

On the twenty-minute ride to Fort Benning, Newberry had a difficult time concentrating. "I've just left her hanging there," he thought. He knew that once he reported to his unit, there would be no chance he could call Rebecca and say: "I'm not going to be back."

She was just left hanging.

When the alert call came to 1st Lt. Loren Ramos, the exuberant executive officer of A Company, he bounded into his car and fifteen minutes later he was in the battalion's special room for reading and discussing operational plans. He'd been there about five minutes, talking with two company commanders and their executive officers, when the battalion operations officer turned to Ramos's company commander and said, "We're going to war."

"Is it really going to happen?" asked the captain.

"Yeah. We're about to make it happen."

Instantly, the battalion planning room became a beehive of activity, staff officers buzzing about. "People were just scrambling to get everything set up," recalls Ramos. "The [battalion intelligence officer] was setting things up and the [operations officer] came in and gave a warning order. We Xeroxed copies of the order, enough to disseminate down to the platoons when we were allowed to do that." Ramos and his company commander sat down to prepare the company warning order and when that was done, moved down to their own war room. They still had not received permission to issue the warning orders to the lower ranks. In that pause, Ramos had a moment to think:

> I don't think it had really sunk in. [I knew] this was going to happen, but I couldn't get too personal about it because it was important for [the company commander] and me to put out accurate information, to make sure that we portrayed an image of self-confidence. Soldiers were still coming in and there was speculation and that's the worst thing, because the boys can have you doing all kinds of things within an hour if you don't just tell them the real deal.

In the momentary quiet, Ramos tried to remember the talks he had had with the previous company commander, Capt. Tony Thomas. Thomas was a veteran of the Grenada operation, Urgent Fury, and Ramos had drawn strength from him. Now, he felt confident. "Capt. Thomas and I talked about it, and you have to look like, hey, we are really going to go down there and slam these folks," says Ramos. "We knew we could do it and we knew that we had to go in there and portray that."

After about four hours of nervous waiting, clearance was given to pass the warning order to platoon leaders and platoon sergeants. Says Ramos: "All the platoon leaders were coming up and asking: 'What's the real deal?' I'd say: 'It's real enough that you don't need to ask a lot of questions.'"

The soldiers already knew it was real. Sgt. Paul Holt was in church that afternoon when he was called back in. He'd been watching the news, and had heard the reports of the killing of Lt. Paz. As he was driving in, he told himself that this is going to be a routine inspection, soon it would be over, soon he could go home for the holidays. "Then I came in and we actually started our sequence," he remembers. "We're getting everyone accounted for, the normal Ranger stuff. But then, it didn't stop, though it should have. The game should have been over. Everybody was still thinking there's got to be a cutoff time, even when the maps came out. Everybody's trying to convince themselves that this isn't going to happen."

When the warning order went out, the company officers huddled with their platoon leaders to work up detailed plans. Ramos and his commander discussed the specific targets they had and divided up the tasks. "We gave the platoon leaders enough latitude—we told them what objective and the fire control measures that applied—to facilitate a company plan but let them work what squad was going to breach an obstacle and things like that," says Ramos. As the plan was fleshed out, the platoon leaders would return to brief their soldiers to prepare them and give them time to draw equipment.

As a fire support NCO, Wayne Newberry was able to sit in on the initial warning order. "I remember walking in and seeing this imagery, the photos and the maps, and thinking, 'That looks like Panama.' But it wasn't Fort Sherman, it wasn't Howard Air Force Base, it was something new. I just was looking at it and wondering, 'Where is this?' I started getting butterflies during the warning order."

What Newberry was looking at were pictures and maps of the Rio Hato compound, about one hundred miles down the coast of the Gulf of Panama from Panama City. But the target had not yet been declassified yet to the point where Newberry could tell the guys in his fire support team. "Walking into our team room they started asking me if they should pack their rucks, is it going to be a road march, or what," says Newberry. "I was kind of caught. When my team gets attached to a platoon, I don't see them again until the mission is over. The only contact I have with them is through the radio. I knew that three days from now we were going to get on airplanes and fly away and the only way I would know if these guys made it was if I heard them on the radio. It was just a weird feeling. It was a couple of hours before we could tell everyone, but I'm sure they could figure it out, at least by the speed with which [the leaders] were pinging off walls."

By midnight, the company had finished its operations order. The first rush was over. A Company had four objectives, to be seized simultaneously, to secure the north side of the Rio Hato airfield. B Company would take other objectives within the same area. The two companies were then to move south toward the rest of the compound, where the regiment's entire 2d Battalion would attack. It would be a night parachute assault, the kind of combat the Rangers had trained for, but tricky business nonetheless.

Newberry called his team together in the moment before the operations order was passed. He tried to give them the overall picture as best he could: "We're going to Rio Hato, going after Noriega," he told them. In a rush, Newberry felt a special bond with the members of his team. "The look on some of their faces was like they weren't any longer subordinates. They were like a family. A friend looked at me and said: 'I'm scared.' He was looking at me for some kind of reassurance, and I was just as scared as they were. I just tried to get them to stay calm, get them through the operations order. The worst thing was to get them all excited."

Sgt. Holt, too, was concerned about his squad and his job in seeing them survive the coming fight. He tried to get his men into a serious frame of mind, when his first sergeant came over to lend a helping hand. "Cut the bullshit," said the senior NCO. "This is Panama. This is no mock stuff here." The first sergeant appealed to the unit's pride. "As a Ranger, your training is designed to keep that to a minimum. If you do go, you know you're going with the best guys."

The effect was instantaneous, says Holt: "It was the big picture. The realism started shooting back into your system. Guys were saying, 'We're going, we're going, we're going.'"

Some Rangers had been sure a Panama mission was just a matter of time.

For members of Sgt. John Hines's unit, the only question was: when? "There was too much going on down there and our training had been too much oriented for that sector for something not to happen," he says. "You'd never turn on the news and have something good happen from Panama. So you put two and two together and know something was going to happen." For a year and more, the Rangers felt their training had been geared for the region. "So every time we would look at the news we'd be wondering: is it going to happen?"

Commanders did their best to force some sort of sleep plan, "so you didn't fall asleep in the middle of Rio Hato," says Ramos. He headed for his office at about 1:00 A.M. Monday morning, 18 December. It was an emotional night. "I lay down on the floor and started thinking about the things that matter most to me: my family, my children. In fact, I got—behind closed doors—very scared and did a lot of soul-searching. My goodness, it was about to come to a head, everything that I ever wanted to do."

What if my commander gets killed? he asked himself.

Loren Ramos is the kind of man who wears his heart on his sleeve. That night, thinking of his wife and children, he felt the urge to leave something for her, for them—a letter—just in case. He wanted to tell her what most mattered to him, what she should do with her life. "I put it in my desk where it wouldn't be found unless someone was cleaning my desk out. I stapled it shut. Unfortunately, my wife found it and opened it up.

It was just a one-page letter: What do you say? You know? What do you say? Just say what comes from your heart, that your kids and your wife are what matter the most to you, and you really believe in what you're doing. What I felt at the time was: Is this a great life or what? All the things that I've done—soccer team coach and pack cub master—and that I'm doing, all those things mattered, and being part of this regiment. That's all I could tell my wife—just go on and have a terrific life, and maybe we'll meet in the hereafter. And I left her a note in the car, before I even knew this thing was happening, saying I love you and the kids.

Ramos eventually fell asleep for a few hours.

When he and the other Rangers awoke Monday morning, it began to dawn on them that they wouldn't be actually going anywhere for about thirty-six hours, and the adrenalin rush of Sunday night began to fade. As Ramos put it, "It kind of lost its initial umph."

Over the course of the next day and a half, the fear and anxiety ebbed and flowed. Says Hines, "When you first came in and had your commander's briefing, saw the maps of someplace you'd never seen before, and the imagery, right then the feeling in your gut was something new. But we had two days before we actually went anywhere and I think everybody digested it."

Many Rangers' minds began to replay the exercises they had just completed. Like other elements of the Just Cause task force, the Ranger regiment had done extensive rehearsals of their parts of the war plan.

For the Rangers, these exercises had been something special. Ranger training is continuous and intense. It's called "joint readiness training," because at the higher unit levels, it demands a large degree of coordination with the Air Force, and in some cases special operations units not only of the Army but other services, with units like the Navy's SEAL teams. But in December 1989, the Rangers conducted their first-ever regimental-level exercises.

Lt. Col. Joe Hunt, commander of the regiment's 3d Battalion, explains:

When we do a joint readiness training, we build up four modules basically. The first three are three company rotations. One's normally an air assault, one's normally an airfield seizure at company level, then a third one is whatever combination of aircraft we have at that particular exercise. The highest level, called Mod-4, is normally a battalion level, bringing all the pieces, all the aircraft together. Since it's joint training, it's training for the Air Force just as much as it is for the Rangers and they'll bring a variety of different aircraft, the C-130s, the C-141s, sometimes a C-5, and we try to put all these pieces to work in one large-scale operation. But on this particular Mod-4, it was a regimental rehearsal of the operational plan.

This difference did not go unnoticed by soldiers who had been in the regiment for some time. "This was the first training mission in my experience that all three battalions and the regimental headquarters were involved in," says Newberry. "I knew that this was more than just the previous Mod-4s we'd done every year."

The exercises were complex. The regiment's 2d Battalion, normally stationed at Fort Lewis, Washington, was to play an important role. While with sophisticated communications gear, the planning was greatly simplified, it still required a number of trips back and forth by the regimental and battalion staffs and commanders. Also, the Ranger battalions maintain liaison officers at each other's posts. "We all worked out our own particular quirks and desires beforehand," says Hunt, "so when it came time to ship the 2d Battalion out here we were all in total harmony in the execution mode."

At the start of the Mod-4 exercises, the 2d Battalion was flown to Lawson Army Airfield, at Fort Benning, Georgia. The 2d and 3d Battalions were then cross-loaded on their transport aircraft. They would be parachuting into Hurlburt Field on the Florida panhandle, where the Air Force stations most of its special operations aircraft, for their assault. Waiting for them at Hurlburt were two companies of the 101st Airborne Division (Air Assault), who were to play the part of the PDF, including the areas where they would be positioned around the airfield. The Rangers' task was to secure the airfield within thirty minutes and then receive airlanded reinforcements.

The regiment had rehearsed the exercise on the ground at battalion level three days prior to the 14 December drop. These run-throughs had been extensive and thorough. Says Hunt, "We went into a formal battalion-level planning and rehearsal prior to the actual exercise, so we had gone out in the field, set up our own area battalion level, rehearsed each one of the teams, gone through it, made sure each one of the guys knew where they were supposed to be, before we launched out into this big exercise."

The rehearsal exercise duplicated the Rio Hato layout in detail.

"We were able to replicate specific objectives in the plan; if a team needed to go over to seize a road, an observation post, all that was replicated in the rehearsal," says Hunt.

> If a team had to go find a particular target, there was something there for them to go after, to see, to go find. That worked out extremely well and all the communications, the link between me, the regimental commander above, that all worked out well. And of course from the Air Force's viewpoint it was a great rehearsal because for the first time, they had to put this tremendous armada in the air and they, too, were replicating true time, true link-up points, refuel and just the command and control of all these aircraft lifting off different places, then getting to specific flight corridors.

There were a lot of aircraft, including thirteen personnel aircraft and two heavy-drop planes loaded with other equipment for the airdrop, followed by five airlanded cargo planes, as well as supporting helicopters and AC-130 Spectre gunships.

The two companies of the 101st Airborne opposing force "gave no quarter," in Hunt's phrase, but were soon overwhelmed and by the thirty-minute deadline, the airfield was secured for the follow-on aircraft landing the Rangers' jeeps and motorcycles. The success gave the Rangers a dramatic morale boost; Generals Stiner and Lindsay had come down to observe the exercise and pronounced themselves more than satisfied. In a brief after-action review, Lindsay said it was as fine an example of an airfield seizure as he had seen.

This boost to the Rangers' confidence was revived when they received their orders to go to Panama for real. "The rehearsal in Florida had the same names of objectives so people were already familiar with them," says Ramos. "The objective was laid out, except for one portion, exactly the same. It was incredible. I applaud those above us for the way they set it up. When I got to reading the plan, it was like, this is close. And it really gave you a good feeling, because there was such a lack of disparity that you knew the soldiers were really going to grab hold of it. The boys knew they could do it."

If the success of their rehearsal exercises helped calm the Rangers' nerves in the waiting period after their initial alert, the tension began to climb again as they moved to Lawson Airfield to prepare to load up for the assault on Rio Hato.

Some were still hoping this was an exercise, or a dream from which they would be wakened. "You were kind of waiting for the switch to be shut off," says Sgt. Hines.

> I was thinking that somewhere along the line the president has said: "Go," and down the line, down the chain of command that has just escalated to where the generals are saying: "Prepare to go," and the colonels are saying: "Let's get ready to go," and it just keeps going down the hill. And I was expecting the president to say: "Whoa! I didn't mean to go!" and I was expecting him to pull the switch: "You got all carried away here. Hold on now, I know it's been twenty years, but hang on." But that never did happen, and when we got to the airfield I knew, Okay it's happening.

The weather was also turning miserable. It was bitterly cold as the Rangers moved about the airfield, drawing ammunition and waiting to board the C-130s, and a soaking rain had begun to fall. Only the reunion of the regiment, meeting comrades on the eve of combat, brightened the mood. "I saw a lot of friends from other battalions," says Newberry. "We went through airborne school and Ranger indoctrination together and then got split, or went to Ranger School and got split. We ran into each other down there. I saw a lot of hugging going on."

The true reality of what they were facing kept being driven home by the changes in the normal procedures of training missions. Says Hines: "There were two things that happened that stepped over a line we'd not stepped over before. One, the incredible amount of ammo we had down at the airfield, and two, right before we left the platoon medics were issued morphine. That is a controlled substance, obviously, and when they got it, that was the point of no return in my book." The Rangers, young men all and prone to the rush of youthful excess, remembered their religions, sought some solace. The airfield was crawling with chaplains and many small services were held and sincerely attended.

The ammunition draw was an impressive sight. There was so much available—and live ammunition is rationed so intensely in peacetime exercises—that the parade of crates became almost humorous. Hines was walking by open crates of ammunition and grenades. He thought to himself: "Well, I could use another one." As he moved along, he walked over to one of the privates in his team who was complaining he didn't have enough grenades. "I just chucked a couple over to him. In training, it's like you're getting all ready for your turn to throw it, and here were are carrying eight of them."

Hines later paid for this profligacy when he had to board an airplane and later jump out of it with a rucksack that weighed more than eighty pounds by his reckoning. Hines's rucksack had to be carried to the plane by two jumpmasters; he could not carry it himself and his parachute.

Ramos made sure his company was more conservative. He had learned a lesson from Capt. Thomas, the previous company commander and a veteran of Grenada. Thomas had told Ramos that in Grenada, rucks had been so heavy "you couldn't carry half of them off the drop zone. And that's a fact. We had people here who shared that with us, but all the companies didn't adhere to it." B Company carried twice as much as A Company did. Ramos limited himself to the basic combat load of ammunition, seven rifle magazines.

> [I] fired maybe four and a half magazines and threw three hand grenades, and that's probably more than most people did. My point was, we had people just leaving rucks all over the place and then we spent half the day trying to recover rucks everywhere. We're loaded down for bear, you can start rationalizing anything. If we need that much ammo, there are going to be enough dead Rangers around that there'll be ammo all over the place. It's not the Battle of the Bulge.

The weather continued to worsen during the ammunition draw, and the wait to board became miserable. The rain would not stop. A supply of blankets was found, and the Rangers were fed chicken soup and cookies. To Ramos, the idea of the blankets was "the best thing I ever saw in my life. It was a very chilly day. Those blankets did two things: first of all they broke the chill of the cold weather, and then they hid the fears that everybody had. It almost took your mind off it for a little while." After hours in the rain, the shelter was welcome.

Just before the aircraft were to be loaded, the Ranger regimental commander, Col. William Kernan, stepped into the gray chill to address his troops. It was an emotional moment. A hush fell over the huddled soldiers. Kernan, who goes by the nickname "Buck," is the living embodiment of the Ranger ethos. His speech struck a chord with his men.

Kernan reminded them of the rehearsals they had just completed, told them they should be confident. Then he said: "We're going down there with everybody here and we're coming back with everybody here."

The speech ended with a great Ranger "Hoo-ah" yell, but Kernan's promise stuck in the minds of his troops. "A kind of hush fell over everybody when he said that," Newberry recalls.

> That's kind of squared away. At least you were coming back, and not going to be left behind somewhere. Sometimes I still think about it. It was just the emotion of it. I don't know if you were listening to what he said or what, or knowing that he'd be on the airplane with you. He would never send us anywhere he wouldn't go himself, wouldn't send us down there to get our butts whipped or anything like that.

By the time it came to load up for the flight to Rio Hato, most of the Rangers were ready for a nap. It had been a long day and afternoon at Lawson, and the chill of the winter air was replaced by the heat and humidity of the jam-packed C-130s. Many Rangers had large and heavy rucksacks. For Rio Hato the transports each were carrying sixty to seventy people. It was cramped quarters.

As it moved south, the air armada grew and grew, until it reached eighty-two aircraft, including the Rangers headed for Tocumen and Torrijos airfields, the command and control aircraft, the Air Force F-15s and other air support, all skimming along at low altitudes to avoid detection by Cuban air defense radars. As this fleet moved into Panama it moved in concert with the hundreds of other helicopters and aircraft already in the air.

The flight itself was smooth and uneventful until about 11:00 P.M., when word came over Kernan's command net that the operation had been compromised and the PDF knew the United States would be striking them. "Oh, shit," thought Kernan, and he paused for a moment, trying to decide whether to pass the information on to his troops. Better they should know what they're up against, he concluded, and the word was passed. Along the dozens of aircraft, a chorus of murmured, "Oh, shit" went up.

Many senior leaders had figured that once the 82d Airborne Division's ready brigade was alerted and moved to Pope Air Force Base, operational security would go with them. "We felt comfortable with getting out here with a little commotion but we knew as time got closer that people would know," recalls 3d Battalion commander Hunt. "I think the guys were ready for that if in fact that was to come about." When word of the compromise came, Hunt wrote it on a card and passed it around his aircraft. "Most of the guys would just read it and go, um, and pass it around," he says. On other planes, it was announced over the intercom.

As the Rangers neared Panama, and word was passed to rig up rucks and hook up for the jump, the planes exploded like a football locker room before a bowl game. "We just went around and started hitting one another on the head and got motivated," remembers Ramos,

> because if anybody deserved to be slammed, [Noriega] was the one. Because he was an evil man. And I'll tell you what, there's very few things worth fighting for in this world, but liberty is one of them. It's inconceivable to me that a person could be down there as long as he was, and take away their freedom, like he did—there was no death wish, but we wanted to get him bad, and he deserved to be got. We are America's kick-off team, if you will, and we were going to get in there and slam this buckaroo.

To Wayne Newberry, also, the flight was like the big silence in the locker room. "And then it was like the coach standing up and saying, 'Let's go get 'em.' The jumpmasters said: 'Up!' and that's when all hell broke loose, everybody came alive."

John Hines took a moment for a heart-to-heart talk with God, a practice he follows before every parachute jump. But he, too, was convinced he was about to do something right. "One thing stuck in my mind," he says.

It might have been May of '89 when they had the election that Noriega subsequently made null and void. And that was to see on the news and specifically on the cover of *Newsweek* those guys getting beaten. I'll always remember the picture on the cover of *Newsweek* magazine. I don't know if it was the president or the vice president that was getting beat up real bad and was covered with blood and was really messed up. I looked at that for a long time—and actually at the time we went through, not an alert, but some training perhaps maybe to go then—that image was always in my mind. Even then I was getting mad. When I was getting scared it came back to me and I started thinking, it's our time, this needs to happen so let's go and do it. So I tried to harness some of that anger, or whatever, to assist me in doing what we were about to do.

After they were strapped in for the jump, the Rangers in each plane chanted the Ranger Creed, something every member of the regiment is required to memorize:

Recognizing that I volunteered to be a Ranger, fully knowing the hazards of my chosen profession, I will always endeavor to uphold the prestige, honor, and high esprit de corps of my Ranger Regiment.

Acknowledging the fact that a Ranger is a more elite soldier who arrives at the cutting edge of battle by land, sea, or air, I accept the fact that as a Ranger, my country expects me to move farther, faster and fight harder than any other soldier.

Never shall I fail my comrades. I will always keep myself mentally alert, physically strong, and morally straight and I will shoulder more than my share of the task, whatever it may be. One hundred percent and then some.

Gallantly will I show the world that I am a specially selected and well-trained soldier. My courtesy to superior officers, my neatness of dress and care of equipment shall set the example for others to follow.

Energetically will I meet the enemies of my country. I shall defeat them on the field of battle for I am better trained and will fight with all my might. Surrender is not a Ranger word. I will never leave a fallen comrade to fall into the hands of the enemy and under no circumstances will I ever embarrass my country.

Readily will I display the intestinal fortitude required to fight on to the Ranger objective and complete the mission, though I be the lone survivor.

Rangers lead the way!

As Ramos was standing, waiting for the duckshuffle characteristic of paratroopers making for a C-130 exit door, he turned to Lt. Justin Whitney, the B Company executive officer who was on the other side of the airplane. Ramos and Whitney had been friends since their days together at officer basic camp. Ramos turned to Whitney and said: "Justin! High five!"

Whack!

"Let's go get 'em."

You're going to go anyway, thought Ramos, so you might as well get in the mood.

Their enthusiasm ran up and down the airplane.

Waiting below at Rio Hato were about 470 to 490 soldiers of the PDF, although how many were actually on post during the night of 20 December 1989 may never be known. They included the 6th and 7th Rifle Companies, accounting for about 440 of the total, and an engineer platoon of perhaps up to 50 PDF. In addition, there was a possibility of up to 250 cadets at the PDF's Herrera-Ruiz Institute, a training facility for Panamanian noncommissioned officers. However, many of the feared soldiers of the 7th Company, the Macho de Monte who had rescued Noriega during the October coup, had been transferred to the Comandancia in Panama City. Brig. Gen. Marc Cisneros interrogated many PDF prisoners after Just Cause, and he estimates that there were no more than a full company's worth of PDF in Rio Hato during the assault (see figure 15–1).

Whatever forces remained were spread among the facilities: the two company and one platoon barracks, two motorpools, a communications center, a training center, the operations complex for the Rio Hato airfield, and an ammunition supply point.

Also nearby was a medical facility of some kind, with a large red cross on its roof. The Rangers did not have exact intelligence on what the facility was—it turned out to be a dispensary—but it was declared a "no fire" zone and caused some adjustments in the Rangers' plan of attack: pre-assault fires were closely controlled to avoid

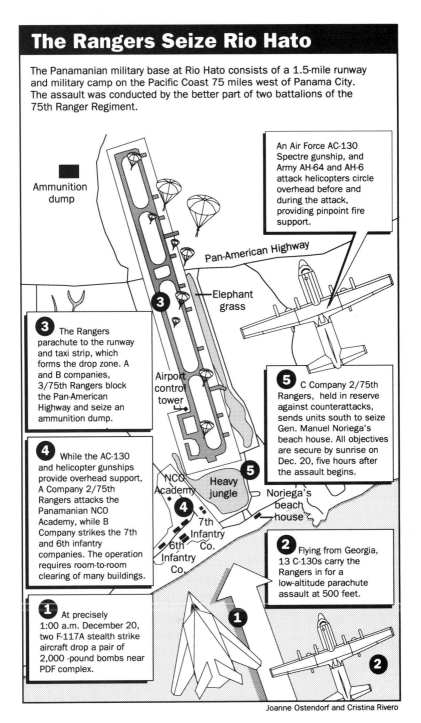

The Rangers Seize Rio Hato

The Panamanian military base at Rio Hato consists of a 1.5-mile runway and military camp on the Pacific Coast 75 miles west of Panama City. The assault was conducted by the better part of two battalions of the 75th Ranger Regiment.

Ammunition dump

An Air Force AC-130 Spectre gunship, and Army AH-64 and AH-6 attack helicopters circle overhead before and during the attack, providing pinpoint fire support.

Pan-American Highway

Elephant grass

3 The Rangers parachute to the runway and taxi strip, which forms the drop zone. A and B companies, 3/75th Rangers block the Pan-American Highway and seize an ammunition dump.

Airport control tower

5 C Company 2/75th Rangers, held in reserve against counterattacks, sends units south to seize Gen. Manuel Noriega's beach house. All objectives are secure by sunrise on Dec. 20, five hours after the assault begins.

4 While the AC-130 and helicopter gunships provide overhead support, A Company 2/75th Rangers attacks the Panamanian NCO Academy, while B Company strikes the 7th and 6th infantry companies. The operation requires room-to-room clearing of many buildings.

NCO Academy

Heavy jungle

Noriega's beach house

7th Infantry Co.

6th Infantry Co.

2 Flying from Georgia, 13 C-130s carry the Rangers in for a low-altitude parachute assault at 500 feet.

1 At precisely 1:00 a.m. December 20, two F-117A stealth strike aircraft drop a pair of 2,000 -pound bombs near PDF complex.

Joanne Ostendorf and Cristina Rivero

FIGURE 15–1

The Rangers Seize Rio Hato.

hitting the building, and each Ranger warned explicitly about the facility, which was nestled among other important targets in the compound.

Whatever the real strength of the Rio Hato garrison, it was well armed. The two infantry companies possessed enough weaponry to cause the Rangers problems. Intelligence estimates gave the PDF 7th Rifle Company about twenty mortars and fifteen motorcycles. Together, these would give the Panamanians the mobility to disappear down the trails that snake through the surrounding countryside and fire harassing mortars while on the run. These could play havoc with the plans to quickly begin air-landing troops and supplies after the airfield at Rio Hato was secured; planes sitting on the runway or on the grass verges unloading large cargoes would be inviting targets. The company also had a number of large caliber, direct-fire weapons: two machine guns, nine bazookas, two recoilless rifles, and perhaps two hundred of the RPG-7 rocket-propelled grenades. The ubiquitous RPGs, of Soviet design and widespread manufacture, while not very accurate at other than close range and in the daytime, nonetheless could also be used for indirect fires.

The 6th Rifle Company boasted an even more formidable order of battle. The unit was estimated to have three V-300 and sixteen V-150 armored cars. The company also had a large number of machine guns, mortars, and recoilless rifles. Perhaps most ominously, they had three ZPU-4 air defense guns. While these guns were of limited range and their gunners limited by darkness, they had the potential to catch the Rangers at their most vulnerable: while still in the plane. The terrible fear of any paratrooper, even more than being shot while descending or while entangled in his chute, is to have his aircraft hit before he jumps. At the low altitudes needed for a quick descent—five hundred feet at Rio Hato—there's little chance if the plane is shot down.

After securing the compound, the Rangers were to back toward the coast to Noriega's beach house, called Farallon. Noriega typically spent a lot of time at the beach house, and the 7th Rifle Company often was called on to serve as a security detachment when he was in residence. The Just Cause plan had called for a Navy SEAL team to assault the beach house on 20 December if Noriega was there, but it was learned he was not and the mission was scrubbed.

The Rio Hato contingent of Rangers, Task Force Red-R, numbered 837 jumpers. The initial drop was supported by two C-130s loaded with heavy drop equipment, including some jeeps, other light vehicles, and command and control gear. Supporting them would be AC-130 Spectre gunships, two AH-64 Apache attack helicopters, and two AH-6 "Little Bird" attack helicopters from Task Force 160. In addition, the Rangers were augmented with a medical unit.

Colonel Kernan would command the task force. Once on the ground, his headquarters, dubbed Team Black and made up of the regiment's principal staff officers, would coordinate fire support from the Little Birds and the Spectres and would serve as the task force's link to Stiner. Directing the fighting on the ground would be a tough task, given the rapid pace planned for the airfield takedown, but it would be Kernan's job to deal with any emergencies.

The Rangers' main Rio Hato force was made up of the regiment's 2d and 3d Battalions, though the latter had given up its C Company for the attack on the Tocumen and Torrijos airfields east of Panama City. Each of the battalions was augmented with special forces, including psychological operations Heavy Broadcast teams, who were to blast surrender demands to the Panamanians before assaults on various buildings, and a civil affairs team.

The two battalions were to split the Rio Hato battlefield, designated Area of Operations Eagle, or AO Eagle. It extended well beyond the airfield area itself, stretching south to the shore to the Farallon beach house. This southern area was the responsibility of the 2d Battalion, commanded by Lt. Col. Alan Maestas. Maestas and his men were to seize the two company compounds and the military institute.

The 3d Battalion, under Hunt, was to clear the runway area to prepare for the airlanding operations to follow. Hunt, commanding A and B Companies plus a team to direct the airlanding movements, was to drop in and secure the northern sector, including the camp headquarters, the communications center, the barracks buildings, and the motor pools. Hunt's battalion also was to sever the Pan American Highway, which bisects the Rio Hato runway. This was the main approach to Rio Hato from the Panama City area, and while the Rangers did not expect much in the way of PDF reinforcements, control of the highway—no more than a two-lane black-top—would prevent the Panamanians from fleeing in their armored cars or sending them into the northern drop zone.

Also up at the northern end of Rio Hato was a recreation center, with a number of thatched-roof buildings and a bullring. At this extreme end is where Kernan's command team would jump and remain during the initial assault.

Despite the fact that the planned H-hour was compromised, the early phases of the Rio Hato assault went like clockwork. At precisely 1:00 A.M., F-117A "Stealth" fighters from Tonapah Test Range Nevada swooped in at four thousand feet to deliver two bombs—the two-thousand-pound "stun grenades" Stiner had ordered to begin the attack and disorient the Panamanians in their barracks—near their intended targets. The first bomb was to land astride the 7th Company headquarters. The second, to follow one minute later, was to hit next to the 6th Company building. Unfortunately, however, lead pilot Maj. Steve Feest dumped his one-ton payload several hundred meters to the north and west of where it was intended; he did not have precise targeting information. The second pilot, orienting on Feest, also dropped his bomb between the two company buildings. The stunning effect intended from the bomb drop was mitigated by the alert given to the PDF as a result of the compromise in H-hour. The two infantry companies had scattered from their barracks. The attack intended to catch the Macho de Monte in their bunks would now find them out in the open.

The Stealth raid had been a controversial element of the Rio Hato plan. Kernan had asked for pre-assault fires on target, not as stun grenades. The Rangers' philosophy is to hit opponents as savagely as possible, and Kernan wanted to hit the PDF as hard as he could. "If I could have gotten it, I would have eliminated that whole thing," he says.

> But there were constraints. What we were looking for is something that would give us the element of surprise—the shock—because we knew how responsive the Panamanians were in the coup. We felt if we dropped something in there real quick—wham!—and disorganized them, it would give our people a chance to get on the ground. If you look our there [across the compound], it's like shooting across

a pool table. We were going to take a lot of casualties if these people were able to marshal their forces as quickly as they had already proven they could. Obviously the decision was made not to totally destroy the place. The agreed-upon munitions by the Air Force were a two-thousand-pound bomb on each target.

The choice of the delivery aircraft was up to the Air Force. Kernan says the bombs were dropped not more than a hundred meters from where he thought they would fall. "I'll take it," he says.

For the soldiers on the airplanes, the sound of the bombs dropping was a big morale boost. Word was passed back from the exits along the lines of paratroopers: "The bombs have dropped! The bombs have dropped!"

As the second Stealth bomb hit, the supporting gunships and attack helicopters struck their targets with laser-homing Hellfire missiles, rockets, and cannon rounds. For ninety seconds, the Rio Hato night was lit up by a fusillade from the Spectres, Apaches, and Little Birds, hitting a range of targets that had been identified in advance, but primarily searching out the ZPU-4 air defense guns, a target easily identifiable with the thermal night sights on the choppers and gunships. Like the display of Stealth firepower, the attack did not take the Panamanians by surprise, and the mobile guns, even with sophisticated sensors, could be hard to find without some idea of where to look for them. But when one of the guns opened up, it was engaged by an Apache. When it was later remanned, Kernan says, the gunner engaged one of the Spectres. "He [the Spectre] put a 105 in his watch-pocket, and that was the end of that guy."

For thirty seconds, there was a lull in the attack. The supporting pilots turned their attention to the drop zones, prepared to attack major PDF formations or weapons systems threatening those areas. In the interval, the lead C-130 swung north across the water to begin the run in for the parachute drop. The attack would come from south to north, with the Rangers' 2d Battalion jumping first. The approach was a tricky one, over the Gulf of Panama and the short space from the water to the Rio Hato compound. Kernan had made his needs clear to the Air Force pilots. "For God's sake, don't give us an early green, because we don't want to be swimming our stuff ashore. And I don't care about a red light because there's plenty of drop zone [to the north]." Kernan wanted to be sure to get his entire force on the ground.

Three minutes after the initial Stealth attack, a small green light went on above the open doorway of the lead C-130. Standing in the doorway, Staff Sgt. Louis Olivera, a jumpmaster with the 2d Battalion, saw tracer rounds searching skyward for the flight of transport airplanes.

After more than seven hours packed like sardines in the cramped C-130s, the Rangers were in no mood to stay aboard any longer. In a few seconds the attackers waddled their rucksacks down both left and right aisles of the chunky cargo planes and leaped into the Panamanian darkness. The drop went just to the right of the runway centerline, and all but ten jumpers got out in time.

The ground fire was intense during the drop. Says Kernan: "We started receiving fire before we hit the drop zone. Eleven of the thirteen aircraft received hits." Many Rangers began to wonder what the odd ticking sound was outside their aircraft. It was the sound of rounds bouncing off the sides of the planes.

The 2d Battalion had the toughest targets and the worst drop zone. The ground around the barracks buildings was broken, and a canopy of jungle trees nearly overhung the area. Staff Sgt. David DeBaere, a jumpmaster like Olivera, suffered the paratroopers' nightmare. Jumping at five hundred feet from the second aircraft, he got caught in a tree and dangling a few feet above a PDF bunker.

Just below him was a thatched roof protecting a Panamanian soldier who continued to fire, as few of his comrades did, at the Rangers landing on the Rio Hato runway. As DeBaere tried to climb down, a branch cracked and alerted the PDF gunner to his presence. Tracer fire ripped through the thatch but somehow missed DeBaere. The American ripped a grenade from his chest and dropped it in the bunker. The explosion silenced the PDF gunner.

DeBaere's nightmare was Loren Ramos's biggest fear: landing in the middle of the enemy. The odds of getting hit in the air weren't good, he reckoned. "If you're shooting at people in the air you couldn't hit them if you tried," he says, "especially at night. I convinced myself I wasn't going to get hit in the air. It's another thing when you're out there." His twelve-second drop seemed to last forever.

Ramos's fire support NCO, Wayne Newberry, could see the tracers in the air as he descended.

> My biggest fear was getting hit before I could get out of the harness, before I could get my weapon," he says. "On the plane I was thinking about landing and hearing something and looking up and seeing nothing but an AK-47 in my face. I at least wanted to be able to roll over and fire back. Let me get my weapon out or a grenade that I could lob over there. I might go with it but at least he wouldn't have the satisfaction of getting me.

The first seconds on the ground are the time when paratroopers are most vulnerable. Rangers are trained to assemble and get organized quickly, but in the confusion of combat in the middle of the night, with fire cutting across the drop zone, they were pumping adrenalin. And the PDF, alerted and out of their barracks, were not organized but seemed to be all over the place. Up at the north end of the drop zone, 3d Battalion was assembling.

"You really couldn't tell which angle the fire was coming from," remembers Ramos. When vehicles would come by on the Pan American Highway, "some brain-dead people would start shooting at these people, though we're all over the place. I'm thinking: 'Shoot out!' Because we're the only ones in the middle of the airfield."

As the Rangers started to assemble and move toward their targets, the airfield rang out with calls of: "Bulldog! Bulldog!" This was the Rangers' way to identify friend from foe. Says Ramos: "You'd run across people, and they'd say: 'Bulldog! Where you going!'"

"I'm going over here!"

"Bulldog to you! That's all you'd hear." As important as the "Bulldog" sign was the distinctive "ragtop" helmet—covered with camouflage—that the Rangers wore, because some of the PDF had American-style helmets. "Luckily, there was a lot of illumination that night," says Ramos.

The Rio Hato task force sustained a fair number of jump injuries, thirty-six, including a broken heel for 2d Battalion commander Maestas. Intelligence on Rio Hato did not include a good understanding of the terrain. "A sporting drop zone," is what the understated Kernan calls it.

Says 3d Battalion commander Hunt:

As I parachute in and I'm looking at telephone poles below me with street lights on, that was the last thing I expected when I came out of the aircraft. The bullets whizzing around didn't bother me. I knew there would probably be some poles there but having street lights on underneath me when I jumped was a little [frightening]—I'm at five hundred feet. I was concerned that they were going in the area that I knew was congested. I knew there were small buildings there. I knew there was potential for small fences. I didn't know quite how bad it was as far as obstacles to parachutists, but every little plot of ground was somebody's personal garden or unit garden or civic group garden and had a wall of some sort around it.

They had all these power lines running down the middle of the area which were hot until the first parachute started arcing over and we had a little light show for a while until the power went out. There were a lot of metal pickets with barbed wire fences that were in the northern sector where I came out in. I wasn't quite expecting all that.

The light show was turned out by regimental commander Kernan. Electricity at Rio Hato was put out when Kernan got hung up in a power line when he jumped in. Suspended about six inches above ground, his parachute caught in the wires. As Kernan released himself, his parachute caught fire and shorted out electricity for the whole camp. "Lightest landing at Rio Hato," says Kernan.

Newberry and Ramos landed just south of the Pan American Highway and halfway between the main runway and the main Rio Hato road. Newberry's big worry was to be separated from Ramos. "We had talked about it on the plane: 'See you on the drop zone, see you on the ground.' We say that every jump and it never seems to happen that way. But I don't think I landed more than twenty meters away from [Ramos]," says Newberry.

His team was supposed to link up at the main Rio Hato gate, a stone structure about twenty-five feet high, and designated Objective Green. The gate turned out to be a two-story archway, with several rooms on the ground floor and a castle-like top. As they got out of their harnesses, they located the gate about one hundred meters away. "We started to get up and go and took fire from both sides of the road," says Newberry. "We saw the tracers and got down. I knew how close those rounds were; they made a distinct sound just above our heads."

Newberry and Ramos lay in the grass until the first fires subsided. Then they began to move on hands and knees—luckily both had knee pads and elbow pads for the jump onto a hard surface. Ramos, with his light load, took the lead, scuttling along followed by Newberry, who was carrying a radio on his back. As they drew close to the gate, they realized that not only was fire being directed at them but that there was a .50 caliber machine gun that was shooting at aircraft also. "I don't think the .50 was shooting at us directly," says Ramos. "He was shooting at movement and sounds and stuff. I never stopped and took that good a look. There was a wall that prevented him from lowering the .50. I fired out three-and-a-half magazines by the time we got there. We'd move, unload a magazine, move, unload another until we got up to the wall."

All Newberry saw was the backside of Ramos. "The first fifty meters or so he'd crawl and lay low, then I'd catch up. And he'd be off again. We both shot back; it was harder for me to roll around with the radio on my back."

When the pair got up against the building, they linked up with Newberry's radio operator and an M60 machine-gunner from the company's 3d Platoon. They had not expected such resistance. "We were expecting to go to Objective Green and set up there," says Newberry.

When they were all together, Ramos said, "We need to take this."

The .50 caliber machine gun was located at the end of the gate building closest to the Rangers. The Americans went around the corner and threw grenades in a ground-floor entrance. As they prepared to peel off and assault one of the rooms, Ramos stepped out into the road and Newberry stepped out after him. Suddenly, Ramos pushed Newberry back and told him to get down. "I remember falling back and this shadow of a vehicle," says Newberry.

A V-150 armored car was speeding down the entrance road. All four Rangers rolled over and opened fire, but the vehicle just kept going. "We saw the tracers firing off it," says Newberry. "It kept going and made a left on the Pan American Highway and took off before we could get a LAW out or anything."

The Rangers went back to the gatehouse and began clearing it room by room. Two PDF soldiers were out front, but ducked inside. "Whoever was on top had a way to get down," says Ramos. "We did not know how the structure went; I didn't pay that close attention to the imagery. We went around that wall and I turned around. I threw the hand grenade in there and it scared the hell out of us. There was a little slit opening, just high enough that you couldn't look in, and you didn't want to put your hand in there, because you knew they were up there."

"You could look at it and tell it was definitely a hole, but it could have been anything," says Newberry.

The PDF then responded with a grenade of their own. After about five minutes, the Panamanian soldiers started to come down out of the tower.

"When they threw the first grenade down, they either thought they got us, or they didn't know which side we were on," says Ramos. "There was only one way out of that thing. When the first guy came out, we shot at the shadow or whatever and he went down. Then we started to go across and then we plugged one on the other side."

Newberry concludes the PDF soldiers got scared. "They just dropped and ran," he says. "They left a helmet up on top, and the .50 cal was hot. They'd probably realized they were overwhelmed and were trying to get out. But they didn't make it."

The PDF machine gun had been hampering the entire Ranger effort, suppressing the whole area near the Pan American Highway. For their efforts, Newberry and Ramos were awarded Bronze Stars.

John Hines's experience at Rio Hato was quite different.

Hines, a large man, was a machine gunner with B Company, and was carrying a heavy rucksack. All through the alert and the flight down, his fears had risen and fallen, but his fear left him when he hit the ground. "For me, the time I was most scared was when I did not have control over my environment," he recalls.

That happened two times. One, when I was in the airplane, and two, when I was parachuting in. I was just there. If the plane gets shot down, hey, I'm going with it. If I'm getting shot coming down, I can steer a little bit, but I'm not going to evade bullets.

Once I got on the ground—I had a bunch of stuff on so I was like a turtle there for a while—and I could move, then I felt better. I could do something to influence my situation. I could shoot back, I could run, I could jump, I could get up. The fear was still there, but it was not the fear you'd experienced before.

Hines's heavy load and the low altitude of the jump left him somewhat disoriented when he landed.

I always seem to come down fast," he says. He tried "to figure out where I was in relation to the airfield. It was behind me. I heard a lot of rounds, and ricochets, but you don't know how close they are to you. I landed in the tall grass, but luckily it was close to the road, and I'd landed in that stuff before when we were training at Fort Sherman, so I knew what it was like. I was on this small road, so I thought: This must lead to a bigger road, so I'll walk down it.

It didn't take too long before he did feel a round was close. Hines got down on one knee and thought. He decided he couldn't be sure if the rounds hissing around him were really close or not, so he figured he'd just get up and walk. "I could have spent all day crawling; I'd still be out there."

In time, Hines linked up with some other Rangers, but nobody from his unit. "Either they moved out before me or I moved out before them," he concluded. The soldiers he did join up with turned out to be from A Company, and when they moved out to a different objective, he stayed with them briefly. "But I knew I had to get where I was supposed to go," says Hines. "My job was to take down a fence near the [Pan American Highway]. I had this great big chain saw because we weren't sure how big the fence was. By the time I finally linked up with my platoon, they'd pretty much cleared their objective, but I still was one of the first from my squad."

If some Rangers were heroes and others dropped out of position, some, too, were casualties. The battle for the airstrip was short, never really in doubt, but confusing and pocked with violent firefights. Staff Sgt. Louis Olivera, the jumpmaster who had spotted the PDF tracers fired at the airdrop transport planes, flirted twice with death.

He was nearly killed during the jump, when his partially opened parachute caught a tree in the heavy jungle canopy near the two PDF company barracks. But it would get worse—much worse. As

Olivera's company moved toward the west end of Rio Hato, PDF soldiers opened fire on every U.S. squad within range. With the fire coming from different directions, the Rangers fanned out into hiding positions. Olivera jumped into a ditch.

The sergeant had barely looked up when he felt a stabbing pain in his shoulder and chest. At least two Panamanians were in the ditch, and one instantly shot Olivera. Cheering over their prey, the PDF began to strip the wounded, but alive, U.S. soldier of his patches, including the Ranger patch on his shoulder. One PDF soldier fired a pistol at point-blank range into Olivera's head, hoping to finish him off. The PDF soldiers then wrapped a black bandana around his rifle and left Olivera for dead. The bandana read "Macho de Monte."

Olivera opened his eyes at about 6:00 A.M. He could not move his arms or legs. He was losing blood fast, and guessed he was in shock. But he was alive. The bullet that was supposed to kill him had blasted through the lip of his Kevlar helmet, penetrated his skin and ricocheted off his skull. The round ripped through his head, exiting behind the sergeant's left ear. But the Kevlar helmet had slowed the bullet, preventing the round from hitting Olivera's brain. The Ranger managed to reach the portable radio in his rucksack and call in a rescue team, which arrived minutes later. The lessons of Olivera's experience, according to one Ranger, are twofold: "Kevlar helmets are great. And if you leave a guy for dead, take his radio, or he'll call in his own search party."

The fight for Rio Hato was over rapidly, with many PDF retreating into the jungle. "I guess the spirited defense ended within two hours," Lieutenant Colonel Maestas says. The runway was cleared within thirty minutes.

The Rangers quickly cordoned off the two infantry companies, but because the operation had been compromised, it was difficult to suppress them all. The Panamanians had scattered out of their barracks. "They were everywhere," says Colonel Kernan. "It was a 360-degree firefight. They were places where we hoped they would not be. Obviously, at 1:00 in the morning, we hoped we'd catch them in their barracks. And if we could contain them down there, it would be a hell of a lot easier to control the objective area. But that didn't occur."

The toughest firefight was in the barracks area. Much of the fighting was laborious, building-to-building, room-to-room. The PDF would retreat out the back of one building, hide in the gullies and washes or broken ground, and ambush the Rangers as they pursued. This tactic cost a number of casualties, and at least one Ranger was killed in this manner. However, in the course of these tense operations, one Ranger recognized that inside one barracks building there were unarmed PDF, and he entered the room without firing or tossing in a grenade. Inside were 167 PDF cadets, ages fourteen to eighteen, who were taking training prior to the Christmas holiday.

One hour and fifty-three minutes after H-hour, Kernan called for the first airlanded troops and supplies; his goal was H-hour plus two hours. "It was ready for airlanding operations a lot sooner than that," he says, "but there were some minor skirmishes still going on, and rather than risk any of those aircraft, we made a decision to hold. We didn't need any of those right away. What they were bringing in was some additional supplies and vehicles for us."

Farallon beach house also was secured quickly. It was defended by a small force of bodyguards who fired upon the Rangers from the roof. In trying to find the best way to get in, the Rangers decided to "use a large key," as one put it, and blew down the front door with a LAW. "Tactically we prefer not to do it that way," says Kernan, but the guards fled and were later picked up at one of the Ranger blocking positions.

In seizing Rio Hato, the Rangers killed 34 Panamanians and wounded an undetermined number of other PDF. They captured 362 soldiers and detained 43 civilians. The Rangers lost four dead, two of those to friendly fire from a Spectre gunship. Eighteen were wounded in the fighting, and twenty-six injured in the jump. They captured many weapons, from armored cars through mortars and machine guns and small arms. Slightly north and west of the airstrip was a major arms cache.

For Buck Kernan, the assault was something of a homecoming. One of his wife's relatives once was a wealthy landowner with extensive holdings, mostly in the Colon area. He forfeited his lands when Omar Torrijos came into power. Kernan has old home movies where Torrijos is a guest at the family's estate at Rio Hato, with Torrijos in his formal white summer uniform. "My exposure to Rio Hato was a little bit different than this guy sitting in his bandstand," says Kernan.

Closing the Loop

With trepidation, the soldiers of 2d Brigade, 7th Division, prepared to venture into the interior of Panama.

They had no idea what to expect, but they feared the worst: that Noriega's staunchest followers, armed to the teeth and with countless more weapons stashed away, would draw the gringos into a protracted jungle war. Another Vietnam.

The brigade had weapons and a plan. The weapons, soldiers would find, were less important. The plan would prove to be a cornerstone of the invasion. Army officials likened it to a carrot-and-stick approach, but without the carrot. The plan was to send Army Special Forces into the airfield of each major city and town. A Spectre gunship, covering them from above, would give the soldiers the authority of deadly force.

The leader of the special forces detachment was to find a phone, dial the PDF, and invite the commander to come discuss an unconditional surrender. However comical telephoning now seems, it was a way to avoid what Army commanders feared could be a bloody confrontation. The PDF would be given five minutes' notice to leave their weapons in the arms room of their cuartel, and assemble outside.

If PDF forces chose to stand their ground, the Americans were prepared to respond immediately with a preview of the fight that would result. Not only would the AC-130 buzzing loudly overhead let loose with cannon fire into an empty area of the cuartel, but a company of the 2d Brigade was standing by on the ground to quash any resistance.

Dubbed the "Ma Bell approach," this strategy proved largely successful in the cities and villages of Panama, aided by the enemy's decision not to resist. It did not finish the job of sweeping the enemy from the country, as the legitimate leaders of Panama and the commanders of Just Cause were all too keenly aware. But it gave them a firmer footing from which to move ahead.

Since D-day, General Cisneros had been on the phone to all the military zone headquarters.

Enlisting the help of Capt. Amadis Jimenez, Cisneros spread the word that the PDF leadership had no choice but to surrender peacefully. He knew it wasn't true, but it was a persuasive approach. "The combat plan was to attack," Cisneros says, "to go in there and fire into the garrisons, and then give them an ultimatum to surrender." Sensing the PDF was not eager to fight, he told his battalion commanders, "See if you can call them first."

"I felt that most of them would not fight. I was most concerned that they would flee in the mountains and the cities and hide all the weapons. Then we would be out for months, looking for those guys." If they surrendered, Cisneros told the PDF commanders, they stood a chance of being included in the new government. The alternative, he said, was bloodshed, destruction, and sure defeat.

Cisneros knew that the PDF would need a way to save face. Presenting surrender as a favor to their country was one way to preserve their pride. He also was aware that many of the PDF, having seen their livelihood destroyed, wanted to secure positions in the new government. As a general in a Latin country, Cisneros knew from his dealings with the Panamanians that his rank commanded respect, regardless of what government he worked for. He could bank on that, and on the loyalty of Jimenez, who was persuaded by the general's argument that a protracted war would further devastate Panama, already wracked by two years of economic sanctions. Endara, Ford, and Calderón agreed to the appointment of Jimenez as the general's liaison to their government.

On the phone, Cisneros let Jimenez do the talking. The ex-PDF captain would start each conversation with his PDF colleagues, then introduce Cisneros at the appropriate time. As a professional military officer who married into a wealthy family, Jimenez had ties to both the PDF and the same stratum of society that produced the newly elected Panamanian leaders. "I was considered one of the rabiblancos [white tails]," he said, a reference to the upper classes.

At the top of Cisneros's calling list was Lt. Col. Luis del Cid, commander of the PDF in Chiriqui, which Cisneros knew was the site of the PDF's largest weapons depot in Panama. He also knew there was a strong spirit of independence among the people of Chiriqui. Cisneros, who grew up in south Texas, thought of Chiriqui as the Texas of Panama.

"I started really putting a lot of work into Chiriqui province," Cisneros says. "That was a redoubt for Noriega." Cisneros felt del Cid, whom he had met once during a military exercise, "was really hanging his hat that Chiriqui would hold on. And yet there were very strong feelings up there in Chiriqui against Noriega."

As often happens in U.S. military offices in Panama, the phone system in Panama was not up to the job. Cisneros could not get through to civilian lines inside the country. Cisneros had to place his calls through the international operator in Miami, who then called the PDF installations long-distance. The general, in consultation with Jimenez, reviewed the list of PDF commanders and decided who commanded the most loyalty. The PDF major in charge of Darien province was one of the first to receive a call from the general. Jimenez considered him the best soldier he had ever met.

Cisneros's plan played well with the PDF. The Darien commander started to call his colleagues to persuade them to surrender. Around 8:00 P.M. the next night, Cisneros got on national radio to encourage the PDF to support the new government. Safe-conduct passes with his signature had been widely distributed in Panama to induce PDF personnel to surrender. "The idea was just to get them to surrender so we could get them under control, find out who they were," Cisneros says.

On Friday and Saturday, 22 and 23 December, four to five thousand PDF soldiers asked to join the new government, Jimenez says. Contrary to PDF expectations, the safe-conduct passes were no guarantee against being arrested, as many were when they approached U.S. military authorities. By the time Cisneros supplied U.S. forces with the phone numbers of PDF garrisons, the soldiers who remained in the garrisons had agreed not to fight.

The Rangers clearly were expected when they arrived in David on Christmas Day to confront del Cid.

Jimenez gave Cisneros the location of a house about ten miles away from David where he knew there was a phone. About 250 Rangers from 3d Battalion, 75th Ranger Regiment, were standing by when the call to the cuartel in David was made from the house outside the city to make sure there was no trap.

"There were a great many questions at my level what we were really flying into," says battalion commander Lt. Col. Joe Hunt, the task force commander assigned to go secure the David area and del Cid's surrender. With Hunt was a special forces detachment of about thirty men to help in the surrender. Hunt sent the special forces into David first in two helicopters, so as to avoid frightening the PDF into a possible firefight. Two Apache attack helicopters and a Spectre gunship were a short distance away, ready to engage the enemy if necessary.

Hunt arranged for del Cid to meet the special forces team at the PDF cuartel. He told the Panamanian lieutenant colonel that a sizable combat force was in the air. "Should there be any problem with this linkup between the special forces element and del Cid, then we would take necessary action," Hunt told him.

The meeting went off "quite insignificantly," Hunt says. The special forces team rented a couple of cars and drove into town to meet del Cid, who agreed to help coordinate the surrender of his military district.

Del Cid, a short, stocky man, whom Hunt described as "very obviously in command," had instructed his men to do as the gringos asked. "When he spoke, people listened. When he directed, people acted immediately," Hunt says. By the time two air assault companies from 7th Division's 2d Brigade flew into the airfield, with the Apaches and AC-130s flying nearby in plain view, they found the special forces team in control. All the PDF at the cuartel in downtown David—between 120 and 150 individuals, by Hunt's estimate—had surrendered and stacked their weapons. "Everything was turned over. It was quite peaceful," Hunt says. "It was very informal."

Del Cid provided the special forces team with information on where weapons were stashed in and around the city. He told them who was absent from the compound and where they could be found. The PDF lieutenant colonel also asked that the police force be allowed to continue functioning, armed at least with pistols to maintain authority. "His concern was hoodlums, local thieves, and thugs," Hunt says. "He appeared to be concerned about the police authority and maintaining law and order within David." Del Cid was taken to his office to pick up some personal items, then was taken to the airfield and flown back to Panama City.

The people of David, staring with curiosity at the camouflaged soldiers in combat gear, wanted to know why U.S. soldiers hadn't come earlier.

Capt. John Sieder didn't know it when he flew into Penonome on 22 December, but he was to about to run a city.

As commander of B Company, 5th Battalion, 21st Infantry Regiment, Sieder became a guinea pig for 2d Brigade's new mission, which assumed the characteristically ordinary name "stability operations." Thus began a phase of Just Cause that turned out to be anything but ordinary for the thousands of infantrymen who had a part in it, including Sieder, who became a de facto mayor in the post-Noriega regime.

Sieder's company conducted an air assault on 22 December into Penonome, which a task force of Rangers and Delta Force commandos had secured earlier that day. The Rangers had expected a fight when they seized a prison in Penonome, but encountered virtually no resistance. The 7th Division's mission was to relieve the Rangers and Delta Force as attackers. "We thought we were going to go in and assault the place," Sieder says. Packed into two CH-47 Chinooks, the company of 110 men encountered no significant resistance. After the first night, his men didn't fire a shot.

Half the company landed in the city by the PDF cuartel, under Ranger control, while the other half landed at the airport. Their first task was to take charge of the many detainees and arms at both locations. The PDF had surrendered two armored personnel carriers at the airfield, as well. The two segments of Sieder's company linked up to move the prisoners and PDF vehicles to the cuartel.

It was at this point, 2d Brigade commander Colonel Burney says, that Operation Just Cause "became a company commander's war." Entering each city, town, and hamlet ready for a fight, the soldiers who carried out stability operations found themselves instead assigned by squad to a variety of missions they had never dreamed of in training, from doling out money for weapons to picking up trash. Combat skills became less critical than "just pretty much common sense," Sieder says.

For the first two weeks of January, 2d Brigade worked sections of the country west of canal. For the next two weeks, the brigade conducted operations to the east.

Unsure whom to entrust with the leadership of Penonome, Sieder tried to communicate to the Panamanians that authority belonged to him and his company. "The big thing we tried to make clear from the start was that we were in charge at that time," Sieder says. "We were pretty cautious who we dealt with and how we dealt with them."

The transition to civilian control took three or four days. On their first day in a town, the soldiers would patrol. The next day, they began joint patrols with Panamanian police. Finally, the soldiers would give the Panamanians sidearms and allow them to patrol on their own.

From his observations, Sieder concluded that the Panamanians themselves seemed the best judges of authority. The soldiers watched and listened to see whom the townspeople hissed at, and whom they applauded. Thus emerged the bad guys, who were removed from responsibility as much as possible, and the good guys, who ended up running the city, if only temporarily. Eventually mayors of cities and towns throughout Panama, sometimes those already in power, were appointed by Ricardo Arias Calderón, Endara's vice president and minister of justice. U.S. helicopters would ferry the new local leaders between Panama City and their city or town, in some cases with special forces to provide security.

The Panamanians proved to be less adept at judging what was needed to restore their city or town to normal. So many things—from basic commodities to expensive machinery—were needed to heal Panama after years of hoarding and corruption led by Noriega. U.S. forces, responsible for establishing security in hundreds of localities over tens of thousands of square miles, had to have a way to reasonably judge what shape a town was in. With that in mind, 2d Brigade developed an evaluation system to analyze dozens of cities, towns and villages where its personnel were assigned.

"There is no format for these kinds of things, so we did what people would normally do: improvise," Burney says.

Every two weeks, he would receive from his troops an overall rating of each locality—red, yellow, or green, in decreasing order of trouble. The soldiers based this broad measure on more than twenty categories of municipal well-being, which they devised after realizing their mission would be far more complex than they anticipated. The criteria for judgment included success in rounding up most-wanted persons; reliability of the mayor; the presence of drugs; the presence of weapons caches; state of the PDF; sanitation; medicine; mail; grocery stores; media; banks and business; and a host of other standards by which a U.S. soldier could rate a community.

The ultimate aim was to decide if it was time to pull the infantry out, leaving only special forces if necessary to start the process of redeveloping the country at the local level.

Far from meeting resistance, U.S. personnel found themselves flooded with good will as they took stock of Panama's hinterlands. They basked in the hospitality of the more remote provinces.

Helicopter pilots from the 7th Division's 3d Battalion, 123d Aviation Regiment, have not yet forgotten the old man in David who kept them supplied with coconuts. He did nothing all day, in fact, but cut coconuts off the trees with his machete. Every afternoon around four-thirty he would bring the pilots a wheelbarrow full of coconuts to eat.

The citizens of Panama also wanted to supply information: an endless stream of leads, rumors, and gossip. Some of it was useful. Much of it was self-serving, however, and became a nuisance for intelligence teams. "People loved to talk," says CW3 Grover McFerran, an intelligence specialist with 7th Division's 107th Military Intelligence Battalion, who was assigned to 2d Brigade operations. Set up in an air-conditioned building in David, McFerran and other intelligence troops would listen to whatever local residents had to say. Many Panamanians brought the soldiers food and beverages, along with stories of stealth and intrigue.

"A lot of it was not good information," McFerran says. "People reported on their neighbors. They'd pay each other back."

Weapons, too, came pouring in when the command announced a few days after the invasion that the military would pay a dollar for each weapon turned in. The cash-for-weapons program produced arms of "just about every description . . . unbelievable things," recalls Col. James Wright, commander of 7th Division Support Command, who had the responsibility of hauling the weapons to a central collection point, sorting through them, and checking them for safety to be shipped back to the States. U.S. forces recovered as many as fifty thousand firearms and hundreds of tons of ammunition in the first six weeks they were in Panama.

"Most of them were AK-47s," Wright says. In addition, "There were a number of crew-served weapons—mortars, machine guns, rocket launchers." A large number of T-65 rifles, a Taiwanese imitation of the M16, also turned up. Add to that sniper rifles, Uzis, pistols, and revolvers, and U.S. forces realized that the Panamanians had the makings of a war, but not the will to fight. There was also a prosaic assortment of antiques: Springfield O-3s of World War I vintage, World War II–era M1 Garands, M1 carbines, and even sabers. "A lot of it was in real bad shape," Wright says. "It was loose: rockets sticking out of rocket-propelled grenades, hand grenades with the pin pulled, rubber bands around it."

One 7th Division major was critically injured when a weapon exploded in his face. He survived, but the accident cost him the rest of his Army career; his injuries forced him to leave the service.

By the end of the first week in January, 2d Brigade located sixteen weapons caches and handed out more than $105,000 in the arms-for-dollars effort. As much as possible, troops tried to locate caches before offering cash for weapons to avoid paying thousands of dollars to recover, gun by gun, what they could seize without paying a dime. They didn't always get to the caches in time although reports of caches came in fast and furious. "People loved to report those because they sounded great, and they thought they'd be paid for the number of weapons," McFerran says. "So if they heard a rumor, they'd field it into a really good story."

The flood of intelligence, combined with a gradual tightening of the rules of engagement, discouraged soldiers from pursuing many spurious leads. At first, U.S. soldiers were authorized to detain essentially anyone who looked suspicious and take them to an interrogation point for questioning. Although they generally had enough to do without unnecessarily chasing after suspicious persons, some were uncomfortable with their vague and sweeping authority. "It seemed like there were almost no rules," says Staff Sgt. Mia Swenson of B Company, 107th Military Intelligence Battalion, who worked with the 3d Brigade in Colon. "If you saw somebody that looked suspicious, you could arrest them. If you saw a house that looked suspicious, you could go in." McFerran found the Panamanians surprisingly accommodating; they seemed to feel that searches and questions were all in a good cause.

Around the first of January, the rules changed, for McFerran's unit at least. From that point, soldiers needed confirming reports of enemy holdouts or weapons stashes before they could enter and search. "And at that point, we lost interest, because you could kill yourself" pursuing leads, McFerran says. "We ended up having to have at least two or three reports of the same (lead) before we'd go out and check it out."

Those assigned to the rural provinces of Panama found they were in charge of their own intelligence operations. Centralized intelligence gathering became impossible with the flood of information coming into dozens of remote outposts. "I would say the processing and gathering of intelligence was the biggest single problem," says Lt. Col. Bob Phillips, 2d Brigade executive officer. "We had overwhelming sources of information . . . four hundred people coming in in one hour."

There was rarely time to filter the intelligence reports through higher headquarters, Phillips says, nor to wait for intelligence from above before pursuing leads. Intelligence units at Joint Task Force headquarters in Panama City typically provided "far, far less than what we needed." "The intelligence we needed, you had to generate for the most part by yourself." For example, in order to track down names of people on the blacklist or cronies of the local PDF, full names, ages to differentiate between Panamanians with the same last name, names of mistresses, property they owned, and addresses, including that of the person's mother were needed. Fugitive Panamanians, soldiers quickly figured out, were most likely to seek refuge with best friends, mistresses, or their mothers.

Details such as addresses proved impossible to get from task force headquarters, Phillips says. "The way we got it was, just open the phone book and read it." Once again, the telephone came through for the soldiers, who simply used the phones and directories in the PDF cuartels.

Once the shooting was over, it became clear that getting Panama back on its feet would be a massive job.

Every kind of transportation was in short supply in Panama, as the soldiers with 2d Brigade discovered when they fanned out around the country. Even after about a dozen additional 7th Division Black Hawk helicopters were flown into Panama in January, the nation-building mission suffered an acute shortage of helicopters and of personnel to unload them.

The helicopter battalions available to Joint Task Force–South, besides having to ferry infantry troops around Panama, had the added task of watching over airports and waterways, particularly rivers around Panama City, with help from the SEALs. Their mission was to keep people on the U.S. military's blacklist from fleeing Panama.

Each helicopter available for transport got maximum use, fortunately with no injury to personnel. Soldiers were packed into helicopters so tightly a crew member would have to lean on the door to shut it. For the air assault on Penonome, 110 soldiers were crammed into two CH-47 Chinook cargo helicopters, each designed to hold about 35. "Needless to say, they were all standing up," says Burney. With so many passengers, rehearsals were critical to loading the helicopter safely; infantry companies practiced getting on and off while the air mission commander briefed the mission.

The cargo-handling crews and equipment could not keep up with the movement of infantry troops around the country. In an effort to make do, soldiers adopted some unconventional ways to deal with the monumental task of unloading, such as tying pallets inside a C-130 to a HMMWV, then driving the HMMWV away from the plane to pull the pallets out. One method used with CH-47s was to have the pilot tilt the helicopter, keeping its nose up and the back tires down, and move forward. "The pilot sort of bumped it along, just like a Cracker Jack box, shaking out cases of Meal Ready to Eats," says brigade logistics officer Maj. Rob Yanichko.

The brigade did not have the hauling capacity it needed, nor were the roads entirely secure. Because of the lift constraints imposed on units that deployed from the States, 2d Brigade had to limit its load to the equivalent of about forty C-141s, one third its requirement. As a result, the brigade had only one-quarter of the vehicles it would normally have—nine or ten, as opposed to thirty-six. For the most part, they were command and control and a few combat vehicles. The support vehicles were mostly ambulances. There were few five-ton trucks with the brigade, and one of those was committed for medical supplies. Most of the lift was oriented towards artillery—one battery for each rifle battalion—which wound up having a relatively minor role in the brigade's overall mission.

The 7th Division was able to tap into several supply sources after arriving in Panama: its own support units that had deployed earlier with 9th Regiment and the 4th Battalion, 17th Infantry Regiment, and the Panama-based 41st Area Support Group. But many trucks had been snatched up for convoys, leaving the Division Support Command (DISCOM) with only a half-dozen cargo trucks in Panama to use in sustaining troop operations. Transportation was "a major challenge" from the beginning, says DISCOM commander Colonel Wright.

Long-range hauling was dependent on C-130s, while short-range hauling was accomplished with a combination of CH-47 slingloads, landing craft, and the few trucks that could be mustered. Where no military transport was available, soldiers became adept at bargaining with Panamanians for their help. Early in its operations, the 7th Division learned how to lease trucks, in the cities as well as the country. Working out of his headquarters at Albrook Air Station in Panama City, Wright mobilized a fleet of twenty Panamanian trucks with drivers, plus fifty general laborers, whom he used for local hauling. The men, directed by a Spanish-speaking Army sergeant, worked for minimal wages—a couple of dollars an hour and three MREs a day—and quickly adopted Army ways. Several put on face paint every day and called Wright "Jefe," or boss.

In the remote regions of Panama, the only trucks available were those that could be rented. Burney's brigade deployed with about $50,000, which was parceled out to various contracting officers with instructions on how to spend it. "There were probably two weeks when that $50,000 was our logistics base," says Maj. Jim Moon, the brigade's operations officer during Just Cause. "We were hiring trucks to transport weapons. We were hiring trucks to transport soldiers. We were getting fuel. Food." Pretty soon the brigade developed a price list; the going rate to have a Panamanian load weapons was $5 and one MRE. Hiring a semi for a day cost $30 and an MRE.

MREs, among the worst military rations can offer, were in tremendous demand in Panama. At one point, the brigade had 2,700 soldiers to feed in remote Panama, not to mention Panamanian workers, captured PDF troops, prisoners of war, detainees, and residents of the penal colony at Coiba Island.

Soldiers also had to bargain with U.S. pilots to bring them fuel at every opportunity, which they stored in fuel bladders. Like the cargo equipment, fuel tankers trailed well behind the infantry's movements. The solution was to persuade C-130 pilots to give up fuel from their tanks that they didn't need to get back to Howard Air Force Base. "As soon as the C-130s would land, we would run up, hook hoses to it, suck out as much fuel as the pilot would let us suck out, and then tell the pilot, 'When you come back, put on more fuel for us to suck back out,'" says Yanichko. Pilots were asked to take cargo, usually weapons turned in by Panamanians, with them back to Panama City. The pilots were remarkably co-operative, Yanichko says. "There was a lot of ad libbing done, but basically when you found a resource, you tapped into it. The logistics support adapted to every operational thing we threw at it." Adds Moon: "Each individual knew what his niche was, and wanted to do as best he could."

Commercial flights into Panama were paralyzed in the wake of the Ranger assault on Tocumen airfield. "We had a lot of debris, a lot of chutes all over the place, so the whole airport closed," says Air Force Master Sgt. Jose Aragon, watch supervisor in the air traffic control tower, 1978th Communications Group. Aragon was given the job of repairing damage at Tocumen—Spectre fire had disabled runway lights, radios, and navigational aids—and organizing its transfer back to Panamanian control. Only airplanes carrying humanitarian supplies were permitted to land while the airport was being restored.

When Aragon moved from Howard to Tocumen on 25 December, having promised to complete his mission within seventy-two hours, he was still getting used to the fact that he was in a war. He stared at the bloodstains inside the terminal, traces of the Ranger assault at H-hour. "You looked at it and said, 'My God, this is real.'"

Nothing in rural Panama prepared the soldiers of the 3d Battalion, 75th Ranger Regiment, for what they found when they assaulted the penal colony of Coiba Island on 28 December.

It was a scene straight out of the movie *Papillon*. The tiny island, south of Chiriqui province, was a desperate place, surrounded by shark-infested waters. The penal colony, which shared the island with a jungle training school, held those criminals Noriega's government deemed least redeemable, including murderers, robbers, and some of the participants in the unsuccessful 3 October coup attempt.

To punish them, Noriega had ordered administrators of the penal colony to prepare a site called Camp Machete for the most dangerous of the coup plotters, according to Cisneros. The camp would consist of small wooden shacks where prisoners could be chained at night. So hopeless was Coiba that a small cemetery had been cleared where, Noriega said, all the prisoners would be buried.

No families were allowed to visit. In Panama prisoners traditionally were fed by their families, who brought meals to them, but the prison colony raised its own food—pigs, cows, and vegetables—in about two-dozen outlying prison farms. Horses were the only means of transportation to some of the farms, since the roads were not passable.

Because of the presence of political prisoners and the potential danger of the truly hardened criminals, the island became a target for U.S. forces. The command wanted to liberate the prison with an eye to incorporating the prisoners whose only crime was opposing Noriega in the new government. Cisneros called the island and found that some of the prisoners had already taken over.

He spoke to Capt. Jorge Balma, whom Noriega had accused of conspiring in the coup attempt. The PDF lieutenant in charge of the penal colony had refused to fight against Balma and other former officers imprisoned by Noriega. Many of the guards were relieved at news of the invasion. Their duty forced them to be away from their families for three to six months at a time, and they had not been paid in months.

The Rangers rounded up the prisoners, who had broken all the locks on their cells. Then they identified the hostile guards and flew them off the island. The Rangers left behind a contingent of civil-affairs personnel and a military police detachment. Two companies and a command element from 7th Division's 2d Battalion, 27th Infantry Regiment, relieved the Rangers on 29 December. With them came the division surgeon, Lt. Col. Robert Bausch, to check out rumors of a dysentery epidemic.

No epidemic existed. Nor did a rumored mass grave. But the squalor was unlike anything the soldiers had ever seen. The penal colony held at least 375 prisoners in grass huts, packed 20 to a hut,

Bausch says. The entire prison used one toilet, which emptied directly into the Pacific Ocean through a long tube. People swam next to the sewage outlet. Medical care consisted of one doctor in one room with twenty box-springs for beds. The doctor gave pills only. Bausch brought with him pills, injectibles, asthma mist meters, and other basics.

For five days, U.S. soldiers tried to create a semblance of decency in the prison colony. Lt. Col. Jeff Rock of the 2/27 Infantry, who became the interim penal administrator, was struck by how ghastly life was in such an idyllic setting. "It was a beautiful island. If they cleared the penal colony off, it would be a Club Med," says Rock, who under the circumstances could not wait to leave Coiba.

Before he could leave, he had to convince SOUTHCOM that the remaining prisoners were under control and a guard force well-established. Finally, after a successful briefing on the penal colony's situation by a lieutenant in the guard force, Rock's battalion departed, leaving the guards with pistols to resume their jobs. Of the U.S. military contingent, only civil-affairs elements remained behind to arrange the handling of the prisoners' legal cases.

An equally strange experience awaited 2d Brigade in Darien province, the easternmost region of Panama.

The brigade set up headquarters in Santa Fe, the provincial capital, with subordinate command posts in La Palma and Yaviza, where the Pan American Highway comes to an end. The only paths of maneuver beyond the highway were rivers and valleys. Movement through the thick jungle canopy was impossible. "We were convinced that dinosaurs lived down there," says Lieutenant Colonel Phillips. Maps, in many cases, were unheard of. Relying on local advice for navigation provided unwise, as the information often was inaccurate.

The soldiers gazed at the Indians, wearing loincloths and bones through their noses, and thought they had stepped into the pages of *National Geographic.* "We were at the end of the world," Lieutenant Colonel Rock says.

Helicopter pilots ferrying troops for the brigade navigated by dead reckoning—flying so many minutes in a particular direction, reporting in, and flying so many minutes in another direction.

Radio communication, too was impossible in some remote areas.

Before moving forward to set up a command post, a unit would send a scout helicopter to locate telephone lines. Again, the telephone became a soldier's best friend, when it was available. From Santa Fe southeast to the Colombian border, there were no telephones. "We quickly realized that telephones were a major asset," says 2d Brigade commander Colonel Burney. Phone change became a supply item of critical importance.

So removed was the province of Darien from the invasion that one farmer did not even know who Noriega was. "If we'd told this guy that he was living in Colombia, he would have believed it," says Staff Sgt. John Kuzmak, who encountered the man on a long-range reconnaissance mission for 2d Brigade shortly after Christmas. The six-man reconnaissance team had stopped the man to ask him if he had seen any armed activity in the area. The farmer had a question of his own. Kuzmak says he asked: "Who is this Manuel Noriega and why do you want him, anyway?"

Several days later, Noriega was in the custody of U.S. drug enforcement agents.

The papal nuncio, Monseigneur José Sebastián Laboa, had convinced him that he could not hope to accomplish anything by remaining indefinitely in the nunciature at Punta Paitilla.[1] The Vatican embassy was prepared to order Noriega to leave if he did not do so willingly, and Noriega would risk his life by striking out on his own. It was clear from the U.S. troops and massive, chanting crowds outside, waving signs with messages such as "Death to the Hitler," "Now We Are Free," and "Justice for the Tyrant," that Noriega had little hope of regaining power—certainly not without considerable bloodshed. His options had simply run out.

Senior U.S. commanders, notably Cisneros, had kept up constant pressure on the nuncio to release Noriega. Rock 'n' roll, blaring for three days straight from U.S. loudspeakers outside the nunciature, electrified the crowd gathered to ridicule Noriega, although the loud music in fact was aimed at preventing reporters stationed on hotel balconies overlooking the embassy from eavesdropping on conversations below. The nuncio finally asked the U.S. military to cease the racket for the sake of his sleep. Noriega, however, had no problems sleeping in his austere room inside the nunciature, despite the fact that the nuncio had shut off the air conditioning.

When he finally gave himself up to U.S. military authorities on 3

January, Noriega looked stunned and submissive. Wearing his PDF uniform —his condition of surrender—he walked onto a plane bound for Hurlburt Field, Florida. As a video camera captured his last movements on Panamanian soil, Noriega patted his hair and then his stomach self-consciously. Then he listened in sheepish silence as Drug Enforcement Administration agents instructed him to step into a dressing room and change into plain coveralls.

A military doctor stepped forward to examine the deposed general for the record as DEA agents catalogued his personal effects. Item by item, an agent patted down Noriega's clothing and laid it down neatly for photographing: a crisply starched uniform shirt with stars on the epaulets, photographed several times; uniform pants; white and red jockey shorts; a watch; a handkerchief; a beaded necklace; and cash.

Noriega stepped out of the dressing room in his coveralls and put his hands up obediently so an agent could wrap a chain around his waist for the trip to Florida. The cunning dictator clearly was not in command here.

After the initial relief at Noriega's flight into the nunciature, the reaction among U.S. soldiers to Noriega's arrest was more subdued.

"A lot of folks were tired. People were relieved, but it wasn't champagne corks," says Capt. Mark Solseth, commander of 7th Division's A Company, 7th Medical Battalion. "My biggest fear was that we'd go down there, kill a bunch of people and then Noriega would disappear and there'd be egg on the faces of U.S. troops."

While Noriega headed for a Miami jail cell to face trial on drug-trafficking charges, U.S. troops in his country encountered the drug problem firsthand, only to find that their hands were tied.

The closer the troops got to Colombia, the closer they got to drugs, confronting them with a mission even murkier than rebuilding a country. Their responsibility in the drug war was undefined.

Drugs, once at the forefront of U.S. policy toward Panama, had become a secondary issue in the post-invasion sweep. In Colon and Panama City, soldiers found a number of sizable drug stashes, from a couple of trashcans stuffed with garbage bags full of marijuana to $2 million worth of heroin packed in two thousand plastic sandwich bags and left in the weeds of a deserted alley. The drug seizures usually were accidental, a by-product of weapons raids or arrests.

Officially, the U.S. military mission in Darien was to show the presence in an area where the PDF was still acting like a military force, Phillips says. The two to three hundred PDF remaining in Darien still wore their military uniforms and decorations. They still raised and lowered the flag ceremoniously. In the towns, they continued to push their weight around. In a region where fresh water is in short supply, they held water pumps hostage. "They were still basically harassing the citizens, stealing things from them," Burney says.

But in terms of numbers and weaponry, the PDF in Darien was not much of a threat, Burney felt. He believed U.S. soldiers could deal with this isolated problem simply by making their presence known, reminding the PDF that they were no longer in control of the country and evaluating the chain of command to determine who should remain in authority.

The PDF put up no resistance to the gringos. Burney was more concerned about reducing the long-term threat of drugs to the stability of the new Panamanian government. His soldiers repeatedly stumbled across evidence of drug trafficking, particularly of cocaine. The province was a known thoroughfare for drug shipments from Colombia to North America. But the soldiers had no authority to pursue drugs at their source, the processing laboratories.

They received a briefing from Drug Enforcement Administration officials in the former PDF garrison at Panama Viejo on what cocaine-processing laboratories might look like, but with the understanding that the DEA would act on any information gathered. "The brigade received no guidance," Phillips says. "We had no overt mission to track down the narcotics traffickers, nor did we." Which is not to say Burney did not want to. He was itching to develop further the leads that kept falling into his soldiers' laps.

The brigade tread a gossamer-thin line at times in its activities in Darien. Burney occasionally sent soldiers, their nametags removed, to watch areas of suspected drug activity. At one point the Joint Task Force command got wind of one of his proposed operations that also involved surveillance of drug factories in Darien and threatened to cancel the entire mission, Burney says. He assured the command he had no intention of sending his soldiers to take on drug lords, and revised his plans.

Burney never knew what became of the intelligence his troops gathered. The brigade turned over its intelligence to the Joint Task

Force, which in turn had the responsibility of turning it over to the DEA. It was one of the most frustrating aspects of Just Cause that the brigade was unable to act on its leads, Burney says. "I think we could have pursued some of the leads and produced hard results. But we were forbidden to even be looking for those kinds of things.

"The drug thing kept coming out, again and again and again, to the point where we couldn't ignore it. But we couldn't go after it."

By the end of January, when most Americans thought Just Cause was over, Burney wanted to stay in the Panamanian countryside for another week or two. He felt the job of weeding out bad influences was not finished. With the rules of engagement becoming increasingly restrictive, Burney felt he was losing valuable time to pursue loose ends, such as leads on hidden ammunition in Chiriqui.

The brigade had developed a plan for rapid deployment of its task force to any hot spot within Panama. The task force implemented the plan once, flying out to David from 15 to 18 January for a series of missions. "We showed whoever might be doubting our resolve or commitment that we could very quickly put this operation together," Burney says.

He did not get his wish to remain in western Panama. The brigade was pulled back to Panama City to support the peacekeeping operation, which Burney thought was a waste of his soldiers' time considering that the PDF in Panama City had largely been routed. The violence in that city "wasn't a threat," he says, just "some idiots with weapons."

"Our attitude was very simple," says Lt. Col. Bob Phillips, brigade executive officer. "And that was, if there was a mission to have three infantry battalions do, fine, then we'd do it. But what we found ourselves doing was a significant amount of public works."

Operations in Panama City and Colon were, in fact, more conventional than in the more remote provinces, but no less demanding.

The MPs set up police precincts in Panama City based on battalion sectors of responsibility. In each precinct, a magistrate was named, a jail established, and joint patrols begun. The patrols, operating twenty-four hours a day, continued to operate checkpoints. The 1st Brigade of the 82d Airborne and the Manchu Brigade of 7th Division had responsibility for Panama City, while the 7th Division's 3d Brigade was in charge of Colon.

The soldiers in Panama City had the advantage of Sheridan tanks in their efforts to dig out the remaining resistance, which included snipers positioned on the roofs of buildings to fire down on the infantry in the streets. The purpose of the tanks in clearing the city was chiefly a show of force. The tank drivers would shine their searchlights on buildings from which they were taking fire, while the infantrymen prepared to take out the snipers.

Not that the tanks were invulnerable. Lt. Col. Jim Granzioplene, commander of 3d Battalion, 73d Armor Regiment, the 82d Airborne unit that supplied the Sheridans, worried that they would make inviting targets for the enemy. Granzioplene arranged with Col. David Hale, commander of the Manchus, to have some of his men provide security for the Sheridans.

Working with tanks was a relatively new experience for the 7th Division light infantrymen. It was a successful match, Granzioplene says. When the tanks moved in and shone their lights, the firing stopped. Snipers would take flight, exposing themselves to 7th Division snipers on nearby rooftops. "The Sheridan, by this time, had gained a pretty good reputation in Panama," the armor commander says. "Guys did not want to mess with a Sheridan."

In Colon, Maj. Luis Guardia became the new police commander, just a few days after surrendering to U.S. forces.

The reincarnation of Guardia, former commander of the PDF 8th Infantry Company, stunned Capt. Barry Keith, deputy provost marshal of the 7th Infantry Division and the MP adviser to Task Force Atlantic. Keith went to an elementary school next to the Colon municipal building to talk to Guardia about the establishment of a joint U.S.-Panamanian police station, to find that Guardia had mustered a number of ex-PDF naval infantrymen in military formation. Many of the former PDF troops had just been released from the central prisoner-of-war camp at Empire Range.

Under Guardia's leadership, "They had already been formed up. They had platoon sergeants designated," Keith recalls. "It shocked me quite a bit. I never really felt threatened, but it didn't seem to be the proper way to do it." He later learned that Joint Task Force Panama had scrubbed plans for the MPs to screen all new Panamanian police. There wasn't time. The country needed a police force immediately.

But, in another twist that would occur frequently in the building of the new government, Guardia's name was added to the most-wanted list after his initial release from U.S. custody. He was arrested and replaced a few days after taking charge.

In Colon and its suburbs as in Darien, former members of the PDF "still thought they were the PDF, saluting each other and the flag, yelling at civilians," says 1st Lt. Jimmy McConico, leader of 2d Platoon, 7th MPs.

While the PDF did not present a serious challenge to U.S. forces, it took about two weeks and a concerted public-relations effort for the people of Colon to trust any police agency. The new Panamanian police force announced a bicycle registration program, an American invention aimed at deterring thieves but, more importantly, at improving the image of Panamanian law and order.

The MPs, spreading out from Colon, made it a point to stop and talk to citizens in the city and adjacent communities of Sabanita and Buena Vista, while members of the Panama-based 549th MP Company stayed behind in Colon as a stabilizing force. "We would get out of the vehicles, buy things from them, and talk to them about anything," says Specialist Bruce MacWhorter, a member of McConico's platoon. Gifts of MREs helped. Gradually the citizens came to trust these soldier-police.

Meanwhile, the city jail, next to Military Zone 2 headquarters, had to be filled. With a capacity for 175 to 200 prisoners, the jail held 400 to 450—until the U.S. invaded, whereupon the PDF released and armed the prisoners to create confusion. It fell to the MPs to round up the prisoners again, using what records they could reconstruct from the police station, with help from informants and former PDF troops who had joined the new police force. Many prisoners with little time left to serve surrendered. Others, proclaiming their innocence, gave themselves up in the hope that the Americans would give them a fairer shake than their Panamanian captors had. The rest had to be arrested again and returned to what the soldiers nicknamed "Fort Apache."

The prisoner-of-war cage at Fort Davis filled more rapidly. It was barely finished on the afternoon of D-day when the first of what would be thirteen hundred prisoners, including eight hundred PDF, started to arrive. After the road to Panama City was secured, the prisoners were transferred to Empire Range. Every day, as soldiers

swept the streets of Colon, another two to three hundred prisoners—PDF, most-wanted suspects, and curfew violators, for the
most part—were sent south to Empire Range.

With the additional responsibilities of organizing a new police
force and managing the city jail, the MPs were hard-pressed to pursue all the leads and sightings reported to them. Reports of Dignity
Battalions, armed with AK-47s, were rampant.

Feeding the prisoners in Colon was a lesson in itself. Panama's
penal system did not include meals for prisoners. They had to rely
on their families and friends for food. When Army officials learned
this, they stopped giving the prisoners MREs, only to find a riot on
their hands. Col. Keith Kellogg, commander of Task Force Atlantic,
was incredulous. "We had to wean them off the MREs."

Even the MPs, professional peacekeepers at home, were not fully
equipped to confront the task of reestablishing law and order in an
essentially friendly country. "It was come as you are," says Sgt. Maj.
James Banks of the 7th MPs. "A lot of people had no idea, 'Where
do I start?'"

Just as infantry company commanders found themselves the new
mayors of remote cities, the MPs were thrust into the position of
organizing a police force from scratch. The template for Colon's
new force was a 1977 organizational chart of the Columbus, Ohio,
police department, which Captain Keith, deputy provost marshal of
the 7th Division, had kept from his studies at Ohio State University.

"It had the same name as Colon," says Keith, who fell back on
his college criminology textbooks to plan the new force. "It was the
only thing I could think of." His wife, Kathy, read him the organizational chart over the phone from their home at Fort Ord,
California.

Leopoldo Benedetti, the provincial governor of Colon, received
daily briefings from U.S. personnel on such measures of progress as
who was in the jail and who had been arrested.

Although many of the new Panamanian police bridled at having
to work under U.S. direction, their own safety was their primary
concern. Accustomed to relying on force for authority, they were
chagrined at having to relinquish their AK-47s after the invasion.
As policemen in the new government, they received .38 caliber
revolvers.

Feeling undergunned without assault rifles, the Panamanian police grudgingly accompanied U.S. soldiers as they cleared buildings in search of suspects or weapons, but they insisted the soldiers go first. "They had lost a lot of face," says Kellogg. "And frankly, I think they were afraid to go out in the street because there were still people looking to beat the hell out of them. They just wanted us there for protection."

At the same time, U.S. MPs found their law-enforcement authority diminishing as the Endara government tried to establish its own authority. In the early days of the invasion, "We were trying to build a democracy, but rights really didn't have a whole lot to do with it. We kind of acted first, " McConico says. After the first week of the invasion, soldiers no longer had the power to arrest anyone carrying a weapon, or appearing suspicious. MPs were ordered to take sworn statements in support of arrests, a practice intended in part to set a new standard for the Panamanian police.

Medically, too, Panama had much to learn from U.S. soldiers. And U.S. soldiers had a lot to learn about medical relief operations.

The Army Medical Department found itself writing a new chapter in military medicine within hours of the first shots fired. Message traffic from Panama made it clear the military was going to have to take responsibility for more than just military casualties, the only kind that had been thoroughly addressed in plans for Just Cause.

The majority of the wounded were treated by members of the 44th Medical Brigade, part of the XVIII Airborne Corps's 1st Corps Support Command, then evacuated in C-130s and C-141s to military hospitals in San Antonio as soon as possible. Triage and stabilizing treatment took place in a tent hospital at the north end of a runway at Howard Air Force Base.

Gorgas Army Community Hospital, on Ancon Hill, played an unexpectedly significant role in treating U.S. casualties. It had been written out of contingency planning because of longstanding friction between the hospital's Army management and its Panamanian employees. Another danger was that the PDF occupied a portion of the same building, walled off from the hospital. It was just too risky, SOUTHCOM planners thought, to rely on a hospital that was open to assault, sitting in the middle of Ancon Hill below Quarry Heights. Unlike SOUTHCOM headquarters at the top of the hill,

Gorgas had no permanent fence or barrier to protect it, although it was guarded by soldiers in armored personnel carriers from 4th Battalion, 6th Infantry Regiment, 5th Infantry Division (Mechanized), based at Fort Polk. Security had stepped up considerably since the 3 October coup attempt; at one point, the mechanized infantrymen, bearing M16s, stared down Panamanian demonstrators who attempted to remove unwieldy concrete sewer pipes set up as a defensive barrier. Demonstrators taunted the soldiers in an unsuccessful attempt to provoke a violent reaction.

A combat hospital had been set up in the medical clinic known as Building 519 on Fort Clayton, in case the staff of Gorgas was forced to evacuate. That never happened, although the hill did come under ineffective mortar fire. Contrary to expectations in SOUTH-COM, many of the Panamanian staff of Gorgas braved the violence to go to work when the invasion began. The first casualties treated there were Panamanian. Among them was a PDF soldier who had been shot in the foot. He and a fellow PDF member had commandeered the car of a Panama Canal Commission employee to get to Gorgas, but surrendered when they saw the APCs of the 5th Mech lined up around the hospital. A ward and clinic were designated specifically for prisoners of war, with U.S. military police posted to guard them. The hospital wound up treating 40 percent of the U.S. wounded, in addition to 250 Panamanian civilians.

Keeping soldiers supplied for civic action projects became the biggest challenge of the medical mission in Just Cause. Requisitions flew through FAX machines in the Army Medical Department. Millions of dollars were spent "without a single question as to whether it was appropriate," says Dr. (Col.) David Sa'adah, the department's clinical advisor for health care operations. "It was a completely new concept for the Army to get into this field so fast, so intensively."

Troop medical units visited all the public hospitals and clinics in Panama's major cities, evaluating their condition and delivering basic supplies such as drugs, instruments, and sterile needles. At Panama City's Santo Tomas and Social Security hospitals, medical personnel found that sanitary standards were extremely low, equipment hadn't been maintained and looters had helped themselves to anything in sight. "Literally they were short on everything," says Capt. Larry Stallings, a logistician with 7th Division's 7th Medical Battalion.

The morgue at Santo Tomas, where Panamanian casualties were taken, was unrefrigerated, according to 7th Division surgeon Bausch. The refrigeration unit was broken. So advanced was the decomposition of bodies that identification by sight was impossible in some cases, further confusing the accounting of casualties. "In that heat, I would think in a day or two, it would become very difficult to identify a body from features," Bausch says.

The PDF suffered no medical deprivations. At the PDF clinic on Fort Amador, "You could see a lot of the cabinets had been fully stocked," says Capt. Mark Solseth, commander of A Company, 7th Medical Battalion. The X-ray and dental equipment was state-of-the-art. But downtown, the clinics were empty.

Panamanians could not get enough from U.S. medics assigned to evaluate the needs of Panama's health care system. Panama had plenty of doctors but no supplies. The U.S. had the supplies, although they had to be ordered in most cases from the States. "I'd get about four or five people at one time, telling me what's wrong with them," says 1st Lt. William Andino of A Company, 7th Medical Battalion. "They didn't want us to leave." In the background, Andino could hear hospital officials discussing in Spanish, apparently unaware he could understand them, how much new equipment they could get from the U.S.

But U.S. medical aid probably paid for itself in intelligence. Counterintelligence teams were dispatched with MEDCAPs, the medical civic action programs that operated street clinics throughout Panama. Soldiers in 7th Division alone treated seven thousand Panamanians in street clinics. Women and children flocked to the clinics for treatment of acute and chronic conditions, from colds to ringworm. In the Indian villages, anyone old enough to have teeth had bad teeth, no doubt because sugar cane was a staple of their diet. "They would come, and as they would warm up to us, we would ask them questions. We would generate a lot of information that way," Colonel Burney says.

Family doctors and physician assistants, while of limited value in patching up combat injuries, found their niche in follow-on operations, particularly in treating the more than three thousand Panamanians who sought shelter in refugee camps because their homes had been destroyed by fighting and vandalism. Family doctors formed the backbone of the mobile clinics deployed with the infantry. Physician assistants, who before Just Cause had only cared for soldiers, also were invaluable in providing basic family medical care.

Sanitation quickly became a major element of the U.S. military's public-health effort in Panama. Army engineers learned that Colon had three pumping stations to move the city's sewage to treatment plants, but none of the pumps worked. They had been broken for five years. In many cases, sewage ran right into the street.

Bausch found that the kitchen in Colon's newest hospital had no stove, so the hospital used the stove in the old hospital, located next door. It was a decrepit gas stove, crawling with roaches. And, if people tracked blood through the kitchen from the morgue next door, that could not be helped.

Based on their experience with stability operations, medical specialists came away from Operation Just Cause convinced that the Army needs to develop a ready-to-ship medical aid package for Third World contingencies. The package would include pharmaceuticals, basic supplies such as bandages and splints, and Third World items such as drugs for malaria, ringworm, and other parasitic conditions.

"We have a lot to learn about civil-military operations," Bausch says. "Basically our mission is to treat soldiers: stop bleeding, build blood volume, and evacuate."

After the battles were fought and won, it became a matter of debate who should assume the role of seeing Panama through to stability. The infantry was not accustomed to mop-up operations, and the personnel trained in peacekeeping and civil action—MPs, civil affairs, and special forces—were in short supply. In the end, soldiers in all specialties shared the burden, but their experience was far from ideal.

The burden thrust upon the military was partly of its own making. Because of the warplanners' desire to keep the invasion a secret, the State Department was shut out of its traditional foreign-assistance role until after U.S. forces had moved on Panama. Newly appointed ambassador Deane Hinton, who had intended to retire from his post as ambassador to Costa Rica before President Bush called on him to head up the embassy in Panama, arrived there on 6 January to find that "the Army was busy implementing a military government."

Having received his new assignment only a week before, Hinton was keenly aware of his lack of preparation to sort through the numerous and often conflicting demands of Panamanian society after the invasion. His conclusion: "There was a major mistake made in the planning. There was no thought that I'm aware of, any civilian inputs to the planning, any consideration of what one does afterwards."

One infantry major who served in the U.S. assault on Grenada wondered where the State Department was when the shooting stopped in Panama. "I didn't see the same effort from the State Department and [the U.S. Agency for International Development] and all those guys that I'd seen in Grenada," says Michael Kerrigan, executive officer of the 7th Division's 5th Battalion, 21st Infantry Regiment, during Just Cause. "And I think, given the situation, we should have been more prepared to do something like that. I'm sure it was obvious to national-level planners at a certain point that Panama was only a matter of time. Whereas Grenada really developed almost overnight."

Kerrigan returned to Panama in April for a normal two-month rotation to find that many of the items local Panamanian leaders had asked soldiers for in January had never arrived. Although he feels he accomplished a great deal just by helping to topple Noriega and the PDF, Kerrigan says he also was frustrated by the U.S. government's "quick-fix" approach immediately after Just Cause. "Okay, the PDF's out, Noriega's out, now what? And it was just kind of, people filling a vacuum on their own."

To Hinton, the decision to swear in Endara, Ford, and Arias Calderon at Fort Clayton was just the first signal that the military, while professing to work towards a nonmilitary government in Panama, saw no harm in managing the new government itself for a time. Nor did Joint Task Force–South see any damaging implications from a swearing-in ceremony on a U.S. military base. "It was considered, but it certainly wasn't thought through in advance," Hinton says. State Department officials, remembering that the U.S. military had educated many PDF officers, saw continued military influence on the new government as jeopardizing its acceptance by the Panamanian people.

Joint Task Force–Panama didn't see it that way. Rather, the command was prepared to call up more civil-affairs personnel from the reserves to handle the rebuilding of Panama. To Hinton, a military uniform was a military uniform.

"This was a free country with a democratic government, and you didn't do it that way," he says. He scaled back plans for more civil-affairs personnel and began developing his own plans to build an aid program virtually from scratch. The embassy staff that would ordinarily have taken on the job had been sent back to the United States after Noriega fired Delvalle.

Thurman let Hinton decide where to assign the civil-affairs personnel that remained in Panama. The ambassador moved them around the country, to the disgruntlement of many Panamanians, who welcomed the soldiers' help and wanted them to stay where they were. In response to Panamanian protests, Hinton relented in some cases.

In the military, the question was which personnel to use, and how many, to "stand up" Panama.

Perhaps MP teams should have gone along with the infantry during the initial process of clearing the cities, then stayed behind to maintain law and order, says Banks of the 7th MPs. "In a low-intensity conflict, you need more MPs than you do infantry, because the MPs can fight as infantry, then they can stay on to reconstruct." In Operation Just Cause, "There just weren't enough MPs," he says. "They were just scattered to the wind," especially in the more populous western regions of Panama.

There is no doubt that the prolonged presence of infantrymen, with all their warrior-like trappings, was not desirable in Panama. The sight of rifle-toting soldiers, camouflaged from their ankles to their eyebrows, could only be a reminder of U.S. aggression and Panamanian weakness. Yet the MPs' approach could also have been more delicate, says one infantry brigade commander.

In the western provinces, MPs took up residence in the old PDF compounds while the infantry company commander set up his command post close to the designated Panamanian local leader, says Burney of 2d Brigade. "They stayed in their police compounds, right away a bad symbol because this was the old PDF compound," Burney says. "And it took a while for them to understand that.

"We worked out of the boroughs into the various areas. They worked out of the compounds into the borough. I think that's a bad tactic for them." Had they devoted more effort to establishing ties with the community, they might have persuaded the citizens to accept the new police force sooner, Burney says.

Burney would have liked to see the infantry units leave sooner, but they could not leave until the town was functioning under civilian control. Besides their natural association with war and unrest, Burney worried that the soldiers would misinterpret the affection and gratitude lavished on them as sexual advances.

Discipline remained tight throughout the brigade's deployment in Panama, with one notable exception that some believe might have been avoided if the soldiers had returned home sooner. On 25 January, more than a month after the invasion, a soldier accidentally shot and killed a Panama City woman. Pfc. Mark McMonagle, of B Company, 5/21 Infantry, was later convicted by court-martial of unpremeditated murder in the death of fifty-year-old Leila Díaz de Panay, making him the first soldier since the Vietnam War to be tried and convicted of murder during a combat operation.[2]

In fact, McMonagle was not engaged in combat when the shooting occurred, although Operation Just Cause did not end officially until 31 January. The court-martial found that McMonagle was helping a fellow soldier, Sgt. Paul Finsel, Jr., cover for the loss of Finsel's pistol in a Panama City bar by shooting into the air. One of those shots killed Díaz de Panay. Finsel, also of B Company, was acquitted of murder but convicted of lesser offenses, including disobeying military orders not to drink alcohol while in Panama. A third soldier in the company, Pfc. Mark Gussen, pleaded guilty to similar charges.

The killing was one of the many things that can go wrong in stability operations, says Capt. John Sieder, commander of B Company. "Stability ops itself is not the ideal infantry operation," he says. "It's a fairly confusing situation, especially the restraint required of soldiers, because we are not trained to exercise that kind of restraint."

Still, only three Panamanians, including Díaz de Panay, were killed at the hands of 2d Brigade soldiers, who had such a large role in "stability operations" in Panama. The other two were shot to death when they ran a roadblock at Rio Hato. Considering that the brigade, more than two thousand strong, was spread out over forty to fifty towns in heavily armed, squad-sized groups, the numbers translate into a highly disciplined use of firepower.

Joint Task Force–Panama sent the bulk of the combat troops home by mid-February. On 8 January, the 82d Airborne's 3d Battalion, 504th Infantry Regiment, arrived home after a month in Panama, the first divisional unit to return. Four days later, having been relieved by soldiers from the 7th Division, two thousand paratroopers made their homecoming jump into Fort Bragg.

Gradually, the 7th Division pulled back its forces in rural Panama, turning over the U.S. role to the special forces. A month later, the first 7th Division troops to go home received a similar welcome at Fort Ord. Commanding General Cavezza conducted a division review. Arriving soldiers basked in the appreciation of their community, which bestowed them with such welcome gifts as food, drink, motel rooms, and football tickets.

As quick a victory as Just Cause was, it was just as quickly forgotten at home. Soldiers who stayed behind in Panama to continue stability operations arrived home to find Panama was old news. "There was no music, no parades," says a bemused Maj. Dennis O'Driscoll, operations officer for 2d Battalion, 27th Infantry Regiment. Arriving in California, "We got on the bus and the bus driver said, 'Where you guys coming from?'"

The soldiers have not forgotten the difficulties of rebuilding Panama. Pfc. Kevin Grullon of the 3/504 Infantry was left with this lasting impression: "If we ever go back to war, it'll probably be back to a city."[3] A year later, Grullon's unit was in Saudi Arabia, preparing for a ground war to drive Iraqi occupation forces from Kuwait. Although that war clearly eclipsed Just Cause, it drew on some of the lessons learned in Just Cause about liberating a foreign country.

Yet the Army's experience in Panama raised as many questions as answers about the infantry's role in policing a foreign country, friendly or hostile. The infantry, for the most part, would have preferred to leave Panama when the combat was over and leave the peacekeeping mission to special forces and MPs.

Burney believes special forces are the ideal soldiers to prop up a foreign country. "They have the linguistic, cultural understanding of what's going on," he says. "The MPs simply didn't have that kind of an understanding. I think we handed it off to them at about the right time."

While attacking and clearing buildings in an urban environment has become a staple of light-infantry training, most infantry commanders would prefer not to take on the murkier responsibilities of stabilizing a country, from searching suspicious persons to assessing the public health. Nor would many soldiers. "I don't think that should be a part of our mission," says Sgt. Henry Howard of 7th Division's B Company, 4th Battalion, 17th Infantry Regiment. "We should have been relieved by MPs." At the same time, recognizing the likelihood he will be called upon for a similar mission, Howard says, "We need some training on that."

Like it or not, Operation Just Cause gave soldiers a glimpse of what to expect if the military is to assume a greater role in post-combat civic action projects. Not every people whose leader the United States seeks to overthrow will provide as friendly a laboratory as Panama did for training in stability operations. The job of rebuilding a larger or more hostile nation can only be more difficult.

"We need to put a lot of time and effort and resources into it," says Lt. Col. Johnny Brooks, commander of the 4/17 Infantry. "You need to expose your soldiers to as many situations as possible. It's a matter of education."

Epilogue: The Makings of a Success

When the last of the invasion force returned to the United States in February, they left Panama in economic and social collapse, but with hopes for a stable democracy.

Some ten thousand Panamanians were left homeless by the onslaught, their houses and apartments destroyed by fighting and arson. The high-rises of El Chorrillo, charred concrete shells in a sea of rubble, were grim reminders of the ferocious battle around the Comandancia. Thousands of businesses in Panama City and Colon had been stripped of their merchandise. Some were physically destroyed, some beyond recovery; most would take months to rebuild.

The war was over, but the streets of Panama City and Colon could hardly be called peaceful. The Endara government's new police force, taken largely from the old PDF, was helpless to control citizens who delighted in defying it. Panamanians could not ignore the fact that many new police officers were the same men who, under Noriega, had wielded rubber hoses and clenched fists.

The police had lost their iron grip on Panama, and they didn't like it. Their bitterness was shared by many civil servants, purged by the newly installed government as it attempted to reshape a bureaucracy bloated by Noriega's generous patronage.

The situation came to a head just weeks before the first anniversary of the invasion, when the Endara government had to call in U.S. soldiers to put down a peaceful rebellion by Panamanian police.[1] It was a scene right out of Just Cause: Panamanian policemen lying prone on the street with soldiers pointing their rifles at them.

Crime, borne of frustration and opportunism, quickly got the upper hand in Panama.

Left jobless by the destruction of businesses and the elimination of civil-service jobs, many Panamanians turned to armed robbery to steal what they could not earn. One in three Panamanians in the capital city—in Colon, one in two—was unemployed. Crime and fear threatened to undo what 27,500 soldiers and their families, not to mention most of the Panamanian people, had waited and worked to accomplish: a just and peaceful society.

The police, feeling undergunned with .38 caliber revolvers, could not or would not enforce order. They lacked the firepower to force their will on people, as they had done with the AK-47 assault rifles they carried under Noriega. They also lacked such basic equipment as radios and patrol cars. The U.S. military supplied what it could, but the police had to make do with pickup trucks and beatup police cars.

There was no shortage of arms for criminals, however. The weapons-for-cash program that the U.S. military created after the invasion could not possibly recover all of the pistols and AK-47s Noriega issued to the Dignity Battalions, nor the weapons that Panamanians stole from PDF installations when the invasion began.

Neither fear of being robbed, nor the fact that the new police officers had sworn allegiance to the new government, could induce the average Panamanian to respect the new "policia." Seizing the opportunity to bask in freedom from oppression, Panamanians openly defied the new police.[2]

Here the Endara government suffered the consequences of its decision to build the new police force from the old PDF. Immediately after the invasion, Endara and his U.S. advisers felt they had no choice. Either they could build a police force using former PDF troops under new civilian control, or they could wait months to establish a training academy and create a new police force. The prospect of the entire PDF thrown out of work, angry, and with weapons at their disposal, was more disturbing than a reincarnated PDF.

Opting for a reconstituted police force, the government decided to receive and investigate charges against former members of the PDF, removing them from the force if necessary. The Endara government immediately retired or suspended all of the colonels in the PDF; 83 percent, or fifteen of seventeen, lieutenant colonels, 30 percent of the majors; 31 percent of the captains; 9 percent of the first lieutenants and 10 percent of the sublieutenants.

Sixty of the two hundred who were refused admission to the new Policia Nacional (Panama), or PNP, were jailed. Those who were given jobs in the PNP received no guarantee of immunity from future prosecution of crimes committed under Noriega, although the safe-conduct passes distributed by the Joint Task Force had implied such a promise. For many of the former PDF officers who sought a place in the PNP, the choice was unemployment or a position of respect in the new government.

"If you are perceived the right way, in this work you will always have a job," one former PDF enlisted man said shortly after the invasion force pulled out. Many of the PDF signed up with the new police force after Noriega took refuge in the papal nunciature on Christmas Eve, when it was clear that the dictator no longer had power.

The paychecks proved to be more regular than under Noriega, and the benefits more generous, but the respect never materialized, as the paramilitary personnel discovered when they joined the PNP. Inside the newly designated precinct headquarters on Cerro Tinajitas, where two U.S. soldiers died and eighteen were wounded in an assault during the invasion, the low-ranking former soldier complained of his lack of authority. The PDF routinely intimidated civilians by demanding identification, but the new police force had little success with such tactics.

"You stop them for identification, they say, 'No, I don't give no frigging identification because I am free,'" he said. "In this country, you've got to show them who's the boss of the moment. If you treat them too soft, your life is in danger."

On one wall of the precinct headquarters, a computer-generated poster bore witness to the kind of police force the United States wants Panama to have. Next to an upturned hand full of cash, the word "NO!" was supposed to remind the police officers that graft was no longer an acceptable fringe benefit.

After the invasion officially ended 31 January, the military was legally prohibited from training the new police. U.S. military police, including American police in the Army reserves, continued joint duty with the PNP, however, in the streets and precinct houses of Panama. About two thousand MPs were assigned to joint operations with the PNP in February. Gradually, the soldiers withdrew from the streets to the precinct houses, eventually turning them over to Panamanian control.

The International Criminal Investigative Training Assistance Program, sponsored by the U.S. Justice Department and run by retired FBI and other law enforcement agents, assumed the job of molding a democratic police force, aided by the MPs' observations. Neither the Endara government nor U.S. officials, keenly aware that the U.S. military had trained many of the PDF, wanted the military training the PNP.

U.S. trainers found a Panamanian police force ignorant of such basic democratic procedures as reading prisoners their rights, handcuffing them, conducting searches, and filling out paperwork. Officially, Panama's paramilitary PDF was history. In reality, it would take years to erase the PDF's tradition of brute force.

Public protection is now the responsibility of the Fuerza Publica, or public force. With 11,500 uniformed members, it is 28 percent smaller than under Noriega, when the PDF numbered 16,000, including a trained military of about 6,000. The new Fuerza Publica is authorized 10,764 police officers, including a border patrol; 351 for a civil air patrol to transport government officials and provide emergency evacuation; 340 for a maritime service to act as a coast guard and police Panama's many islands; and one antiterrorist SWAT team of 50 people, the only members of the Fuerza Publica to carry AK-47s, who also are to handle hostage and kidnapping situations.

Police hiring, promotions, spending, procurement, and internal investigations all are under civilian control. The new force also is more compartmented. While Noriega's PDF encompassed a variety of public services, including customs and the postal service as well as law enforcement and national defense, many of those functions were shifted to the new government's Ministry of Government and Justice. The PNP took over responsibility for traffic control from the DNTT, but many of the other traffic functions the DNTT used to control, such as taxi regulations and drivers' licenses, fall under a separate civilian department. The notorious DENI, loosely compared to the FBI, was to become even more like its U.S. counterpart with the establishment of lawyers at its head.

No army, navy, or air force is part of the new government of Panama, leaving it to the United States to defend the tiny country against armed aggression. "We do not anticipate an invasion from anywhere, so why have an Army?" says Raul Arias, comptroller of the Fuerza Publica.

A year after the invasion, joint U.S.-Panamanian police operations were to cease altogether. Then former police chief Eduardo Herrera Hassan, second in a series of four chiefs since Operation Just Cause, threw the Endara government off-balance by escaping from jail and taking over PNP headquarters.

Herrera, surrounded by about fifty policemen loyal to him, staged what he called "a movement . . . not a military coup." Journalists were allowed to come and go during the takeover in what had once been DNTT headquarters, near Albrook Air Station. Describing members of the police force as "humiliated," Herrera said he was seeking greater respect on their behalf.

An aide, confidant, personal bodyguard and admirer of Torrijos, Herrera had been a favorite candidate to lead a U.S.-sponsored coup against Noriega, but no plan ever materialized. He faded into the background until after Just Cause, when he became police chief in the Endara government. But he never reconciled himself to the PDF's loss of power under civilian control, says Cisneros, who talked to him extensively about plans for the new police force.

His rebellion lasted less than a day. At Endara's request, about five hundred U.S. soldiers mobilized to put down the revolt, taking Herrera and dozens of his compatriots prisoner. A month later, USARSO announced MPs would begin "courtesy patrols" with Panamanian police.

As predicted, a flood of charges has rushed in against individuals in the new police force and former members of Noriega's government. Three police chiefs have been ousted, two crimes committed under Noriega, since the Endara government took office. The first was charged with theft of government money; the second with civil-rights violations; and the third with slandering the editor of *La Prensa* by accusing him publicly of incest.

Many more public figures under Noriega stand accused of crimes ranging from extortion to murder, but the court system is paralyzed.[3] More than forty thousand accusations have been filed in Panamanian courts against members of Noriega's government, on charges ranging from outright theft of public property to human rights violations. Rogelio Cruz, attorney general of Panama, had submitted almost fourteen hundred cases for prosecution as of 1 August, 1990. Six months later, not one had come to trial.

"Hundreds of arrest warrants haven't been followed through," according to Otilia Koster, director of the Center for Human Rights Investigation and Legal Aid in Panama City.

Part of the paralysis stems from post-invasion damage. The country's supreme court building was ravaged by fire and looting during the invasion and has remained boarded up. Files on pending cases simply disappeared. The U.S. government for many months denied the Endara government access to still more files—15,000 boxes of documents seized during the invasion—that prosecutors said would help them punish some of Noriega's cronies. In the meantime, many suspects were freed from jail for lack of evidence.

"There has been practically no justice," says Koster. Only the Noriega-era criminals apprehended during the invasion have been jailed, she says, calling the lack of further action "a mockery" of Panama's supposed freedom. Some of those criminals are not getting the punishment they deserve, many Panamanians feel. Koster, for one, was infuriated to see Luis "Papa" Cordoba, for example, formerly a PDF colonel and Noriega's right-hand man, freed from jail to drive himself to a doctor's appointment. No police guard was in sight, she says.

The Panamanian legal system may have to be rewritten, a monumental task begun a year after the invasion, before it will function smoothly. A judge in the United States has the power to admit or dismiss legal arguments. In Panama, a lawyer has a set period of days to present any argument. The opposing lawyer then has a certain number of days in which to present a rebuttal, after which the judge is given another period in which to rule. Critics say the process allows cases to drag on indefinitely.

Outside the confines of U.S. military bases, Americans feel only slightly safer than they did when Noriega's police ruled the streets. Bars, discos, nightclubs, and casinos remained off limits to U.S.

troops for more than a year after the invasion troops returned home.

The restriction was put into effect after the 2 March, 1990 bombing of My Place, a popular Panamanian nightclub. The bomb killed a soldier and injured fifteen U.S. soldiers and twelve Panamanians.[4] It was the first and last night for at least a year that soldiers were allowed to go to downtown bars after hostilities ended. At least three groups claimed responsibility for the bombing, but U.S. military officials called the claims questionable.

U.S. service personnel and their families once again frequent Panamanian stores and restaurants, but they are mindful of the instability in Panamanian society. "During the daytime, I think you're relatively safe, especially if you're where there's a lot of people and you don't carry your money in your purse," says Lettie Raab, wife of Col. Larry Raab, commander of MPs in Panama. The Raabs lived on Fort Clayton.

"After dark, we don't go off post much" because of the large number of armed robberies in Panama, she says. "I think we've gone to one function downtown at night. I'm not in fear for my life or anything like that, but I don't think it's particularly prudent to be out." When Americans go downtown, "they still take their jewelry off," she says.

The fear is not as pervasive as it was under Noriega, however. The first time Raab went to Fort Amador after arriving in Panama in July 1989, a PDF officer trained an automatic weapon on her car. The Raabs went to Amador to enjoy the tranquil ocean view.

The crisis in criminal justice, and the resulting sense of insecurity, have eroded support for the Endara government, despite its landslide victory in May 1989. Demonstrations against the Endara government are a regular event in Panama, although their size is nothing compared to the demonstrations supporting the Endara ticket against Noriega. Furthermore, the violence that greeted previous demonstrations is no longer a regular feature of public dissent.

Now that the dictator is gone, Endara himself is under scrutiny. The new president has hardly endeared himself to the populace by attacking the still-beloved Torrijos in the same breath with Noriega, as equal players in twenty-one years of dictatorship.[5] Members of the Panamanian upper class, Endara and his government ministers are in many of his countrymen's eyes an inept team of rabiblancos, or white tails, elitist members of Panama's oligarchy.

A September 1990 poll commissioned by *La Prensa* brought a resounding vote of no confidence in the new government, particularly the Fuerza Publica.[6] Of eight hundred Panamanians interviewed for the poll, 75 percent expressed no confidence in the new public force. More than half, 57 percent, said it was not a true civilian force. Almost 55 percent said the PNP was the PDF in disguise. A subsequent poll, published six months later, found public faith in the government had only declined.

Those polled were more optimistic about the economy. More than half were certain or somewhat certain that the economy had rebounded in the first few months of 1990. In Panama City, the economic heart of the country, businesses rebounded as soon as the Bush administration lifted economic sanctions. The resurgence came in spite of the insurance industry's refusal to pay a nickel on the losses suffered during the looting, on the grounds that the looting was a result of an act of war.

After the scare of economic sanctions, during which Noriega severely restricted bank withdrawals, the flow of deposits back into the banks has been surprisingly vigorous. Small businesses have popped up everywhere. The situation is not so cheery in Colon, the country's second-largest city and an economic backwater since the canal treaties reduced the U.S. military presence there. Unemployment, widely considered to be Panama's number one economic problem, is estimated to be significantly higher than the national average of 20 percent, and the reopening of businesses has been slower.

As to the prospects for recovery, Panamanians have confidence in the country's economic future, but less faith in their government. A majority is certain the future is quite promising. But the *La Prensa* poll registered serious doubts that the government had a viable economic plan.

Given the recent period of dictatorship in Panama, *La Prensa* president Roberto Eisenmann was not surprised by the poll results. "Everybody in the Endara government is basically an amateur in governance," he says. "These people won an election overwhelmingly, but they did not conquer power. Power fell on them one day."

Eisenmann attributes the Panamanian people's unhappiness to a desire for immediate improvement now that a democratically elected government is in office. "People are now losing patience," he says. "They want to see efficiency and they want to see things happening."

Amid the dissension and criticism of the Endara government, the United States has kept a low profile. Six months after the invasion, SOUTHCOM had sent home all but about ten thousand personnel, the number stationed in Panama before Bush started building up forces in early 1989.

The Military Support Group, formed as the invasion came to a close and Operation Just Cause became Operation Promote Liberty, was scaled back to a handful of officers a year after the invasion.

The military effort contributed more than $25 million worth of labor, equipment, donations, and transportation to build a democratic Panama. Soldiers assisted in, and in many cases organized, road building, school repairs, ditch digging, drainage improvements, medical and dental clinics, and numerous other public-works projects. Such efforts were to continue through the summer of 1991, with U.S. Army National Guard units working jointly with Panama's civilian ministries.

The State Department assumed the lead in rebuilding Panama after the invasion officially ended. The Agency for International Development estimated that 10,000 Panamanians were left homeless during the invasion, although other estimates ranged as high as 25,000. Some of the homeless moved in with family and friends, others to the refugee camp set up at Albrook Air Station. Many government employees were also displaced, their offices scoured by looters who left them without furniture and phones, much less cars or computers.

Congress approved $48 million in emergency aid almost immediately after the invasion, mainly for housing, employment, the recovery of small businesses, and the restoration of public services.

After much debate over the United States's proper role in Central and South America, Congress in April 1990 approved an additional $420 million to help pay off Panama's international debt, provide loans to businesses and start long-term projects designed to strengthen democratic institutions in Panama. The assistance for democratic institutions was intended to take such forms as university programs to train journalists and the overhaul of Panama's court system.

In most of the various aid programs created by the United States, money has started to flow. At least 450 displaced families have moved back into the apartments at El Chorrillo. Hundreds of others have moved into modest cement-block houses built with U.S. aid.

Further U.S. aid to Panama is expected to be on a much smaller scale than after the invasion, although many Panamanians still look to the United States to guide their country through its insecurity. The *La Prensa* poll found that the vast majority of Panamanians are relying on the United States for help.

Ambassador Hinton anticipates additional aid to be "very limited . . . $10 million, $20 million. We said jumpstart, we meant it."

Miraculously, the United States so far has managed to avoid being a lightning rod for Panamanian discontent, says Eisenmann, himself a long-time critic of the United States. Public opinion, in fact, is still very strongly in favor of the *yanquis*.

"I am surprised that nine, ten months after the invasion we still did not have any major anti-U.S. movement or body of opinion at all," Eisenmann says. "We are plainly convinced that the population of Panama considers the U.S. invasion a liberation."

Was the invasion worth it?

Twenty-three U.S. soldiers and 3 American civilians died to rid Panama of Noriega. Another 324 were wounded. At least 314 Panamanians died defending him, by SOUTHCOM's estimate, and half again as many were wounded. The invasion also cost the lives of at least 202 Panamanian civilians, according to a rough count by SOUTHCOM. That estimate immediately came under criticism from human-rights groups, who figured at least 300 civilians died.[7] Reports of several thousand civilians killed or wounded have received little credence.

An uncounted number of Panamanian civilians were wounded in Just Cause. Thousands of Panamanians lost their homes and thousands more their jobs in the destruction of businesses and the reorganization of Panama's civil service.

Even considering the loss of life and livelihood, most Panamanians will say yes. The invasion was worth it. No longer are they subject to the sadistic whims of a brutal dictatorship: the vindictive arrests, the beatings with rubber hoses, the late-night visits by PDF thugs. Noriega, facing trial in Miami for drug trafficking, is out of their lives. Many of his cronies remain in Panama, but without the terrible power they enjoyed before the invasion. Instead of repressing the rights of citizens, the police force is designed to protect them.

For the first time in twenty-one years, Panama has a legitimately elected government with a popular mandate. A supreme court has been established that truly is independent of the government, although it has a long way to go before it operates smoothly. The country's treasury no longer is the personal bank account of the head of government, as it was to Noriega, who impoverished his country to make himself a millionaire. Businesses are coming back to life. The press enjoys new freedom, and diversity of opinion is no longer punished.

If that diversity creates havoc in the new government, that is nonetheless better than the rubber-stamp parliament that existed to serve Noriega.

Panama's crime rate is falling, although it is hard to measure because the government has only recently begun to collect data on crime. In any case, Hinton notes, the murder rate is nowhere near that of many U.S. cities. In short, Panama has all the ingredients of a democracy, although it might take years to reestablish economic and political stability in the country.

Perhaps those could have been achieved in time without the invasion. That is impossible to say with any certainty. But if those who had the most to lose are any judge one year after the invasion, Operation Just Cause accomplished its goals.

Conclusions: Lessons Learned

How to understand Operation Just Cause? Unquestionably an overwhelming military victory, it holds more ambiguous lessons about the role of the armed forces as a tool of U.S. strategy.

It is Gen. Carl Stiner's conceit that there were no lessons learned from Just Cause. Meeting with reporters two months after the invasion or responding to questions about looting, casualties and the F-117 Stealth fighter missions, he maintained that Just Cause justified the training, the doctrine, the quality of U.S. soldiers and their equipment. The overall direction of his Army had been validated, he said.

In the sense that "lessons learned" has come to mean "mistakes made," Stiner is close to the truth, although Just Cause was not error-free. Above all, it is important to understand what made Just Cause unique, and what will stand the test of time, especially for an Army seeking to reshape itself to meet uncertain challenges. Success can be as costly as failure if it blinds the victor to the fleeting nature of victory.

Operation Just Cause marks a significant change of mission for the U.S. Army and, to a lesser extent, its sister services, from containment of the Soviet Union and the defense of western Europe to something less well-defined. Only weeks after the first cracks appeared in the Berlin Wall, Just Cause revealed capabilities that U.S. military forces will need in the evolving post–cold war world. The Army already is sure to be smaller and rely less on forward deployments. It will be called on to resolve political disputes not defined by the certainties of the forty-five-year struggle between the United States and the Soviet Union.

On a strategic level—based on what the United States wishes the world to be—Operation Just Cause represented a break from the heavy focus on containing communism that dominated U.S. policy in the cold war. While there were elements of anticommunism in U.S. policy toward Panama, they were sometimes dwarfed by conflicting theater and regional concerns. Diplomacy is not the focus of this book, but it must be said that U.S. policy towards Panama had become hopelessly entangled in the latter months of the Reagan administration and first months of George Bush's presidency. Noriega was adept at playing the competing goals of U.S. policy against one another while wrapping his own strategy in a less successful appeal to Panamanian nationalism. Panama, as home to U.S. Southern Command, played an important role in regional efforts at containment, as witness SOUTHCOM's role in supplying the Nicaraguan contras and efforts to train the El Salvadoran army. As Noriega's relationship with the United States deteriorated, he turned increasingly to the Cubans and Nicaraguans for help. Cubans advised the PDF and were instrumental in constructing the Dignity Battalions.

But containment has been only a passing influence on U.S. strategy in Panama, compared to the security of the Panama Canal. The United States could not allow this important avenue of commerce to fall into hostile or unpredictable hands, as it would have if Noriega and his newly appointed canal administrator had remained in power. The stability and good will of the government of Panama are vital for U.S. interests after the canal reverts completely to Panamanian control at midnight on 31 December, 1999.

A third and clear goal of U.S. strategy that played a critical role in Just Cause is to ensure the safety of Americans abroad. The cold war aside, protecting Americans abroad is increasingly important as a sign of strength in the face of terrorism and hostage taking. In Panama as in Grenada, this concern provided a casus belli when Marine Lt. Robert Paz was killed on 16 December, 1989.

Beyond the clear beacons of containment, control of the canal and the safety of Americans, U.S. strategy enters the murkier world of the Latin American theater. The United States has always had a fondness for stability in its regional neighbors, but has been ambivalent toward the repressive excesses of autocratic regimes in Guatemala, El Salvador, and Nicaragua. But since the Carter presidency, promoting democracy and human rights has been an important theme of American policy in Latin America, although it has been difficult to reconcile sometimes with containment. As containment of communism becomes less important, human rights are likely to become more so.

How to achieve stability in the western hemisphere without insulting Latin nationalism remains a troublesome issue for U.S. strategists, but one of growing importance throughout the Third World. The principle of nonintervention is particularly important to Latin Americans, and an article of faith for the Organization of American States. Yet the principle has yet to prevent the United States, the region's only superpower, from acing unilaterally. Nonintervention was, however, an inhibiting factor that delayed U.S. military action in Panama. After the invasion, U.S. military advisers went to considerable lengths to avoid charges of "yanqui imperialism," although not far enough from the point of view of U.S. diplomats.

A sixth goal of U.S. strategy, emerging only recently, has been to attack the South American drug trade. Panama is a significant link in the growth, production, refinement, and shipment of cocaine and other drugs. U.S. commitment to the fight has ebbed and flowed, but in recent years it appears that controlling the drug supply, particularly by the Colombian drug cartels, has become a serious, long-term strategic goal that points toward more foreign interventions.

By the last year of Reagan's presidency, these conflicting strategic interests had so confused American policymakers that the State Department and Defense Department were at odds. Against the background of a paralyzed bureaucracy, Reagan was unable to make a decisive choice. Just Cause was such a choice. The operation created new opportunities, but whether the United States can take advantage of them remains to be seen.

By eliminating the PDF, Just Cause removed the institution that controlled Panamanian political life. For twenty-one years military dictatorship proved a robust institution, created and nurtured by General Omar Torrijos and brought to full, if monstrous, flower under Noriega. Hatred of Noriega may have been a driving factor in the Bush administration's policy toward the PDF, but he was very much a creature of the institution. It is hard to imagine Noriega enjoying his sweeping powers without the instrument of the PDF.

To the extent Just Cause eliminated the PDF as an institution—although former PDF troops make up a majority of the restructured public forces—it offered Endara and his country a blank page upon which to compose a new, more democratic and just society. It will take years to write the score, but without Just Cause, it may never have been conceived.

Perhaps with time, the institution of the PDF would have collapsed on itself. That was the hope of those who counseled against U.S. intervention. But Panamanian nationalism is a more fragile institution. The 3 October, 1989, coup led by Maj. Moisés Giroldi was not to establish the popularly elected Endara government or any other form of democracy. It was a struggle for power within the PDF, a struggle for the spoils. Those who hoped a coup would topple Noriega focus too much on his particular evils and not enough on the evils of the PDF.

Considering the risks, Just Cause clearly served U.S. strategic goals in the region. Noriega is in U.S. custody to stand trial on multiple corruption and drug-trafficking charges, although no one has ever shown him to be a kingpin of the drug cartels. While there is evidence that drug profits are once again flowing into Panamanian banks, the cartels undoubtedly suffered a setback as a result of Just Cause. The United States, in any case, now is in a position to press for stricter banking controls in Panama.

Second, U.S. attempts to promote democracy and human rights within the region have seldom come so right. Whatever struggles the Endara government faces pale in comparison with the climate of blatant abuse under Noriega and the PDF. The Panamanians still look to the United States as a crutch, and will for the foreseeable future. Endara summoned U.S. forces, not Panamanians, to put down the most serious rebellion in his first year as president. The Panamanians desperately want U.S. aid. The administration and Congress were too slow and too stingy in approving aid after Just Cause. But the final burden of proof is with the Panamanians, who are not likely to get another financial care package of that size. Instead, Just Cause has given them a chance to reshape their own economy.

Third, Just Cause demonstrated U.S. resolve to protect its citizens abroad. This rationale may have proved hollow as a prelude to action in Grenada, but certainly was no exaggeration in Panama; American soldiers and civilians were in danger. The shooting of Paz was merely the culmination of a long pattern of abuse. By December 1989, Noriega's ability to control anti-Americanism among his forces was in serious doubt.

Fourth, Just Cause may actually have bolstered efforts at containment, such as they were. The Sandinistas were voted from power in Nicaragua less than three months after Just Cause. A case can be made that the operation demonstrated U.S. determination to pursue its strategy to the point of military action. The so-called Vietnam syndrome—a reluctance to act militarily—appears to be a thing of the past, a major development in U.S. foreign policy.

Only in its violation of the principle of nonintervention does Just Cause fail to make the grade. But it must be noted that while most Latin American nations deplored the U.S. military strike, few repercussions have emerged. Many Latin leaders privately have expressed relief that Noriega is gone from power. He represents a strain of brutal Latin militarism that has outlived its popularity in the region.

But while Just Cause fits well within the main themes of U.S. strategy, it raises disturbing questions about the process of making foreign policy. The leaders in Just Cause came almost exclusively from the Pentagon. Thurman abhorred a vacuum, and he moved into one when he assumed command of SOUTHCOM. His predecessor, Woerner, had also complained of a "policy vacuum" in the Reagan administration regarding Panama, a remark that helped to alienate him from the Bush administration. In developing a plan for Just Cause, Thurman accomplished a task that had thus far proved impossible amid the bureaucratic bickering of Washington policymakers.

Powell translated Thurman's solution into a form that made it acceptable to Bush and his administration. Even as the decision to invade was made, members of Bush's inner foreign-policy circle searched for options other than a full-scale assault. Without Powell's popularity in the White House and his political sensibilities, it is possible that the Just Cause plan would have died on the vine. The two generals seem, in retrospect, to have been the only figures who could respond decisively to such an ill-defined strategic situation, without the comfortable certainties of cold war strategy. Perhaps Just Cause need not have been the only option.

Measured as a military operation, Just Cause was clearly a success, even a masterpiece, of *operational art,* the term coined by analyst Edward Luttwak to describe the level of military art between strategy and tactics. It translated confusing strategic goals into lucid military objectives. Now its successful execution has opened new strategic values.

Just Cause was a campaign consisting of two ambitious operations. The goals of the first were to protect American lives and installations, to secure other key sites within Panama, to capture and deliver Noriega into competent legal hands, and, most importantly, to shatter the Panama Defense Forces. The second operation, which was to begin almost simultaneously with the first, was to replace Noriega's rule with the democratically elected government of Guillermo Endara and to rebuild the PDF. As Stiner put it, he intended to knock down the PDF one night, then offer it a helping hand the next morning.

The first of these operations went remarkably well. The assault on dozens of targets simultaneously, in the middle of the night, and with overwhelming force, left Noriega and his supporters little hope of response. Stiner's insight that the PDF was a highly centralized organization, capable of only modest action without direction from Noriega or his chief lieutenants, proved to be true, and was vital to the success of the assaults.

As commander of the Army's XVIII Airborne Corps, Stiner was perhaps in a unique position to hit upon this fundamental element. The rapid and efficient application of combat power within hours of an alert is the trademark of the corps, permeating the thinking of its war planners. Stiner's superiors, Thurman and Powell, also were drawn to the concept of a quick, hammerhead attack, having served in Vietnam where they saw the crippling effects of a piecemeal, tit-for-tat application of force.

It is not surprising that with their preference for decisive action, Thurman and Stiner made it a point to emphasize the role of special forces in Just Cause. Having commanded the Joint Special Operations Command from 1984 to 1987, Stiner had the respect of both conventional and special forces communities. For his part, Thurman made major changes to the command structure in battle plans for Panama, replacing a separate-but-equal relationship between the conventional and special-operations communities with true integration. The result was a special operation writ large, rather than a series of unconventional and conventional operations stitched together.

Thurman and Stiner were not the only ones to share a common conception of the operation. The operations staff at XVIII Airborne enjoyed a similar harmony of outlook with other planners at Fort Bragg and elsewhere in the Army's light infantry community. Some of this sympathy was based on personal familiarity; crisscrossing careers have taken officers and NCOs from the 82d Airborne Division to the 75th Ranger Regiment to the 7th Infantry Division (Light) and back again. But among the war-planning staffs, there was another commond bond: the Army's School of Advanced Military Studies at Fort Leavenworth, Kansas, from which many of the officers had graduated with a common frame of reference and discourse. Their mutual trust was critical not only in the conception of the plan, but in its acceptance by a wide array of units, from paratroopers to aviators to special operations personnel.

Stiner's analysis of the role of the PDF in Panamanian society meshed neatly with the intention to use swift, overpowering force to accomplish the Bush administration's goals in Panama. More than strictly a military organization, the PDF permeated every aspect of Panamanian life. It was organized along provincial lines, acting as the agent of the central government in the rugged outback of such regions as Chiriqui province on the Costa Rican border. It served also as a police force, down to the function of writing traffic tickets. Most importantly, it was a sort of Mafia, distributing the spoils of bribery and corruption to its members. To belong to the PDF was to be a cut above the rest of Panamanian society. Membership was a key to status for ambitious youths not born into the business aristocracy.

In drawing their conclusions about the PDF, Thurman and Stiner broke ranks not only with others in the Defense Department but also with many in other cabinet agencies. Some of the principals of the Just Cause task force contend still that the operation confronted a problem better left to the Panamanians alone. Even as they prepared to execute Just Cause, high officials in the Bush administration hoped instead that PDF troops would wage a successful coup against Noriega and remove that problem from the U.S. agenda.

But once it began, the combat operation was conducted with a minimum of interference from above. Thurman left Stiner alone to plan and conduct the combat, and Stiner resisted the inevitable suggestions from outside the task force. The Joint Chiefs of Staff gave Thurman the freedom he wanted, while Powell protected him from interservice rivalry. Powell's strong presence as JCS chairman was made even stronger by the Goldwater-Nichols Defense Reorganization Act, which made the chairman the spokesman for all the joint chiefs. Goldwater-Nichols also vested more authority in the warfighting commanders in chief.

Bush and his advisers refrained from tinkering with the plan. In return, they got a plan sensitive to strategic policy goals. The result was that the strong personalities of Thurman and Stiner had the added authority to avoid lowest-common-denominator solutions to the problems posed by an invasion of Panama. Just Cause was not a horse designed by a committee. Thurman and Stiner made Noriega fight their kind of war, not his. In a paradoxical way, the rapid, overwhelming application of combat power ended the fighting as soon as possible with a minimum loss of life. It was an elegant work of operational art.

In moving from combat to stability operations, the Army went from strength to relative weakness. With the PDF gone, Panama was in disarray. Civil affairs, psychological affairs, all the talents that come under the military term "nation building," were tried with modest success and little consistency in Vietnam and subsequently suffered by association. In the Army at large, civil affairs became the purview of reservists or special forces, neither an institution of great bureaucratic clout, although in recent years special forces have gained in stature.

While the stability phase of Just Cause was perhaps doomed by previous doctrine to be a poor relation to battlefield operations, Thurman and Stiner at least understood the need for such efforts. They felt that if the fighting went well, the task of putting Panama back together would be that much easier. The worst possible situation would be trying to pacify and rebuild Panama City and care for its inhabitants while tracking down guerrilla bands in the remote provinces or negotiating for the release of hostages. The risk of several days' looting was a price worth paying for the ability to concentrate on eliminating the PDF.

There was widespread looting in the week after the initial combat was over. The pacification of the entire country took several weeks, straining military police and civil affairs units to their limits. Nor is the job completed. More than a year after the invasion, the new police force of Panama had yet to prove itself a competent law enforcement agency. As this is written, the organization, made up largely of former PDF personnel, is on its fourth chief. The Panamanian people do not trust their own policemen. No doubt it will take another year—or longer—to exorcise the malevolent influence of Noriega's PDF.

It is clear that coordinated stability operations must become part of the U.S. Army's repertoire. How to handle the problem—creating a sufficient active force to deal with the need or demonstrating a greater willingness to call up reserves—may not be as important as confronting it in the first place.

The Just Cause campaign was an overall success when measured against its stated goals. But certain advantages make it an imperfect model for future campaigns. One bonus was an extremely friendly reception by the Panamanians. Noriega's attempts to whip up anti-American feelings among his people failed miserably. The invading soldiers were welcomed as liberators; Noreiga was truly reviled, as Panamanians proved when they helped hunt down the dictator and his lieutenants. Secondly, the PDF was in no way organized to respond to so many challenges in so many places in such short order. The response of PDF leaders was to empty their magazines and run away, although in some attacks they proved difficult to subdue. It would have taken monumental tactical incompetence to prevent Just Cause from achieving success against such bad soldiers. Third, the U.S. military drew rare advantages from its decades-long presence in Panama, actually rehearsing assaults right under the enemy's nose and gathering information on Noriega and the PDF, although that same advantage suggests that intelligence on the Panamanians should have been better than it was.

But it is no stroke of luck that the battlefield was conquered so rapidly; securing an entire nation within eight hours is almost unheard of. In the end, success came from a combination of tactical and operational advantages. U.S. forces held almost all the cards, from the competence of individual soldiers to their training, schemes of maneuver, mobility on the battlefield, the volume of precise fire support, and the ability to conduct extensive rehearsals.

Certainly the biggest tactical advantage was the ability of U.S. forces to fight at night, with near-complete freedom of maneuver. The ability to fight at night has become deeply ingrained in the U.S. Army. It's not just that a few elite units feel comfortable in the dark, or that most soldiers are capable of limited night fighting. Most of today's Army is equipped with sophisticated night-fighting equipment and has been trained to operate at night. The Army has been through several generations of night vision goggles. They are now common at the squad and platoon levels. Several stages of development have produced a goggle small and light enough to be standard soldier gear. While there are limitations to night vision goggles for pilots, Just Cause clearly showed the importance of these devices in training and combat. Large numbers of helicopters were able to fly in tight formation with their running lights blacked out because of the pilots' ability to see in the dark. More than 170 choppers were in the air for extended periods of time during D-day operations without any accidents due to poor visibility.

Army forces also made good use of thermal imagers on the AH-64 Apache attack helicopters and special operations aircraft. While these infrared devices are integral to the aircraft's weapons systems, they also serve well in reconnaissance. Regrettably, there were too few aircraft with such capability. Both the Army's Panama-based and U.S.-based aircraft fleet lacked the "D" model of the OH-58 scout helicopter. This small chopper packs a similar thermal sight capability into a much smaller airframe than the Apache, and can also tie into artillery data networks. One older, "C" model OH-58 was shot down during the assault on Fort Amador, killing one of the pilots. Had the more modern model been in use, the pilot may have been able to stand out of range of PDF guns.

The success of night operations in Just Cause resulted as much from training as from the devices themselves, though this training is so expensive that the Army is hard-pressed to build an adequate corps of aviators with night-fighting skills. U.S. Army South suffered a significant shortage of night-qualified pilots and door gunners; qualified flight crews had to be stripped from other Army units to bring Just Cause combat units up to strength. The shortage was the result of a U.S. policy that encouraged U.S. soldiers to rotate out of Panama more rapidly than they could be replaced, and SOUTHCOM's traditional place near the bottom of Army manning and equipment priorities. SOUTHCOM units lacked not only pilots, but also infantrymen. A pair of helicopter crashes in Panama early in 1990, attributed to inexperienced pilots flying beyond their trained capabilities, was part and parcel of this problem.

Even more important than the ability to fly effectively at night is the ability to maneuver on the ground. U.S. Rangers, paratroopers, and infantrymen receive extensive training in night fighting. Airborne units routinely jump at night. Such skills paid off impressively in the Rangers' seizure of the Rio Hato and Torrijos/Tocumen airfields. At Rio Hato, the 6th and 7th Companies of the PDF, the soldiers who had put down the 3 October coup attempt, were alerted to the coming invasion and scattered from their barracks to defend the installation. The PDF, fighting on home turf, put up tough resistance near the barracks, but the Rangers rallied quickly after their jump, moved without hesitation to their objectives, and secured the airfield within two hours. A similar success played out at Torrijos/Tocumen, despite PDF attempts to take cover among passengers from a Brazilian airliner.

While the Rangers are perhaps the Army's most highly trained light infantrymen, Ranger skills are widely taught throughout the Army, especially in the 82d Airborne and 7th Infantry divisions. The Ranger tab, certifying successful completion of the Ranger School, is not only a status symbol but an important boost to an infantryman's career. A pocked-sized manual called the *Ranger Handbook,* outlining small-unit practices in cookbook form, has long been a popular item throughout the Army. While no substitute for training, the handbook is a boon to junior officers and their NCOs.

The difference between attacking at night and in the daytime can be measured in lives lost in the air assault at Tinajitas. Because elements of the 82d Airborne left Fort Bragg late, delayed by an ice storm, the air assault was delayed until the following morning. Though the assault succeeded in routing a PDF infantry company, two soldiers died in the attempt within minutes of hopping off the assault helicopters. Eighteen were injured.

The ability to fight at night was not confined to the light units. The troops of the 5th Mechanized Infantry Division, who assaulted

La Comandancia, also seized their objective in the dark. The movement to and fighting around La Comandancia was extremely violent. The PDF headquarters, in downtown Panama City, was surrounded by a warren of slums and narrow streets—a far cry from the desert or the plains of Europe, where mechanized forces are more in their element. The cordoning off of the Comandancia was perhaps the toughest engagement of Just Cause.

Although the assault was successful, it also underscored a number of shortcomings that the Army needs to address. Only recently has doctrine emerged on the use of armored and mechanized forces in an urban or built-up environment; classic doctrine stresses the need to avoid or bypass towns and cities. Yet there was an obvious requirement to protect armored personnel carriers around the Comandancia, where the use of weapons had to be restricted. The armored vehicles were vulnerable at the makeshift roadblocks thrown up by the PDF. If Panamanians had been better shots with their antiarmor rockets, casualties might have been greater still. The PDF was well outfitted with these cheap weapons, which can tear up an M113 or a Sheridan light tank. But it remains unclear how accurate they are and thus how much danger they pose. The issue was hotly debated during the dispute over the vulnerability of the Bradley Infantry Fighting Vehicle. The battlefield effectiveness of rocket-propelled grenades against mechanized forces also is not well understood.

Conversely, U.S. soldiers appear to have been relatively accurate gunners with LAWs and AT-4s, claiming a number of first-round hits on PDF armored cars and trucks. These weapons may be inherently more accurate, but it seems probable that U.S. gunners were better trained.

The night-fighting capabilities of Just Cause forces would have been greatly enhanced had the Vietnam-era M551 Sheridan light tank not been the only armor available. The Sheridan has none of the thermal viewers or sophisticated fire control systems of modern main battle tanks, and its 152mm main gun is far from ideal. Yet the Sheridan, in use for twenty-five years, is still the workhorse of the 82d Airborne's armor unit. It is also the only tank-like vehicle the Army owns that is light enough to be air-dropped. The Army has struggled unsuccessfully to field a replacement for a decade, through various Army-Marine and Army-only programs.

Beyond the ability to fight at night and to shoot more accurately, the need for a rapidly deployable assault gun that can be air-dropped has been apparent for years. If paratroopers are to defend an airstrip they've assaulted, they need some organic tank-killing ability of their own. Apaches are helpful, and infantry antitank missiles essential, but a Sheridan replacement would better serve this need. The Sheridan is not a true tank.

Other kinds of fire support played important roles in Just Cause actions. Perhaps the most salient were the AC-130 Spectre gunship, on station for just about every assault and in universal demand, and the AH-64 Apache attack helicopter. But while they usually provided highly accurate firepower, two incidents of casualties were a sober reminder of the potential dangers. The first occurred at Rio Hato, where two Rangers were killed by Apache fire. Just what happened is unclear; the Rio Hato battlefield was very confused, and Rangers intermingled with PDF all over the airstrip. The second incident took place around the Comandancia. No one was killed, but twenty-one U.S. soldiers were wounded and more pinned down by their own gunships. In both cases, it is apparent that the reflective tape and distinctive rag-top helmet camouflage that helped infantrymen on the ground distinguish friend from foe did not do so for the Spectre gunners.

It is hard to put reports of friendly fire casualties in the proper context, for Just Cause marked the first time they were classified as such. The Army said the two Rangers' deaths at Rio Hato were the only friendly-fire casualties of twenty-three soldiers killed in action. How this compares with previous conflicts is impossible to judge.

In many other cases, the Spectres did yeoman work. At Rio Hato, they eliminated PDF air defense guns; at the Pacora River Bridge, they decimated a PDF column moving toward a small special operations force. By the time U.S. forces moved to round up the PDF in the west, just the threat of the circling Spectres helped persuade the Panamanians to surrender.

The gunships are an integral part of Ranger, light infantry, and special operations training, but are not often exercised with the heavy forces like those that assaulted the Comandancia. If light-heavy force mixes are desirable, then greater integration of all possible forces should be a goal. Shortly after Just Cause, the Army assembled many of the elements of the Just Cause task force to participate in exercises at the National Training Center at Fort Irwin, California, the Army's premier training ground for heavy forces. Spectre gunships played a role in those exercises.

The Apaches and AH-6 special operations attack helicopters also gave U.S. forces highly accurate fire support. There were problems with AH-64 maintenance, sorely testing the small fleet during the first few hours of combat. But both pilots and infantry say the Hellfire laser-guided missile proved itself quite accurate and reasonably useful, although it had limited effect against the steel-reinforced walls of the Comandancia.

Stiner made a special effort to limit the use of indirect fire weapons, with the result that mortars and artillery played very little role in Just Cause. This was important in controlling collateral damage, which despite widespread looting and the destruction of slum housing around the Comandancia, was one of the chief accomplishments of Just Cause. Howitzer fire required approval from a battalion commander or above, and 105mm guns were used only in direct fire. Because Howard Air Force Base, the main logistics head for Just Cause, was within range of PDF mortars, artillerymen in the task force had concentrated heavily on counterbattery fire in their preparations for the assault. But the few PDF mortar shots in Panama City were directed at Fort Clayton, not Howard. Known mortar positions were suppressed with Spectre and Apache fires.

A clear tactical improvement by U.S. forces over previous operations was the integration of its signals effort. Stiner made a priority of the so-called Joint Communications and Electronics Operating Instructions. After months hammering out these procedures, all parts of the task force were able to talk to each other when needed. Unit commanders and their radio operators carried small notebooks that assigned frequencies and call signs to everyone on every network. There was an alternate system in case the first was compromised.

The performance of individual soldiers in Just Cause is especially difficult to judge. The war was short, the advantages many. From an infantryman's perspective, there were moments of chaos. Yet surely the most important benchmark to consider is that for the vast majority Just Cause was an introduction to battle. The 82d Airborne and the Rangers both played key roles in Grenada, but many of the individuals involved did not take part in Just Cause.

During the 1980s, the Army became dramatically more attractive to brighter and better educated soldiers. The percentage of high school graduates enlisting in the service skyrocketed from less than 50 percent a decade ago to more than 90 percent. The change is reflected in much higher scores on Army entrance tests.

The Army also improved greatly both the quantity and the quality of its training, to a level higher than at any point in American history. Initial entry and advanced individual training is physically rigorous. Beyond basic training, combat training is stressed constantly. Success in combat exercises is woven into the very fabric of a soldier's career; a junior enlisted man cannot be promoted to sergeant in today's Army without completing the Primary Leadership Development Course, which for combat arms personnel centers on warfighting tasks. It would have been difficult to find a sergeant participating in Just Cause who had not attended the course. In addition, the introduction of sophisticated training aids like the Multiple Integrated Laser Engagement System, or MILES, has produced a realism in maneuver training that previously was available only under live fire. MILES training, a form of laser tag, has convinced many a soldier that if he exposes himself on the battlefield, there's a good chance he'll get hit. It also teaches soldiers the need to maneuver.

As valuable as small-unit maneuvers are, they were not altogether successful in Panama. An assault by Navy SEALs on the Paitilla airstrip cost four lives and left eleven others wounded. The mission was appropriate for SEALs, as the airstrip was on a peninsula, but the SEALs' performance on the ground remains questionable. Whether the incident at Paitilla reveals an institutional weakness, a one-time fatal mistake, or just an accident in the fog of war is still unclear. Some within the special operations community have suggested that the training of elite units tends to concentrate too much on the method of insertion and not enough on maneuvering on the objective. An initiative is underway to set standards within the U.S. Special Operations Command whereby the techniques of experts— Rangers in the case of light infantry tactics—become the standard for other units.

Beyond small-unit maneuvers, the Army exposes a large portion of its soldiers to the effects of large-scale engagements at its combat training centers at Fort Irwin, California; Fort Chaffee, Arkansas; and Hohenfels, Germany. At these centers, soldiers learn how to fight and survive against the power of armor and artillery. Smaller-level battalion exercises provided by the Battalion Command Training Program give staff officers vital experience.

Peacetime preparation of this caliber is not "shake and bake" training. In Just Cause, soldiers had not only the personal courage to fulfill their tasks, but also the knowledge, developed over years of constant training, to do their jobs quickly and efficiently. Disciplined fire, a hallmark of Just Cause, was a direct result of such preparation.

It is significant, however, that the soldiers' proficiency was greatly enhanced by detailed rehearsals conducted before the operation began. From the Sand Flea exercises to air movements to the detailed special operations rehearsals just days before Just Cause, soldiers came to understand their tasks thoroughly. While the soldiers had the lucky opportunity to see much of the battlefield before the battle started, rehearsals are also a normal part of unit training, which attempts to simulate real-world operations.

Live-fire training was another important factor in the tactical successes of Just Cause. It is the most expensive kind of training, but also paid off the most in combat. Just Cause aggravated doubts about whether increased use of simulation will erode the skills and the confidence that live-fire training imparts. Will infantrymen be willing to push an attack in the dark of night without the reassurance that their buddies won't shoot them in the back?

Because it was over so fast, Just Cause did not test unit cohesion in sustained combat. No one can say whether units would have held up if numerous senior NCOs and junior and senior officers had been wounded or killed.

Just Cause did, however, tread new ground in mixing different kinds of units. The task force encompassed a broad range of units, from special operators to paratroopers to light infantry to mechanized infantry. The Army only recently began to experiment with such groupings in its training center rotations, to mix and match capabilities to the mission at hand. The successes and shortcomings of Just Cause in this regard should reinforce the need for mixed-force training. The unquestioning confidence that senior commanders had in each other in Just Cause can be instilled among all ranks, particularly between the unconventional units—special forces, Delta Force, and SEALs—and more conventional forces. In Panama, Stiner's credibility among both communities carried the day, but such trust needs to be institutionalized by command and field exercises.

Perhaps the broadest tactical frontier opening up after Just Cause is the area of stability operations. Because of the shortage of military police troops and civil affairs units, the burden of "nation building" fell predominately on the infantry, particularly the 82d Airborne and the 7th Infantry Division (Light). Though the infantrymen performed reasonably well in their peacekeeping role, virtually all of them wished for more guidance and training. They found themselves in the awkward position of making up doctrine as they went along.

The transition from soldier at war to policeman on the beat was disturbingly swift for most Just Cause participants. Within three or four days of the initial attack, U.S. soldiers found themselves working side by side with former members of the PDF, newly sworn by the Endara government to secure the streets. One of the first difficulties U.S. forces encountered was in trying to disarm Panamanian society. Under Noriega, the isthmus had become something of a Dodge City, with thousands of assault rifles distributed to the Dignity Battalions and tens of thousands more stashed in caches around the countryside. Panamanians played on this effort to exact revenge on neighbors and rivals. As a result, U.S. soldiers often found themselves in the middle of long-simmering personal feuds and vendettas. Certainly arbitration was not part of their training.

Even further removed from combat were many tasks needed to put Panamanian society back on its feet, such as caring for refugees. The necessary rules of engagement—ask questions before shooting—sometimes allowed PDF stragglers to get their shots in first, as in the celebrated incident that formed the core of the murder charge against Master Sgt. Roberto Enrique Bryan, who shot a Panamanian whose companion had just thrown a grenade at a group of U.S. paratroopers. The acquittal of Bryan, who was expecting to receive the Panamanians' surrender when the grenade was thrown, vindicated his response to suspicions that another grenade might be thrown, but the trial renewed the debate over how an occupying force should respond to threats of violence.

If soldiers are to be peacekeepers and social workers—and it seems unlikely that a shrinking Army will find room for sufficient

MPs or civil affairs specialists to do the job—they deserve more detailed training. The Army has begun to tackle such tasks in its training on Military Operations in Urban Terrain, but units such as the 7th Infantry Division and the 101st and 82d Airborne divisions need thorough schooling in such duties.

Spanish-speaking skills also require greater emphasis. The Army has many Hispanic soldiers who are fluent in Spanish. But the soldiers are not necessarily prepared for operations in Spanish-speaking countries, as the 7th Infantry Division discovered when its soldiers were called to Panama. Because its primary focus has been on reinforcing Korea, its intelligence troops were schooled in Korean, not Spanish. Hispanic soldiers, in turn, were called on for a variety of tasks in Panama that they were not trained for. Perhaps simply identifying those soldiers who can converse in Spanish and distributing them among units would solve the problem. More broadly, perhaps foreign-language skills should be rewarded in some way as a secondary specialty.

Looking beyond military issues, one issue still festering from Just Cause is the role of the press in wartime coverage. The so-called Pentagon press pool, a limited group of reporters allowed immediate access to military actions on behalf of other reporters who cannot safely approach the battlefield, is a critical asset in wartime, for news coverage certainly shapes public attitudes toward a war. Just Cause revealed how wide the gap between the military and the media remains, and both parties must share the blame. The Pentagon did a poor job in assembling the pool for Just Cause, with the result that pool reporters did not arrive in Panama soon enough and then were not given timely access to troops. The fighting was never really covered as it happened.

There is some question as to whether the pool was necessary, however. There was a sizable contingent of reporters already stationed in Panama before Just Cause began. The Pentagon might have accomplished the same purposes by providing reporters already in country with whatever escorts were necessary and allowing those reporters to cover the fighting.

Members of the press also contributed to bungling the pool arrangements. For example, *Time* magazine, represented in the pool, was notified at a Christmas party that the group was being activated. In the course of finding a correspondent to fill the assignment, virtually the entire Washington staff of the magazine learned of the operation. Some correspondents in the pool showed up for the flight to Panama without passports or the proper equipment, according to NBC Pentagon correspondent Fred Francis, the network's reporter in the pool.

In lieu of a full-time war to cover, the media need to devote the time and effort to training competent military correspondents. News organizations that wish to participate should be required to assign reporters to a more permanent pool organization, which would be exercised regularly, perhaps as part of National Training Center rotations and to include outfitting correspondents with MILES gear to give them a feel for the dangers of combat. As Fred Francis put it, "Combat is no time for on-the-job training." The American tradition of combat reporting has withered, with defense reporting having become just Pentagon reporting, another Washington beat. There are few David Halberstams, Peter Arnetts, or Neil Sheehans among the Pentagon reporters.

Another blunder in the coverage of Just Cause occurred when a second wave of reporters overwhelmed SOUTHCOM as abruptly as the Just Cause task force fell on the PDF. When Air Force Col. Ronald Sconyers permitted NBC to land one charter airplane of reporters at Howard Air Force Base, he anticipated a small puddle-jumper with a handful of reporters and crew members. What he got instead was a wide-body L-1011 jet packed with hundreds of television and print journalists, all clamoring to find a local angle on the operation. With scattered battles being fought around Panama, Sconyers and his public affairs staff were prepared only to park the unhappy group of reporters inside the operations center at Howard. Frustrated in their hopes for a scoop, half of them left Panama on the first plane they could find, with little good to say about their treatment. In an age of mini-cams and easy satellite hook-ups, reporters have a mobility the Pentagon must anticipate. Given the small scale of Operation Just Cause, this problem was only exacerbated.

The unique aspects of Just Cause aside, an Army that is smaller, increasingly based in the United States rather than abroad, oriented toward a range of threats rather than the Soviet menace and sent to resolve ill-defined political conflicts would do well to adopt many of the traits of the Just Cause task force. In the words of Gen. Carl

Vuono, Army chief of staff, the future force must be versatile, deployable, and lethal. In a January 1990 white paper, Vuono argued that "the nature of the United States's interests around the world, and its coalition-based strategy, will require that U.S. forces be globally deployable, often with little or no warning, from the United States or from forward bases." He might have been describing the capabilities of the units that conducted Just Cause.

Appendix A: Glossary

AH-1 The Cobra attack helicopter was first developed during the Vietnam war and remains central to the Army's attack helicopter fleet. Armed with rockets, TOW missiles, and a 20mm gun, the Cobra lacks the modern night-flying and targeting devices of the **AH-64** Apache.

AH-6 A light special-operations helicopter, modified from an OH-6 observation helicopter. Called "Little Birds," these helicopters pack an array of sophisticated electronics, missiles, and machine guns in a very small airframe.

AH-64 The Army's premier attack helicopter, called the "Apache." The AH-64 is armed with laser-homing Hellfire missiles, rockets, and a 30mm automatic cannon. Pilots use a sophisticated array of targeting and night-fighting sensors to engage targets at long range and to fly at night and in adverse weather.

AK-47 An assault rifle designed by the Soviet Kalashnikov works and used throughout the world; the Soviet counterpart to the U.S. M16.

AT-4 An 84mm rocket that one soldier can carry and fire alone. The AT-4 is often called a "bunker-buster," meaning that it is useful against small enemy positions or lightly armored vehicles, but is incapable of penetrating the frontal armor on a modern main battle tank.

Bangalore torpedo A piece of pipe filled with C4 plastic explosive, commonly used to clear a path through barbed wire or to detonate land mines.

Battalion 2000 An elite fighting unit made up of 200 of Noriega's most loyal soldiers. Based at Fort Cimarron, the unit was equipped with armored combat vehicles.

Black Hawk The Army's primary assault helicopter, designated the UH-60, has a crew of three and can carry eleven or more fully loaded infantrymen. The Black Hawk first was introduced into the Army inventory in the late 1970s and early 1980s, and has proved much tougher than the Vietnam-era UH-1 "Huey."

Blue Spoon The name given to the combat operations phase of the Prayer Book series. This plan included troop lists and a wide range of military options, from surgical strikes to full-scale assaults.

Boyd-Roosevelt Highway   The main highway linking Colon with Panama City.

Bridge of the Americas   The bridge spanning the Panama Canal, linking Fort Clayton and Howard Air Force Base.

Coco Solo   Headquarters of the PDF naval infantry, just outside of Colon on the Atlantic side of Panama.

Delta Force   The Army's secret counterterrorism unit(s), specializing in hostage rescue.

Dignity Battalions   In his final years as PDF commander, Noriega organized local militia he called "Dignity Battalions," though U.S. soldiers referred to them as "DigBats" or "DingBats." These were little more than mobs organized to perpetuate Noriega's rule by frightening the political opposition. Though fairly well armed, these units had no military training to speak of.

Dobermans   Noriega's personal plainclothes riot police.

Fissures   Plans favored by General Frederick Woerner, then-commander of U.S. Southern Command, to facilitate the removal of Noriega without resorting to the use of the U.S. military. The plans sought to oust Noriega with a PDF coup or a strengthening of the civilian opposition.

Fort Amador   A joint U.S.-Panamanian military installation along the Pacific coast near downtown Panama City.

Fort Espinar   Home of the PDF 8th Infantry Company near the northern end of the Panama Canal.

Golden Pheasant   A March 1988 emergency deployment of U.S. troops to Palmerola Air Base in central Honduras. The force, consisting of soldiers from the 82d Airborne Division and 7th Infantry Division (Light), was deployed to ensure stability in Central America, but was also a test of the compatibility of the units leading the troop roster in the military planning for Panama.

High Mobility Multipurpose Wheeled Vehicle, or HMMWV   Pronounced "Hum-vee," this wide-tracked four-wheel-drive vehicle has all but replaced the Jeep as the Army's basic all-purpose truck. The HMMWV comes in a variety of configurations, from a combat model equipped with machine guns and antitank missiles to a small medical facility.

Howard Air Force Base   The primary U.S. Air Force base in Panama, on the opposite side of the canal from Fort Clayton, headquarters of U.S. Army South.

Improved TOW Vehicle, or ITV A modified version of the ubiquitous M113 fitted with a mechanism for firing Tube-launched, Optically-tracked, Wire-guided antitank missiles. The launcher, which soldiers commonly call a "Hammerhead," contains a sight that is raised to fire the missiles, then folded down for cross-country movement.

Joint Communications and Electronics Operating Instructions Plans drawn up to establish frequencies to be used by specific units. Designed to prevent two units from using the same radio frequency.

Joint Special Operations Task Force The planning and command headquarters for U.S. special forces prior to and during Operation Just Cause. Commanded by Maj. Gen. Wayne Downing, who reported directly to Lieutenant General Stiner.

Joint Task Force–South, or JTF-South The headquarters and planning cell for Operation Just Cause, run by the Army's XVIII Airborne Corps and commanded by Lt. Gen. Carl Stiner.

La Comandancia The walled main headquarters of the PDF. The concrete-reinforced building in the center of downtown Panama City was a primary target of U.S. forces during Operation Just Cause. It was dubbed Bravo One.

LAW 80 Light Antiarmor Weapon. (LAW) A British-built, shoulder-fired antitank weapon system widely fielded throughout the U.S. Army.

Light Armored Vehicle, or LAV An eight-wheeled, lightly armored car developed for the Marine Corps, the LAV comes in many variants, the basic model mounting a 25mm cannon and carrying a squad of Marines.

M113 A tracked, armored personnel carrier, the M113 has been the primary vehicle for U.S. mechanized infantry since Vietnam. Now being replaced by the better-armed and more capable M2/3 Bradley fighting vehicle, the M113 looks like a metal box on tracks. It weighs thirteen tons, mounts a .50-caliber machine gun, can carry eleven soldiers, and has been made for countless other uses. Commonly called a "track."

Macho de Monte The self-chosen nickname of the vaunted PDF 7th Infantry Company, based at Rio Hato. Loosely translated to mean "Mountain Men," these elite soldiers were the most loyal to Manuel Noriega and rescued him during the 3 October coup attempt. Following the failed coup, Noriega reassigned much of the Macho de Monte to La Comandancia.

Madden Dam A critical structure that controls the level of the canal; maintains a balance between the Atlantic and Pacific Oceans, which are at different levels.

National Military Command Center   The Joint Chiefs of Staff command center in the Pentagon, from where the U.S. military monitors world events and its operations.

Nimrod Dancer   A May 1989 deployment of 1,881 soldiers and Marines to Panama in response to the beating of opposition candidates by Noriega loyalists following the marred national election. The operation sent to Panama the headquarters of the 1st Brigade, 9th Regiment, 7th Infantry Division; an infantry battalion and battery of towed field artillery from the 7th Infantry Division; a battalion of mechanized infantry with armored personnel carriers; tracked mortar carriers and one hundred other combat vehicles from the 5th Infantry Division (Mechanized); and a Marine company of 165 infantrymen with Light Armored Vehicles.

OH-58   The Kiowa scout and observation helicopter is another Vietnam-era aircraft still in active service. The basic OH-58 has been upgraded, with "C" and "D" models now forming the bulk of the fleet. However, there is a huge gap in the capabilities between these two models, with the "D" version, developed under the Army Helicopter Improvement Program, possessing far greater sensing and targeting capabilities, better engines, and more protection against small arms fire than any previous scout.

Operation Plans 90-1 and 90-2   The formal name for the written drafts of the Blue Spoon combat plan. Operation Plan 90-2 would become the guidebook for Operation Just Cause.

Pacora River Bridge   A critical juncture along the Pan American Highway providing the Battalion 2000 at Fort Cimarron its only pathway to Panama City. The bridge would become a special forces target.

Panama Defense Forces, or PDF   Noriega's forces were more than regular military units. They included a wide range of units from the DENI, a kind of cross between the U.S. FBI and customs police, and the DNTT traffic police to the UESAT special operations forces.

Panama Viejo   The site of the first European settlement in Panama and home of the PDF 1st Cavalry Squadron. The unit was equipped with V-150 and V-300 armored cars.

Prayer Book   The contingency plan for Panama, superseded by what became Just Cause. It contained a number of elements: Klondike Key, for evacuation of noncombatants to ensure the safety of the U.S. citizens living throughout Panama during the assault; Post Time, calling for an incremental buildup of U.S. firepower in Panama, and Krystal Ball and Blind Logic, covering stability operations and civil affairs operations to be conducted after the military invasion was over.

Rio Hato The western Panama headquarters of the PDF 7th Infantry Company, better known as the *Macho de Monte*, some of the better trained and most loyal of Noriega's military. Rio Hato is about one hundred miles from Panama City on the Pacific Coast.

Rocket-propelled grenades, or RPGs These rounds, shot from the end of an assault rifle, are common weapons throughout the world and give an infantryman some protection against thin-skinned personnel carriers and light vehicles. Accurate only at short range, they are cheap but deadly in close quarters, especially in city fighting.

Rodman Naval Station U.S. Navy headquarters in Panama.

Sand Fleas Provocative exercises conducted by U.S. troops from the summer of 1989 to gain a psychological edge over Noriega and the PDF and to practice the routes detailed in the Blue Spoon combat plan. Named for the sand flea, a pest endemic to Panama.

SEALs Navy Sea-Air-Land special operations forces participated in many aspects of Just Cause, especially the attack on Paitilla airport. These teams specialize in unconventional missions initiated from the sea.

Sheridan light tank The M551 Sheridan was developed as a light tank for the Vietnam war and remains the primary weapon of the armored units of the 82d Airborne Division. Its primary virtue is its ability to be air-dropped, but its old gun-and-missile main armament and weak armor are major drawbacks.

Spectre, or AC-130 gunship These special operations gunships are modified versions of the C-130 cargo plane, mounting sophisticated sensors, a 20mm Gatling gun, and 40mm and 105mm cannons. These provided the most effective fire support for Operation Just Cause.

The Tank The Joint Chiefs of Staff meeting room where much of the highly secretive detailed war planning takes place.

Task Force Atlantic A U.S. force consisting of the 7th Infantry Division (Light) from Fort Ord, California, deployed during Operation Nimrod Dancer; a battalion that was undergoing training at the Jungle Operations Training Center; military police; and special forces. The task force was responsible for targets in central and northern Panama.

Task Force Aviation Largest helicopter element in Operation Just Cause. Commanded by Col. Douglas Terrell, who also commanded the 7th Infantry Division's Aviation Brigade, the task force was the controlling headquarters for all conventional aviation forces in Panama. It blended elements of the 7th Division, 82d Airborne Division and the Panama-based 1st Battalion, 228th Aviation Regiment.

Task Force Bayonet A U.S. force consisting of the 193d Infantry Brigade and the 4th Battalion, 6th Infantry Regiment of the 5th Infantry Division (Mechanized) from Fort Polk, Louisiana. Task Force Bayonet's mission was to secure La Comandancia.

Task Force Black The 3d Battalion, 7th Special Forces Group, which would seize the Pacora River Bridge and a television tower at Cerro Azul, and perform reconnaissance missions.

Task Force Gator Consisting of B and D Companies of the 4th Battalion, 6th Infantry Regiment, 5th Infantry Division (Mechanized), and C Company, 1st Battalion, 508th Infantry Regiment (Airborne), this task force was the main assault element charged with isolating and seizing La Comandancia, the main PDF headquarters building in downtown Panama City.

Task Force Green This force consisted of members of Delta Force who were to rescue Kurt Muse, an American radio operator, from the Carcel Modelo in downtown Panama City.

Task Force 160 This is a special operations aviation unit based at Fort Campbell, Kentucky. Nicknamed the "Night Stalkers," the unit often flies air cover for other special operations forces.

Task Force Hawk The task force, constituted from 7th Division assets, rotated through Panama regularly, starting in April 1988. Made up of an assault company and an attack company, Hawk was commanded by Lt. Col. Howard Borum, commander of 7th Division's 1st Battalion, 123d Aviation Regiment. The task force had D-Day assault missions at Fort Amador, Panama Viejo, Tinajitas, and Fort Cimarron.

Task Force Pacific This force consisted of the ready brigade of the 82d Airborne Division and would secure Torrijos-Tocumen airfields, and then launch subsequent attacks on Panama Viejo, Fort Cimarron, and Tinajitas.

Task Force Red This force consisted of the 75th Ranger Regiment, which would seize Rio Hato and Tocumen/Torrijos airfields.

Task Force Red Devil A, B and Headquarters companies of the 1st Battalion, 508th Infantry (Airborne), assigned to air assault into Fort Amador at H-hour. The mission of the task force was to ensure the safety of U.S. civilians living on the post and to neutralize the PDF 5th Infantry Company across the fairway.

Task Force Semper Fi   The force consisted of the U.S. Marines in Panama, who were responsible for establishing a series of blockades along the Bridge of the Americas and around Howard Air Force Base. They were also required to secure towns near the Howard airfield, including Arraijan, and to use LAVs to fire on La Comandancia.

Task Force White   This force, consisting of Navy Sea-Air-Land (SEAL) Team 4 and elements of SEAL Group 2, Little Creek, Virginia, was tasked to secure Paitilla airfield in Panama City and to block potential sea-based escape routes for Noriega.

Tinajitas   A large PDF base, home to the 1st PDF Infantry Company in eastern Panama City.

The Tunnel   A command facility buried hundreds of yards deep into Ancon Hill in the middle of Panama City. The tunnel, which sits under the Quarry Heights headquarters of the Southern Command, is reserved for the most highly classified military planning.

UESAT   Noriega's most elite special forces commandos, trained by the Israelis in counterterrorist and other elite missions. Headquartered on Flamenco Island, off Fort Amador.

U.S. Army South   The largest fighting element of the U.S. Southern Command, consisting of a single brigade of two battalions.

U.S. Southern Command   The American unified command in Latin America. Preceded by the Panama Canal Department and the Caribbean Defense Command, the headquarters averages a total of ten thousand personnel. Its main mission is to defend the Panama Canal.

V-300 or V-150   Many PDF units were equipped with these four-and six-wheeled armored cars. Made by Cadillac Gage, an American company, these vehicles are popular with governments throughout Latin America and the Third World, as much for controlling their own people as for purely military uses.

Vulcans   Rapid-fire air defense weapons using two 20mm Gatling guns.

XVIII Airborne Corps   This is the U.S. Army's quick reaction corps headquartered at Fort Bragg, North Carolina. As planning for Just Cause intensified in the late 1980s, the corps became the planning nucleus. The 82d Airborne Division, elite paratroopers, are a key element of the corps.

ZPU-4   A towed, four-barreled air defense gun of Soviet design and manufacture. The primary air defense weapon of the PDF.

Appendix B: Principal Characters

Abrams, Elliott U.S. assistant secretary of state for inter-American affairs from 1985 to 1989.

Arias, Arnulfo Served as president of Panama three times between 1940 and 1968, the third term lasting only eleven days. Arias was a fascist and a populist and an admirer of Hitler and Mussolini. He was ousted by the military.

Armitage, Richard Assistant secretary of defense for international security affairs in 1988.

Banks, Sergeant Major James Sergeant major to the 7th Infantry Division (Light) provost marshal.

Barletta, Nicolás Ardito President of Panama from 1983 to 1985. Widely believed to be a puppet, Barletta was removed from power when he confronted Noriega concerning the death of opposition leader Hugo Spadafora.

Bastidas, Rodrigo de Led Spanish discovery of the area now known as Panama in 1501.

Bausch, Lieutenant Colonel Robert Stephen Division surgeon, 7th Infantry Division (Light).

Beech, Captain Mike Commander, A Company, 4th Battalion, 17th Infantry Regiment, 7th Infantry Division (Light). Led H-hour assault on PDF 8th Infantry Company outside Colon and 22 December mission to secure Colon Free Trade Zone.

Borum, Lieutenant Colonel Howard Commander of Task Force Hawk and commander of the 1st Battalion, 123d Aviation Regiment, 7th Division.

Boylan, Captain Pete Commander, A Company, 3d Battalion, 504th Parachute Infantry Regiment, 82d Airborne Division. His company conducted an air assault at H-hour to drive PDF units from the town of Gamboa and protect Americans there.

Brooks, Lieutenant Colonel Johnny   Commander, 4th Battalion, 17th Infantry Regiment, 7th Infantry Division (Light). Led assaults on PDF installations outside Colon and the mission to secure the city.

Bryan, Master Sergeant Roberto Enrique   First sergeant of D Company, 3d Battalion, 504th Parachute Infantry Regiment, 82d Airborne Division. Bryan was acquitted of court-martial murder charges stemming from the 23 December fatal shooting of a Panamanian at Madden Dam.

Burney, Colonel Linwood   Commander of 2d Brigade, 7th Infantry Division (Light). In charge of removing the PDF from bases of power outside the Canal Zone after the initial U.S. assaults, and of numerous missions to stabilize those regions.

Calderon, Ricardo Arias   A vice-president of Panama.

Campbell, Captain John   Commander, D Company, 3d Battalion, 504th Parachute Infantry Regiment, 82d Airborne Division. His company conducted an assault at H-hour to secure Madden Dam, a key power station for the Panama Canal zone.

Cavezza, Major General Carmen   Commander of the 7th Infantry Division (Light).

del Cid, Lieutenant Colonel Luis   Commander of PDF regional headquarters in Chiriqui and a member of Noriega's war-fighting council. A key figure in the PDF command.

del Cid, Major Mario   Commander of PDF Military Zone 2 headquarters in Colon.

Cisneros, Major General Marc   Spanish-speaking commander of U.S. Army South during Operation Just Cause. Cisneros also drew up the battle plans for the operation as director of operations and plans under General Woerner at the U.S. Southern Command.

Coggin, Major Jim   Executive officer of 4th Battalion, 17th Infantry Regiment, 7th Infantry Division (Light), which conducted several H-hour assaults around Colon.

Cortizo, Captain Moisés   Commander, PDF 5th Infantry Company, Fort Amador.

Crowe, Admiral William   Chairman of the Joint Chiefs of Staff from 1985 to 1989.

DeBlois, Sergeant Michael   A member of 2d Platoon, C Company, 1st Battalion, 508th Infantry Regiment (Airborne), part of 193d Infantry Brigade, stationed in Panama. Killed in the assault on La Comandancia.

Delvalle, Eric Arturo   One of Panama's wealthiest businessmen and president of Panama from 1985 to 1988. He was ousted by Noriega.

Díaz Herrera, Roberto   A military and political leader of Panama who rivaled Noriega, his cousin, for power until he was arrested in 1987.

Downing, Major General Wayne   Commander, Army Special Operations Command, and ground commander of special operations forces during Operation Just Cause.

Dyer, Captain Bryan   Commander, B Company, 3d Battalion, 504th Parachute Infantry Regiment, 82d Airborne Division. His company conducted an air assault at H-hour to seize the central PDF logistics station and explosives school at Cerro Tigre, then a ground assault on 22 December on a DENI station in Colon.

Endara, Guillermo   President of Panama. Campaigned against Noriega from 1988 to his ouster in December 1989.

Etheridge, Captain Michael   Commander, D Company, 4th Battalion, 6th Infantry Regiment, 5th Infantry Division (Mechanized), Fort Polk, Louisiana.

Evans, First Lieutenant Dan   Executive officer, A Company, 4th Battalion, 17th Infantry Regiment, 7th Infantry Division (Light). At H-hour his company seized the headquarters of the PDF 8th Infantry Company and secured Fort Espinar. Two days later the company secured the Colon Free Trade Zone.

Fitzgerald, Lieutenant Colonel Billy Ray   Commander, 1st Battalion, 508th Infantry Regiment (Airborne), part of the 193d Infantry Brigade, Panama.

Flynn, Captain Timothy   Commander, C Company, 1st Battalion, 508th Infantry Regiment (Airborne), part of 193d Infantry Brigade, stationed in Panama.

Ford, Guillermo "Billy"   A vice-president of Panama.

Ford, Command Sergeant Major Rupert   Sergeant major, 4th Battalion, 6th Infantry Regiment, 5th Infantry Division (Mechanized), Fort Polk, Louisiana.

Foss, General John   Commanded XVIII Airborne Corps, Fort Bragg, North Carolina, in 1988, and as a result, was involved in the planning for what would become Operation Just Cause. Foss later became commander of the U.S. Army Training and Doctrine Command, Fort Monroe, Virginia.

Franks, Corporal Larry   Member of A Company, 4th Battalion, 17th Infantry Regiment, 7th Infantry Division (Light). His company took part in the H-hour assault on PDF 8th Infantry Company at Fort Espinar and subsequent mission to secure Colon.

Galvin, General John   Commander in chief of U.S. Southern Command from 1985 to 1987. Galvin is currently Supreme Allied Commander Europe.

Gardner, Major Greg   Operations officer, 3d Brigade, 7th Infantry Division (Light). Participated in planning and executing Task Force Atlantic missions.

Giroldi, Major Moisés   Former chief of security for the Panama Defense Forces. A Noriega aide who turned on the military strongman and led the failed 3 October 1989 coup against his boss. Giroldi was killed shortly after the coup attempt.

Gragg, Sharon   Wife of Colonel Larry Gragg, military community commander in Panama, and mother of two children. Lived on Fort Amador.

Gray, Sergeant First Class Charlie   Platoon sergeant of 3d Platoon, 549th Military Police Company. Shot PDF guard in self-defense, accelerating the H-hour assault on Coco Solo.

Grazioplene, Lieutenant Colonel Jim   Commander, 3d Battalion (Airborne), 73d Armor Regiment, 82d Airborne Division. His unit supplied Sheridans for 82d Airborne and 7th Infantry Division operations in Just Cause.

Guardia, Major Luis   Commander of 8th Infantry Company at Fort Espinar. Fled post before H-hour and later surrendered to U.S. troops.

Halder, Captain Matthew   Commander, Headquarters Company, 3d Battalion, 504th Parachute Infantry Regiment, 82d Airborne Division. Led H-hour mission to secure PDF's Espinar School and prevent its students from taking up arms.

Hale, Colonel David   Commander, 9th Regiment (Manchu Brigade), 7th Infantry Division (Light). His men had responsibility for securing a large segment of Panama City.

Hartzog, Brigadier General William   Director of operations, U.S. Southern Command, during Operation Just Cause. Hartzog now serves as commander of U.S. Army South.

Healy, First Lieutenant Robert   Helicopter pilot, A Company, 3d Battalion,

123d Aviation Regiment, 7th Infantry Division (Light). Flew in D-day air assaults on Panama Viejo, Cerro Tinajitas, and Fort Cimarron.

Helms, Senator Jesse   Republican senator from North Carolina since 1973. Helms is an outspoken opponent of the 1977 Carter-Torrijos treaties.

Higgins, Major Kevin   Commander, A Company, 3d Battalion, 7th Special Forces Group. Led attack against Pacora River Bridge.

Hinton, Ambassador Deane   U.S. ambassador to Panama, replacing Arthur Davis on 6 January 1990.

Holt, Sergeant Paul   Squad leader, A Company, 3d Battalion, 75th Ranger Regiment.

Hort, Captain John   Commander Headquarters/Headquarters Company, 1st Battalion, 508th Infantry Regiment (Airborne), 193d Infantry Brigade, Panama. Participated in assault on Fort Amador.

Howard, Sergeant Henry   Member of B Company, 4th Battalion, 17th Infantry Regiment, 7th Infantry Division (Light). Took part in H-hour mission to secure bottleneck and later mission to secure Colon.

Hunt, Lieutenant Colonel Joseph   Commander of 3d Battalion, 75th Ranger Regiment. His battalion participated in the assault at Rio Hato. He also commanded a task force assigned to secure the city of David and accept the surrender of PDF commander del Cid.

Huntoon, Major David   Operations planner for the XVIII Airborne Corps, teamed with Lieutenant Colonel Tim McMahon to map out the details of Operation Just Cause.

Hutchinson, Zulema   Resident of Colon who witnessed the U.S. assault on Coco Solo and subsequent U.S. operations in Colon.

Jacobelly, Colonel Jake   Commander, Special Operations Command–South, based in Panama but responsible for all special forces activities in Latin America. Also commanded Task Force Black in Operation Just Cause.

Jimenez, Captain Amadis   Commander of PDF naval infantry company at Coco Solo. Later appointed as Cisneros's liaison to PDF commanders still at large.

Johnson, Captain Derek   Commander, C Company, 3d Battalion, 504th Parachute Infantry Regiment, 82d Airborne Division. His company conducted an H-hour air assault to seize Renacer Prison and liberate the prisoners.

Johnson, Major General James   Commander, 82d Airborne Division.

Jones, Captain Timothy   Commander, B Company, 1st Battalion, 123d Aviation Regiment, 7th Infantry Division (Light). Participated in Task Force Hawk and was shot down by hostile fire over Fort Amador on D-day.

Keith, Captain Barry   Deputy provost marshal of 7th Infantry Division (Light) and military police adviser to Task Force Atlantic.

Kellogg, Colonel Keith   Commander, Task Force Atlantic, the group with responsibility for fifteen H-hour missions in the northern and central portions of the Panama Canal zone, including the city of Colon.

Kelly, Lieutenant General Thomas   Director of Operations, Joint Chiefs of Staff. Now retired.

Kernan, Colonel William "Buck"   Commander, 75th Ranger Regiment. Head of Task Force Red during Just Cause.

Kirk, Second Lieutenant Dan   Leader, 2d Platoon, C Company, 4th Battalion, 17th Infantry Regiment, 7th Infantry Division (Light). His platoon seized the PDF naval infantry headquarters building at Coco Solo.

Kreeger, Staff Sergeant Edward   Member of B Battery, 7th Battalion, 15th Field Artillery Brigade, 7th Infantry Division (Light). Battery conducted direct fire on DENI headquarters in Colon, one of only two instances of direct artillery fire in Just Cause.

Kubick, Private First Class Patrick   Member of C Company, 3d Battalion, 75th Ranger Regiment. Participated in securing of La Comandancia.

Kusinski, Staff Sergeant James   Leader of 2d squad, 3d Platoon, B Company, 4th Battalion, 17th Infantry Regiment, 7th Infantry Division (Light). Participated in mission to secure the Colon bottleneck.

Laboa, Monseigneur José Sebastián   Panama's papal nuncio, or Vatican ambassador. Played key role as intermediary between Cisneros and Noriega.

La Fountaine, Colonel Edward L.   Special assistant to the 61st Military Airlift Group commander. During Just Cause he was deputy commander for air operations of Howard Air Force Base.

Legaspi, Sergeant Joseph   Fire team leader with 3d squad, 1st Platoon, C Company, 4th Battalion, 17th Infantry Regiment, 7th Infantry Division (Light). Participated in H-hour assault on complex housing PDF naval infantry headquarters.

Lindsay, General James   Commander, U.S. Special Operations Command, the agency that oversees the special operations forces of all services. Now retired.

Loeffke, Major General Bernard   Commander, U.S. Army South from 1987 to 1989. Later president of the Inter-American Defense Board in Washington, D.C.

Marcinkevicius, Private First Class Darin   Member of 2d Platoon, D Company, 4th Battalion, 6th Infantry Regiment, 5th Infantry Division (Mechanized).

Maylin, Lieutenant Colonel Anibal   Commander of PDF Military Zone 2, headquartered in Colon.

McConico, First Lieutenant Jimmy   Leader of 2d Platoon, 7th Military Police Company. Played key role in establishing new police force in Colon after Endara government took power.

McMahon, Lieutenant Colonel Tim   Operations staff, XVIII Airborne Corps. Played a key role in the detailed planning of Operation Just Cause.

Miller, Specialist Darrel   Member of A Company, 4th Battalion, 17th Infantry Regiment, 7th Infantry Division (Light). His company took part in H-hour assault on PDF 8th Infantry Company at Fort Espinar and subsequent mission to secure Colon.

Moon, Major Jim   Operations officer, 2d Brigade, 7th Infantry Division (Light). Brigade had responsibility for securing outlying regions of Panama.

Moore, Lieutenant Colonel Lynn   Commander, 3d Battalion, 504th Parachute Infantry Regiment, 82d Airborne Division. The battalion, training at the Jungle Operations Training Center at the outbreak of Operation Just Cause, conducted several H-hour assaults in the central portion of the Panama Canal zone.

Mowatt, Sergeant Rick   Leader of 1st squad, 1st Platoon, C Company, 4th Battalion, 17th Infantry Regiment, 7th Infantry Division (Light). Led H-hour assault to stop PDF naval infantrymen from fleeing Coco Solo in their boats.

Muir, Captain Tom   Black Hawk pilot and commander, A Company, 3d Battalion, 123d Aviation Regiment, 7th Infantry Division. Shot in D-day air assault on Cerro Tinajitas, where he was flight leader.

Muse, Kurt   Clandestine radio operator whose networks formed a rallying point for Panamanian opposition to Noriega. Liberated from prison in a daring raid by special operations forces on the night of Operation Just Cause.

Needham, Colonel Tom   Director of operations, XVIII Airborne Corps.

Newberry, Staff Sergeant Wayne   Fire support NCO, A Company, 3d Battalion, 75th Ranger Regiment. Awarded Bronze Star for bravery in assault on Rio Hato.

Noriega, Manuel Antonio   Commander of the Panama Defense Forces and effectively the dictator of Panama.

Nuñez, Captain Pedro   Intelligence officer, 1st Battalion, 508th Infantry Regiment (Airborne), part of 193d Brigade, stationed in Panama.

Paredes, Rubén Darío   A senior Panamanian military leader from 1968 to 1983. His aspirations to become president of Panama were dashed by Noriega.

Paz, First Lieutenant Robert   Marine shot to death by PDF at a roadblock 16 December 1989. His death led to the decision to launch Operation Just Cause.

Phillips, Lieutenant Colonel Bob   Executive officer of 2d Brigade, 7th Infantry Division (Light). Brigade had responsibility for securing outlying regions of Panama.

Pote, Barbara   Wife of Major Rob Pote and mother of an infant girl. The family lived on Fort Clayton.

Pote, Major Rob   Executive officer of Panama-based 1st Battalion (Airborne), 508th Infantry Regiment, 193d Infantry Brigade (Light). Two companies from his battalion conducted the H-hour assault at Fort Amador, and the third participated in the H-hour assault on the Comandancia.

Powell, General Colin.   Chairman, Joint Chiefs of Staff, during Operation Just Cause.

Powers, Second Lieutenant Harold   Leader of 2d Platoon, D Company, 4th Battalion, 6th Infantry Regiment, 5th Infantry Division (Mechanized).

Quezada, Major Fernando   A Panama Defense Forces officer who led an unsuccessful coup attempt against Noriega on 16 March 1988.

Raab, Lettie   Wife of Col. Larry Raab, commander of U.S. military police in Panama, and mother of two. The family lived on Fort Clayton.

Ramos, First Lieutenant Loren   Executive officer, A Company, 75th Ranger Regiment. Awarded Bronze Star for bravery in assault on Rio Hato.

Reagan, Captain William   Commander of A Company, 1st Battalion, 508th

Infantry Regiment (Airborne), part of the 193d Infantry Brigade, Panama. Involved in assault on Fort Amador.

Reed, Lieutenant Colonel James   Commander, 4th Battalion, 6th Regiment, 5th Infantry Division (Mechanized). Commander of Task Force Gator in Operation Just Cause.

Rizzo, Captain Chris   Commander, C Company, 4th Battalion, 17th Infantry Regiment, 7th Infantry Division (Light). Led the H-hour assault on the PDF naval infantry company at Coco Solo.

Rodríguez, Francisco   Noriega-appointed civilian president of the provisional government from August 1989 to December 1989.

Rosser, First Lieutenant George   Leader of 3d Platoon, A Company, 1st Battalion, 508th Infantry Regiment (Airborne), part of 193d Infantry Brigade, Panama. Led final building-clearing assaults at Fort Amador.

Ryan, Major Tom   Operations officer for 4th Battalion, 17th Infantry Regiment, 7th Infantry Division (Light), the battalion that assaulted PDF installations outside Colon and led the mission to secure the city.

Shultz, George   U.S. Secretary of State from 1982 to 1988.

Snell, Colonel Michael   Commander, 193d Infantry Brigade, Panama.

Spadafora, Hugo   A romantic revolutionary who was a long-time enemy of Noriega. He openly opposed the general, and was brutally murdered on 14 September 1985.

Stiner, Lieutenant General Carl   Commander, XVIII Airborne Corps, and overall military commander of Operation Just Cause. Later promoted to general and given command of the U.S. Special Operations Command, MacDill Air Force Base, Florida.

Thorp, Captain Doug   Commander, B Company, 4th Battalion, 17th Infantry Regiment, 7th Infantry Division (Light). Led the H-hour mission to secure the Colon bottleneck.

Threadgill, Private First Class Anthony   Member of B Company, 4th Battalion, 17th Infantry Regiment, 7th Infantry Division (Light). His company had the H-hour mission to secure the Colon bottleneck.

Thurman, General Maxwell   Commander, U.S. Southern Command, Quarry Heights, Panama, from 2 October 1989 to 21 November 1990.

Toohey, Lieutenant Commander Patrick   Commanded detachment of Navy SEALs in the assault on Paitilla airfield.

Torrijos, Omar   Panamanian general and political leader who in 1968 masterminded a coup that would give the military control of the Panamanian government until late 1989. Died in a plane crash in 1981.

Vallarino, Bolívar   A top general who headed the Panamanian Guardia Nacional in 1968. He was the last military leader to come from the upper classes.

Villahermosa, Corporal Ricardo   A Marine killed in a crossfire between U.S soldiers and Panamanian hooligans at the Arraijan Tank Farm in April 1989.

Watkins, Captain Dwight   Commander, B Battery, 7th Battalion, 15th Field Artillery Brigade, 7th Infantry Division (Light). Battery conducted direct fire on DENI headquarters in Colon, one of only two instances of direct artillery fire in Just Cause.

Whitt, Lieutenant Colonel Earl, Jr.   Chief of operations and training, 24th Composite Wing. During Just Cause he was director of the Air Operations Center at Howard Air Force Base.

Wilderman, Lieutenant Colonel David   J-3 operations officer, Special Operations Command—South.

Woerner, General Frederick   Commander in chief, U.S. Southern Command from 1987 to 1989. He is now retired.

Wright, Colonel James   Commander of 7th Division (Light) Support Command, with responsibility for logistics support to 7th Division operations in Panama, including hauling captured weapons and preparing them for shipment.

Yanichko, Major Rob   Logistics officer for 2d Brigade, 7th Infantry Division (Light). Brigade had responsibility for securing outlying regions of Panama.

Zebrowski, Captain Robert   Commander, B Company, 1st Battalion, 508th Infantry Regiment (Airborne), 193d Infantry Brigade, Panama. Involved in assault on Fort Amador.

Appendix C: Operation Just Cause—The Cost

Navy Deaths

Lieutenant Junior Grade John Patrick Connors, 25, Naval Special Warfare Group Two, Little Creek, Va.

Chief Engineman Donald Lewis McFaul, 32, Naval Special Warfare Group Two, Little Creek, Va.

Torpedoman's Mate Second Class Issac George Rodriguez, III, 24, Naval Special Warfare Group Two, Little Creek, Va.

Boatswain's Mate First Class Christopher Tilghman, 30, Naval Special Warfare Group Two, Little Creek, Va.

Marine Deaths

Corporal Garreth C. Isaak, 22, 2d Light Armored Infantry Battalion, Camp Lejeune, N.C.

Army Deaths

Staff Sergeant Larry Barnard, 29, B Company, 3d Battalion, 75th Ranger Regiment, Fort Benning, Ga.

Private First Class Roy Dennis Brown, Jr. 19, A Company, 3d Battalion, 75th Ranger Regiment, Fort Benning, Ga.

Private First Class Vance "Troy" Coats, 18, C Company, 1st Battalion, 508th Infantry Regiment (Airborne), Fort Kobbe, Panama.

Private First Class Jerry Scott Daves, 20, B Company, 1st Battalion, 504th Parachute Infantry Regiment, Fort Bragg, N.C.

Sergeant Michael DeBlois, 24, C Company, 1st Battalion, 508th Infantry Regiment (Airborne), Fort Kobbe.

Private First Class Martin Doug Denson, 21, B Company, 1st Battalion, 504th Parachute Infantry Regiment, Fort Bragg, N.C.

Specialist William D. Gibbs, 22, B Company, 4th Battalion, 17th Infantry Regiment, Fort Ord, Calif.

First Lieutenant John Wessel Hunter, 30, Headquarters and Support Company, 160th Special Operations Aviation Group (Airborne), Fort Campbell, Ky.

Specialist Phillip Lear, 21, B Company, 2d Battalion, 75th Ranger Regiment, Fort Lewis, Wash.

Specialist Alejandro Manrique-Lozano, 30, D Company, 2d Battalion, 504th Parachute Infantry Regiment, Fort Bragg, N.C.

Private First Class James William Markwell, 21, Headquarters and Headquarters Company, 1st Battalion, 75th Ranger Regiment, Hunter Army Airfield, Ga.

Chief Warrant Officer Second Class Wilson B. Owens, 29, B Company, 160th Special Operations Aviation Group (Airborne), Fort Campbell, Ky.

Corporal Ivan D. Perez, 22, B Company, 4th Battalion, 6th Infantry Regiment, Fort Polk, La.

Chief Warrant Officer Second Class Andrew P. Porter, 25, B Company, 1st Battalion, 123d Aviation Regiment, Fort Ord, Calif.

Private First Class John Mark Price, 22, A Company, 2d Battalion, 75th Ranger Regiment, Fort Lewis, Wash.

Private First Class Scott Lee Roth, 19, 401st Military Police Company, Fort Hood, Texas.

Private Kenneth Douglas Scott, 20, A Company, 4th Battalion, 6th Infantry Regiment, Fort Polk, La.

Private James Allen Tabor, Jr., 18, Headquarters/Headquarters Company, 4th Battalion, 325th Parachute Infantry Regiment, Fort Bragg, N.C.

Appendix D: Notes

Chapter 1

1. Frederick Kempe, *Divorcing the Dictator,* (New York: G.P. Putnam's Sons, 1990) page 62.
2. Ibid., page 59.
3. Ibid., page 58.
4. John Dinges, *Our Man in Panama* (New York: Random House, 1990), page 142.
5. Ibid., page 152.
6. Abrams testimony before House Select Committee on Narcotics, confirmed in interview.
7. Seymour Hersh, *The New York Times,* 12 June 1986, page A1.
8. Charles R. Babcock and Bob Woodward, *The Washington Post,* 13 June 1986, page A1.
9. Dinges, *Our Man in Panama,* pages 259–62.
10. Ibid., pages 262–63.

Chapter 2

1. Statistics and other details concerning the firefight at the Arraijan fuel tank farm near Howard Air Force Base taken from United Press International report in the SOUTHCOM newspaper, *Tropic Times,* 18 April 1988, page 1.
2. UPI report in *Tropic Times,* 8 April 1988.
3. Marine 1st Sgt. Alexander Nevglovski interviewed by UPI, *Tropic Times,* 18 April 1988, page 1.
4. Article by Sgt. Joe Patton, *Tropic Times,* 8 April 1988.
5. A fuller account of these meetings is in Kempe's *Divorcing the Dictator,* pages 309–14.
6. Ibid., page 312.

Chapter 3

1. Fuller account of Bush-Delvalle meeting in *Divorcing the Dictator,* page 348.
2. Elaine Sciolino, "General Sees Lack of Panama Policy," *The New York Times,* 24 February 1989, page 1:3.

3. J. Paul Scicchitano, "Soldiers, families living in fear," *Army Times*, 27 March 1989.

4. Kempe, *Divorcing the Dictator*, p. 352.

5. "Carter condemns election fraud," interview by *Tropic Times*, 12 May 1989, page 1.

6. Kempe, *Divorcing the Dictator*, page 356.

7. Margaret Roth and J. Paul Scicchitano, "Showdown in Panama," *Army Times*, 22 May 1989.

8. George C. Wilson, "Bush Turns to Gunboat Diplomacy in Move to Protect U.S. Lives," *The Washington Post*, 12 May 1989, page A27.

9. "US Should Consider Military Solution," *Tropic Times*, 10 July 1989.

Chapter 5

1. Molly Moore and Joe Pichirallo, "Cheney: U.S. Was Willing to Take Custody of Noriega," *The Washington Post*, 6 October 1989, page A36.

Chapter 7

1. Molly Moore and Patrick Tyler, "Strike Force Struck Out," *The Washington Post*, 23 December 1989, page A1.

2. Barbara Starr, "Comms failure blights SEAL operation," *Jane's Defence Weekly*, 5 May, 1990, page 834.

3. Neil C. Livingstone, "Danger in the Air," *The Washingtonian*, June 1990, page 92.

4. Ibid.

Chapter 11

1. The Associated Press, 21–22 December 1989.

2. William Booth, *The Washington Post*, 23 December 1989, page A7.

3. David E. Pitt, "U.S. Reported To Find Body of an Abducted American," *The New York Times*, 30 December 1989, page 1:6.

4. *Quotes & Notes*, Quarry Heights Officers' Wives Club, No. 9, pages 25–27.

Chapter 12

1. 1st Lt. Clarence Briggs, *Operation Just Cause—Panama December 1989: A Soldier's Eyewitness Account*, pages 55–56.

2. Ibid., pages 68–70.

Chapter 14

1. William Branigin, *The Washington Post,* 30 December 1989, page A1.
2. Douglas Jehl and Bob Secter, *Los Angeles Times* report reprinted in *Fayette-ville Observer,* 28 December 1989, page 1D.
3. Rich Browne, *Fayetteville Observer,* 11 January 1990, page 1D.
4. Column by Janet Thompson in *Army Times,* 16 April 1990, page 23.
5. *Quotes & Notes,* Quarry Heights Officers' Wives Club, No. 9, pages 34–35, 42.
6. Bill Baskervill, "Soldier Charged in Panama Invasion Says He Was Doing Duty," The Associated Press, 23 July 1990.
7. Patrick Tyler, *The Washington Post,* 22 July 1990, page 1.
8. J. Paul Scicchitano, *Army Times,* 10 September 1990, page 14.

Chapter 16

1. Richard Boudreaux, *The Philadelphia Inquirer,* 5 January 1990, page 1A.
2. Kevin Howe, *Army Times,* 9 July 1990, page 20.
3. Elizabeth Rathbun, *Army Times,* 22 January 1990, page 10.

Epilogue

1. Margaret Roth, *Army Times,* 17 December 1990, page 8.
2. Margaret Roth, *Army Times,* 4 June 1990, page 12.
3. Linda Robinson and Peter Cary, *U.S. News & World Report,* 30 July 1990, page 29.
4. J. Paul Scicchitano, *Army Times,* 19 March 1990, page 12.
5. Linda Robinson and Peter Cary, *U.S. News & World Report,* 30 July 1990, page 29.
6. *La Prensa,* 9 September 1990, special supplement.
7. *The Laws of War and the Conduct of the Panama Invasion: An Americas Watch Report,* May 1990, page 8.

Index

A-37 aircraft, 50

AC-130 (Spectre) gunship, 86, 90, 109, 115, 119, 121, 126–129, 132, 137, 143–144, 146, 149–152, 154, 158, 162, 173, 189, 190, 193, 194, 199, 202, 229, 231–232, 313, 320, 330, 339, 341, 349–351, 353, 361, 405–406

AH-1 (Cobra) helicopter, 174, 217, 220, 222–227, 229, 272–274, 279, 282–283, 292

AH-6 (Little Bird) helicopter, 132–133, 148–149, 173, 189, 190, 193, 194, 199, 205, 339, 341, 406

AH-64 (Apache) helicopter, 86, 91, 156–158, 217, 223, 227, 229, 230, 339, 341, 353, 402, 405, 406

AK-47 assault rifle, 46, 94, 112, 117, 125, 143, 144, 154, 170, 172, 206, 211, 224, 232, 246, 251, 257, 265, 270, 278, 289, 308–310, 313, 320, 343, 357, 370–371, 382, 384

AT-4 antitank weapon, 115, 127, 128, 172, 178, 179, 230, 243, 254, 259, 266, 274, 276, 279, 283, 286, 404

ABC, 231

Abrams, Elliott, 9–10, 13–14, 16, 21, 31, 33, 34, 38, 41, 42, 65

Aguas Buenas, 109

Albrook Air Station, 385, 389; operations phase and, 119, 122–125, 153, 173, 234, 309, 312–313, 360

Alexander, Michael, 220

Almeida, James, 136

Alto de Golf, 111

American Chambers of Commerce, 42

Ancon Hill, 3, 70–71, 84; operations phase and, 141–143, 147–149, 154–157, 371–372

Andino, William, 373

Andrews Air Force Base, Maryland, xvi

Apache. *See* AH-64 helicopter

Aragon, Jose, 361

Arias, Arnulfo, 2, 4–5, 7

Arias, Raul, 385

Arias Calderón, Ricardo, 44, 46, 122, 351, 355, 375

Armacost, Michael, 38

Armitage, Richard, 38

Arnett, Peter, 411

Arraijan: operations phase and, 185–187; planning phase and, 184; tank farm raids, 32, 85, 183

Associated Press, 230, 311

Axson, Harry, 231

Baba, Satya Sai, 11

Baha'i Temple, 123; operations phase and, 223

Baker, James, 98–99

Balboa, 13, 84, 86; operations phase and, 120–121, 123, 153, 154, 169–170

Balboa High School, 43, 48

Balboa, Vasco Núñez de, 1

Balma, Jorge, 362

Bangalore torpedo, 265

Banks, James, 370, 376

Barletta, Nicolás Ardito, 7–10

Bastidas, Rodrigo de, 1

Battalion Command Training Program (U.S. Army), 408

Battalion 2000, 9, 72–74, 86, 139; operations phase and, 124, 190–191, 214, 227, 229, 307

Bausch, Robert Stephen, 239, 240, 362–363, 372, 374

Beck, Bruce, 272

Beech, Mike, 260, 262, 266–267, 298, 303

Beliz, Anel, 234

Benedetti, Leopoldo, 304, 370

About the Authors

Thomas Donnelly is editor of *Army Times,* an independent newspaper covering a full range of Army interests, from weapons and strategy issues to pay, promotion and personnel policies. Donnelly has been editor of *Army Times* since October 1987. Before that, he was deputy editor of *Defense News* and its land warfare correspondent since the newspaper's inception in 1985. He lives in Washington, D.C.

Margaret Roth is editor of "Life in the Times," the features section of *Army Times* and its sister publications, *Navy Times* and *Air Force Times.* During most of her 14-year journalism career, she has been a reporter, including a two and one half year stint at *Army Times,* where she wrote extensively about the deterioration of U.S.– Panamanian relations and the aftermath of Operation Just Cause. She lives in Fairfax County, Virginia.

Caleb Baker is the land warfare correspondent for Defense News, a weekly publication devoted to covering U.S. and NATO military strategy and its impact on industry. Previously the naval warfare correspondent, Baker also specializes in special operations, helicopters, unmanned aerial vehicles, chemical warfare, Asia, and Central America. He lives in Montgomery County, Maryland.